Can Robots Love God and be Saved?

CAN ROBOTS LOVE GOD AND BE SAVED?

A Journalist Reports on Faith

JOHN LONGHURST

CMU PRESS
WINNIPEG, MANITOBA
2024

CMU Press
Canadian Mennonite University
500 Shaftesbury Blvd.
Winnipeg MB R3P2N2
www.cmupress.ca

CMU Press is learning and striving to create an inclusive and welcoming space for people of many identities and communities. We work on land which is the ancestral home of the Anishinaabe, Cree, Dakota, and Métis peoples. We are grateful for their stewardship of this place.

Project editor: Katie Doke Sawatzky
Copyeditor: Sue Sorensen
Editorial assistance: Felipio Abrenica, Phil Waldner
Interior design and layout: Jonathan Dyck
Cover design: Judith Rempel Smucker
Photos by John Longhurst

Printed in Canada by Friesens Corporation, Altona, Manitoba.
ISBN 978-1-987986-19-8

Library and Archives Canada Cataloguing in Publication

Title: Can robots love God and be saved? : a journalist reports on faith / John Longhurst.
Names: Longhurst, John (Journalist), author.
Description: Includes bibliographical references.
Identifiers: Canadiana 20240360559 | ISBN 9781987986198 (softcover)
Subjects: LCSH: Faith.
Classification: LCC BV4637 .L66 2024 | DDC 234/.23—dc23

Contents

3. MANY FAITHS

4. CHURCH LIFE

5. CHALLENGING SCRIPTURE

6. THE CANADIAN CONTEXT OF FAITH

7. PRACTICES, TRADITIONS AND NEW WAYS FORWARD

8. WHAT'S GOING ON?

Foreword
Paul Samyn

The *Winnipeg Free Press* is one of the last papers left in the country to have a faith page, a commitment which ensures we are part of the discussion on issues shaping not only the lives of many of our readers, but also our society.

The *Free Press* is blessed to have John Longhurst help us do the heavy lifting of keeping our faith page lively, relevant and diverse through his experience and expertise forged over decades of service as a journalist specializing in faith-focused reporting.

Whether reporting from the Vatican on a historic mission involving Indigenous Manitobans seeking a papal apology, taking stock of concerns of antisemitism at a local synagogue, or explaining the rhythms of Ramadan, John delivers stories that matter.

"In today's world, [the work of journalists] is, in every sense, not just a job; it is a mission," Pope Francis wrote in 2018.

John has lived that mission with every word he has written for the *Free Press*. And it was his sense of mission that enabled us to expand our coverage of religion by working with the faith community to fund an initiative unique among Canadian newspapers. Since the launch of that project in 2019, there have been more than one thousand articles published which focus on every faith and creed in our city and province—many of which land on our front page.

We live in a time when many institutions of faith don't command the respect they once did. Throughout his impressive career, however, John has always commanded respect for his articles of faith, many of which you will be able to bear witness to in this collection.

Preface

Can robots love God and be saved? That's the question raised by Christopher Benek, a Presbyterian pastor in Fort Lauderdale, Florida who describes himself as a "techno-theologian." It's also one of many questions I have asked as a faith columnist at the *Winnipeg Free Press* since 2003.

Over the past 20 years, writing that column has given me the opportunity to ask all sorts of questions—the kind you might not ask in most churches or other places of worship. Questions such as: Is God Christian? Before settlers arrived, what was God saying to Indigenous people in Canada? Can a pacifist wear a poppy? What do witches actually believe? How do Hindus feel about everyone wanting to do yoga? Do rocks have rights? And, was Jesus really born in a stable?

Those are a few of the questions you will find raised in this collection of columns—selections from the over 900 I have written for the *Winnipeg Free Press*. My goal has always been to gently raise interesting and provocative issues and then invite readers to ponder and reflect on them—and do so in a way that is generally positive and inclusive and encourages readers to explore deeper into various subjects.

As for how I got to be a faith page columnist in the first place, credit—if that's the word—goes to Nicholas Hirst, publisher of the *Free Press* from 1996-2006. When Mary Lou Driedger moved on as columnist after three years, Nick, who I had been annoying for years about the need for better religion coverage in the paper, asked me to take her place. At first, I shared the page on a biweekly basis with Karen Toole. When Karen moved on, the *Free Press* asked me to write every Saturday—something I continue to do today.

When I started, I joined a number of very fine reporters and columnists on the faith beat in Canada—people like Tom Harpur, Gordon Legge, Bob Harvey, Douglas Todd, and Harvey Sheppard, all of whom inspired and encouraged me. They have all since retired or passed away or, in the case of Doug Todd, largely moved on to other beats. At the same time, the faith page has also disappeared in this country. In fact, the *Free Press* may be the only daily newspaper in Canada that still has one. Since 2019, it has engaged two freelancers to write stories about local faith groups and individuals. Credit for that goes to former publisher Bob Cox and current editor Paul Samyn, and to about 25 local faith groups and many hundreds of individuals who contribute financially to make it possible.

Finally, thanks also goes to my wife, Christine, who proofreads my columns before I file them—catching mistakes and anything that is hard to understand. Thanks also to my very first editor, Harold Jantz, who mentored me long ago at my first writing job as an intern reporter at the *Mennonite Brethren Herald*.

As for whether robots can love God and be saved, well, you'll just have to read on.

John Longhurst, February 2024

Can Robots Love God and be Saved?

Introduction: What makes for good religion?

"Sometimes you find religion in the most unusual places." That's what I wrote in January 2004, my second year of being a faith page columnist for the *Winnipeg Free Press*. In the column, I wrote about an article in the sports section of the paper where ESPN college football analyst Bill Curry was quoted as saying: "A good offence is like a good religion. It should have an answer for everything."

"It's a great quote," I wrote. "It's pithy. It's humourous. It's wrong."

Of course, I didn't mean football—maybe all good football offences really do have answers for everything the opposing team will throw at them. But the quote was wrong about good religion. Good religion has as many questions as answers. Maybe more.

That perspective is what has governed my work as a columnist at the *Free Press*. A good religion makes us think and gives us room to admit when we just don't know.

But where did Curry get the idea that religion provides answers for everything? From religious people, of course. Christians, for instance, in well-meaning efforts to reach out to non-believers, sometimes dumb down faith. They pass out booklets with simple formulas for finding God. They write books about prayers that promise to grant our heart's desires. They preach sermons that say all problems will be solved if people get right with God. Or they promote the idea that people can be happy, healthy, and wealthy if they only believe hard enough (the infamous "name it and claim it" school of Christianity).

The result? Instead of attracting thinking non-believers, they repel them. They make religion sound like something suitable only for children. In so doing, they unwittingly suggest Sigmund Freud was right when he likened religion to a "childhood neurosis" that has to be outgrown since "men cannot remain children forever."

That's not how historian and social critic Christopher Lasch saw religion.

In a speech to students at New York's Jewish Theological Seminary in 1991, he said: "What has to be questioned here is the assumption that religion ever provided a set of comprehensive and unambiguous answers to ethical questions, answers completely resistant to skepticism; or that it forestalled speculation about the meaning and purpose of life; or that religious people were unacquainted with existential despair."

Religion isn't for the intellectually timid—it has room for questions and doubt. As Frederick Buechner once put it: "Whether your faith is that there is a God or that there is not a God, if you don't have any doubts, you are either kidding yourself or asleep. Doubts are the ants in the pants of faith. They keep it awake and moving."

Indeed, choosing to believe in a God is now a more radical and challenging act than deciding not to believe at all. It's easy to write off belief in God because there is so much suffering in the world, or for any other reason, and then never trouble yourself to think about the subject again. Keeping the faith takes a lot more energy and thoughtfulness. This is something philosopher Jonathan Rée has recognized. In the Winter 2002 issue of *Index on Censorship*, he noted that being an atheist was hard in the past—it required courage to think independently and go against the norm of religious belief. Today, however, with participation in organized religion waning, atheism is the "default position" for many, often "nothing more than a 'do not disturb sign' hung out by the intellectually inert." Meanwhile, he said, thoughtful believers are the ones leading the way in trying to find "appropriate ways of attending to the rough and arbitrary finitude of our existence."

That's the thing about good religion; it doesn't have an answer for everything. Instead, it reminds people they are finite—we can't know everything, and God's plans may be different from how we think things should work out. As Christopher Lasch said: "It is just this comfortable belief—that the purposes of the Almighty coincide with our purely human purposes—that religious faith requires us to renounce. Religion reminds us of the inescapable limits on human power and freedom. Far from endorsing comfortable superstitions, it undermines the most important superstition of all—that the human race controls its own destiny . . . We have no special claim on the universe, and our prayers are only answered when we surrender that claim: Such is the true meaning of religious faith."

So, is your religion like Bill Curry's good football offence—does it have an answer for everything? If your answer is yes, then maybe it's time for you to start asking some hard questions.

Like some of the ones you will find in this book.

I

FAITH AND SOCIETY

"Life is still difficult": Faith and mental illness

"LIFE IS DIFFICULT." That's the first line of the book *The Road Less Traveled* by psychiatrist and author M. Scott Peck. After it was published in 1978, the book became a bestseller and was also well-known among religious people. This was partly due to Peck's belief in a higher power, which was crystallized later in life when he became a Christian, but also to the fact that Peck spoke a truth we all know but sometimes fail to hear in worship services—that just believing in God doesn't make life perfect and wonderful, or make us happy "all the day," in the words of the old hymn, "At the Cross," by Isaac Watts.

In 2003, Peck wrote, "The most common response I have received to *The Road Less Traveled* in letters from readers has been one of gratitude for my courage, not for saying anything new, but for writing about the kind of things they had been thinking and feeling all along, but were afraid to talk about."

Why the fear? "For many Christians, there is a sense that they should not be struggling," says Todd Sellick, a marriage and family therapist in Winnipeg. "If they are, they think they've failed." Part of the problem, he says, is the message from some churches that everything should go well for believers and, if it doesn't, "there's something wrong with them." But that's completely false, he states. "You may be forgiven, and God is with you, but it doesn't mean you won't struggle in life."

The problem is exacerbated when people who experience difficulty go to church looking for help. "Some churches can be very unwelcome places for people who are failing," says Sellick, when they should be "the safest and most grace-filled places. We hardly know how much we have damaged people though this kind of church culture."

The church Sellick attends knows about peoples' struggles—a number of people in the congregation are facing health-related issues. "We are riddled with cancer," he says. "All we can do is pray, offer support, and bury our dead. There is a lot of pain, and there are no platitudes for that. But even in the darkest places, we trust and believe that God is walking with us, is part of our journey."

Eckhard Goerz was CEO of Eden Health Care Services in Winkler, which assists people struggling with mental illness, among other things. One of the challenges he faced there was helping Christians understand that faith in God isn't a guarantee against mental health issues. "There's no reason to expect that people of faith should be anymore immune to mental illness than anyone else," he says. "After all, Christians aren't immune from cancer or other diseases."

Goerz says faith groups can play an important role for individuals experiencing mental illness, and for their families, by "standing by them and being supportive, and by demonstrating the love of God in all the messiness and challenges of mental illness." They can also break the stigma by talking about mental illness from the pulpit and by welcoming people who are experiencing mental health issues.

The fact of the matter is that everyone struggles or faces difficulty at some point in life—people of faith included. What's that famous quote? "Be kind, for everyone you meet is fighting a great battle," said John Watson, 19th century Scottish theologian. Or, as Joshua Halberstam, author of *Everyday Ethics*, puts it: "When you judge other people, remember one overriding axiom: Everyone is having a hard time. Everyone is insecure. Everyone is hassled. Everyone is tired—we all need more sleep. Everyone wishes he had more courage, more money and better social skills. Everyone wants more glamour in life, and we all desperately need more laughter. Few can figure out how they ended up living the life they lead. Don't be misled by flippant talk; it's a battle for everyone out there . . . Give people a break. It's not easy doing a life."

October 2005

"They hate taxes more than they love Jesus"

Do Christians have a religious duty to pay taxes?

In 2004, the Roman Catholic Church in England and Wales said yes. Not only that, the churches said Christians should be happy to do it. But wait, there's more: they said wealthier Christians should pay more taxes, in order to ease the burden on the poor.

"Taxes are very much based on the principle of solidarity, which is based on the commandment to love your neighbour," Bishop Howard Tripp told Reuters at the launch of *Taxation for the Common Good*, a 40-page document designed to spark discussion about taxation and public services in the United Kingdom. According to Tripp, Christians should "rejoice" in the chance to contribute towards the sort of society that they want. "This document is suggesting taxes are a way to play our part and it is something we should be pleased to do," he said. "It's all part of our duty to our neighbour."

"Taxation is a sign of social health, a moral good. Our willingness to pay it is a sign of our solidarity with one another, and of our humanity," said the Most Reverend Peter Smith, Archbishop of Cardiff, head of the committee that created the report.

One person who tried to put this kind of thinking into action in the United States was Alabama Governor Bob Riley. An evangelical Christian and Republican, Riley stunned many of his conservative supporters in 2003 when he advocated a tax-reform plan that would have shifted a significant amount of the state's tax burden from the poor to wealthy individuals and corporations. In trying to rally support for the plan in the heavily religious state, Riley argued that it was a matter of Christian duty to reform a tax system in which a family of four making as little as $4,600 a year paid more taxes, percentage wise, than the richest of the state's residents. "I've spent a lot of time reading the New Testament," said Riley, "and it has three philosophies: Love God, love each other, and take care of the least among you. It is immoral to charge somebody making $5,000 a year in income tax."

Under Riley's proposal, which critics called the "How would Jesus Tax Us?" plan, just the top third of income earners, plus corporations and large farm and timber operations, would pay more taxes. Anyone earning less than $20,000 a year would pay no income taxes at all. Christians in Alabama were divided over the plan, with some church groups in favour and others attacking it.

"Never in Scripture does it say, 'Render unto Caesar so he can take care of the poor,'" said John Giles, president of the Christian Coalition of Alabama, which opposed the plan. "It is the church's responsibility."

When Riley's tax reform plan was defeated by Alabama voters in a special election, one observer was prompted to remark that "for all the moral high ground Christians claim," their opposition to the proposal showed that "they hate taxes more than they love Jesus."

Given concerns of government waste, the last thing many people of faith in Canada want to hear is that we have a religious duty to give politicians our hard-earned money. But maybe the English and Welsh bishops have a point; maybe there is a moral and religious foundation to taxation that includes Jesus' command to love our neighbours, whoever they are, and wherever they live. It's a shared commitment to creating a society that serves the common good, with a special concern for the neediest among us.

So if you're up late this month trying to calculate your income tax, maybe it will help if you don't think of it as a burden. Maybe you will feel better if you see it as a way to serve God and love your neighbour. But I think you will be forgiven if you don't feel happy about it.

March 2014

Do pets go to heaven?

"Goodbye, Kitty" was the subject line of an email I received from a friend. In the message, she shared the sad news that her beloved cat, named Kitty, had died. I sent her a short note, expressing my sympathy. She thanked me for the reply, saying she wasn't sure how people would react to the news. She worried some people might not understand how deeply her cat's death affected her—it was just an animal, after all. As someone who owns a dog, I know that isn't true.

We got Rikki, our mutt, from a pet rescue shelter in 2001. Her previous owners had left her tied up in the backyard when they moved away. (Hard to believe, I know!) She has grown from an anxious, frightened animal into an affectionate and much-loved member of our family. We can't imagine life without her; we will be devastated when she dies.

Why do our pets affect us so strongly? There are lots of reasons, but I think it's partly because they help make us better people. Looking after a being that is totally reliant on you for food and care makes you more responsible and considerate. Observant owners can draw a parallel between the way a pet depends on them for everything, and the way humans depend on God. But that's not all animals can teach us; they can also help us learn more about the life of the spirit.

At least, that's what writer Jon Katz has discovered. Katz lives on a New York farm with a 3,000-pound steer named Elvis. Elvis, he says, has taught him as much about spirituality as any book on the subject or worship service. "I've attended churches, Quaker meetings, synagogues, and Buddhist temples," Katz wrote. "I've taken yoga and read Joseph Campbell, Thomas Merton, C.S. Lewis, St. Augustine, and the Bible. I pray often. But I had an unsettling realization recently, which is that my steer, Elvis, already has the spiritual equanimity I have been seeking. He is comfortable within himself, has no discernible anxiety, rolls with life as if it were a gentle wave, is uncomplaining, generous and loyal to his mate, and trusts and accepts people."

Cold, rain, snow, flies, ticks, mud, and muck—none of this disturbs him, Katz noted. "He is as peaceful covered in ice as he is taking in the sun with the Guernsey steer, and his pal, Harold." Elvis "doesn't have to work at acceptance or retrain his mind to accept the bad with the good," he adds. "This, I think, is the spiritual centre of animals like Elvis, the thing that they can teach us and show us."

Thomas Merton, Katz notes, "wrote that one of the most important and neglected elements in the beginnings of an authentic and interior life is the ability to see the value and the beauty in ordinary things. Elvis seems to have that. I do not."

I have a feeling that Katz will be sorry when Elvis dies. Maybe he might want a prayer like the one below, which I found on the Internet. I sent it to my friend following the death of her cat: "Thank you, God, for lending her to me. Because of her I learned a little more about loving, a little more about taking care, a little more about letting things be. Thank you, God. She is one of the nicest ways that I have ever met you. I really miss her. But I'm looking for some new sign of you. Please help me find it. Amen."

My friend replied with thanks, saying, "I sure hope animals get to go to heaven." When I think of my dog, all I can say is: me, too.

December 2014

"You have searched me and known me": Government surveillance and religion

"You have searched me and known me. You know when I sit down and when I rise up; you discern my thoughts from far away. You search out my path and my lying down, and are acquainted with all my ways. Even before a word is on my tongue, you know it completely."

No, that's not a description of how governments around the world are conducting surveillance. As many Christians and Jews know, these are the opening verses of Psalm 139, a song of wonder at the omniscience, or all-knowing, of God. In general, believers seem OK with that. But how do they feel about governments practicing an earthlier kind of all-knowingness by spying on their citizens?

Much of the discussion about electronic spying takes place in the realms of law, politics, and the military—are hackers stealing state secrets? Are other countries listening in on sensitive conversations? Less is said from the point of view of religion. Daniel Schultz, in an article for *Christian Century* on US government surveillance, addresses the subject from a religious perspective. He suggests that people of faith should be wary when governments say they do this kind of spying because they say they want to keep us safe. "Only God can provide ultimate security," he says, adding that anything else is an idol. Belief in God's omniscience doesn't mean we will be kept safe from all harm, he states. Instead, it provides a "transformative support and presence amid our vulnerability . . . we do ourselves a disservice when we give in to the temptation to make ourselves as safe as possible at the expense of freedom."

Timothy George, dean of Beeson Divinity School in Birmingham, Alabama, writing for the religious magazine *First Things*, says that "persons of faith should be deeply concerned" about government spying "not because privacy is an absolute end in itself, but rather because it points to and safeguards something else even more basic and fundamental, namely, human dignity." Citing Article 18 of the United Nations' Declaration of Human Rights, which says that everyone has the right of freedom to practice religion, he says that such spying is an affront to religious freedom, which "presupposes the recognition of privacy."

But is it such a big deal? Who cares if the government knows if you go to worship services, or what you believe? If you happen to be a member of a faith group that is lumped in with international terrorism, it can be a big deal. It can also be a big problem for people of faith who oppose militarism, nuclear weapons, or who are critical of various government policies on the environment or refugees.

Followers of the major monotheistic religions—Judaism, Christianity and Islam—believe that everything we do is known by God. But some are becoming less comfortable with governments trying to do the same thing. As Timothy George notes, people of faith don't mind being watched. We just want to be people who "only want to look up, not over shoulders."

February 2015

Can robots love God and be saved?
Artificial intelligence and religion

TRUCK DRIVERS, ACCOUNTANTS, barbers, taxi drivers, roofers, bricklayers, umpires, journalists, even surgeons—these are all occupations that face the possibility of being replaced by artificial intelligence. When it comes to clergy, websites like www.willrobotstakemyjob.com and www.replacedbyrobots.info, which calculate the risk of losing your job to a robot, indicate that priests and ministers are safe, with some putting the risk at zero and others at less than one per cent.

Unless you live in Japan, that is. Nissei Eco and SoftBank in that country offer a robot priest for end-of-life rituals and you can't beat the price: a monk or priest may cost 240,000 yen ($2,200 CAD), while the robot only costs 50,000 yen ($450 CAD). That may sound strange to some, but it raises the question: what if you could ask Siri on your iPhone to pray for you? Would God hear it? Does God hear prayers spoken by any intelligent being, robot, or phone, or just prayers uttered by humans?

Meantime, if advances in AI find chatbots like ChatGPT producing some passable sermons and homilies—who needs a preacher anymore? Maybe this can be the answer for congregations that are too small to afford a pastor.

These are the kinds of questions being asked these days by people interested in the intersection of artificial intelligence (AI) and religion. One person exploring this subject is Jonathan Merritt. In an article for *The Atlantic* he suggests the rise of AI raises some "fundamental questions" for adherents of Christianity. One of those questions is what happens if robots develop the ability to make ethical decisions—something that only humans (currently) are able to do.

Merrit notes that we already have driverless cars that make decisions based on traffic around them: slow down, move left, stop. But what if those cars could also make moral decisions? This is something Google is working on. In the future, cars may be able to decide what to do if a child runs in front of a driverless car with four passengers. Should it swerve and risk the lives of those in the vehicle, or hit the child—one life instead of four?

And what if the robots become fully sentient, rational agents—beings with emotions, consciousness, and self-awareness? Merritt quotes Kevin Kelly, author of *The Inevitable: Understanding the 12 Technological Forces that Will Shape Our Future*, who writes that the day will come when there will be "a spiritual dimension to what we're making . . . If you create other things that think for themselves, a serious theological disruption will occur."

Kelly adds: "If humans were to create free-willed beings, absolutely every single aspect of traditional theology would be challenged and have to be reinterpreted in some capacity." Would this include the Christian idea of salvation? If artificially intelligent machines can think and make decisions, could they also establish a relationship with God?

Christopher Benek, a Presbyterian pastor in Fort Lauderdale, Florida, who describes himself as a "techno-theologian," thinks they could. "I don't see Christ's redemption limited to human beings," said Benek in an article in *Gizmodo*. "It's redemption of all of creation, even AI. If AI is autonomous, then we should encourage it to participate in Christ's redemptive purposes in the world."

Christians aren't the only ones asking these questions. In an article titled "Are you ready for robot prayer quorums?" in the Jewish online newspaper *Times of Israel*, Adam Soclof asked if a self-aware robot could hold a conversation, would it qualify to be counted for a minyan, a quorum of ten men (in some synagogues, also women) required for traditional Jewish public worship?

Soclof quotes Rabbi Mark Goldfeder, a fellow at Emory University's Center for the Study of Law and Religion in Atlanta, Georgia, who thinks they could. "When something looks human, and acts human, to the point that I think it might be human, then *halachah* [the collective body of Jewish religious laws derived from the written and oral Torah] might consider the threshold to have been crossed."

Goldfelder doesn't think we are anywhere near that point now. But it's coming. "I do think that Jewish thinkers should start tossing around the questions, because we're probably 30, not 100, years away."

Kevin Kelly feels the same way. What would happen if a free willed, thinking, AI machine says: "I want to believe in God"? At that point, he states, "we should have a response."

September 2017

Could religion combat the loneliness epidemic?

In 2018, the British government created a new portfolio called the Minister for Loneliness. The idea arose out of research conducted by the Red Cross that found about nine million Britons—14 per cent of the population—were lonely. In developing the new portfolio, the British government found that loneliness cuts across all age groups, but it is particularly hard on the elderly, with over a third of older people in the UK reporting being overwhelmed by loneliness. About half of those over 75 live alone, with many saying they can go days or even weeks with no meaningful social interaction.

The situation is similar in Canada, where as many as 1.4 million elderly Canadians say they are lonely. Overall, between 25 to 30 per cent of Canadians describe themselves as lonely, young and old alike. And being lonely is hard on mental health, but also on physical health. Researchers say being lonely increases the chance of premature death by 14 per cent.

So what's behind the epidemic of loneliness? Some blame our high rates of mobility—people move a lot today, disrupting long-term relationships. And when children move to faraway cities, parents are left behind and on their own. Others blame social media. Although it's never been easier to connect with people, it can also lead to fewer physical encounters with actual human beings. And then there's the general decline of participation in civic life—decreasing involvement in service groups, parent-teacher associations, labour unions, political parties, places of worship, and the like, as outlined in Robert Putnam's groundbreaking book *Bowling Alone: The Collapse and Revival of American Community* (2001).

Thinking about the epidemic of loneliness, I wonder: Could a decrease of participation in faith groups also be part of the problem? After all, studies show that regular participation in worship services and other religious activities can protect against loneliness. And being part of a worshipping community is associated with higher levels of social integration and support—things that help people feel less lonely. As more and more people drop out of religious groups, perhaps loneliness is an unintended consequence. But beyond having someone to talk to or be part of a group, is there something more? What about the spiritual dimension?

That's the question I posed to Delmar Epp, associate professor of psychology at Canadian Mennonite University in Winnipeg. From a psychological perspective, he says, people do "have a need to belong." People of faith would say that "being created by God with a need to be in relationship with others

. . . is fundamental to who we are as human beings." But where does God fit in? Epp pointed me to Lee Kirkpatrick's work on attachment theory, as it pertains to religion.

I am not going to pretend I can do a good job of explaining attachment theory in a short column, but here goes. In short, attachment theory holds that humans form deep and abiding bonds with their caregivers when they are young. This provides us with a sense we are secure because someone who is strong will keep us safe. In Kirkpatrick's view, for believers, God becomes an attachment figure—someone to have a relationship with and to turn to when we feel unsafe or distressed. "People can view God as their friend and companion, a comforter, and protector," Epp says, adding that through prayer, worship, and meditation, people can feel close to God and not so alone. Of course, it doesn't always work out so neatly. People who have bad experiences with caregivers when young can struggle to form an attachment to God when older. And if your own parents were harsh and neglectful, it can be tough to believe in a heavenly parent who cares for you.

Places of worship aren't perfect, either. They can be lonely experiences for those who don't feel they can be open and honest with others about their struggles for fear of being judged. Yet there's still something about religion that seems to make a big difference in loneliness and overall health. As millions of people try drugs, therapy, treatment programs, and workout routines to improve their mental health, religion might provide the support and connection they seek. But I don't expect any Western government to create a Minister for Religion and Health anytime soon.

February 2018

Religion and aliens, or, where is everybody?

"WHERE IS EVERYBODY?" Famed physicist Enrico Fermi asked the question in 1950, about the absence of contact with alien life. Today the question is known as the Fermi paradox. It describes the apparent contradiction between the probability that the vast universe must certainly be home to other earth-like planets and civilizations—and the absence of any evidence they exist.

Over the decades, there have been many attempts to explain the Fermi paradox. Some say alien life is either not able to contact us or is unwilling to do so. Others say we are not sophisticated enough as a species to communicate with them. Underneath it all is a feeling that we just can't be alone in the universe—there must be something, or someone else, out there.

But now a team of researchers says no. According to a paper released in June by Anders Sandberg, Eric Drexler, and Toby Ord of the University's of Oxford's Future of Humanity Institute (FHI), and titled "Dissolving the Fermi Paradox," there is a high probability "of there being no other intelligent life in our observable universe, and thus that there should be little surprise when we fail to detect any signs of it." This result, they go on to say, "dissolves the Fermi paradox, and in doing so removes any need to invoke speculative mechanisms by which civilizations would inevitably fail to have observable effects upon the universe."

The authors do not make a definitive claim about whether or not aliens exist. They suggest that the preponderance of evidence indicates we are likely alone. Such a conclusion has a number of implications for science—none of which I am qualified to explore—but also for religion.

The question of whether human beings are unique and have a special relationship with God has prompted a great deal of speculation about what it would mean for religion if aliens existed. David Weintraub, professor of astronomy at Vanderbilt University, wrote a book on the topic, titled *Religions and Extraterrestrial Life* (2014), which explores the views of over two dozen different religions—Christianity, Islam, Judaism, Hinduism, Buddhism, and others.

Weintraub concludes that Asian religions would have the least difficulty accepting the discovery of extraterrestrial life, citing some Hindu thinkers who have speculated that humans may be reincarnated as aliens. Meanwhile, Buddhist cosmology includes thousands of inhabited worlds. As for Islam, there are passages in the Qur'an that appear to support the idea that spiritual beings exist on other planets, but these beings may not practice Islam as it is practiced on Earth. Weintraub finds very little in Judaic scriptures or rabbinical writings on the subject. He quotes a Jewish scholar, Michael Ashkenazi, who asserts that the discovery of extraterrestrial intelligence wouldn't change the special relationship God has with the Jewish people.

When it comes to Christians, it is Roman Catholics that have done the most thinking about the possibility of life on other worlds, while Protestant thinking is all over the map—in keeping with the thousands of different denominations that make up the Protestant world. Some are open to it, while others deny it could be possible. One commonality across Christianity is the belief that the need for salvation is universal, and the saving power of God must apply everywhere.

All of this may be moot, of course, if there is nothing and nobody else out there. But that only raises another question for people of faith: If this planet is indeed all that there is when it comes to intelligent life, how should we be treating it? Right now, there are significant debates about fossil fuels, pipelines, use of plastics, and climate change—not to mention the ongoing threat of nuclear war. What is the religious response to those issues? What is our religious responsibility to this planet?

I don't know if aliens exist—and neither do the world's top scientists. Until we hear differently, I'm inclined to side with Carl Sagan who writes in his book *Pale Blue Dot: A Vision of the Human Future in Space* (1997): "In all this vastness, there is no hint that help will come from elsewhere to save us from ourselves. The Earth is the only world known so far to harbor life . . . the Earth is where we make our stand."

July 2018

Want to become more spiritual? One day there might be a pill for that

For people of faith, reaching the heights of religious devotion, enlightenment, virtue, spiritual and moral betterment, or oneness with God requires effort—things like studying sacred scriptures, praying, meditating, going on pilgrimages, or sitting at the feet of great spiritual masters and teachers. It's a journey, a discipline, a process that can take years, decades, or a whole lifetime. Or you could just take a pill and instantly be more moral, spiritual, and virtuous.

Sound far-fetched? Not according to Moira McQueen, Executive Director of the Canadian Catholic Bioethics Institute. Speaking at a Canadian Council of Churches webinar titled, "Faster, Higher, More Moral? Moral Bioenhancement and Christianity," in 2020, McQueen—who also teaches moral theology at University of St Michael's Graduate Faculty of Theology at the University of Toronto—noted researchers are currently working on ways to biochemically make people more moral and virtuous. "We know that our brains can be altered," she says, referring to drugs like Ritalin, which can reduce negative behaviours like aggression. But should pharmaceuticals also be used to promote pro-social behaviours such as empathy, cooperation, generosity, morality, and trust?

McQueen is not convinced. But others are, including philosophers and ethicists Julian Savulescu and Ingmar Persson. The two think such bioengineering may be the only way for humanity to survive. According to them, human beings evolved to live and deal with problems in small groups. We aren't equipped evolutionarily for a complex and interconnected issue like climate change. Maybe we could educate everyone to take it more seriously but, they argue, we don't have time for everyone to accept the need to change the way they live so we can save the planet.

"Our knowledge of human biology—in particular of genetics and neurobiology—is beginning to enable us to directly affect the biological or physiological bases of human motivation" about things like climate change, Savulescu and Persson write in their book *Unfit for the Future: The Need for Moral Enhancement* (2012), adding "enhancing our moral motivation would enable us to act better for distant people, future generations, and non-human animals." By using these techniques, they stated, we can "overcome the moral and psychological shortcomings that imperil the human species."

During the pandemic, Parker Crutchfield, associate professor of medical ethics at Western Michigan University, proposed in an article for *The*

Conversation, using moral bioenhancement to solve the problem of "coronavirus defectors"—people who refuse to take the virus seriously. "Like receiving a vaccine to beef up your immune system, people could take a substance to boost their cooperative, pro-social behavior," he said, suggesting such a drug could even be put into the water supply.

Currently, research into what some call "morality pills" is in its early stages. But, McQueen warns, interest in the technology is growing—and it raises questions for people of faith.

While she believes there is a role for drugs that help people overcome challenges they can't handle on their own, moral bioenhancement raises important questions such as what it means to be human, what is the role of free will, and who gets to decide what is better and more moral. Then there's also the question of privilege and affordability; if it becomes acceptable, will only wealthy people be able to afford to become morally enhanced? But the bigger question for Moira McQueen is whether morality is "God-given or artificially induced . . . are we more than our bio-chemical networks?"

Also participating in the Canadian Council of Churches webinar was Tracy Trothen, a professor of ethics at the School of Religion at Queens University. If the goal of moral bioenhancement is to make us more moral, she says, then the question is "is it moral to make us more moral?" For her this research touches on the question of what it means to be human, and the role of faith in developing morality in human beings.

Trothen is also concerned about the negative outcomes of bioenhancement. What if along with learning how to make people more empathetic, researchers learn how to make them more hateful and aggressive towards others? We could get "better at creating good things, but also at creating bad things," she says. Increasing virtues such as empathy and self-sacrifice might also get in the way of how faith traditions sometimes need to muster righteous anger in the face of injustice by "standing aggressively" against actions that harm marginalized and vulnerable people, she notes. For both Trothen and McQueen, bioengineering people to be more moral raises questions about what it means for humans to be created in the image of God, the issue of free will, and the importance of community in spiritual formation.

The apostle Paul was one person who struggled with doing the right thing. In the book of Romans, chapter seven, he lamented: "I do not understand my own actions. For I do not do what I want, but I do the very thing I hate." If Paul were alive today, maybe he could look forward to taking a pill for that.

November 2020

Preach, robot, preach!

LIKE MANY OTHERS, I am fascinated by ChatGPT—the artificial intelligence that can write essays, letters, poems, and just about anything else you ask it to do. But can it write sermons? I decided to find out.

I asked ChatGPT to write a sermon about the Good Samaritan: What the parable meant in its original context and what it means for Christians today, with reference to those who are marginalized. Here's what it created:

> As we know, the story of the Good Samaritan is told by Jesus in response to a question about eternal life. A man asks him, "What must I do to inherit eternal life?" Jesus replies with the story of a man who is beaten and left for dead on the side of the road. A priest and a Levite, both religious leaders, pass by him without stopping to help. But a Samaritan, who was considered an outcast and an enemy by the Jews, stops to help the man, bringing him to an inn and caring for him.
>
> In the historical context of the time, this parable was a shocking and revolutionary message. Samaritans were seen as second-class citizens, and their religious beliefs were considered to be heretical. Yet, in this story, Jesus shows that it is the outsider who acts with compassion and humanity, while the religious leaders pass by without helping.
>
> So what does this parable mean for Christians today? First and foremost, it is a reminder of the importance of loving our neighbours as ourselves. This means reaching out to those who are vulnerable and marginalized in our communities, including the houseless, drug addicts, sex workers, 2SLGBTQ+ people, Indigenous people, and others who are often ignored or mistreated by society.
>
> But loving our neighbours is not just about offering practical help, such as food and shelter. It's also about treating them with dignity and respect, listening to their stories, and breaking down the barriers of prejudice and discrimination that divide us. In doing so, we demonstrate the love of Christ to the world and bring healing to broken communities.
>
> Another important aspect of this parable is the reminder that we are all called to be good Samaritans in our own lives. This means being proactive in seeking out opportunities to serve and care for those in need. It means taking the initiative to reach out to those who are marginalized and showing them kindness, compassion, and respect. And it means recognizing that our actions, no matter how small, can make a big difference in the lives of others.

> Let us strive to live out the message of the Good Samaritan in our own lives. Let us love our neighbours as ourselves and bring hope and healing to those who are vulnerable and marginalized. And let us remember that in doing so, we fulfill the call of Christ to love one another as he has loved us.

As sermons go, it's not bad! But what do preachers think? I decided to find that out, too.

"Augustine said that the purpose of the sermon was to teach, to delight, to persuade," says Michael Wilson, minister at Charleswood United Church. "This example may pass the first element, but I would suggest it fails to address the second and third."

Maybe some future programmer will address that shortcoming, Wilson says, but it can't replace the role of the preacher in a congregation. Preachers, he says, are "sent by a community to the Word in order to come back and share what was found. I wonder if an AI sermon can wrestle with a text, putting it into the context of a community's life and add the weight of the tradition and theology. This example does not."

A sermon is also preached in the context of a worship service and is an act of worship, Wilson adds. "It is supported by and contributes to that which has come before and after the sermon. That is in part a reflection on the incarnational nature of the Christian community."

Andrew Rampton, rector at Holy Trinity Anglican Church in downtown Winnipeg, has also been playing around with ChatGPT. "I don't think it's something that preachers need to worry about as a potential replacement. At least, not in its current form." For Rampton, its main strength is collecting, organizing, and reproducing data in the requested format. "That could be incredibly useful in lots of ways," he says, but what it lacks "is the relating of the data in a contextual way. It doesn't know my congregation, it doesn't know me."

Rampton argues this doesn't mean it isn't useful; it could help preachers with prompts or to overcome writer's block since it can help organize ideas into words: "Being able to punch into an app a request to outline some data around a particular passage and set of theological ideas might be the spark that gets the fire going."

Jeff Loach is the minister at St. Paul's Church, a Presbyterian congregation in Nobleton, Ontario. He also thinks ChatGPT has the potential to serve pastors as a research tool, "but not as a replacement for themselves or for good preaching." For him, AI can't replicate—at least, not yet—the "pastoral role in preaching," because "the machine does not know the people who will hear or read it." It is the task of the preacher to craft a sermon for his or her congregation that can "explain the Scriptures with their people in mind, their various issues and struggles and joys," he says, adding that a pastor knows "the culture of the church in a way that no robot does."

If the goal was only passing along information, "I suppose AI could kick me out of the manse," Loach says. "But the goal is also formation, and that doesn't happen in a vacuum of ones and zeroes."

February 2023

Time for a quantum theology?

IN 2022, DR. Frank Wilczek, a professor at the Massachusetts Institute of Technology, won the Templeton Prize. The prize is given annually to a person who uses science to "explore the deepest questions of the universe and humankind's place and purpose within it."

For Wilczek, 70, the goal is to try to understand the universe through the lens of quantum mechanics. He started on that path when he couldn't reconcile traditional religious teaching "with how the world really works," he says in an interview with www.religionunplugged.com. For him, scriptures written thousands of years ago aren't sufficient for understanding the universe today. All they can do, he says, is represent the contemporary human knowledge of ancient times—the writers could only write about what they knew, observed, and understood about the world around them.

"The ancient texts, which are the basis of most of the traditional religions, don't do justice to what we know about the universe now," he said in an interview for *The Daily Hatch*. "They don't have a notion that the universe could be enormously large, much less that it could contain extravagant numbers of dimensions and quantum mechanics, or that it's so very old." That knowledge "left a void," he says. "It left me with a hunger that I've been trying to satisfy ever since."

His comments sparked my curiosity. I am not a scientist, and I know little about quantum mechanics, also known as quantum physics. I wondered if it had any implications for religious belief, and our understanding about God, so I did some research. That's when I found a term I had never heard before: quantum theology. But before that, a basic overview of quantum mechanics: In quantum mechanics, objects have dual natures. They can be both waves and particles; they can be in more than one state at once; and you can't know exactly the location and velocity of a quantum object. (The latter is an example of Heisenberg's famous uncertainty principle, which posits that the observer, by simply observing something, changes the thing that is observed—something that renders the exercise unavoidably subjective.)

The quantum universe is a world of probability, not certainty; it is indeterministic, not deterministic; possible, but not predictable. This is in contrast with the Newtonian worldview, which posited a clockwork universe that functions according to predictable patterns and predetermined laws, with all phenomena understood, no matter how complex, in terms of those laws.

What does this have to do with theology?

While thinking about this, I realized the theology and view of God I was brought up on was based on a Newtonian view of the universe, with its framework of knowability, certainty, objectivity, and predictability. It was a world of true/false, either/or, yes/no. The quantum worldview is not like that. Things can be both/and. And certainty is no longer certain.

What does this mean for religious belief, and, in my own case, for Christian belief? Since I'm not smart enough to figure this out, I looked for people who are. That's how I found Arnold Sikkema, a professor of physics and mathematical sciences at Trinity Western University in Langley, BC. Sikkema has given this some thought. He agrees the ancient scriptures can't do justice to the universe as we know it now—much larger, older, and more complex than those writers thousands of years ago could know or possibly imagine. And he doesn't think of God as a micro-manager of world events and individual lives with a preconceived and predictable clockwork-type plan. "If everything is determined, we are not able to choose," he said.

But this new quantum world is not a problem for him or his faith. He still believes in God. But "how God works in the world is not clear," he said, adding, "I'm comfortable with that mystery." Rather than a cause to jettison faith, Sikkema sees a quantum world of unpredictability and uncertainty as a good fit for Christianity. "People have choices to make," he said. "We are not predestined or just going through the motions . . . there is a resonance between Christianity and quantum physics."

John Polkinghorne, an English Anglican priest and theoretical physicist, noted in his book *Science and the Trinity: The Christian Encounter with Reality* (2004) that the quantum world "must be encountered on its own terms and in accordance with its Heisenbergian uncertainty . . . there is no universal epistemology." By that, he means there is no one-size-fits-all approach for trying to explain the world, or an all-encompassing theory of knowledge for who God is and how God works. In this quantum world, it would be "epistemically disastrous" to try to insist on the Newtonian sense of certainty and clarity about religious belief, he writes.

Where does this leave us? I'm not exactly sure. But in a world where the old certainties about the universe are being swept away, maybe we need a different approach to knowing who God is and how God works—a new quantum theology.

June 2022

Different approaches to Medical Assistance in Dying

SHOULD CLERGY BE condemned or supported if they accompany people who choose Medical Assistance in Dying (MAID)? Some Christian groups in two countries are taking markedly different approaches.

In Canada, the head of the Evangelical Fellowship of Canada (EFC) doesn't believe pastors should walk alongside members who choose MAID. In a column in the May-June issue of *Faith Today*, EFC president and CEO David Guretzki, acknowledges it is natural for clergy to want to be with people dying a natural death. But MAID is different, he said. "My moral conviction is that any intentional ending of a person's life apart from divine permission is a form of murder," he states. "Even though pastors aren't the ones carrying out the procedure, they will need to answer, before God and their flocks, whether their presence is a form of permission or blessing to the person opting to have their life ended," he adds. When I asked Guretzki if maybe that wasn't a bit harsh. He replied: "The column stands as is."

Meanwhile, Dutch Mennonites are taking a different approach to MAID for their clergy. Though not without controversy, MAID—legal in the Netherlands since 2002—has become generally accepted by the population, including the country's 5,000 or so Mennonite church members. Instead of condemning clergy who walk with members who choose to end their own lives, Mennonites are looking for ways to incorporate it into pastoral care as part of church life, says Dutch Mennonite pastor and theologian Pieter Post, who researched MAID in the Netherlands in 2021. "Mennonite pastors here believe the church should be there when people choose euthanasia, to give their death meaning and significance," he shares. "A pastor should be there with the person who is dying."

Post, who is pastor of the United Mennonite Church of Heerenveen and Tjalleberd, and taught at the Mennonite Seminary in Amsterdam, worked as a nurse before he became a pastor in 1985. In that capacity he talked to people who wished they could end their lives to ease their suffering. As a pastor, he has been at the bedside of three people who requested MAID. Post notes that Dutch culture is one of tolerance for individual choices. "We have this idea that we should try to respect each other's decisions and accommodate each other," he says. "We believe decisions about euthanasia are the responsibility of individual believers. They have the right to self-determination."

Even though people have the right to decide for themselves, Post says, he hopes they do it in conversation with their pastor and others. "We want people to be part of the community. We want them to make their decision about dying through conversation with others in the church," he says. Through his research, Post came up with three principles for clergy in responding to requests for euthanasia. First, listen. "Be open and be there, don't judge and tell them they are wrong," he said. Second, offer pastoral support. "Walk with them as they move towards their death," he said. "Be there with them." Third, work with them to create a service for their passing. The need for that became clear to Post when he was called to be at the deathbed of a woman who chose MAID. When he got there, he realized he had no liturgy for the occasion. "That prompted me to want to create something for other pastors to use," he said, adding the liturgy he will create will include scripture, prayers, confession, and hymns.

Post noted that doctors he has talked to expressed gratitude for having pastors there when they administered the procedure. "They told me they felt alone with such a great responsibility," he says. "They were glad a pastor was there to provide spiritual support to not only the person who was dying, but for them, too."

Doug Koop is a spiritual care provider in Winnipeg who has been present during MAID deaths. He believes clergy have a role to play at those times. "We need pastorally sensitive people to be there in the valley of the shadow of death alongside people who are suffering," he says. "You have to be there genuinely for the people. And be there without an agenda. That's when real spiritual healing occurs."

When it comes to MAID, there are many important questions, but one thing seems clear: when someone decides that MAID is their best or only option, the last thing they need is for their clergy to abandon them due to some higher theological principle. Or, as Koop put it: "My role is to be a compassionate presence. My primary purpose is simply to be a companionable soul to a person who has decided it is time to go."

May 2023

Denominations divided over 2SLGBTQ+ inclusion and affirmation

IT'S ONE OF the biggest issues rocking Protestant churches in North America today: welcome and affirmation of 2SLGBTQ+ people. Denominations are dividing over it, hardening their stances, or expelling congregations that break from traditional beliefs about sexuality and marriage.

In the US, more than 6,000 churches have decided to leave the United Methodist Church (UMC) because they believe the denomination is becoming more open to ordaining 2SLGBTQ+ ministers or performing same-sex weddings. That's a fifth of the total number of UMC congregations in that country. In fact, the denomination currently does not permit the marriage or ordination of 2SLGBTQ+ people. But two 2SLGBTQ+ bishops have already been elected and each of its five jurisdictions voted last year to aspire to become a church where 2SLGBTQ+ people will be "protected, affirmed, and empowered."

Where the UMC is becoming more open, the Christian Reformed Church, which has congregations in the US and Canada, voted last year to take a harder stance against 2SLGBTQ+ welcome and affirmation. "The church must warn its members that those who refuse to repent of these sins . . . will not inherit the kingdom of God," the denomination stated. "It must discipline those who refuse to repent of such sins for the sake of their souls." Over the years, the denomination had given its churches a degree of latitude with regards to 2SLGBTQ+ people. Now the denomination has signalled there is no room for things like same-sex marriage or inviting 2SLGBTQ+ people into leadership. That decision could prompt a divide the opposite way of the UMC, with more liberal congregations voting to exit the denomination.

Another American denomination feeling the pain of division is Mennonite Church USA, which officially supports marriage only between a man and a woman but allows individual congregations to decide their stance on the topic. It has gone from 840 congregations to 509 and from 113,000 members to about 50,000 since 2001, largely over the issue of 2SLGBTQ+ inclusion and affirmation. Mennonite Church Canada, MC USA's counterpart, has not seen the same large exodus, but some churches have left over how MC Canada lets individual congregations decide their approach to 2SLGBTQ+ inclusion. Those include two in Manitoba: Carman Mennonite Church and Springfield Heights Mennonite Church in Winnipeg.

The Canadian Conference of Mennonite Brethren Churches is also dealing with congregations that want to be more open to 2SLGBTQ+ people. Like its Christian Reform counterpart, Mennonite Brethren have pushed a hardline stance against churches that violate its opposition to same-sex marriage. Three churches have been expelled so far—two in Ontario and Jubilee Mennonite Church in Winnipeg. River East Church—my home congregation—has been suspended by the denomination because of its decision to become affirming and welcoming of 2SLGBTQ+ people, with suspension being the first step towards expulsion.

A church moving more towards more full inclusion is the Anglican Church of Canada, which recently approved a liturgy for people who are transitioning genders. The decision was welcomed by the Diocese of Rupert's Land, which covers southern Manitoba and northwestern Ontario. But the Diocese of the Arctic, which covers Canada's north, issued a statement to its clergy and members saying it is "committed to the clear teaching of scripture" on this topic and that they should not use the new liturgy in their churches.

Other denominations are also dealing with this topic, like the Canadian Baptists of Western Canada which has felt compelled to reaffirm their opposition to same-sex marriage. But two other Baptist groups in Canada—the Gathering of Baptists and the Canadian Association for Baptist Freedoms—are openly promoting 2SLGBTQ+ affirmation and welcome. In fact, the latter group ordained its first openly 2SLGBTQ+ minister earlier this year.

Late author and theologian Phyllis Tickle predicted this state of affairs in her book *The Great Emergence: How Christianity is Changing and Why* (2012). She popularized the idea that every 500 years Christianity has a garage sale—selling off the ideas and beliefs and practices that no longer fit. The last one was the Reformation in the sixteenth century. Tickle maintained we are now in the midst of the next upheaval. Christians are jettisoning things they no longer believe necessary in order to be faithful—things like institutional church structures, buildings, and traditional beliefs about sexuality and marriage.

The opposition we are seeing today to 2SLGBTQ+ affirmation and inclusion is, Tickle says, "the last playing piece" in the fight over how Christians view the Bible. Previous playing pieces that have already been dealt with include slavery, divorce, and women in ministry—topics that once were very contentious and split Protestant denominations, but are not considered divisive or controversial today. (Although some evangelical churches today are still reluctant to allow women to be clergy.) This current battle over 2SLGBTQ+ inclusion, Tickle says, would be "the bitterest, because once it is lost, there are no more fights to be had" over how people read the Bible—whether it is to be taken literally as a black-and-white book of rules, or if it should be seen as a product of its time that can provide only inspiration for current belief and behaviour.

Whether Tickle was correct about the 500-year timeline or views of the Bible, one thing she got right was about the fight. It is bitter, and it is dividing churches and denominations. What remains for these denominations when the fight is over is not yet clear.

July 2023

Muslim singer's faith overlooked following her death

WHEN THE SINGER who was born as Sinéad O'Connor died on July 26, there was a lot of emphasis in the media about her singing career and her strained relations with the Roman Catholic faith—the faith she was born into. Less attention was paid to something that had become very important to her in the last few years of her life: her conversion to Islam in 2018.

This omission was noted by Muslim commentators. They also noted the global media rarely used the Irish singer's preferred name: Shuhada' Sadaqat, the name she took for herself after converting to Islam five years ago. If religion was mentioned at all, it was mostly about her conflict with the Roman Catholic Church. This included the time, in 1992, she ripped up a photo of Pope John Paul II on *Saturday Night Live* to protest the church's handling of the issue of sexual abuse by priests.

Little was also said about how her burial rites were not Catholic but Muslim, or that the person who eulogized her was Sheikh Umar Al-Qadri, an Islamic scholar and the chief imam at the Islamic Centre of Ireland. As someone tweeted out following her death: "You'd be forgiven for missing that Sinéad O'Connor passed away as a Muslim named Shuhada' Sadaqat, as almost all posted photos are from before her converting and there's entire big media obituaries not using her chosen name even once."

For Anna Piela, a visiting scholar in religious studies and gender at Northwestern University, and author of *Wearing the Niqab: Muslim Women in the UK and the US* (2021), this represented "a seemingly willful ignorance" on the part of the media that were "more interested in her reputation as a rebellious and even sacrilegious celebrity."

When Sadaqat converted to Islam, she says it was "the natural conclusion of any intelligent theologian's journey." In an interview in 2019, she said it was while reading the Qur'an that she discovered "I've been a Muslim all my life and didn't realize it . . . I realized, 'Oh my God, I am home.'" She chose the name "Shuhada'" because it referred to the idea of bearing witness, as she hoped her life would be a witness to truth, justice and mercy.

Her conversion prompted supportive comments from Muslims. In response, Sadaqat thanked them, saying, "You can't begin to imagine how much your tenderness means to me." But there were also negative comments from non-Muslims. The Islamophobic comments were, she said, "disgusting." But most of that was missed by media reports following her death. In so doing, the media not only failed to explore "the religion that eventually brought her peace after a tumultuous faith journey," Piela says, they also missed "a chance to challenge Islamophobia." By overlooking her Muslim faith, they were disrespectful of her human and religious agency, Piela adds. "Her religious choice, belief, practice and identity . . . was seen as an afterthought."

In a statement about the singer's death, the Council on American-Islamic Relations (CAIR) noted many of the photos used in her obituaries were prior to her conversion where she had bare arms and her head uncovered. Those photos, it said, would have been counter to how she would have wanted to be depicted after converting, when she often wore a hijab and abaya in public. CAIR went on to urge the media to "respect her acceptance of Islam by acknowledging the name she chose for herself and using recent photos that depict how she chose to present herself."

In an interview with NPR, Al-Qadri, the imam who aided her conversion, acknowledged the public lack of interest in her Muslim faith bothered him. Noting this is a time when society is increasingly willing to address people by their preferred pronouns, Al-Qadri noted she didn't get the same respect or treatment by the media, who didn't use her Muslim name. She had "embraced Islam. She had accepted the identity. She had changed her name. And if one wants to honor her, let's honor her comprehensively, her personality comprehensively. And she was a proud Irish woman, but also, she was a proud Irish Muslim woman. And I think that should be acknowledged," he says. Speaking about her death, Al-Qadri said Muslims were sad because of the loss of someone who had had such a global, cultural impact. But they were also sad because they had "lost a sister in faith."

August 2023

Are liberal ideas winning the culture war?

"Liberals Have Won the Culture War." That was the title of an article published in August by Ryan Burge, an American political scientist, statistician, and Baptist pastor on his blog *Graphs About Religion.*

Associate professor at Eastern Illinois University, Burge is known for his work charting trends in the religious landscape of the US. Considering the news about all the states that have passed or proposed laws against abortion, trans people, and drag shows, you would be forgiven for thinking the US is moving to the right on these issues. But opinions in America about these hot-button topics have moved left since the early 1990s, he maintains. One of the reasons for that is religion—or its lack.

Burge traces the start of the culture wars in the US to a speech by Pat Buchanan on August 17, 1992. Buchanan, who had failed in his attempt to secure the Republican nomination to be president, delivered a speech to that party's convention announcing that America was headed in the wrong direction on things like gay rights and abortion. "We must take back our cities, and take back our culture, and take back our country," he stated. His goal, along with that of his supporters—including many on the religious right—was to stop what he saw as a leftward drift in America.

According to Burge, Buchanan failed. "I've looked at the data and it's clear to me that Christian conservatives failed miserably in this endeavor," he writes. "On every single social issue, the average American is more liberal today than they were just two decades ago." Burge comes to that conclusion by using the General Social Survey, which charts American opinion on various subjects such as drugs, same-sex marriage, and abortion.

For example, in the 1990s only about 20 per cent of Americans supported legalizing marijuana. Today 74 per cent do. When it comes to same-sex marriage, just 12 per cent were in favor in 1988. Today it is 73 per cent. On abortion, 40 per cent of Americans supported making it legal 30 years ago. Today 54 per cent favour it for any reason. One reason for the change, according to Burge, is that the US "is becoming a heck of a lot less religious" today.

Today in that country, 30 per cent say they are "nones"—people who have no religious affiliation. Since "nones" tend to be more socially liberal, the rise in the size of that group is having an affect on issues like abortion and same-sex marriage. Added to that is decreasing interest in religion in America. A recent Gallup poll found that membership in a church, mosque, synagogue, or other place of worship has fallen to 47 per cent of people in the US, down from 70 per cent in 1999.

But it's not just that American society is becoming less religious. "Even religious people are becoming more left leaning on these types of issues," he writes. For example, in 2004, just 12 per cent of evangelicals were in favour of same-sex marriage. By 2021, 35 per cent of evangelicals felt that way. For evangelicals between the ages of 18-35, that figure was 56 per cent. "It seems inevitable that a majority of evangelicals will support same-sex marriage in the next two decades," Burge observes.

Mainline Christian support for same-sex marriage is even higher, at 68 per cent, up from 33 per cent in 2004. There has also been an increase in support among Catholics, from 38 per cent to 66 per cent. "It's hard to look at these numbers and not be astonished at how fast opinion has moved on this topic, even among religious groups like evangelicals and Catholics where the church's teachings haven't moved at all," he writes. There has also been dramatic movement on marijuana. "Today, a majority of every major Christian tradition is in favour of legalized weed," he adds. When it comes to abortion, most religious people agree it should not be illegal in all circumstances, Burge says.

Of course, Burge is writing about America. Canada is at a very different place on these issues. Yet we are hearing some of the same culture-war rhetoric being preached by Canadian religious leaders or advocated by politicians who are against 2SLGBTQ+ and trans rights, abortion, and other issues. But if Burge is right about the US, all the preaching and laws about 2SLGBTQ+ people, trans people, and drag queens won't ultimately mean a thing in his country, when it comes to what people really believe. It looks like Americans, including many religious Americans, have moved on from traditional views on many social issues—despite what their ministers and leaders say.

September 2023

2

ON RECONCILIATION AND JUSTICE

Decolonizing Christian faith

In April 2022 when I was in Rome with a delegation of Indigenous people, I reported on their request to the Pope for an apology for how the Roman Catholic Church has treated Indigenous people in Canada. Four months later, I heard him deliver that apology in Alberta on July 25. It's been over a year and I'm still processing my response to those events.

On those trips, I was humbled and horrified to hear the stories of pain Indigenous people recounted about their experiences at residential schools. I heard people talk about being taken away, as young as four years old, crying all the way to the school. I heard people tell me about witnessing or experiencing physical and sexual abuse at the hands of school officials, including priests. I met people who lost their language, culture, and connection to family and home.

At the same time, I was impressed by their strength, dignity, and resilience—despite those horrific abuses—and how their Indigenous spirituality and traditions give them the ability to carry on. One question that has remained with me since then is how I, as a Christian, should respond. I wasn't there, at the schools; I didn't participate in the abuse; I'm not even Catholic. But surely I need to do something.

That something, it seems to me, is to decolonize my faith. But how does one do that? For me, it means starting by acknowledging that the Christian religion in Canada—the one I grew up in—is based on European and white colonial perspectives and practices. What we call Christianity didn't fall from the air in an unvarnished and neutral form or come straight from the Bible to Canada. Most of us have inherited the cultural, political, economic, social, and gender ideas of Christians who shaped the religion in Europe and then brought it to this country generations ago. As my Indigenous friend Kyle Mason notes,

"Many Canadian Christians aren't aware of how their view of faith was formed from a European or western mindset. God is bigger than that."

Decolonizing faith also means acknowledging that, while the Christian religion has been good news for many in Canada, it has been decidedly bad news for others—especially for Indigenous people. And not only Indigenous people: women and members of the 2SLGBTQ+ community also struggle to live full, meaningful, safe, and dignified lives because of how Christianity has been interpreted and applied.

This is hard for many Christians to admit. It's common for people to quickly point to all the good Christianity has done in Canada—hospitals, shelters, food banks, working with disadvantaged youth, responding to natural disasters, or alleviating poverty around the world, to name a few. All those things are true and good, but they don't let Christians off the hook for the wrongs done to those who have experienced the religion as harmful and hurtful.

Decolonizing faith also means listening to Indigenous people. It means taking time to understand the Indigenous approach to life, with its emphasis on community, cooperation, and the sacredness of all creation—and then asking what we might learn from it. It also means not seeing Indigenous people as objects of Christian conversion. As my friend Kyle puts it: by listening to Indigenous people, we can "become more inclusive of Indigenous views of spirituality and move away from the old missionary idea of taking God to Indigenous people."

There are also structural implications to decolonizing faith. Do churches and denominations promote safe spaces for conversation between Indigenous and non-Indigenous peoples? Do they foster those conversations? Or are only certain people welcome to speak and share, and only about certain topics?

If Christianity in Canada is to decolonize, then it needs to take to heart what American theologian James Cone suggests in the context of race relations in the US: those who have done the oppressing need to listen to those who have been oppressed if they are to truly change perspectives. The oppressed, Cone says, deeply understand the ways the dominant system is flawed, since these flaws have consequences that directly impact them. This first-hand knowledge can help fix the system that keeps one group down while elevating the other.

As for me, an older, white, straight, male Christian, I still have much to learn. I have only started on this journey of decolonizing my faith, my trips to Rome and Alberta giving me strong impetus. I am ready to keep trying.

November 2022

Before Christmas on Turtle Island, what was God saying to Indigenous people?

At Christmas, Christians celebrate how they believe God came into the world through Jesus. But before God came into the world 2,000 years ago in Palestine, as Christians believe, what was God saying to Indigenous people in North America?

After all, it's not like Christians believe God wasn't doing anything to communicate to human beings prior to that Christmas event. This would have to include Indigenous people, who have been living in North America for as long as 12,000 years. And if that's the case, what was God saying?

That's the question I posed to my friend Terry LeBlanc, an Indigenous Christian leader and director of the North American Institute for Indigenous Theological Studies. While affirming the traditional Christmas story of God breaking into the world as a baby in a particular place and time to provide redemption and restoration for all creation, Leblanc notes this doesn't mean God wasn't also speaking to Indigenous people before that event. While the history we read about in the Bible was unfolding, "there was an historical timeline of equal length unfolding here and in other places of the globe," he says.

This doesn't mean "God, as Jesus, was here (in North America)," he adds, although he says there are Indigenous prophecies "of the arrival of the message of Jesus." But God "as Creator and God as the Spirit were here," he states, speaking to Indigenous people through things like the seven teachings: love, respect, courage, honesty, wisdom, humility, and truth.

As an "Indigenous follower of the Jesus Way," as he describes himself, the biblical story qualifies "the notion of the Creator's sufficient revelation to Indigenous peoples in the past," Leblanc said. "For whatever reason, God chose to enter God's own creation in human form to perform the ceremony of redemption and restoration, through a particular people group, from a particular land, at a particular time, and that this was for all of creation," he adds.

That's not how Europeans saw it when they arrived on this continent. They assumed North America's Indigenous people were heathens, people with no prior knowledge whatsoever of God—at least as they conceived of God. But Indigenous people weren't heathens, Leblanc says; they had a different way of understanding Creator.

Christian missionaries assumed those stories "were irrelevant and/or replaceable by the biblical narrative, instead of recognizing the universal applicability of those [Indigenous] narratives," he says. Blinded to the Creator's presence among Indigenous people, and conflating Christianity with their own culture, the European missionaries sought to convert them to their way of being Christian. "It is this theologically aberrant understanding that has been thrust upon Indigenous peoples," Leblanc says.

Indigenous people need to free themselves from that view, LeBlanc says, and so do non-Indigenous Christians—a process called decolonization. As he puts it: "Decolonization is just as needed for Euro-centric Christianity at Christmas as it is for Indigenous peoples. Only then will we be able to see a Christ-filled celebration that is not devoid of culture, but rather expressive of the intent of God through all cultures that have emerged through time." For him, that intent is "the redemption and restoration of all things . . . whatever hinders or redirects that intention needs either to be decolonized or set aside entirely."

What would it mean for non-Indigenous Christians to decolonize Christmas? One way to start is by remembering the radical idea behind God's coming to Earth was to upend all rulers, structures, cultures, and economic and political systems. Another is to remember how Jesus, during his ministry, discomfited the political and religious elites of his day, overturning cultural norms and challenging theological certainties by doing things like eating with prostitutes, befriending tax collectors, and re-defining the concept of "neighbour." As Christian author Jonathan Martin puts it: if this Christmas the Jesus you worship "makes emperors feel comfortable and oppressed people feel unsafe, it's time for a grand reversal."

December 2019

A call for faith groups to apologize for the mistreatment of women

When recorded derogatory comments made by Donald Trump about women became public, I posted an apology to my female friends on Facebook. In it, I said I was appalled by what Trump said and did. But what disturbed me more, I wrote, "was hearing from my female friends that this kind of thing is normal—it has happened to so many, including to many who grew up in Christian churches."

To all of them, I expressed my sadness and outrage. I went on to ask if this was a topic I should write about on the Faith Page. The answers came quickly: Yes. "Please do, John," said one woman. "It is time that we stop accepting this as normal and a woman's lot."

"You have no idea how prevalent sexual harassment of young girls and adult women is in our Christian circles," said another.

I then asked if some would share their stories and those came quickly, too. A female pastor spoke about entering a room full of her congregants and having an older man say, "Come sit here on my lap."

"I just laughed it off, but it made me very wary of him," she said. Several women wrote of being inappropriately touched by male relatives back in the 1960s and 70s—men who were respected leaders in their churches.

"It was done in plain sight," said one woman of what happened to her. "There was an apathy among Christian adults in the generation before us, to look the other way."

Another woman wrote about her father, also a highly respected church leader, who regularly touched her and her sisters in sexual ways. "He treated us like we were inferior, all the while being an elder of the church. You can't begin to know the devastation it caused!" There were more stories: a professor of religion who touched his female students in inappropriate ways; men who exposed themselves to women on buses; men who rubbed against women and girls in crowded places; men who hugged too tightly and for too long.

Reading the messages, I couldn't believe how many women I knew had experienced those things—and I was probably only scratching the surface. It made me angry and sad. We can't fix the problems of the past, but maybe we can say sorry. Surely it's time for Canadian faith groups that haven't already done so to issue apologies—to say sorry for the harm their religions have caused to women over the centuries. What can they apologize for? Here are a few ideas:

They can apologize for not believing women when they complained about harassment and abuse. They can apologize for not holding abusers accountable for their actions. They can apologize for how they have selectively interpreted the Bible to justify silencing women and treating them as inferior. They can apologize for taking so long to let women use all their gifts in the church in service to God. They can apologize for excluding women from the boards and committees that shaped the mission and vision of their denominations. And they can apologize for not speaking out against injustice towards women in broader society—things like paying women less because of their gender, and denying them promotions.

I'm sure there are other things that could be named, and other religions would have their own unique additions to the list. One leader in promoting equality for women in religious groups is former US President Jimmy Carter. In a speech in 2009 he summed it up this way: "The view that the Almighty considers women to be inferior to men is not restricted to one religion or tradition," he said. "Women are prevented from playing a full and equal role in many faiths, creating an environment in which violations against women are justified."

The truth, he stated, "is that male religious leaders have had—and still have—an option to interpret holy teachings either to exalt or subjugate women. They have, for their own selfish ends, overwhelmingly chosen the latter." It is time, he stated, "we had the courage to challenge these views and set a new course that demands equal rights for women and men, girls and boys."

Let's begin with an apology.

October 2016

Misogyny in religion, or, things Christian women hear

CONSIDERING HOW THEY'VE been treated, why do so many women stick with religion? For centuries they have been told by men to shut up, cover up, and put up with countless rules and regulations governing how, where, when, and why they may or may not participate in religious roles or rituals of one sort or another. Oh, and how they had to dress while doing it.

I honestly don't know how so many of them manage to keep their faith. If the shoe were on the other foot—if men faced the same limitations and restrictions based on interpretations of selected verses from ancient texts—most of them would be out of there in a minute. But somehow, and for some reason, many religious women hang in there.

All I feel is awe.

What got me thinking about how women have been treated by religious groups was the hashtag #thingsonlyChristianwomenhear, which went viral on Twitter this spring. Canadian author Sarah Bessey began the conversation about the sexist and toxic things Christian women hear. According to Bessey, who wrote the book *Jesus Feminist: An Invitation to Revisit the Bible's View of Women* (2013), it was just something she wanted to talk to her Twitter followers about. But the hashtag quickly went viral, amassing hundreds of responses from women sharing things they had heard in churches or from church leaders.

Examples include: "You are an amazing leader! You'd make an excellent pastor's wife someday!" And, "Women are too emotional to be leaders and pastors. It would never work." Or, "OK, you can teach this, but there has to be a male leader in the room when you do. We'll send someone." Not to mention, "Your clothes can cause boys to sin." And the clincher: "You have tremendous leadership gifts . . . it's too bad you weren't born male."

Writes Bessey on her Facebook page: "This hashtag is pulling back the curtain on the everyday lived experiences of women within the church." She adds that the responses were "illuminating, sad, infuriating, ridiculous, funny . . . we still need to speak about freedom and expose the lies and amplify the voices of women who have too often been silenced." In an interview with *HuffPost* she goes on to say, "I love the church but I also know that we can't fix what we refuse to acknowledge . . . I look forward to the day when women with leadership and insight, gifts and talents, callings and prophetic leanings are called out and celebrated." She stated in a subsequent tweet: "Nobody is attacking the church. We're attacking the patriarchal spirit that has a death-grip on the throat of the beautiful bride of Christ."

There was pushback. Author and speaker Rebekah Lyons urged women to avoid making the hashtag a "megaphone for bitterness." That prompted *Christianity Today* editor Katelyn Beaty to respond: "I don't know . . . it seems to me when men name structural problems it's prophetic. When women name structural problems it's bitterness?"

Of course, many church groups are welcoming of women as leaders. But I bet some of those women also have experienced sexism while trying to follow God's call in their lives. And it's not just a religious issue—women hear similar things in many parts of society. Another Twitter hashtag, #thingsonlywomenwritershear, gained traction at the same time as *The Handmaid's Tale*, was beginning its run on TV. In the series, based on the novel by Canadian author Margaret Atwood, men in the future theocratic country of Gilead use religion as a basis to subjugate women. Just fiction, right? In fact, Atwood based her book, published in 1985, on real-life events throughout history, such as the traditions of seventeenth-century Puritans, the experience of women in some Muslim-majority countries, and the rise of the religious right in the US.

One can only hope that the imaginary country of Gilead will remain a fantasy. The comments of women today show there's still work to be done.

June 2017

Time to remove statues of white Jesus?

Like many other Canadians and Americans, I reacted positively to the removal of statues of Confederate generals and leaders in the US. It's time to see those old symbols of racism go; taking them down is a good first step in promoting healing and reconciliation in that country.

But what about statuary and paintings of Jesus that show him as a white man? Should those go, too? That's what some African Americans in the US are calling for in the wake of the killing of George Floyd by police on May 25 in Minneapolis, Minnesota. This includes Black Lives Matter supporter Shaun King, who posted on Twitter: "I think the statues of the white European they claim is Jesus should also come down. They are a form of white supremacy. Always have been. In the Bible, when the family of Jesus wanted to hide, and blend in, guess where they went? EGYPT! Not Denmark. Tear them down." Added award-winning Nigerian American author Nnedi Okorafor, also on Twitter: "Blond blue-eyed Jesus IS a form of white supremacy."

Both King and Okorafor are reacting to the traditional way Jesus has been pictured for centuries, especially in North America and Europe—as white and European, not as the Middle Eastern man that he was. For many Christians, the one picture that has come to personify Jesus more than any other is Warner E. Sallman's *Head of Christ*. Painted in 1940, the famed image of a very white-skinned, brown-blonde Jesus was found in many homes throughout the US and Canada, including mine when I was growing up. The image spread widely throughout the twentieth century, found on paintings, prayer cards, clocks, bookmarks, and in magazines. It could be found in a wide range of churches. This included Black churches in the US, where people like Anthea Butler, associate professor of religious studies and Africana studies at the University of Pennsylvania, saw it as a child.

Sallman's Jesus was "the Jesus you saw in all the Black Baptist churches," Butler told Religion News Service. But, she adds, he didn't look like Black Christians. Instead, Jesus looked "like the people who were beating you up in the streets or setting dogs on you." That Jesus sent a message that told Black people, "If Jesus is white and God is white, then authority is white," she says.

Edward J. Blum, co-author of *The Color of Christ: The Son of God and the Saga of Race in America* (2014), would like to see that painting, and others, removed. "If white Jesus can't be put to death, how could it possibly be the case that systemic racism is done?" he told Religion News Service. "This is one that just seems obvious. This one seems easy to give up."

But is it? The angry reaction to Shaun King, after he tweeted out his call to get rid of statues and paintings depicting Jesus as white, suggests the answer is no. A survey by pollster Rasmussen Reports found 69 per cent of American adults in the US opposed removing statues and paintings depicting Jesus as white.

An American Christian publication expressing support for a change in the way Jesus is depicted is the *National Catholic Reporter*. In a column, the editorial staff write that King and his supporters have a point. "As a Palestinian Jew, Jesus was not white, and the ubiquitous depiction of Jesus as not only white, but often blonde-haired and blue-eyed as in the famous Warner Sallman illustration *Head of Christ*, is not without consequences, both theological and psychological," the newspaper says. An exclusively white Jesus "not only narrows our understanding of him, it sends a message that connects Jesus to the powerful, not the oppressed."

Noting how, in the Catholic tradition, Jesus, Mary, and many of the saints are represented differently in societies across the globe, the paper asks, "How many of us think of these faces in our daily prayer lives? How many of us are confronted with the image of Jesus in a Black body at our parishes? How many of us are uncomfortable with the fact that God chose to become incarnate in a body that was not white, but likely brown?"

The editors do not call for the elimination of depictions of Jesus as white, but for more balance. They suggest dioceses across the country host art contests, inviting people to create different images of Christ and featuring them in churches in each parish.

"Symbols matter," they conclude. "The versions of Jesus that white US Catholics see in their parishes will surely influence how they look at their non-white neighbours and whether those white Catholics will stand up to oppose sinful structures of racism . . . there are at least as many faces of God as there are people on Earth. Our churches should depict the multitude."

July 2020

White Christianity and Disney princess theology

"White Christianity suffers from a bad case of Disney Princess theology." That's how a meme circulating on social media began. Created by Erna Kim Hackett, executive pastor of The Way church in Berkeley, California, and a woman of colour, the meme was prompted by Black Lives Matter protests in the US in 2020.

Hackett's social media post went on to say when white Christians read the Bible, "they see themselves as the princess in every story. They are Esther, never Xerxes or Haman. They are Peter, but never Judas. They are the woman anointing Jesus, never the Pharisees. They are the Jews escaping slavery, never Egypt."

For Americans in particular, she continued, "the citizens of the most powerful country in the world, who enslaved both Native and Black people, to see itself as Israel and not Egypt when it is studying Scripture is a perfect example of Disney princess theology. It means that as people in power they have no lens for locating themselves rightly in Scripture or society—and it has made them blind and utterly ill equipped to engage issues of power and injustice. It is some very weak Bible work."

As a Canadian, I have never thought of myself as a citizen of a superpower—or as a Disney princess, for that matter. But as a white person who is a citizen of a wealthy country, with all the advantages of my race and privilege, I admit I have read the Bible in the way Hackett suggests.

When I hear the stories of many Black and Indigenous people in this country, I am reminded that Christianity—instead of bringing good news—has caused great harm, suffering and oppression to them and their ancestors. When they read the Bible, it is more likely they identify with the poor and oppressed in its pages—unlike me.

I'm not the only white person who recognizes, belatedly, how privileged my viewpoint has been. So does Brian Zahnd, lead pastor of Word of Life Church in St. Joseph, Missouri. In a 2014 article published on his website titled *My Problem With the Bible*, Zahnd, who is white, writes about how hard it is for him to truly understand the Bible today.

As someone who is white and privileged, Zahnd says, he can't read the Bible through the eyes of those who lived it: Hebrew slaves suffering in Egypt, conquered Judeans deported to Babylon, first-century Jews living under Roman occupation. As a citizen of a superpower, it is challenging for him to read the Bible since it is "a narrative told from the perspective of the poor, the oppressed, the enslaved, the conquered, the occupied, the defeated . . . I was born among the conquerors. I live in the empire. But I want to read the Bible and think it's talking to me. This is a problem."

The Bible, he notes, is a revolutionary document. Through Jesus, it calls for a new way of seeing the world from the bottom-up. To help others understand what he means, Zahnd asks American Christians to imagine what would happen if a compelling and charismatic figure arrived on the world scene today, amassed a great following, and then announced the arrival of a new economic order for the world—those at the bottom economically and racially would rise to the top, while those at the top would be forced to the bottom.

How one reacted would depend on whether you are at the top or the bottom, he says. "I can imagine the Bangladeshis saying, 'When do we start?!'" he writes. "And American Christians saying, 'Hold on now, let's not get carried away!'"

During Black Lives Matter protests, US streets were filled with people protesting racism, poverty and injustice. I'm guessing if Jesus were around then, he would have been marching with those crowds and telling them God was on their side—on the side of the poor and the oppressed. He might have even joined them in pulling down statues of Confederate generals and other racist figures.

If you are white and privileged like me, you may experience discomfort when considering Jesus' revolutionary reordering that Zahnd describes in his article. Or you might find you suffer from a case of Disney princess theology as laid out by Erna Kim Hackett. Maybe your ancestors, like mine, were never enslaved or sent to residential schools. Maybe you, like me, don't suffer the effects of racism today. Or, like me, you don't fear the police.

If that's the case, perhaps it's time to take out your Bible and have another look.

June 2021

Christians called to be ministers of reconciliation

Delegates and supporters from the Assembly of First Nations, the Métis National Council, and Inuit Tapiriit Kanatami gathered on the roof of their hotel Monday morning for a sunrise ceremony before the first meetings with Pope Francis in Rome in April 2022. The ceremony was led by Fred Kelly, a citizen of the Ojibways of Onigaming of the Anishinaabe Nation in Treaty 3 and an Elder in Midewiwin, the Grand Medicine Society of the Anishinaabe. Treaty 3 takes in land from just west of Thunder Bay to just east of Winnipeg.

The ceremony, with the famous church of Santa Maria Maggiore as a backdrop, included a pipe, strawberries, water, the burning of sweetgrass, and drumming and singing. Before the ceremony, Kelly explained that the word "Ojibway" means "roots." Just as trees and plants have roots, Indigenous people "have a special relationship to the land," he said. "We belong to the land, but we don't own the land. The dominant society in Canada sees it differently, they think they can own it."

The morning ceremony was preceded the night before by a Mass for delegates, their supporters, and others. Presided over by Bishops Raymond Poisson of Saint-Jérôme, Quebec, William McGrattan of Calgary, Richard Smith of Edmonton, Donald Bolen of Regina, and Richard Gagnon of Winnipeg, the Mass included prayer for the delegates' visits to the Pope that week.

In his homily, Bishop McGrattan said every Christian is called to be a "minister of reconciliation" and that achieving reconciliation requires people to "walk together" while "taking very small steps." The meeting with the Pope, he said, is one of those steps. It is "like a seed, but it can bear the fruit of healing and forgiveness." After the homily Bishop McGrattan prayed that the visits would create a "path to repair the injustices of the past."

April 2022

"I am very sorry," Pope tells Indigenous people from Canada

SAYING HE WAS "deeply grieved by the stories of the suffering, hardship, discrimination, and various forms of abuse" First Nations, Métis, and Inuit experienced in residential schools operated by the Roman Catholic Church, Pope Francis told delegates from those groups, "I join my brothers the Canadian bishops in asking your pardon." In Rome on April 1, he said, "With all my heart, I am very sorry," adding he also "asked for God's forgiveness."

Hearing his words were the 32 delegates representing First Nations, Métis, and Inuit, who had met privately with him earlier in the week. They were accompanied by seven bishops and over 100 secondary delegates and supporters including Elders, spiritual advisors, survivors, and others. The stories the survivors told him of being robbed of their identity, culture, and spirituality were "chilling," the Pope said, causing him to feel "indignation and shame." He felt indignation, since it is not right to "accept evil," and sorrow and shame for "the role a number of Catholics have had in all these things that wounded you, and the abuses you suffered and the lack of respect for your identity, culture, and spiritual values." All these things, and the "deplorable conduct" of some members of the Catholic church, are "contrary to the Gospel of Jesus Christ," he said. "Jesus taught us to welcome, love, serve, and not judge," he said, adding "it is a frightening thing then when in the name of the faith, counter- witness is rendered to the Gospel."

The meeting began with prayers from each of the First Nations, Métis, and Inuit delegations in their own languages, including by Elder Fred Kelly, a member of the Anishinaabe Nation in Treaty 3 territory, which extends from west of Thunder Bay to just east of Winnipeg. The prayers were remarkable in themselves, since those they were once forbidden for Indigenous people to say in public.

Along with the prayers, the three delegations gave gifts to the Pope: a beaded leather stole made by Therese Dettanikkeaze from the Northlands Denesuline First Nation in Manitoba; traditional handmade snowshoes; a book of stories from Métis survivors; a cross made of baleen from a bowhead whale; and a sealskin pouch. The Pope gave a bronze olive branch, a sign of peace and reconciliation, to the three delegations.

In his remarks, Bishop Raymond Poisson, president of the Canadian Conference of Catholic Bishops, acknowledged the Church's history in Canada "is marked with stigma of mistakes and failures to love our neighbour, in particular towards members of those nations who have been present in Canada for centuries." By coming to Rome, the Church was showing its desire for reconciliation with Indigenous people, he said, adding the Pope's "warm welcome as pastor of the universal Church" was important for "all Canadians on this road of reconciliation." The Pope's positive reply to the invitation to come to Canada "warms the hearts of the Canadian faithful," he said, adding "we are ready today to help you pack your bags!"

April 2022

"Creator does things in Creator's time"

"Do YOU THINK it's appropriate for Indigenous people, especially elderly residential school survivors, to have to travel all the way to Rome to meet the Pope? Why couldn't he have met them in Canada?" Pixie Wells, who is Métis from Abbotsford, British Columbia, was asked this question by a reporter in St. Peter's Square, after the Métis National Council delegation visited with Pope Francis in April at The Vatican in Rome.

Wells, who is president of the Fraser Valley Métis Association, acknowledged the trip was arduous for some of older people. But, she noted, for a number of delegates, older and younger, the trip was a highlight of their lives because of their Catholic faith. For them the trip "was worthwhile" and a special spiritual moment because they got to meet the Pope, she said.

Antoinette LaFleur, 79, of Saskatchewan feels a similar way. LaFleur, a residential school survivor, was one of three from the Métis delegation asked to share their stories in the audience with the Pope. She admits to having lost her faith in her younger days following her ten years at residential school. "During that time, I didn't pass it on to my kids," she says. But as a committed Catholic today, her meeting with the Pope was a special experience. "He made us feel comfortable," she says, adding she never dreamed she would one day have a chance to meet him. "He radiated calm."

Brianna Lizotte and Alex Kuturok lead the Métis delegation from the Vatican.

As the delegates from the Métis National Council delegation filed into the library where the meeting was held, the Pope was at the door greeting each person with a handshake. "I told him I'm not going to wash my hand for a week!" LaFleur says with a laugh, adding the Pope laughed at her remark.

Emilien Janvier, 74, also from Saskatchewan and part of the Métis delegation, felt the same way. He also spent ten years at a residential school but kept his Catholic faith. Meeting the Pope was "a chance of a lifetime," he says, admitting he was nervous before the meeting. "But he made us feel comfortable." A highlight for Janvier was being asked to pray in Dene, his language, before the meeting started. "I prayed for guidance and strength so we can move forward," he says.

LaFleur and Janvier are not alone in their Catholic beliefs. Many Métis are Roman Catholic or practice a mix of Christianity and traditional Indigenous spirituality. Statistics Canada's most recent census data from 2011 shows over 500,000 Indigenous people out of the over 1.6 million in Canada are Roman Catholic.

Wells is not a member of the Catholic Church, but she has a profound sense of spirituality that is shared by many of the Inuit, Métis, and First Nations delegates in Rome. For her, spirituality is revealed as a deep trust and belief in Creator. In response to queries about whether this meeting with the Pope should have taken place a long time ago, Wells said: "Creator does things in Creator's time. Creator made the timing right for us to be here now." That includes the postponement of the trip from December 2021 to April 2023 due to the rise in Omicron infections around the world. "We may not have been ready then," said Wells, of the delay. "Creator doesn't make any mistakes."

April 2022

"For the children"

It's almost 9,000 kilometres from the Vatican to Kamloops, British Columbia, but for Rosanne Casimir, Kúkpi7 (Chief) of the Tk'emlúps te Secwépemc in that interior BC community, the two places are strongly linked. "Many believe we wouldn't be here (in Rome) without the discovery of the graves," she said, referring to the visit in April 2022 between delegates from First Nations, Inuit, and Métis communities and Pope Francis.

For Casimir, like for many others on the trip, the 2021 discovery of unmarked graves at the former Kamloops residential school was a turning point in Indigenous relations with the Roman Catholic Church. It helped create the conditions for the "historic" meeting with the Pope, she says, adding she came to Rome with a "deliberate message from my people to have the Pope acknowledge the harm" done by the residential schools.

That admission, and an apology in Canada, will be the first step towards reconciliation with the Church, Casimir says. "A lot of other things also need to take place," she says, adding there would be follow up with the Canadian Conference of Catholic Bishops when the meetings are over. This includes

"acts of contrition" so "wrongs can be made right for our people." Members of her community differ on their willingness to pursue reconciliation with the Church, Casimir says. "Some are ready, some aren't," she says, noting the meeting with the Pope is a first step on that journey.

For Casimir, the Pope coming to Canada and apologizing is mandatory. She would like him to do it in Kamloops, which some call "ground zero" for the current level of awareness about the abuses of residential schools. Although she acknowledges not everyone in her community supported her trip to meet the Pope, she "feels good" about the visit, believing it "will make a difference for our community. It can start the healing."

Before she left for Rome, Casimir participated in a ceremony with Elders and other community members to prepare herself mentally, emotionally and spiritually. "I felt supported as we sang and prayed together," she says. "It was the good medicine I needed." She also had to fit in a speech at a camp for Indigenous children just before she left. "It was good to be around the children," she says. "It reminded me of the purpose of the trip going forward, for the children."

April 2022

Singing so the spirits won't be lonely

My time in Rome in April 2022 was filled with many more stories than I could write. I experienced an ocean of information and emotion from my front row seat watching history in the making as Métis, First Nations, and Inuit delegates shared their stories with Pope Francis—and received a personal apology in return.

It was a profoundly religious experience. Each day began at 6:30 a.m. with a mass conducted by one of the five bishops on the trip, followed by a traditional Indigenous sunrise ceremony. Each meeting with the Pope began with prayer, often conducted in the language of the Indigenous person doing the praying. Press briefings were infused with references to the divine, God, or Creator. Sometimes they included songs, prayers, and sacred ceremonies. Delegates recognized there was something beyond humankind at work during the week. As Dene National and Assembly of First Nations regional Chief Gerald Antoine put it: "There are powers greater than us out there, working their ways to line things up the ways they need to be."

On one of the days, four women sang and drummed in St. Peter's Square

before the First Nations delegates emerged from their meeting with the Pope. When asked why, one said: "Our artifacts are nearby [in the Vatican Museums]. They contain our ancestor's spirits. We are singing so they won't be lonely."

Calgary's Archbishop William McGrattan said of the time in Rome: "This work is divinely inspired, beyond our human ability to understand and recognize. I think we all sensed the presence of God, of Creator."

While there were heavy times, filled with emotional stories of horror and trauma, there were also many lighthearted moments. The delegates loved to laugh. They clearly enjoyed being together, and many new friendships were formed.

Meeting the Pope was a huge highlight for many, especially for the Catholics on the trip—and there were many among the delegates, generating some memorable experiences. When one delegate shook the Pope's hand, she clasped her other hand over his and held it there for a moment. Her takeaway? "He has soft hands, like bread," she said with a smile.

Lots of media were present from Canada, the US, and Europe. About 75 reporters were in Rome for the visit; the media scrums in St. Peter's Square were tight and packed. Reporters could be an overbearing group at times, pushing cameras and microphones into the faces of delegates. But the delegates were patient in taking time to answer questions, even when it was hard. Not only that, they thanked us for telling their stories to the world. More than one remarked it was the worldwide coverage of Kamloops that helped them get the attention they needed to begin the healing journey. For journalists who are accustomed to mostly receiving criticism and hate mail, that was an unexpected and gratifying experience.

While the delegates agreed the visit was worthwhile, they were aware not everyone back home did. Their Facebook pages were filled with angry and vitriolic criticisms of the trip. At one dinner, a delegate implored the others to turn off social media; it wasn't good for their souls or for the goals of the trip, he said. That anger is real, and it needs to be taken into account—by the delegates, and also by the Church. It will take a long time to heal the wounds of the past. Some will never find healing.

The story isn't over. Everyone agreed the visit, and the papal apology, was just the beginning of a long road ahead. Indigenous people and the Church will need to continue to be in conversation in the months leading up to the Pope's visit to Canada—perhaps as early as this summer—and beyond.

The final audience with the Pope was filled with all the solemnity one would expect from such an occasion, but when it ended, the Pope stood up, waved at the delegates and said, "Thanks for the visit. Bye-bye." It was a special human moment, one that made everyone smile.

April 2022

A bus filled with hurt and hope

It was a bus filled with hurt and hope. Sponsored by the Archdiocese of Saint Boniface, in Manitoba, it carried 41 residential school survivors from the First Nation communities of Poplar River, Berens River, Bloodvein, Little Grand Rapids, Pauingassi, Hollow Water, Manigotogan, and Sagkeeng to Alberta to hear the Pope's apology. The hurt came from the survivors' experiences at residential schools—painful memories sparked by the trip. But for some, hearing the Pope apologize also prompted feelings of hope that things could maybe now get better. That they could heal.

As a reporter from the *Winnipeg Free Press*, I was invited to come along to hear their stories and share their experience at Maskwacis, where Pope Francis issued his historic apology on Monday, July 25, and at Lac Ste. Anne, a site of ancient pilgrimage for Indigenous people in Canada. For me, it was a bookend to a trip I took earlier, in March and early April, to report on the visit by Indigenous delegations to the Pope in Rome. In both places, it was a privilege to hear survivors tell their stories. In Alberta, it was a chance to learn what the papal apology on Canadian soil means to those who have suffered so much.

There's no denying it; it was hard to hear the stories. There is so much pain. At times I offered to let survivors stop sharing; I didn't want to be responsible for opening up old wounds. But they wanted to talk. It meant a lot that someone wanted to listen. For some, it was part of their healing. While often overwhelmed by the depth of their sorrow, I was also impressed again and again by their strength and resilience; they have overcome so much.

I also enjoyed hearing them laugh—and they liked to laugh! Whether it was telling jokes or entertaining with funny stories, humour was as much a hallmark of the trip as sadness. It was also moving to hear some say they are now prepared to grant the Pope, and the Roman Catholic Church, the forgiveness he asked for and look for ways to move on.

It will take time. Indigenous people in Canada are divided over whether the apology said enough or went far enough—if it will ever make up for the pain they endured in residential schools. Yet, as some noted, they have to do it—they have to forgive in order to break the cycle of anger and blame for the sake of younger generations.

As for me, I also need time to process what I saw and heard. The stories below are glimpses from the trip, snippets of lives broken and torn apart by a cruel, church-supported residential-school system that, in the end, failed in its goal to break the spirit of proud and noble peoples. Now non-Indigenous

Canadians need to listen and find ways to support Indigenous neighbours as they use the papal apology to start a new path forward, for themselves and with all of us. *Meegwetch* to the survivors who welcomed me aboard their bus, who shared their hurt and their hope. I hope I am a better person because of it.

Humanity taken away

"They took us from our homes, cut our hair, strapped us," says Verna Prince, 81, of Sagkeeng First Nation. She was sent to a residential school at age six. She was there for seven years. "Our humanity was taken away. It hurts us still. I'm still mourning," she says.

For Prince, going on the trip is a way to honour those who have died and cannot hear the apology. "Most of those my age who went to residential school are gone," she says, adding she asked Creator what she could do now that she is older. "Creator told me I have to stand up and tell the story," she says. She appreciates the Pope's apology, and his request for forgiveness. But it will take time to process it. "Those who weren't at residential school can't know how hard it was," she says. "It's going to take a while to forgive. I need time to think about it."

Break the cycle of anger

For Rose Klippenstein of Poplar River, the trip is something she can do to honour her mother and older siblings, all of whom went to residential schools. "They didn't talk about it," says Klippenstein, 64, noting they have all passed away.

Klippenstein, who has stayed with the Catholic Church, went to residential high schools as a teen in the late 1970s. When she went, things were better, she says. Her main memory is "the loneliness." Hearing the apology prompts a sense of relief. "Finally, he apologized," she says.

Forgiving the Church "will be hard," she says, noting many Indigenous people are deeply angry about what happened at the schools. "We need to break that cycle of anger," she says. "We can't get stuck in the past. If we stay there, we won't get anywhere." At the same time, younger Indigenous people need to know the history of the schools, and what they did to First Nations people. "It's our responsibility to educate them about it," she says.

Attacking from a place of pain

Cynthia Bunn of Sagkeeng First Nation believes "God had a reason" for everyone who was on the bus, even if some have doubts about going—including her. "I told the Archbishop I didn't want to go because of my osteoarthritis," she says. "I worried it would be too hard on me." But Bunn, who attended a residential school for four years, is glad she went to hear the Pope's apology in person. "I felt his sincerity," she says, pointing to her heart. "I believe he wants to walk with us."

It hurts to see some Indigenous people criticize aspects of the papal visit (for example, the gift of a headdress, which the Pope willingly accepted) but she says she understands where it is coming from. "They are attacking from a place of pain," she says. "Many have had a hard life, been beaten down."

"I saw things"

Stafford Bruce of Poplar River is also on the trip. A quiet, dignified man, he breaks down when he talks about his time in residential school. "I saw things," the sixty-eight-year-old says. One of them was watching supervisors in the dorm at the school beat a teenage boy. "I was only 15 at the time," he says, wiping his eyes. "It still brings tears to my eyes."

He appreciates the papal apology, but all he could think of when the Pope was speaking was that boy. It was "not enough" for that boy, he says. "It will never be enough."

Pope's words "help me in my healing"

Susan Daniels, 68, was just six years old when she and her two older siblings were taken to a residential school. Originally from Fairford, Manitoba, and now living at Sagkeeng First Nation, she remembers a black car coming to her house and then being driven over four hours to the school. "It was very scary," she says. "We cried all the way."

Daniels spent seven years in residential school. "It was a bad experience," she says. "I have bad memories." Her siblings—a brother and sister—are both deceased. "I'm here for them," she says.

When the Pope apologized, "I cried," she says. "It was very emotional." Of her own journey, she says the Pope's words "help me in my healing. I have forgiven my abusers. I have learned to put it behind me so I can move forward. But I will never forget." She gets her strength to forgive and move on from Creator, she says. "We have to learn to be a forgiving people, so we don't pass the anger down to the next generations," she adds.

A better world for the children

Norman Meade, 78, sees the trip as a way to pass on hope to younger generations. That's why he brought his eight-year-old granddaughter, Everlee, with him. "We need to create a better future for our children," he says. "That's why I went on the trip."

Meade didn't attend a residential school but his wife, Thelma, did. "Everlee is a second-generation survivor," he says. It will take time, but Indigenous people need to use the apology as a way to start the work of making the world "a better place for our young ones than it was for us," he says.

A "hard time growing up"

Bradley Bushie, 60, attended a day school. But he lived with the effects of residential school through his alcoholic father. "I had a hard time growing up," says Bushie, originally from Bloodvein but now living in Poplar River.

When his father was drinking, he would often hit and "slap around" his children, Bushie says. "He treated me the way he was treated as a boy," he adds. "Drinking was the way he coped." When Bushie heard the Pope apologize, "I was thinking about my dad," he says, noting he died in 2000. "I had mixed feelings. I was thinking how my dad would have felt to have heard it."

"An honour to have your friendship"

In his final address to the group before the bus arrived back in Winnipeg, Archbishop Albert LeGatt—who had arranged the trip to Alberta—told the group how wonderful it had been for him to be with them to witness the Pope's apology. "It shows us a way forward," he says, adding "I have hope that will happen."

"Thank-you for coming with your memories," LeGatt says, expressing gratitude to residential school survivors for coming on the trip. "It is an honour to have your friendship . . . Now we can find a new way of walking together. May it be so."

July 2022

"I felt so proud": Reflections on the Pope's visit to Canada

For starters, there was the grand entrance of the chiefs at Maskwacis on July 25.

The chiefs—hundreds of them—marched proudly into the powwow grounds, resplendent in the headdresses and ceremonial regalia, the crowd cheering and applauding their entry, war songs and victory songs in the air. Awaiting them was Pope Francis, small and stooped in his white chair, weak and frail due to poor health, relying on a wheelchair to get around.

Watching the procession, I couldn't help but think of the stark contrast between the present and the past; for hundreds of years the church has held the commanding position in its relationship with Indigenous people, forcing them into a position of weakness and supplication.

But the tables have turned, the Pope contritely coming to Indigenous people as a supplicant, asking their forgiveness for the way the Church has treated and abused them in Canada for generations.

To their credit, the chiefs responded generously, offering a headdress to the Pope. As for the Roman Catholic Church in Canada more broadly, it, too, is greatly weakened. In 1985, an average of 77 per cent of Canadian Catholics attended religious services or gatherings at least once a year. In 2022 that figure plummeted to 18 per cent, with only 14 per cent saying they go once or twice a month. Of course, the pandemic makes it hard to know exactly what is happening today, but scholars who study religion in Canada say the decline will not be reversed; if anything, the pandemic simply sped it up. This decline in attendance has implications for giving. If people aren't in church, it's hard to appeal to them for donations—including to the Indigenous Reconciliation Fund fund meant to help Indigenous people with their healing journey.

As for Indigenous people, maybe this is their time to be in the ascendant. As one woman told me about the grand entry of the chiefs: "I felt so proud watching them come in. I was proud to be Indigenous." If that's the case, the Pope's visit is a turning point, a before-and-after moment that future historians will see as the time when Indigenous people began to heal and reclaim their place in Canadian life.

Perhaps this is also a learning moment for Roman Catholics and Indigenous people together, a time when they can help each other. After all, features of healthy relationships are reciprocity and mutual support. Maybe a weakened Roman Catholic Church can find strength and renewed purpose through reconciliation with Indigenous people, by engaging with their teachings and walking together with them to serve Creator.

Then there is the Doctrine of Discovery, which was a main sticking point during the Pontiff's five-day visit. Would he renounce it? He came close, but he did not officially condemn the old idea. That's how non-Indigenous Canadians tend to think of it—as some ancient, historical document, but it has in fact become part of the legal system in Canada and the US. This makes it hard to denounce.

The first time it came up was in the US in 1823, when that country's Supreme Court ruled that two Native American communities in the Ohio River valley had no claim to land ownership due to the Doctrine of Discovery—their land belonged to the federal government. It was invoked again in 2005 when the late Justice Ruth Bader Ginsburg—yes, that icon of liberal values—used it to deny an Indigenous community's claim to land. In Canada, the doctrine has been referenced by the courts in 1888 and again in 2014. I don't say that to justify it, but simply to show it has become part of jurisprudence in both Canada and the US. A statement by the Pope condemning it can't change those legal facts.

Or could it? Maybe someone has to take the lead, even symbolically, since Roman Catholic officials note the doctrine is no longer part of Church teaching: it has no legal or moral authority for Roman Catholics. Canadian bishops are working with the Vatican to come up with a statement about the doctrine to try to clear things up. Perhaps a forceful statement by Pope Francis and the bishops will set the stage for productive new discussions on this important subject.

Finally, it may be tempting for Christian denominations that didn't operate residential schools to see this as just a Catholic issue, but they may have things to apologize for. I'm thinking especially of evangelical churches that sent missionaries to the north to plant churches—with the result that some small Indigenous communities have five or six Christian churches of different stripes, negatively impacting Indigenous communities by fracturing them along denominational lines. Maybe one day evangelical leaders will issue their own apologies for seeing Indigenous people merely as a mission field, and not respecting their unique beliefs, customs, and traditions. That would also be an important step along the road of reconciliation.

August 2022

3
MANY FAITHS

Grappling with religion's failures

When cartoons about the Prophet Muhammed were published in France, I was sorry for the hurt they caused Muslims, and then for the violence that resulted from their publication. But what I also grieve in the wake of the shootings of the *Charlie Hebdo* newspaper staff in Paris, is how religion is portrayed, once again, to non-religious people around the world.

Like most people of faith, I believe religion is a good thing. I believe the world would be a poorer place if it weren't for believers who perform acts of service and compassion. But I wonder if many non-religious people see it that way.

I'm guessing that when many non-believers think of religion, they are more likely to think of it as something destructive—systems of beliefs that cause people to justify bombing abortion clinics, killing doctors and nurses who perform abortions or to fly airplanes into buildings. When they think of religion, they may be inclined to think of it as something people use to support their claim to a piece of land, to say that it was given to them—and only them—by God. They see it used by political leaders to justify war, or as motivation and inspiration by suicide bombers. And now they see it as something that would shut down and curtail free expression, even if some forms of expression are better off left unexpressed.

While believers tend to think of religion as a force for good, many non-religious people are more likely to see it as something to be feared. It doesn't matter how many times believers of various faiths say that Islam is a religion of peace, that Jesus is the Prince of Peace, or that all Yahweh desires is *shalom* among all the nations—the evidence on the ground often suggests otherwise.

Where does this tendency of religious people to act violently come from? In his book *The Destructive Power of Religion: Violence in Judaism, Christianity, and Islam* (2007), J. Harold Ellens argues that these three major religions merged with pagan influences to see the world composed of two forces—Good versus Evil. This, he says, leads to an unhealthy form of religion that instils within followers a willingness to use violence to fight off what they consider to be evil.

For Ellens, the problem lies with the Old Testament, a collection of books esteemed by Judaism, Christianity, and Islam. That collection of books, he says, offers a violent metaphor, borrowed from Persian Zoroastrianism, of a cosmic contest between the forces of absolute good and absolute evil. "That metaphor has settled into the centre of the psyche of the communities of faith we know as Judaism, Christianity, and Islam," he says, adding that unless these three great religions renounce "this destructive story and its vicious metaphors," the world will hurtle toward "the impending prospect of a final cataclysmic Armageddon, closing out history."

Martin Marty, one of the organizers of the Fundamentalism Project, puts blame for the violence not on religion itself, but on fundamentalists in all religious groups. These are people who, he says, "cannot tolerate paradox, contradiction, ambiguity, and choice. They rebel against a world of many competing signals and build figurative walls around themselves . . . The modern world comes at them in commerce, enterprise, international interactions, often corollary relativism, and pluralism, and they close the door on as much of these as they can and gather into enclaves . . . they are sure that their God is calling them to be militant in defending their own faith and keeping all others at a distance."

Karen Armstrong, author of the books *A History of God* and *The Battle for God*, says that the problem is people who misinterpret the purpose of religion. "There are some forms of religion that must make God weep," she says. "Just as there's bad cooking or bad art . . . you have bad religion too—religion that has concentrated on egotism, that's concentrated on belligerence rather than compassion . . . These are people who acknowledge compassion is an important religious virtue, but who wonder 'what's the point of having religion if you can't disapprove of other people?' And sometimes we use religion just to back up these unworthy hatreds."

However people of faith got into this situation, the immediate goal must be to get out of it. Can the faithful show the world that religion is not what others see on the TV news? Can they live in ways that allow them to hear, understand, and accept other points of view? Are they able to renounce the desire to have their side "win"? As philosopher and theologian Jacques Ellul stated: "Neither exaltation of power nor the search for vengeance will ever solve any human situation. In accepting death, Jesus Christ showed us the only possible way." If we reject that option, he says, "we are left with one alternative—increasing the sum of evil in the world."

Roman Catholic theologian Hans Küng put it this way: "There can be no peace on earth without peace among the religions." Or, to use the words of the old song, "Let there be peace on earth, and let it begin with me."

February 2015

Can Allah make Muslims funny?

After the September 11, 2001, attacks, Brian Whitaker, Middle East editor of *The Guardian*, was asked by a group of Muslims in England what they could do to stem the growth of "Islamophobia and media stereotypes portraying Muslims as violent, misogynistic, stern, and humourless people," he wrote in a column for the paper in 2005.

"The most useful thing they could do about that, I suggested—only half-flippantly—was to collect jokes and amusing anecdotes and publish them as the Bumper Book of Muslim Humour," he wrote. "After all, Jewish humour is renowned, and it has probably done more over the years to counter anti-Semitism than all the efforts of the Anti-Defamation League."

Whitaker has a point. One way that Jews have dealt with anti-Semitism is by using comedy to skewer stereotypical notions about their community. It is similar for Black people in the US, with comedians like Dick Gregory using humour to deal with subjects such as racism and poverty. More recently, people from other racial groups and people with disabilities have taken the stage, employing comedy to dispel stereotypes.

So is it Islam's turn to step up to the mic and tell jokes? Bryant Moss says yes. The American comedian, who goes by the stage name Preacher Moss, is part of the "Allah Made Me Funny" tour, which crossed North America in an effort to dispel the notion that Muslims are a dour bunch who never have any fun. "Post-9/11, we wanted to do something to bring the Islamic community into the mainstream," Moss says, adding that the tour uses humour to bridge the gap between Muslims and non-Muslims. "It's an opportunity to have some dialogue and to make people, Muslims and non-Muslims, feel enlightened and entertained. Through comedy, we're able to break down a lot of walls very quickly and establish a connection."

For Moss, laughter is a way to show that most Muslims aren't like the people on the evening news. "I can honestly say that the Muslims that are portrayed on television, I don't know those guys," he says. The jokes the comics tell are wide-ranging, dealing with idiosyncrasies of Muslim behaviour, sound systems in mosques, and media portrayal of Islam.

Azhar Usman, a member of the tour, is a stand-up comic from Chicago who is known as "the Ayatollah of Comedy." "Everything the media says about Arabs and Muslims, it has something to do with violence," he says on stage. "If they show up here tonight and write an article about me, they'll be like, 'Muslim Comic Bombs.' And I can't win because even if I do well, they'll be like 'Muslim Comic Kills!' or 'Audience Explodes With Laughter!'"

Bryant Moss bemoaned the fact that the media don't tend to portray many smiling Muslims, especially since September 11. He quips the media always show the same angry guy who is ranting and waving his arms because "somebody just parked a tank on his house." The tour also dealt with the touchy issue of terrorism. "I am an American Muslim," says Usman as part of his set. "That's right. I consider myself a patriotic American Muslim, which means I would die for this country—by blowing myself up."

The tour does have boundaries. The comedians won't tell jokes about the Qur'an, make fun of Allah or the prophet Muhammed, and they don't swear. But they will tell jokes about how their religion is practiced or about the idiosyncrasies of an imam. Plus, they insist that no alcohol be sold at clubs where they perform. This has resulted in some poor weekday timeslots, but the comedians are unrepentant. "We've taken our lumps, but we are standing by our guns," Moss said, adding that while Muslims don't drink, they do eat. "We eat like a horde of locusts," he says, noting that clubs with kitchens fare very well with a Muslim crowd.

Usman notes not everyone in the Muslim community approves of the tour. He says that although the prophet Muhammad is said to have liked jokes, "there are a lot of very conservative Muslims" who don't approve of stand-up comedy. However, he says his act was cited as "praiseworthy" by a Muslim religious scholar who ruled that stand-up comedy is allowed if it is "to make people laugh" and "accompanied by noble intentions."

The early-twentieth-century English author G.K. Chesterton said that "a test of a good religion is whether you can joke about it." By poking fun at themselves, their communities, and the prejudice Muslims face, the "Allah Made Me Funny" tour is a way to show that Muslims can pass that test—and break down stereotypes at the same time.

August 2009

The commercialization of Buddhism, or, eaten any Dharma burgers lately?

HAVE YOU HEARD about the Buddha Bar?

According to an ad in the *Winnipeg Free Press*, people who patronize Winnipeg's newest drinking establishment can expect to find "chic interiors" and "exotic electronic beats" to go along with the usual cocktail, beer, and wine specials. One thing they shouldn't expect to find there, though, are actual Buddhists. At least, they won't find any who take their faith seriously—adherents of this ancient religion are forbidden to drink alcohol.

Winnipeg's Buddha Bar is just one more example of what has come to be called "Dharma Burgers," a phrase made popular by Rod Meade Sperry of the Buddhist pop-and-culture website *The Worst Hope*. According to Sperry, a Dharma Burger is "any example of Buddhist ideas or imagery in the marketing or production of (usually non-Buddhist) services and consumables." Other examples on Sperry's website include Guru energy drinks, Buddha beer, Buddha briefs, Zendough (a new way "master your finances"), and Karma soap.

How do Buddhists feel about seeing their religion used to sell stuff? I posed that question to Sensei Fredrich Ulrich of the Manitoba Buddhist Temple. "Most Buddhists don't relish them, but seldom take offense," he says. Buddhists did draw the line a few years ago when Victoria's Secret introduced a "Buddha bikini," with an image of a Buddha-like figure on the crotch. "Using the Buddha to sell erotic garments is a misuse of the Buddha image," Ulrich states. As for all the other "Dharma Burgers," he is resigned to seeing more businesses using his religion to make money. "As Buddhism becomes more popular, such things will become more numerous," he says.

Some Buddhists, like Scott A. Mitchell of the Institute of Buddhist Studies in Berkeley, California, are worried by the growing trend. "Far from being harmless kitsch, these products are redefining Buddhism in terms palatable to a consumer-driven, capitalist culture," he writes in his essay, "Buddhism, pop-culture, and the homogenization of the Dharma," presented at the International Association of Shin Buddhist Studies in 2009.

One of the ways Buddhism has been redefined by non-Buddhists is by the way it is so often linked with meditation. "What these representations of Buddhism do is reinforce the stereotype in the West that all Buddhists meditate," he says, noting that it is just one practice among many for Buddhists. At the same time, it promotes the idea that Buddhism is a passive and detached way of life characterized by "not rocking the boat, not upsetting the status quo," he says. In fact, Buddhism promotes a serious critique of consumerism and materialism, he points out. "If Buddhism were to stand its ground, so to speak, and define itself in its own terms, it might suggest something radically contrary to the capitalist system."

It's not just Buddhism that is being co-opted by consumer culture; it's happening to other eastern religions, too, as British religion scholars Jeremy Carrette and Richard King point out in their book *Selling Spirituality: The Silent Takeover of Religion* (2004). "From feng shui to holistic medicine, from aromatherapy candles to yoga weekends, spirituality is big business," they write.

What bothers Carrette and King is how these great religions have been cheapened as ways to achieve self-fulfillment, health, and fitness. In fact, Asian religious traditions can be "easily read today as profound critiques of consumerism and a 'spirituality of the self' rather than an endorsement of them," they write. Instead of being seen as engaging that critique, eastern religions have been co-opted by a "western society that is oriented toward the individual as consumer and society as market."

For Christians, this is old news. The Christian faith has been used and misused for centuries in the service of commercialism. Who hasn't seen ads for "Jesus junk"—things like the Stock Car Racing Edition Bible, "fruit of the spirit" health drinks, Christian flip-flops, a Jesus air freshener, Gospel shoes, Jesus guitar picks, disciple sunglasses, biblical breakfast cereal, or the Jesus night light? (Now the Light of the World lights up bathrooms, too.)

What—if anything—can be done? The simplest course of action is not to buy anything that cynically trades on religion to sell merchandise. Which means that if you feel like having a drink, don't go to any place called the Buddha Bar.

April 2010

If we want more peace, maybe we need fewer sacred spaces

It's hard to imagine religion without sacred spaces. These sacred spaces can be hills, mountains, rivers, caves, cities, trees, and, of course, buildings—temples, mosques, cathedrals, and other places of worship. For believers, these places are sacred because something religiously significant happened there, usually hundreds or thousands of years ago. Visiting these places is an opportunity to draw closer to God or the divine, to find inner peace and fulfilment, or to experience something deep and supernatural.

For others, however, they are reasons to fight and kill. Instead of promoting peace, they are sources of conflict. That's what happens too often in Jerusalem, over the Al-Aqsa mosque. The mosque, the third holiest site in Islam, is located on what Jews call the Temple Mount—the holiest site in Judaism—and what Muslims call Haram al-Sharif, or the Noble Sanctuary. Many Muslims believe that the Prophet Muhammed was carried on a flying horse from Mecca to Al-Aqsa during his miraculous night journey. While there, he prayed with Abraham and Jesus on the rock that is now said to be inside the Dome of the Rock, the golden roof of which dominates the Jerusalem skyline. Many Jews, however, believe this to be the site of Solomon's temple, later destroyed by the Babylonians and rebuilt as the Second Temple in the fifth century BCE, only to be destroyed again, this time by the Romans, in the first century of the Common Era.

Over the past 50 years, the site has been a source of tension between Palestinians and Israelis. It is said the Second Intifada, from 2000-2005, which saw over 4,000 people killed, was sparked by a visit to the mosque by Ariel Sharon, then-candidate for Prime Minister of Israel. In the summer of 2014, the site was the source of unrest and conflict after Israeli authorities restricted Muslim access to the mosque following the murders of two Israeli police officers. In response, Palestinians gathered to pray and protest—mostly peacefully—in the streets surrounding the area.

Of course, the conflict is over more than what people believe happened on the site centuries ago. Israelis view it as a matter of security and safety, while Palestinians see it as part of a larger effort to control and humiliate them. Both sides can justify their actions. But I still wonder: are these principles worth killing and dying over? I posed that question to a Palestinian friend.

He agreed that any deaths arising from the unrest were terrible, but said answers are "not so easy when everything has been taken away from you." He noted that, over the centuries, Palestinians have welcomed and incorporated people from many nationalities and faiths—Arabs, Turks, Berbers, Greeks, and Jews, among others. "Those who came as pilgrims and refugees found space on the land. But an occupation is a different story," he says.

This is indeed a different story, for Israelis and Palestinians alike. The site in Jerusalem is much more than a holy place for both groups. People on both sides, each for their own political reasons, seem to be looking for confrontation rather than calm. Lest Christians think they are above this sort of controversy, the Church of the Holy Sepulchre proves otherwise. The Church, which is said to contain the tomb of Jesus, is administered by six Christian groups under a centuries-old agreement. They squabble constantly over who is responsible for what part of the church, sometimes resulting in fist fights between monks. So bad are the relations between them they don't even trust each other with the church keys; a Muslim family opens and closes the church each day.

As for me, my mind keeps going back to the prophet Isaiah, who delivers a message from God about sacred spaces. In chapter 66, verses 1-2, God says through the prophet: "Heaven is my throne and the earth is my footstool; what is the house that you would build for me, and what is my resting place? All these things my hand has made, and so all these things are mine. But this is the one to whom I will look, to the humble and contrite in spirit, who trembles at my word." I don't know about you, but I think the world would be better off if we had more of those kinds of people today, and maybe fewer sacred spaces.

August 2017

Budgets are moral documents

"Budgets are moral documents. They reveal priorities and values, and as a society, they are the primary way that we care for one another, especially for the vulnerable. That is why the church takes them so seriously."

That's what American Jesuit priest Father Travis Russell said in 2021 about the budget proposed by the US government. In that, he echoed what the United States Conference of Catholic Bishops said in 2017, when they argued that "a central moral measure of any budget proposal is how it affects 'the least of these.' The needs of those who are hungry and homeless, vulnerable and at risk, without work or in poverty should come first . . . a just framework for the federal budget cannot rely on disproportionate cuts in essential services to poor and vulnerable persons."

If that's the case—if budgets are moral documents—then people of faith should be concerned about the one just passed by the governing Liberals that cut foreign aid by $1.3 billion. That is a 15 per cent reduction in spending to help feed, clothe, shelter, and educate people in the developing world.

For Canadian aid groups, the cut is disappointing at a time of enormous global need. "The decision by the government to cut foreign aid comes amidst a world facing multiple crises around climate change, hunger, conflict, and an erosion of human rights and democratic values," says Cooperation Canada, the umbrella group for 95 international relief and development groups.

"At a time when the world is calling on Canada to step up and deliver on the vision and leadership it promised, this government chose to step down," adds Julia Anderson of CanWaCH, a coalition of organizations working on women's and children's health outcomes.

Elise Legault, Canada Director of the ONE Campaign, says, "We made a promise to the world to increase international assistance every year, and instead there is a 15 per cent cut in the middle of an unprecedented food crisis and countries crumbling under the effects of climate change. This isn't the leadership that Canadians or the world expects."

Of course, budgets are complex things. There are many different needs, priorities, expectations, and constituencies to satisfy. It's not like Canada isn't doing anything to help people in the developing world; it will still spend $6.8 billion on foreign aid, up from the $4.6 billion it spent in 2015-16. Nor is it the case that the budget doesn't contain things people of faith can feel good about, like efforts to combat climate change, to support newcomers and refugees, and to support organizations that serve marginalized women in Canada. But it still should sting to see a wealthy nation like Canada send less money to help poor people around the world.

All major religions have some version of the "Golden Rule"—to treat others the way they would like to be treated. If we are poor, hungry, thirsty, or in need of help due to war, climate change, or natural disasters, we would hope other countries would come to our aid, just like we should want to help them.

The truth is that foreign aid is the easiest thing for governments to cut; poor people in other countries don't vote. That was a point made by Carl Hétu, executive director of the Canadian Catholic organization Development and Peace – Caritas Canada, as he reflected on the cut. "I just know that once again cutting international aid is the least politically costly for a government," he says.

While people in poor countries don't vote, people of faith who care about Canada's role in the world do; they can be a voice in Ottawa. If the cut to foreign aid concerns you, now's the time to contact your Member of Parliament. When the next election rolls around, you can remind those running for office about your desire for Canada to keep the needs of the world's poor in mind. You can also signal your concern by donating to groups like Mennonite Central Committee, Canadian Foodgrains Bank, or Canadian Lutheran World Relief—all headquartered in Winnipeg—or other aid organizations. Many aid groups could see their government funding cut due to the reduction in aid spending. If you already donate to an aid organization, consider giving more. A 15 per cent increase this year sounds about right!

April 2023

Settler or Indigenous: Who owns the land?

It is customary today for gatherings to begin with an acknowledgement of the traditional lands of Indigenous groups on which the events take place. Universities, arts groups, public schools, city councils, and even sports teams are doing it.

In religious settings, the United Church of Canada has been a leader in this area. For them, "acknowledging the territory where we gather and the people who have traditionally called it home for thousands of years is a way to continue to live out the church's Apologies to the First Peoples of North America." It also "supports our calls to others to pay respect to Indigenous peoples" and is a way the church can "work toward right relations" with Indigenous people.

I heartily endorse the practice, but while it is good and right to openly acknowledge that the lands on which we meet were once home to Indigenous peoples, from a theological perspective it doesn't feel like the whole story. Why is that? Because for people of faith the land—indeed, the whole planet—doesn't belong, and never belonged, to anyone. It belongs to God.

For Christians and Jews, the words of Psalm 24 make this clear. The earth, it says, "is the Lord's, and all that is in it, the world, and those who live in it; for he has founded it on the seas, and established it on the rivers." For Muslims, the Qur'an states that "Allah created the heavens and the earth, and all that is between them." Hindus believe that Vishnu is the creator, sustainer, destroyer, and then re-creator of the universe. Sikhs believe the universe was made by Waheguru who created Earth and all forms of life on it. Buddhism has no concept of a creator god to explain the origin of the universe. It teaches that everything is co-dependent with everything else in the universe. But a similar idea to the other religions is still present: people are not at the centre; there are other forces at work beyond humankind.

Without getting into a debate about how the earth was made—creation versus evolution—all the world's major religions acknowledge earth was made by, and belongs to God, or gods, or to forces and factors beyond human beings. For these reasons, I like what my church does. The weekly bulletin acknowledges the historical connection between the land we are meeting on and Indigenous people. But it also affirms a broader theological perspective. It goes like this:

> We affirm with Psalm 24 that the earth's is the Lord's and everything in it. We humbly acknowledge that our worship takes place on Treaty One

> land, the traditional territory of the Anishinaabe, Cree, Oji-Cree, Dakota, and Dene peoples and the homeland of the Métis Nation. We pray for justice and reconciliation.

That works for me. But does it work for Indigenous people? I asked a couple of my Indigenous friends. They both found it quite acceptable. In fact, one said it is similar to Indigenous beliefs about how the creator made the earth, and how humans—Indigenous and non-Indigenous alike—are responsible to care for it.

Of course, there is much work to be done beyond acknowledgements. This includes taking seriously the Truth and Reconciliation Commission's calls to action. One of them invites faith groups to "develop ongoing education strategies to ensure that their respective congregations learn about their church's role in colonization, the history and legacy of residential schools, and why apologies to former residential school students, their families, and communities were necessary." An acknowledgement is one small way to work towards that goal. So is acknowledging that we all have an obligation to care for this earth we share, together.

October 2018

"Pharisee" as pejorative is offensive, says rabbi

Democratic presidential hopeful Pete Buttigieg got into trouble with American Jews in March. That's when, in an interview with the *Washington Post*, he accused US Vice-President Mike Pence and other Republicans of being "Pharisees."

What he meant, of course, is they were hypocrites—that they don't practise the values they preach. "When you see someone, especially somebody who has such a dogmatic take on faith that they bring it into public life, being willing to attach themselves to this administration for the purposes of gaining power, it is alarmingly resonant with some New Testament themes, and not in a good way," he said, noting "there's an awful lot about Pharisees in there."

As someone who grew up going to church, as Buttigieg apparently did (he's Episcopalian and an avowed Christian), I understand where he is coming from. In Sunday school and sermons, I was taught to see the Pharisees as harsh, rules-based, judgemental, and hypocritical. But that's not necessarily how Jews view the Pharisees, as the episode with Buttigieg soon showed. His comment prompted a number of Jews to write in defence of the ancient group, one of a number of Jewish sects that existed during the time of Jesus.

One critic is Rabbi Jeffrey K. Salkin of Temple Solel in Hollywood, Florida. For Jews, he says, "'Pharisee' is a fighting word," adding the way it was used by Buttigieg was "bigoted, and narrow, and dated, and painful." The history of its use in a derogatory way dates back 2,000 years, he says, noting it has come to mean "a kind of narrow, petty, rules-intoxicated religiosity. That is the way that the New Testament uses it, especially because the texts juxtapose Jesus with the Pharisees." But it can be seen differently. Pharisees, he says, laid the important groundwork for what Judaism has become today.

According to Salkin, the Pharisees and their spiritual descendants created the texts that have kept the Jewish faith alive over the centuries—things like the Mishnah, Judaism's law code; the Talmud, the interpretation of the Mishnah; various collections of interpretations of the Bible; and Jewish liturgy. Because of the Pharisees, he says, "Judaism survived and grew."

For Rabbi Salkin, it is tragic they are seen by many today "only through the bias of the New Testament. Clearly, the gospel writers wanted to separate themselves from Jewish custom and interpretation. But, because of that inner, political need, the Pharisees have been getting a bad rap." Worse, he adds, using the word in that way can be a subtle doorway to anti-Judaism by Christians—reinforcing a view that the Jewish religion is only about laws and rules.

Salkin acknowledged that some Pharisees were, in fact, hypocrites—just like in any other religion. In fact, some ancient Jewish sources indicate criticism of Pharisees who ostentatiously displayed their piety, knowledge, humility, generosity, purity, or love for God. But others were deeply respected for how they loved God and delighted in God's law. So when someone acts hypocritically today, instead of calling them a "Pharisee," Salkin suggests just calling it what it is: "religious hypocrisy." No other word is necessary, he notes.

Belle Jarniewski, executive director of the Jewish Heritage Centre of Western Canada, feels similarly about use of that word. "The term 'Pharisee' has been typically used in a pejorative way to refer to a person who is hypocritical and/or dishonest," she says. "Given the pejorative use, I think it is high time that Christians and any others stop using the term," she adds. "We Jews today are the descendants of the Pharisees, and the pejorative use of the term increases anti-Semitism."

Buttigieg's misstep is a reminder to be careful when it comes to the words we use. Words that sound normal and right in conversation for some religious groups can be seen as insensitive or offensive for members of others—words like "guru," "karma," "zen," "jihad," or "pagan." As for Buttigieg, he will no longer use the word "Pharisee" to refer to those he deems religious hypocrites, a campaign official said. "We appreciate the people who have reached out to educate us on this," the campaign tweeted. "While intended to highlight political hypocrisy, we listened and learned and won't be using it going forward."

June 2019

If religion is good for mental health, is atheism bad?

STUDIES HAVE REPEATEDLY found that religion is good for mental health. People who are religious or spiritual report being happier, less depressed, and more satisfied with their lives. Does that mean the opposite is true—that atheists are less happy and more depressed?

Finding answers to those questions was the aim of "Godless in the Great White North: Assessing the Health of Canadian Atheists," a new study by David Speed, professor of psychology at the University of New Brunswick. Using information from the 2012 Canadian Community Health Survey, Speed and co-researchers Caitlin Barry, also of UNB, and Ryan Cragun of the University of Tampa, compared the mental health of those who said they were highly religious and those who said they were atheists.

The results? While the data showed people who are actively involved in their places of worship reported better mental health outcomes, so did atheists. "We know higher levels of religiosity equals good mental health, but that doesn't mean lower levels of religiosity means poor mental health," Speed says in an interview.

Why do religious people report better mental health outcomes? The answer, says Speed, is social support—people feel better if they are actively involved with others in a church, mosque, synagogue, temple, gurdwara, or other place of worship. As he puts it, being religious itself is not the reason for better mental health, but it is indirectly responsible since it can "provide a warm and supportive social environment." People who are not religious can get the same benefit, Speed says, by regularly spending time with others—meeting regularly with friends, playing on a sports team, being part of book clubs, or other activities. "Atheists who had strong social networks had strong mental health outcomes."

At the same time, Speed—who is not religious—recognizes that religion has some built-in advantages when it comes to providing social support such as an organized system of looking after its members. This includes having pastoral staff whose job it is to look in on or connect with people on a regular basis, or designated volunteers who provide various kinds of interaction and care when people are sick or under stress. Then there are the regular services, potlucks, home groups, and other gatherings that ensure people have someplace to go to meet others and find the social support they need.

Of course, the quality of the social support provided by a religious community is key. If it is a bad or toxic environment—if there is conflict, dispute over theology and practice, oppressive leadership, or if the group's beliefs make some people feel unwelcome—it can be bad for mental health. Speed's study is one of a growing number starting to research the impact of declining religiosity in Canada and the US. This includes examining the rise of the "nones"—people who claim no affiliation with any religious group. By going deeper into data, researchers like Speed are discovering nones aren't a homogenous group. Not everyone who claims to be a none is an atheist, he says; many are still spiritual. These people have been dubbed "theistic nones," people who still have a strong belief in God.

Interestingly, at least one study has found the level of certainty in beliefs—either for or against the existence of God—is a factor for predicting positive mental health outcomes. According to Luke Galen, a professor of psychology at Grand Valley State University in Michigan, who is researching this subject, both ardent believers and committed atheists report greater overall well-being than either believers or atheists who were unsure or confused about their belief in God. Those getting the least benefit are those in the middle, people who "might have a certain amount of distress or anxiety related to the lack of coherence in their worldview," says Galen, in a feature for the American Psychology Association's Monitor.

In other research, Galen finds that atheists could get the same benefits as religious people by being active in humanist or atheist groups—something echoed by Joseph Baker, a sociologist specializing in religion at East Tennessee State University. In an interview with Religion News Service, Baker says while atheism can give people as strong a sense of identity as religion can for believers, and it may help with their mental well-being, the challenge for them is "think consciously and seriously about where they will find community—and organize accordingly," he says.

As for David Speed, he hopes more research will be done about the question of religion, atheism, and health. "Atheists are not well studied," he says. "But there is an explosion in this area with the growth of nones."

March 2021

Is God Christian?

I CONFESS I had never asked myself the question, is God Christian? Then I heard about a new book by Archbishop Desmond Tutu, titled *God Is Not a Christian: And Other Provocations* (2011). It's a collection of sermons, speeches and interviews given by the well-known South African pastor, who rose to prominence in the 1980s as a vocal and determined opponent of apartheid.

According to Tutu, the answer to the above question is "no." "God is clearly not a Christian," he says in the book. "His concern is for all his children. To claim God exclusively for Christians is to make God too small and in a real sense is blasphemous. God is bigger than Christians and cares for more than Christians only." Some Christians might object to that line of thinking. Tutu anticipates their objection. For them, he has a question: "Can you tell us what God was before he was a Christian?"

In a speech in 1989 to leaders of different faiths—the speech is included in the book—Tutu elaborated on this idea, beginning with a story of someone who crossed a street to ask a pedestrian a question. Asking which side of the street was the "other side," the pedestrian answered, "That side, of course." The first person said that it was strange, since when they were on that side, others told them this side was the other side.

For Tutu, "where the other side of the street is depends on where we are. Our perspective differs with our context, the things that have helped to form us; and religion is one of the most potent of these formative influences, helping to determine how and what we apprehend of reality and how we operate in our own specific context." His point, he goes on to say, "seems overwhelmingly simple: that the accidents of birth and geography determine to a very large extent to what faith we belong. The chances are very great that if you were born in Pakistan you are a Muslim, or a Hindu if you happened to be born in India, or a Shintoist if it is Japan, and a Christian if you were born in Italy."

The lesson to be drawn from these accidents of birth, he suggests, is not to "succumb too easily to the temptation to exclusiveness and dogmatic claims to a monopoly of the truth of our particular faith. You could so easily have been an adherent of the faith that you are now denigrating, but for the fact that you were born here rather than there." This realization, he states, should make Christians open to learning from people of other faiths. "We must acknowledge them for who they are in all their integrity, with their conscientiously held beliefs; we must welcome them and respect them as who they are and walk reverently on what is their holy ground, taking off our shoes, metaphorically and literally," he states.

But that doesn't mean giving up one's own deeply held convictions, Tutu adds. "We must hold to our particular and peculiar beliefs tenaciously, not pretending that all religions are the same, for they are patently not the same. We must be ready to learn from one another, not claiming that we alone possess all truth and that somehow we have a corner on God." At the same time, he believes that members of all faiths should look for commonalities. "We have enough that conspires to separate us," he states. "Let us celebrate that which unites us, that which we share in common."

For Tutu, this means acknowledging that the "supernatural and divine reality we all worship in some form or other transcends all our particular categories of thought and imagining" and that "what we call the Spirit of God is not a Christian preserve, for the Spirit of God existed long before there were Christians, inspiring and nurturing women and men in the ways of holiness, bringing them to fruition, bringing to fruition what was best in all."

June 2011

Holocaust survivors tell their stories: Who will listen?

"In Auschwitz I swore that if God let me stay alive I would tell my story again and again until my breath died out so that no one could say it never happened."

That's what survivor Perla Ovitz said about her experience during the Holocaust. Ovitz and her family of 12 Romanian Jews were deported to Auschwitz in 1944. Since seven of the children were about three feet tall, they drew the attention of the infamous Dr. Josef Mengele. Fascinated by their genetic condition, Mengele conducted regular medical experiments on members of the family. As a result, they all survived.

I never had a chance to interview Perla, who died in 2001. But during my time as religion reporter and columnist at the *Free Press* I have been fortunate enough to talk to other Holocaust survivors who, like her, dedicated their lives to telling their stories. One of them was Stefan Carter of Winnipeg, who was 14 the last time he saw his mother alive. On that September day in 1942, Carter and his mother, Janina, were ordered by the Nazis to leave their workplace and assemble at the Umschlagplatz, or collection point, in the Warsaw Ghetto. With a nod of his head, an SS soldier sent Stefan—who was tall for his age—back to the factory. "They thought I would be good for labour," he says.

His mother was sent to a train at a nearby railway siding and, ultimately, to her death at the Treblinka concentration camp. "She may have died on the train on the way, or in the camp. I don't know," Carter says. For him, those memories from long ago are still fresh in his mind. For that reason he tells people about his experience, warning about the dangers of anti-Semitism and Holocaust denial and distortion. "We have to constantly keep talking about it," he says, adding if future Holocausts are to be prevented "the stories of survivors have to be told over and over again."

Then there is Angela Orosz-Richt, the youngest Canadian survivor of Auschwitz—she was born in the death camp in 1945. For decades, she hid those memories away. "I was busy making a living, looking after my family," she says, adding "it was too painful to remember."

All that changed when she returned to Auschwitz on the 70th anniversary of the liberation of the camp. "I woke up," she says of the visit. "I realized God spared me for a reason. It opened my eyes to the need for me to tell my story." Now Orosz-Richt speaks regularly about the Holocaust. "As the years go by, I see how important the work of education is," she says. "We need to tell people the Holocaust is true, it happened."

In 1944, when she was 11, Winnipegger Susan Garfield started writing a diary about her life as a Jew in Hungary. In it she recorded how her parents were taken to work camps, where they both died. Alone, she went into hiding as a young teen and managed to survive.

Later, she was miraculously re-united with her diary. In 1947, she began writing in it again, catching up on her life in hiding and her decision to immigrate to Canada. For Garfield, a mother and grandmother, the publication of the diary is a way to "counteract those who say it didn't happen. I am here to say it did. I saw it." She also wants to "speak up for those who died, and for those who are still suffering because of their experiences during the war."

Listening to those stories, and others, I am in awe and not a little overwhelmed as they share experiences that are still, all those years later, extremely painful. At the same time, they are also exceedingly patient with a reporter who needed to get the facts right, asking awkward questions like: "What year was your mother murdered?" and "When did you find out most of your family was killed?"

I could tell, as they spoke, they were driven by some tremendous force or deep sense of responsibility to share what they had seen and experienced—out of obligation to the dead, certainly, but also so future generations won't have to go through the same things. There is a tinge of anger on their part; why is it still necessary to counter claims the Holocaust never happened? Not to mention their bewilderment at the rising number of antisemitic incidents taking place in Canada today. Have we learned nothing from the past?

Not everyone will be so fortunate to talk to a Holocaust survivor. But everyone can read and learn more about their experiences, even online. I'm sure Perla, Stefan, Angela, and Susan would be grateful if you did.

October 2021

Kindness overcomes hate

I WAS STANDING at the busy intersection of Henderson Highway and Chief Peguis Trail in Winnipeg, waiting for a light to change. It was June 2022. Cars sped past me, just a metre or so away, as I waited on the curb. It suddenly occurred to me I wasn't afraid that any of those cars would deliberately veer out of their lane and strike me—as happened to the Afzaal family in London, Ontario, in 2021. On June 6, the family of five were out for an evening walk when, in an act of what the police called anti-Muslim hatred, a man drove a truck into them, killing Talat Afzaal, Salman Afzaal, Yumna Afzaal, and Madiha Salman. A young boy survived.

The event shocked the nation and focused attention on Islamophobia—fear of and hostility toward Muslims. As a straight, white, Christian male, I am privileged; I have no idea what it is like to be Muslim, Sikh, or Black—or identify as 2SLGBTQ+ and worried for my safety and well-being. But members of those groups know it only too well. Not just through horrific acts like the murders in London, but in everyday slights, glances, words, or more overt discrimination.

Earlier this year, Manitoba's Muslim community took stock of the situation facing members of that group. The Manitoba Islamic Association released a report that finds Manitoba isn't that friendly a place for many Muslims. MIA's report, titled "Friendly Manitoba: Community Experiences with Islamophobia," finds that 62 per cent of Manitoba Muslims say they have experienced Islamophobia in public spaces, schools, at work, or online. Islamophobic behaviours ranged from verbal attacks to racial profiling and physical assaults.

The group most affected are Muslim women, with 73 per cent saying they experience it, most likely because of wearing a traditional covering like a hijab. Other groups more likely to experience Islamophobia are Black people and those from the Middle East. Most troubling for the researchers are the number of incidents in schools, with 43 per cent of respondents saying it happened to them there. Among those most impacted in educational settings are Muslim girls; if teachers make ill-informed remarks about the wearing of the hijab, such remarks are then repeated by students. The report also finds that only 18 per cent of Manitoba Muslims report feeling very safe wearing garments that identify them as Muslims in public.

MIA's report offers suggestions for ways to combat Islamophobia, such as developing toolkits and curriculum resources for teachers on Islam; providing reasonable religious accommodations for Muslim students so they can perform daily prayers in a safe space at school; and equipping school libraries with a wide selection of resources on Islam and Muslims appropriate for the K-12 age range.

For Shahina Siddiqui—who might be the closest thing the Manitoba Muslim community has to a senior statesperson—the report isn't surprising. "It's true some people don't like us," she says, acknowledging Islamophobia in Manitoba is real. But Siddiqui prefers not to dwell on the negative or spend her energy being angry when people say or do hateful things. "I want to be proactive, not reactive, I want to transform the community," she says. "I don't just want to think about the fears."

Siddiqui's guide in this is the Islamic ideal of reciprocity, similar to what others call the Golden Rule—treat others the way you want to be treated. "I ask myself, what am I doing to make others feel welcome?" she says, suggesting acts of kindness can help overcome hate if people with racist thoughts are treated kindly by someone from another race or religion. And when someone does something Islamophobic, she resists the urge to paint all members of that group as the same. "Let's not fall into the trap of demonizing people," based on what few do or say, she adds.

Another way to tackle racism is for marginalized groups to collaborate. "Marginalized people need to come together," Siddiqui says, noting the Muslim community has reached out to the Indigenous community for inspiration and mutual support. Education is also key. "Many people simply don't know about Islam, they don't know any Muslims," she says. In this, the media have an important role to play, she adds, through something called "solutions journalism"—not just reporting the news but giving people ideas for solutions. Reporters shouldn't "just say how bad things are, but how we can make it better," she suggests. The media can also "talk about the positive things that are being done" to promote harmony and good relations, she says. "There is also good news in Manitoba when it comes to being good neighbours."

Overall, Siddiqui is hopeful, for two reasons. First, she is inspired by the next generation of Muslims in the province. "Nothing is going to stop our grandchildren!" she says, and second, "the Manitoba I love has good soil, the good outweighs the bad."

June 2022

When Good Friday was a day of hate for Jews

Jews across North America were in a state of high alert February 25, 2023, the so-called "day of hate" against members of that community. Although the day was directed at Jews in the US by white supremacist and neo-Nazi groups, it's likely Jews everywhere were more careful and cautious than normal as they went to synagogue or carried out their normal daily activities.

Fortunately, nothing happened. But it reminded me of another day of hate directed at Jews for centuries in the past: Good Friday. Yes, the holiest of days for Christians was often a day of fear, persecution, and death for Jews around the world in centuries past. On that day, Jews in the Middle Ages would close their businesses and stay inside their homes for fear of mobs of Christians who—motivated by inexpert readings from the Gospels—were intent on doing harm to those they viewed responsible for the crucifixion of Jesus.

"The crucifixion of Jesus has mostly been a source of pain for Jews," says Adèle Reinhartz, who teaches religious studies, with a focus on the New Testament and early Jewish-Christian relations, at the University of Ottawa. The reason for that are verses in the Gospels, such as Matthew chapter 27, where Pilate takes no responsibility for Jesus' death. "I am innocent of this man's blood," he is quoted as saying as he washes his hands. Then the crowd answers, "His blood be on us and on our children!" That "anti-Jewish statement" has led to centuries of antisemitism, death, and destruction against Jews, Reinhartz says.

For her, and for other New Testament scholars, there are questions about that account: did it really happen that way? Why did Matthew chose to put it in there? "We don't know how much of it is historical, how much of it was rooted in animosity by Christians towards Jews when it was written down," she says, noting stories about the life and crucifixion of Jesus were compiled many years after it occurred.

One thing that doesn't make sense, Reinhartz says, is the portrayal of Pontius Pilate in Matthew. In Matthew's account, he comes across as an agreeable, sympathetic, and even decent man put into an untenable position. Someone who, almost against his will, is forced to deliver Jesus to his death. But the other main source of information about that time period, the first-century historian Josephus, described Pilate quite differently—as a cruel, vicious, and violent person, not beyond doing exactly such a thing. "The Gospels present us with a kinder and gentler Pilate than we know from other sources," Reinhartz says.

Although little is known about Pilate, the few accounts that exist indicate there was tension and violence between the Jewish population and his administration, with many incidents involving ways that offended the religious sensibilities of Jews. According to Josephus, he was actually removed from office because of the especially violent way he suppressed an armed revolt against the Roman occupation. So why was Pilate given a pass and the Jews blamed for the death of Jesus in the earliest Christian literature?

According to Reinhartz, it may have been a way to preserve the fledgling Christian movement; blaming the Romans for the death of their leader would not have been a good move. "It could have been dangerous to write a story blaming the Romans for the death of God," she says. As for the Jewish perspective at that time, there are almost no Jewish sources that refer to Jesus, nothing that suggests why they would want to kill him. "We don't have any way of knowing what they thought about Jesus," Reinhartz says. "I suspect most Jews didn't know about him and didn't care." If that's the case, it didn't save Jews, over centuries, from suffering because of what is written in the Gospels. Google "Good Friday pogroms" and you get 230,000 results.

Christians have tried to ease tensions with the Jewish community over the crucifixion accounts. The most notable was in 1965 when, as part of the Vatican II council, the Catholic Church published *Nostra Aetate*. It argued that modern-day Jews should not be held accountable for Jesus' crucifixion—a big step forward in the history of Christian attitudes toward Jews. Today, few Christians would believe their Jewish friends and neighbours are responsible for the death of Christ, and it's less likely the verses read on Good Friday create anger towards Jews. But antisemitism is nevertheless on the rise again around the world. As Good Friday rolls around again this year, perhaps Christians can, firstly, think about how Jews might hear those Gospel accounts, read from pulpits, or dramatized in plays. Secondly, they can think about what they can do, individually and collectively, to show members of the Jewish community that they stand with them against hate of all kinds—on Good Friday or any other day of the year.

March 2023

4
CHURCH LIFE

Has your church been visited by the Mystery Worshipper?

YOU'VE HEARD ABOUT mystery shoppers—people who evaluate how staff treat customers in various stores. You know about restaurant reviewers, who keep their identities secret so they can evaluate food and service. Now get ready for Mystery Worshippers—people who surreptitiously review worship services at churches.

The Mystery Worshipper Project is sponsored by the *Ship of Fools*, an online Christian magazine based in the UK. The aim of the project is to help people know what goes on in various churches, and to "give the churches themselves a shot in the arm by showing them how they look to outsiders." According to the magazine's editors, "we have no hidden agenda. What we ideally look for are honest, searching, and (above all) amusing reports which are critically aware of the good and bad aspects of modern worship."

Anyone can be a Mystery Worshipper—all you have to do is fill out an application on the magazine's website. There are about 180 Mystery Worshippers around the world, including at least two in my hometown, Winnipeg. They are given a 20-question survey that includes questions about the warmth of the welcome, the length of the sermon, the quality of the preaching, and whether the reviewer would consider attending that church regularly. They are also asked to indicate what part of the service was like being in heaven, and what part was "like being in . . . er . . . the other place." The only clue that a Mystery Worshipper has visited your church is a calling card, dropped discreetly into the collection plate. The review is then published on the *Ship of Fools* website, which receives about 1.7 million visits a month.

Why would anyone care what Mystery Worshippers think? The World Wide Web—that's why. Lots of people use the Web today to find information, including about churches. If you Google a church, there's a chance the Mystery Worshipper review will come up high in the list. It may be the first impression for many people seeking information about a congregation.

The idea of the Mystery Worshipper does raise the question of what people—especially un-churched people—are looking for in a church. According to US Christian pollster George Barna, it isn't "stirring worship music" because "worship isn't even on their radar screen." What about snazzy Sunday morning services with high production values? "Church events cannot effectively compete with what the world has to offer," the research group states.

According to Barna, "the only thing the church can provide that no one else has is a life-changing, practical encounter—and on-going relationship—with the living God and with people transformed by similar encounters." Focusing on "features, programs, and benefits other than such a life-shaping encounter is more likely to lose ground than to gain it."

There's nothing mysterious about that.

May 2004

Is it time to get rid of sermons?

I WAS DAYDREAMING the other Sunday during the sermon, and got to thinking about, well, sermons. Specifically, I wondered if talking *at people* is the best way to communicate in today's attention-deficient world.

I'm not sure. I can't think of very many other times when people are required to sit still, be quiet and listen to someone speak for 20 to 30 minutes. In most cases—like a university lecture, for example—people are welcome to ask questions, seek clarification, or add comments. But not at church.

Some preachers are amazingly gifted and can pull off long sermons. They have an ability to hold a congregation in thrall. One preacher friend of mine has an Irish accent, an unfair advantage. He could read a phone book and make it sound interesting. But most preachers aren't so lucky with their place of birth. And we, as listeners, don't make their jobs any easier—many of us have the attention spans of gnats. Or maybe goldfish.

Ted Selker of the Massachusetts Institute of Technology studies how people browse the web. He says that some people spend about nine seconds checking out a web page—the same attention span as a goldfish. Most browsers spend less than 60 seconds on a web page before moving on. "If we spend our time flitting from one thing to another on the web, we can get into a habit of not concentrating," he told the BBC in 2002. "Our attention span gets affected by the way we do things."

It's not just the Internet that makes us less attentive—everything today seems to be cut into smaller pieces. As Nancy Miller states in *Wired* magazine: "Music, television, games, movies, fashion: we now devour our pop culture the same way we enjoy candy and chips—in conveniently packaged bite-size nuggets made to be munched easily with increased frequency and maximum speed. This is snack culture—and boy, is it tasty."

For most of us, she goes on to say, "media snacking is a way of life. In the morning, we check news and tap out emails on our laptops. At work, we graze all day on videos and blogs . . . In between are the morsels that fill those whenever minutes, as your mobile phone carrier calls them: a 30-second game on your Nintendo DS, a 60-second webisode on your cell, a three-minute podcast on your MP3 player."

Does all this mean the sermon is dead? Not necessarily—but preachers do need to be creative to keep their listeners engaged. Sharon Bowman is author of the book *Preventing Death by Lecture!* (2001). She says research shows that "if you leave a group of adults sitting, listening for more than seven minutes, their minds begin to drift." Her solution? Speakers should break their presentations into seven-minute segments. In between segments, they should move about the stage, ask questions of the audience, write a key message or thought on a blackboard or flipchart, tell a story or a joke, show a picture, get people to stand up and stretch—anything to keep listeners engaged.

Not everyone will be comfortable with those ideas, but there are other ways to hold the attention of a congregation. In an article in *The Salvationist*, titled "How to Prevent Death by Sermon," Kim Garreffa gives examples of ways preachers have tried to engage their congregations.

She writes of one pastor who found a novel way to illustrate the idea of Christ as the bread of life. Before church started, he placed bread machines throughout the sanctuary, timing them to bake loaves of bread during the service. While he spoke, the aroma of fresh bread wafted throughout the congregation; at the end of the service, the members used the bread for communion. "Although this congregation had participated in communion many times before, guess which service they never forgot?" she writes. "And what happened the next time they sniffed the aroma of freshly baked bread?"

At another church, Garreffa and other attenders were handed pieces of charcoal and told to hold it throughout the service. "As the service progressed, our hands became black," she writes. "Eventually we were led in a devotional on sin and confession that related the contamination of our hands to the contamination of sin in our hearts. We then practised a time of confession by laying our charcoal at the base of a cross and washing our hands in bowls provided for us. Six months later I can still vividly recall that service."

Garreffa quotes Bowman: "Learning is not a spectator sport . . . the person doing the most talking is doing the most learning. We remember 20 per cent of what we hear, but 90 per cent of what we say and do." Or, as an old saying puts it: "I hear and I forget. I see and I remember. I do and I understand."

May 2005

In defence of Christian introverts

Do you find excuses not to join a care group at your church, or not to go on a congregational retreat or participate in a potluck? Do you like to leave quickly after a service so you don't have to talk to others? Do you get nervous when the person leading a church meeting decides to break the congregation into small groups to discuss a topic or, worse, to pray? If you answered yes to those questions, you might be a Christian introvert, and there's a book just for you.

Called *Introverts in the Church: Finding Our Place in an Extroverted Culture* (2009), the book examines what it's like to be introverted in churches that place a high value on being extroverted. "The extroverted bias of our larger culture has crept into church practice, especially those churches that associate with the evangelical tradition," says author and admitted introvert Adam McHugh. The result is that some churches "unintentionally equate faithfulness with extroversion." This, he says, can lead to the idea that the ideal Christian is someone who likes to share openly and deeply, is gregarious and eager to participate in activities, and is willing to take on leadership roles. That, says McHugh, sounds "suspiciously like an extrovert" to him. Add in the "talkative, mingling informality of many churches" and you've got an environment that can be intimidating for introverts, he adds.

As an introvert myself, I identify with McHugh. Like him, I sometimes find going to church to be an intimidating experience. I don't like sharing about my spiritual journey, or other personal issues. I find it hard to talk to people in the foyer after a service. And heaven help me if the worship leader or preacher is moved to ask the congregation to break into small groups to pray; it's all I can do not to find the nearest exit.

Of course, it's not just church where introverts might feel uncomfortable; society, as a whole, seems to favour extroverts. For example, when someone is outgoing, they are praised for being a people person. But if you are quiet and reserved, you might be considered a loner, or worse, arrogant. For introverted church-goers, an added twist is that it can lead to questions about the quality of your spirituality. How deep are your beliefs if you don't open up to others? Are you really committed to the church if you don't like to participate in church activities? Can you truly be a Christian if you don't like to talk to strangers about your faith?

McHugh's goal is to help introverts feel more at home in church, and to help extroverts understand people like himself better. "Many extroverts assume that introverts need to be constantly 'drawn out,' and that if we are alone, we are just waiting for someone to come over and chat us up, because we are languishing in self-pity and isolation," he says. In fact, "one of the hallmarks of introverts is that we find energy from solitude, and that even though we may enjoy social interaction, those experiences drain us."

He also wants to help church leaders make sure they don't overlook introverted members. "Many churches reflect our society as a whole, valuing gregarious, action-oriented, assertive people," he says. "But introverts are relatively quiet, often hovering around the fringes, preferring to observe and reflect before entering into the action. We generally do not have the same 'presence' when we enter a room as many extroverts do. We are not likely to share our opinions until we have considered them and we are uncomfortable interrupting others to make our voices heard."

Finally, McHugh hopes churches will see and value the gifts introverts bring to the church, such as the gift of listening. "People in our culture so rarely have the experience of being truly listened to—having not only their words taken seriously, but also having their feelings, questions, and doubts underneath those words paid attention to," he says. Introverts, he suggests, "have a head start on listening. Because we process internally, and take up less social space, we can offer a nonjudgmental posture that frees people to open up to us."

It's McHugh's sense that other religions, "especially of the eastern traditions," may be friendlier to introverts since they have "a quieter, more contemplative bent to them." He hopes churches that emphasize a more assertive approach to Christianity might also adopt contemplative practices to make introverts feel more at home.

Hey—it could be an outreach opportunity. It's estimated between 25 to 30 per cent of a given population are introverts. That means there could be a lot of people looking for a little more quiet when it comes to religious practices. Or, as McHugh says, "churches need to acknowledge a diversity of personality types, patterns, habits, and experiences. I want for extroverts, especially those in leadership, to acknowledge that there are different, and equally valuable and viable, ways of following Jesus."

March 2010

What makes for a good Christian funeral?

IT'S NOT OFTEN that a whole nation is talking about funerals. But that's what happened when Jack Layton received his final send-off. His funeral, on August 22, 2011, was moving, inspiring, poignant, personal, funny, and sad. With Layton's funeral in mind, this might be a good time to ask: What makes for a good funeral, anyway? What makes for a good Christian funeral?

Thomas Long is the author of the book *Accompany Them With Singing: The Christian Funeral* (2013). For a long time, he writes, Christian funerals followed a fairly similar pattern—prayers, songs, a simple eulogy, and a sermon. The main focus was not on the life of the deceased, but on God's activity in the world. The primary metaphor was the deceased as a baptized saint on a lifelong, baptismal journey of faith toward God.

"It's a fairly simple picture, but it's actually very profound theologically," he writes. "It involves honoring the body and the identity of the deceased, but it also involves the deceased moving toward a new community—the communion of saints. So the funeral becomes a piece of 'community theatre' in which people act out what they believe about life and death."

But that's not what happens at many Christian funerals today—at least, most of the ones I've attended. Those funerals are apt to be celebrations of the deceased's life; some of them feel more like a celebrity roast, but without the subject alive in the room. In place of a simple eulogy, those funerals feature a number anecdotes about the deceased shared by various people, and what he or she meant to them. Very often, there are also poems, tributes, readings, and special songs. Increasingly, they also feature PowerPoint presentations about the deceased's life, from birth to death, usually accompanied by music. Of course, there is a sermon, too, but by the time we get to it, it almost seems like an afterthought. Even if it is really good, the congregation is so exhausted by everything that's gone on before that we can hardly wait for the minister to finish so we can go home.

For Long, this style of funeral represents a "dramatic and fairly sudden departure from classic Christian funeral practices." In place of liturgy, ritual, worship, and the central role of clergy, Long says, today's church funerals are more like memorial services instead of funerals, focusing more on the deceased than on God. "The trend lines are clear," he states. "It is apparent that funeral practices for all Christians, as a part of the larger culture, are moving at various rates of speed toward this new pattern."

What is wrong with celebrating the life of the deceased? Nothing, says

Long; it should just be done separate from the funeral—at the viewing, after the service, or during some other special event. The goal of the funeral, he says, is to reflect on the "the grand cosmic drama of the church marching to the edge of eternity with a fellow saint, singing songs of resurrection victory and sneering in the face of the final enemy."

The change in funeral practices isn't a North American phenomenon, or even a Protestant one; the Catholic Church in Australia has created guidelines banning football club songs, PowerPoint presentations, and pop or rock music at funerals. According to the guidelines, the wishes of the deceased, family, and friends should be taken into account, but the church should "moderate any tendency to turn the funeral into a secular celebration of the life of the deceased."

In a pastoral letter published on his website last year, Denis Hart, Archbishop of Melbourne, noted that "our funeral services are getting overloaded—a lengthy combination of a commemorative event, a wake, a liturgy . . . the result is that the funeral can become more like a secular memorial service with several eulogies or audiovisual presentations with secular readings and songs." The goal of a Christian funeral, he goes on to say, is to "acknowledge where families are at in their faith journey in life, but also to lift up their hearts to discover how deep is God's love through the proclamation of the Scriptures and the sharing of the Eucharist."

Does that sound like what you want your funeral to be like? If yes, then maybe it's best to leave instructions now about what you want your final send-off to be.

August 2011

The other side of church growth, or, do we need a theology of retreat?

CHURCH GROWTH IS a popular topic. A Google search for that topic returns millions of pages. You can find institutes, seminars, conferences, movements, and lots and lots of books about starting or growing churches. But church death? It's not as popular a subject.

Yet the fact of the matter is that churches not only get born—they die. Every year hundreds of churches in Canada close their doors as members age and attendance declines. The United Church of Canada alone is closing about one a week; in the US, it's reported that 50 churches are shut down each week.

Despite this, it's rare to hear much about church death. And that, says Philip Jenkins, is unfortunate. "I sometimes ask audiences how many people have ever read a book on the growth or establishment of a church, and many people raise their hands," says the author of *The Lost History of Christianity: The Thousand-Year Golden Age of the Church in the Middle East, Africa, and Asia—and How It Died* (2009). "Then I ask how many people have ever read a book on the death or extinction of a church, and virtually nobody does. But in history, church death is a very common phenomenon."

In his book, Jenkins explores the rich history of Christianity in Asia, Africa, and the Middle East. "Its sheer scale is astonishing," he writes of the Nestorian, Chaldean, and Jacobite churches that were thriving and growing at a time when Europe was emerging from the middle ages. "Looking at the world in 850 or so, few observers would have doubted that the Christian future lay in the Middle East and Asia, rather than in the barbarian-ravaged lands of Western Europe," he says.

And yet, those ancient churches are gone. All that's left are small remnants in places like Iraq, Syria, Egypt and—growing smaller every year—Palestine, home to the original Christian church. "There is a major theological issue that nobody addresses, the theology of extinction," says Jenkins. "How do Christians explain the death of their religion in a particular time and place? Is that really part of God's plan?" he asks. Or maybe, he adds, "our time scale is just too short, and one day we will realize why this had to happen." Whatever the reason, "nobody is really discussing these questions," he says.

The disappearance of these ancient churches runs counter to conventional thinking about Christianity. Christians, especially in North America, are accustomed to thinking about their faith in terms of growth and outreach and mission. But churches also die. And when they die, very little is usually said about it. It's sort of embarrassing—after all, nobody likes to admit failure. "We have a theology of mission, not a theology of retreat," states Jenkins.

A central tenet of Christian faith is that the church belongs to God. Whether it lives or dies is not up to us. But that may not be very comforting to people who are seeing their membership decline. How can denominations help them makes sense of it all? Maybe Jenkins is right; perhaps we need a theology of retreat, after all.

September 2011

Time for a divorce ceremony?

A FRIEND OF mine who is going through a divorce compared it to death.

The difference, she says, is that when someone dies there is a funeral and a public way to mark the end of a life. But when a marriage dies there is "no commemoration of a life that you lived, there is no respectful acknowledgement of passage, and there is no announcement in the paper . . . it's an odd thing for a Christian to have to grieve the death of marriage by divorce. I feel very alone in the grief."

I feel for her, and wish she attended a church that holds divorce ceremonies, like the one I attended a number of years ago. I was visiting a Mennonite church in Pennsylvania. Near the end of the service the pastor asked the congregation to stand to read a "blessing of separation" for two members whose marriage had come to an end. As a congregation, we read a litany that invoked God's blessing on the former couple as they went their separate ways. It was a sad occasion, yet hopeful at the same time. Later, I was told that this couple had tried counseling. They had worked on their issues, but in the end everyone agreed that divorce was inevitable.

That Mennonite church is not unique. Methodist, Presbyterian, Lutheran, United Church of Christ, Unitarian, and Episcopalian churches offer blessing ceremonies or special prayers for people who divorce. For some people, any talk about blessing divorced people is tantamount to surrendering to modern culture's belief that nothing is permanent and marriage vows are meaningless. But none of these groups have abandoned their belief in life-long marriage. They are simply coming to terms with reality—Christians get divorced, too. But it's still a leap from there to actually conducting divorce ceremonies. So why do it?

In their book *A Healing Divorce: Transforming the End of Your Relationship with Ritual and Ceremony* (2001), authors Phil and Barbara Penningroth note that faith groups have lots of rituals to mark transitions from one stage of life to another—christenings, baptisms, weddings, and funerals. But there's little for divorce, which is a huge transition for couples, their families, and their friends. "Whether one sees [divorce] as a failure or as a sin, it is without question a major life transition for millions of couples and their children," they write. For many this transition is "handled coldly and impersonally by law and the courts," leading to anger, bitterness, and pain. By "reframing divorce as a life transition and using ritual to facilitate the divorce process," they believe it can be an occasion to "heal hearts and transform lives."

Divorce ceremonies vary. In one, a couple simply repeats their vows, replacing the words “I do” with “I’m sorry.” In another, each person confesses to each other where they failed, asks forgiveness, and blesses the other as they began their future apart. At that point, the pastor pronounces them free from their marriage vows.

After a friend’s husband left her for another relationship, she asked her pastor and some church members gathered in her home to read scripture and pray. During a short ceremony, she took off her wedding ring and she replaced it with a new ring to symbolize a new beginning. “It was an incredibly emotional” experience, she tells me, “but healing as well.”

Couples who want help preserving their marriages often turn to the church. But where is the church when marriages end? Churches need to find ways to provide healing and care for people experiencing divorce. Or, to put it another way, if marriages start in the church, maybe they can end there, too.

November 2014

You've heard about the "nones"; get ready for the "dones"

Many people are familiar with the "nones"—people who, when asked by census takers about their religious affiliation, say they don't belong to any religious group. Not as well-known are the "dones." These are people who still identify strongly with their faith, but have given up on going to services.

They are a growing phenomenon. According to sociologist Josh Packard, co-author, with Ashleigh Hope, of the book *Church Refugees: Sociologists Reveal Why People are DONE with Church but Not Their Faith* (2015), and head of The Dechurched Project, which explores the move away from institutional church by both parishioners and pastors, the dones used to be some of the most dedicated and active people in their congregations. But somewhere along the way they stopped wanting to attend worship services.

Why are they done? One reason, Packard says, is that people are weary of sitting in pews and going through the same motions every Sunday—they're bored. Another reason is the sermon-centred style of most worship services today. As one person tells him, "I'm tired of being lectured to." For others, it's about all the work and energy needed to run a congregation. "I just kept thinking that Jesus has to be bigger than subcommittees," says another to Packard.

"Dones" desire to be more engaged in the community. "Now that we're out [of church] we have time and energy to spend on our community," says one. "We do a lot more volunteering with civic groups around town." Adds a pastor who quit on church: "I didn't want to be part of the machine anymore. I wanted to change the focus of my life to relationships."

In 2014 the Barna group, a US organization that researches faith and culture, published a list of five reasons why people say they are done with the church: they find it irrelevant; they don't find God there; they don't feel that doubt and honest questioning are welcome; they don't understand the sermons; and churches don't feel friendly.

It's not just an American phenomenon. It's happening in Canada, too. Doug Koop, the former editor of *ChristianWeek*, wrote about it last summer for the Canadian evangelical magazine *Faith Today*. In his column about how many of his 50-something peers are disengaging from the church, Koop noted many used to be active in their congregations, but now are "making the institutional church more of a back-burner item, less of a lifestyle." For some, he writes, it was the result of a crisis of faith, but for most, there was a simpler explanation: "They realize that weekly worship service attendance no longer provides them with the sanctuary and inspiration it previously delivered." Instead of going to church on Sundays, "they are largely content to worship more serendipitously and attend Sunday services irregularly," he writes.

Ontario pastor and blogger Carey Nieuwhof has also been following this trend. Among the reasons he gives for Christians stopping attending church are the general busyness of life, the ability to access what you want to know about theology on your smartphone, and a failure to see a direct benefit from attending services. He also cites the disappearance of guilt. There was a time, he writes, when Christians felt bad if they didn't go to church. Today, he says, "the number of people who feel guilty about not being in church on Sunday shrinks daily." For Nieuwhof, the rapid fall in church attendance is a "truly radical change, the kind that happens only every few centuries," on par with "what happened to the church after Constantine's conversion or after the invention of the printing press."

In her book, *The Great Emergence: How Christianity is Changing and Why* (2012), Phyllis Tickle suggests the church periodically holds a garage sale, getting rid of the things it no longer wants or needs. "About every 500 years the empowered structures of institutionalized Christianity, whatever they may be at that time, become an intolerable carapace, or hard shell, that must be shattered in order that renewal and new growth may occur," she writes.

Tickle writes that the last big garage sale was during the Reformation. If she's right, that means we are in the midst of the next one, and it looks like Christians are letting go of the way churches hold worship services today.

March 2015

Reasons why don't people go to church

JOEL THIESSEN, A sociology professor at Ambrose University in Calgary, wants to know why people don't go to church. To get some answers, he decided to interview some non-churchgoers. From those conversations, he heard eight reasons why Canadians today don't go to church.

At the top of the list is the feeling that church is too exclusive in its beliefs and practices—that it is out of step with Canadian values of inclusivity and tolerance. This would be especially true of things like not allowing women to be leaders, or not accepting or affirming people who are gay. Next is life transitions. People today move a lot. They find it hard to put down roots in a church. It can also be because of transitions like divorce, or the death of the family member who made sure everyone went to church.

Teenage choice is third. When I was a teenager, staying home on Sunday mornings wasn't an option. Parents today increasingly let their teenage children decide whether they want to go to church or not. As Thiessen notes, "most teens opt out at that point." Busyness is fourth. With most families having two working parents today, with kids involved in multiple extracurricular activities, it's hard to find time to empty the dishwasher and do the laundry—much less go to church. Plus, Sunday morning might be the only time you have to shop for groceries or simply relax.

Disillusionment over church sex scandals comes in fifth on the list, along with religiously inspired violence. Sixth is the inability to reconcile religious beliefs with science, or with evil in the world. "A church might say that God is love, but if your child dies of a disease or accident, it's hard to reconcile that with your personal experience," Thiessen says. A bad experience in a church is seventh. This can be anything from not feeling welcomed to experiencing tension with another church member, or just feeling let down by the community. Last on the list is social ties: if your friends and family frown upon your involvement in a religious group, chances are you will stop going.

Many of these reasons are beyond the control of churches to address, says Thiessen, who details his findings in his new book *The Meaning of Sunday: The Practice of Belief in a Secular Age* (2015). But even if churches try to change the things they can control—if they are friendlier, less exclusive, or have fewer scandals, it likely wouldn't change things, he maintains. "Demand for greater involvement is not strong" among non-churchgoers, he says, no matter what churches try to do to fix the problem.

Thiessen points to the United Church, which was the first major Canadian denomination to welcome gay people. Attendance did not improve because of that decision. "The fact is that most of those who are not regularly involved are fairly content with their levels of involvement, and any lip service paid to desiring greater involvement is just that—lip service," he says.

There are always anecdotal stories that tell a different tale, he notes, "but on the whole I don't think the demand for religion or religious involvement is as great as many think." The central premise of his book is that Canada is "becoming increasingly secular, and there's no reason to believe that trend won't continue . . . simply put, fewer Canadians identify with a religious tradition or desire to attend worship services regularly."

There are major implications from this change, and not just for churches. Studies in Canada and the US show that regular attendance at worship services is strongly tied to giving and volunteering, and that people who are more religiously active tend to also give more than those who don't attend worship services. For charities that depend on regular churchgoers for donations—both religious and non-religious alike—declining attendance means they are going to face some big challenges. "If the donor pool is shrinking, it will necessitate some creative thinking about how to fundraise," says Thiessen.

February 2016

Converts and "nonverts"

If a convert is someone who has been persuaded to change their religious faith or beliefs, what's a "nonvert"? According to Stephen Bullivant, professor of theology and the sociology of religion at St. Mary's University, Twickenham in London, a nonvert is a person who grew up in a religious home, but drifted away—who once identified with a religion, but now says they have none.

The number of British nonverts who experience "nonversion" is growing. Altogether, 48.6 per cent of Britons say they have no religion, according to data from a 2015 British social attitudes survey and a 2014 European social survey. "The striking thing is the clear sense of the growth of 'no religion' as a proportion of the population," Bullivant told *The Guardian* in 2016. "The main driver is people who were brought up with some religion now saying they have no religion . . . the rise of the non-religious is arguably the story of British religious history over the past half-century or so," he said.

In his 2016 report titled, "The 'No Religion' Population of Britain," Bullivant notes that more than 60 per cent of the nonverts were brought up as Christians, mainly Anglican or Catholic. Non-Christian religions have better retention levels; overall, only two per cent of nonverts were raised in religious homes other than Christian. According to Bullivant, the "nonversion" rate is 14 per cent for Jews, 10 per cent for Muslims and Sikhs, and six per cent for Hindus.

But what about people going the other way—converting from no-faith to being religious? The news isn't good on that front; the number of the non-religious who convert to faith is small. Just over five per cent of what Bullivant calls "cradle nones" report becoming Christians. Only two per cent joined non-Christian faiths. Or, to put it another way, for every person brought up in a non-religious household who becomes religious, 26 people raised as Christians became non-religious.

Other findings from Bullivant's report showed that 67 per cent of Britons identified as some kind of Christian in 1983; in 2015, it was 43 per cent. Over the same period, members of non-Christian religions have more than quadrupled. Those who no longer identify with religions are younger on average—35 per cent of the "nones" are under 35, compared to just six per cent of that cohort who say they're Anglicans.

If there is any good news for religious groups, Bullivant says that after consistent decline the proportion of nones in Britain appears to have stabilized over the past few years. "Younger people tend to be more non-religious, so you'd expect it to keep going," he told *The Guardian* in May. "But it hasn't. The steady growth of non-Christian religions is a contributing factor, but I wonder if everyone who is going to give up their Anglican affiliation has done so by now? We've seen a vast shedding of nominal Christianity, and perhaps it's now down to its hard core." And that may be another source of good news for religious groups, he suggests.

While many people have left Christianity, a "creative minority" of committed Christians remain, Bullivant notes in an article in *Church Times*, an Anglican newspaper in the United Kingdom. This group is strongly committed, he says, and since they are "swimming against the tide" are often stronger in their faith. This may lead to a rise in the number of people who are committed to religion in the future, he adds, since they will be more intentional about bringing their children up in the faith.

What does this mean for Canadian religious groups? Attendance at religious services is also declining in this country, as is affiliation with various religious groups—"nones" make up 24 per cent of the population, one of the fastest growing faith categories in Canada.

In the meantime, one lesson to be drawn out of the British experience might be to pour fewer resources into outreach, or what Christians call evangelism, since it doesn't appear to be working—in the UK, at least. What might be more effective is investing in things like family ministries, children's programs, youth groups, creative ways to be relevant and community-minded, and providing more support for religious colleges and universities. Maybe that way there will be fewer nonverts in the future.

July 2017

Is your church (really) welcoming of seniors?

"I'D LIKE TO comment on your column regarding the topic of loneliness among seniors and the church," begins an e-mail I've received from a reader.

The writer, a senior herself, is a widow. She finds churches to be very unwelcoming places for older, single people. "I find myself marginalized," she writes. "The church certainly isn't a part of the solution. It is by and large the problem. Families organize around themselves and their significant others. It would be the extreme exception for a family to embrace a senior that wasn't their grandmother."

Although the writer has been widowed for over 25 years, she has received few invitations to the homes of others from people who are members of churches. "The Bible teaches that Christians are to look out for widows, but I doubt very much if it is ever mentioned in churches," she writes. Non-church-going people, on the other hand, "are much more inclusive of outsiders," in her experience. As a result, she doesn't see church as a solution to the growing number of lonely people in Canada today, including many seniors. "Quite the opposite," she writes. "I think they will feel more lonely there."

I suspect this writer's situation isn't unique. It would be a rare place of worship that didn't say they are welcoming of anyone and everyone; I randomly checked the websites of half-a-dozen churches, a synagogue, and a mosque here in Winnipeg, and all had the word "welcome" on their home pages. But is that how people experience them? Is everyone really welcome or are those just words?

About the same time I received the e-mail from the lonely senior, I was in Ontario on a speaking tour. When I came to the Thamesville United Church in Fullarton, I found an interesting sign in the foyer. It read:

> All are welcome here. But we extend a special welcome to those who are single, married, divorced, gay, confused, filthy rich, comfortable or dirt poor. We extend a special welcome to wailing babies and excited toddlers.
>
> We welcome you if you can sing like Pavarotti or just growl quietly to yourself. You're welcome here if you're just browsing, just woke up or just out of prison. We don't care if you're more Christian than Mother Teresa, or haven't been in church since Christmas 1977.
>
> We welcome those who are over 60 but not yet grown up, and to teenagers who are growing up too fast. We welcome keep-fit moms, football dads, starving artists, tree-huggers, latte-sippers, vegetarians, junk-food

eaters.

We welcome those who are in recovery or still addicted. We welcome you if you're having problems, are down in the dumps, or if you don't like "organized religion." (We're not keen on it, either.)

We welcome those who think the earth is flat, work too hard, don't work, can't spell, or are here just because mom or grandma is in town and wanted to go to church. We welcome those who are inked, pierced, both or neither.

We offer a prayer to those who could use a special prayer right now, had religion shoved down their throats as kids, or got lost on their way to a cottage and ended up here by mistake. We welcome pilgrims, tourist, seekers, doubters, young, old—and you!

A bit of research reveals that the sign is not unique to that church; it can be found, with different words and localizations, on the websites of many churches in England, the US, and Canada. Some also include it in their bulletins and orders of worship. Nobody seems to know where it originated; the earliest mention appears to be around 2012 in a church in Colorado. But the where and when of the sign doesn't matter. What matters is how neatly it sums up what "welcome" could really mean—if places of worship really mean what they say.

May 2018

When "Everyone Welcome" at church doesn't really mean everyone

A FEW YEARS ago, a friend of mine who identifies with the 2SLGBTQ+ community expressed interest in going to church and asked me, what congregation might I recommend?

I could immediately think of lots of churches that were friendly, engaging, had great music, and good programs. But were they welcoming of 2SLGBTQ+ people? I didn't want to send her someplace where she would feel condemned and rejected. After some searching, I came with a short list of churches to suggest to her—places where she might feel at home. I wish I had known about *Church Clarity* back then. That would have made things much easier.

Founded in 2017, *Church Clarity* is a website that rates churches in the US and Canada on how clear they are about their policies towards 2SLGBTQ+ people and women in leadership. Since many people today visit websites when looking for a new church, the idea behind *Church Clarity* is to help churches be as clear as possible about whether everyone is truly welcome to participate fully in the life of their congregation.

Churches are rated by the volunteer-run organization in two ways: they can either ask to be evaluated, or someone can recommend them. After receiving a request, volunteers visit a church's website and assign a score of clear, unclear, or undisclosed when it comes to how transparently they communicate their stance on 2SLGBTQ+ people or women in leadership. After assigning a score, *Church Clarity* reaches out to a church to verify its rating and invite feedback before publishing its findings.

To date, the website has rated over 3,600 churches across North America. Fourteen are in Winnipeg. I reached out to Kai Ngu, co-founder of *Church Clarity*, to find out more. "We created it to fill a gap," they say, noting that churches commonly say "everyone is welcome" but may not, in fact, extend that welcome to 2SLGBTQ+ people or women who feel called to be leaders. "We want churches to be clear about who is welcome and who isn't," they say.

At the same time, *Church Clarity* wants to take the burden off individuals trying to figure out where a church stands on these issues. "It can be risky for them to try to figure out if they are truly welcome," Ngu says, adding it can be hard to go a pastor and try to get an answer—without revealing more than they wish to share about themselves. They continue, "We want to empower people by giving them the information they need to make good decisions about where to attend."

Ngu is adamant the goal of *Church Clarity* is not to advocate for changes in policies around 2SLGBTQ+ or women in leadership. "We don't want to convince churches to change their theology, but just to be clear about it," they state.

Most of the Winnipeg churches on the *Church Clarity* website are United Church and Anglican. One is Mennonite. Eight are clearly welcoming and affirming of 2SLGBTQ+ people. Five are unclear, one is clearly not open to 2SLGBTQ+ people, and another is undisclosed, which means you can't tell one way or the other from its website.

I reached out to Winnipeg churches on the list. Those "verified clear" for their welcome said they were happy to be listed. Some that are unclear said they are still in the process of working through the issue. A few indicated they were open to 2SLGBTQ+ inclusion but couldn't say that on their websites since their denominations aren't open to it. The one that is clearly not welcoming did not respond, nor did the one that is undisclosed.

For Loraine MacKenzie Shepherd, minister at Westworth United Church, my query about her church's rating on *Church Clarity* came at an interesting time—her congregation is in the process of considering becoming affirming. "I'm including your email in my sermon—quite timely!" she wrote me, adding "our hope is to bring this to a congregational vote about a year from now. We have had three sessions on lesbian, gay, transgender and non-binary, identity. We are now moving to other types of marginalized identities, as we understand affirming to be much larger than just LGBTQ+."

February 2020

Pressures of the job and clergy suicide

Clergy suicide—two words you don't expect to see in the same sentence. But that was the news making the rounds this month after the death of a much-loved minister in the UK.

Her name was The Reverend Canon Anna Matthews, and the 44-year-old was the priest at St. Bene't's Anglican Church in Cambridge. She left behind her husband, Stephen. A statement on her church's website says: "Anna's death was tragic and sudden, and we are now able to confirm that she took her own life."

In a follow-up statement, the church says: "This will be a difficult time for us as a congregation as we navigate the tremendous chasm in the life and worship of St Bene't's that Anna's sudden loss brings and the feelings of deep grief we all share." Nothing has been shared about why Matthews took her own life, but her death is a reminder of the pressures many clergy face, especially during the pandemic.

Writing about Matthews on Facebook, Mike Rayson, the worship pastor at Main Street United Methodist Church in Alton, Illinois, says: "To be brutally honest with you all, I understand some of this. Often times, clergy are placed under enormous pressures and when the load becomes more than we can bear, we don't know who to turn to." Unburdening themselves to their congregants often isn't an option, he writes. "We are sent to serve communities, not rely on communities to support us," he shares. "And all it takes is one slip of the tongue from a trusted parishioner, and the whole church is on fire." Clergy can turn to other ministers, but that can also be hard, Rayson adds. "In my own experience, there's also a deep sense of shame that I can't deal with my own 'stuff.'"

"Clergy face unbelievable pressure from all sides all the time," he writes. "To ask for help, any help, even just to ask another clergy friend to lend an ear over a cup of coffee and a cookie feels dangerous and has the ability to cast yourself as a failure in the eyes of the church and in the eyes of God." Rayson knows this because he's experienced it: "There have been times I've stayed in bed for days ignoring the phone and not responding to text messages. Who do you turn to when life throws an enormous load of stuff at you?" he asks. Matthew's death is not unique, he goes on to say: "I've attended a couple of funerals for colleagues who simply saw no other way."

Jakob Topper is pastor at North Haven Church in Norman, Oklahoma. Writing for Baptist News Global, he notes how difficult the pandemic was for many clergy—what with the debates among members over closures and mask mandates. Navigating a hyper-partisan political culture in the US was also hard. After writing an earlier article about the stresses many clergy were experiencing, and how it led some to suicide, he began to hear from the families of ministers, who wanted him to do the memorial. "I officiated six of these services and turned down a dozen more," he writes. "Clergy mental health is a life-or-death matter."

His advice to struggling clergy? Ask for help if needed, and don't assume because the pandemic is over that mental health will automatically get better. "It might," he says. "It might not. It might even get worse. I know several ministers who are experiencing just this, and it's perfectly normal. The deep reserves that carried you this far may be empty, and it's time to fill yourself up again." Congregants, Topper adds, should "practice grace and mercy with their ministers . . . they are not gods. They're just people under immense pressure. How we treat people when they are vulnerable tells us everything we need to know about our true Christian beliefs."

I asked some local denominational leaders and clergy if they were aware of any ministers in Manitoba who had taken their own lives due to stress. The answer was no. But, as one put it, "that is not to say that mental health concerns do not affect clergy. There has been an increase in the need to talk about mental health, especially during and following COVID-19 shutdowns." One way his denomination is responding is by offering seminars for clergy about coping with stress during COVID-19, and significantly increasing counselling benefits clergy can access.

A final word from Mike Raynor to members of congregations: "Take good care of your pastor, so that they can take good care of you."

March 2023

5
CHALLENGING SCRIPTURE

What do you do with a hole-y Bible?

How do you dispose of an old, worn-out Bible? It doesn't seem right to throw it into the garbage—it feels disrespectful and irreverent. Is it better to burn it? Or should you bury it? Or maybe put it in the recycling bin?

"I don't think there is any formal practice for the disposal of old Bibles for most church groups," said George Shillington, a former New Testament scholar at Winnipeg's Canadian Mennonite University. Checks of official church websites and calls to various church offices suggest that he is right.

The only group that has guidelines for the proper disposal of old Bibles are Roman Catholics. According to Joanne Struch of the Archdiocese of Winnipeg, "a Bible, especially one that has been blessed, should be burned. This is if the Bible is absolutely unreadable anymore. If it is simply a matter of not using the Bible anymore, it can be given away to missions, or taken to a used bookstore."

Wondering what to do with worn-out scriptures isn't a problem for Jews, Muslims, and Sikhs; members of these three groups have precise rules and rituals for disposing of sacred texts. Jews, for example, bury any Torah scroll, Torah cover, wooden roller for the Torah parchment, and any other holy book or piece of paper with the Hebrew word for God written on them.

Muslims burn old copies of the Qur'an, although disposing of them in the ocean is also acceptable. Some also bury worn-out copies of their holy book, but they have to make sure they do it in "pure soil"—on high ground, where there is little chance that animals or humans might despoil it.

Sikhs also burn old copies of their scripture. Called the Guru Granth Sahib, it is considered by them to be a living Guru and is the supreme spiritual authority for the Sikh religion. According to Hakam Singh Johal, past president of the Sikh Society of Manitoba, copies that can no longer be used are sent to Vancouver, where Sikhs have a special place for burning them. "It's done respectfully, and with a proper ceremony and prayers," he says.

These rules for the disposal of worn-out scriptures shows the reverence that Jews, Muslims, and Sikhs have for their sacred texts. So why haven't Christians, who also revere the Bible, created any special rituals for its disposal? According to Shillington, it may be because Christians have tended to view the Bible more as a book of instruction. "We don't have the same view of the sacredness of the text as some other religions," he says, adding that "maybe a little more respect for the Bible would be helpful."

So, what should you do with your old, worn-out Bible? Burning seems to be an option, but it might feel a bit strange. After all, the idea of burning books is viewed by many people as censorship, which isn't the message you might want to communicate. Then there's the problem of where to burn it; if you don't have a fireplace, do you take it out to a campground and throw it in a campfire? That might require tricky explanations when the wind picks up partially burned pages of the Gospel of John and deposits them on neighbouring campsites.

Recycling is a possibility, especially since it embodies the Christian ideal of being transformed into something new. If the Bible isn't too worn, you could give it away. That's what Mark Ruge, a spokesman for the Jehovah's Witnesses in Canada, does; if, during his door-to-door visits, he meets someone who doesn't have a Bible but wants one, he offers one of his old Bibles. "That way, it continues to be useful," he says.

Maybe burying an old worn-out Bible is the best idea. After all, Jesus talked about planting seeds and the need for something to die in order to produce new life. Burying your old Bible in the garden might be a respectful and even biblical way to dispose of it—and help create new life—in the form of flowers or vegetables—at the same time.

But the last word goes to Wayne Weissenbuehler, pastor of Bethany Lutheran Church in Cherry Hills Village, Colorado, and former bishop of the Rocky Mountain Synod of the Evangelical Lutheran Church in America. Writing in *The Lutheran*, in response to a question from a church member about how to dispose of a worn-out Bible, he says: "Oh, how I wish this were a problem for us. We (Lutherans) have too many Bibles in wonderful mint condition."

April 2004

God is my snowplow driver, and other new images for God

"THE LORD IS my snowplow driver. My path shall be clear."

That thought came to mind one May day, when a huge and unexpected spring snowstorm hit the province of Manitoba. My wife and I were traveling home to Winnipeg from rural Manitoba, the storm at its height. Visibility was nil; we couldn't see the road at all. The only option seemed to be to pull off the road. But then a snowplow turned on to the highway right in front of us, clearing a path for our car. We followed the snowplow almost all the way home.

Later, I thought of how our experience with the snowplow parallels the way we sometimes experience life: when we can't see the way, God appears and clears a path. God, in other words, is like a snowplow driver.

You won't find God described that way in the Bible, but there are lots of other images: rock, eagle, hen, wind, fire, water, cloud, rock, mother, father, bread, landowner, gardener, potter shepherd, judge, king, and architect, among other things. Of course, God is none of these things. They are images that help us understand God's attributes.

Many of the Bible's images for God are rural or agrarian. But as people today become increasingly urbanized, images that were meaningful to the mostly rural and nomadic people of the Bible's time are harder to understand. As Donald Miller says, in his book *Blue Like Jazz*, "all the vocabulary about God" seems to come from "ancient history, before video games and the Internet."

Take the image of shepherd. Most of us have never met one. We certainly don't understand what a shepherd does. In 1974, Phillip Keller tackled this problem with his best-selling book *A Shepherd Looks at Psalm 23.* Keller, who developed and managed sheep ranches, helped modern urbanites see this familiar Psalm in a new way by explaining what those pastoral images really meant.

For example, Keller explained that the verse about God preparing a table does not mean that God has prepared a banquet. Rather, for a shepherd, a table is the top of a hill where sheep are taken for summer pasturage. And the verse about anointing heads with oil? That was done to ward off pests—not to confer some special privilege or blessing. Both verses reveal what God's care for people is like, if you understand their imagery.

But, for some, even more contemporary images are hard to comprehend. Donald Miller was abandoned by his father as a young child. "Today I wonder why it is God refers to Himself as 'father' at all," he writes. "This, to me, in light of the earthly representation of the role, seems a marketing mistake. Why would God want to call Himself Father when so many fathers abandon their children?" Miller goes on to say that "as a child, the title Father God offered an ambiguous haze with which to interact. I understood what a father did as well as I understood the task of a shepherd."

One antiquated image that remains popular today is that of king. That worked well in Bible times, and even until a hundred years ago. But today few people live in countries ruled by absolute monarchs. In fact, we have seen an explosion of democracy worldwide in the last 25 years, according to Freedom House, an organization that tracks the growth of democracy around the world. Today 121 out of 192 countries have some form of electoral democracy. For those of us who live in North America, the idea of what a king is like is limited to fairy tales, Disney movies, and the English monarchy.

This disconnect between the image of king and our daily lives was addressed by William Johnson Everett in a 1989 article for *Christian Century*, "Sunday Monarchists and Monday Citizens?" In it, he noted that Christians across North America talk and sing about worshipping a king on Sundays but live in democracies the rest of the week. "How has this fervent Christian anomaly survived two centuries of democratic development?" he wondered, adding: "Isn't it time we that we reconstructed our Christian thought in order to engage the world in which we actually live?"

But what would we use in place of king—president or prime minister? Given the state of US and Canadian politics today, that may seem a stretch. But perhaps there is a kernel of truth in it. According to Everett, that way of thinking is consistent with the life and ministry of Jesus, "whose presidency was powered by listening, whose republic was founded in covenant bonding, and whose election was rooted in self-sacrifice."

For many, the old images work just fine. But new images are always helpful. One that might help younger generations understand God's transcendence and all-knowing power is this: God is like Google, the web's most powerful search engine. Like all images, it has limitations, but perhaps it can help some people understand God's attributes. Or, for those of us who live in Canada, or the northern US, God as snowplow driver works just fine too.

May 2005

666, or, waiting for the end of the world

If you're reading this, it means the world hasn't ended. That's what a few people worried would happen as June 6, 2006, drew closer. For them, it was an ominous date—or would that be *omenous*?—the sixth day of the sixth month of the sixth year of this century: 666.

Some people claimed it could be a day of satanic power, marked by a comet hitting Earth. Others believed it could signal the start of Armageddon, or maybe The Rapture—the belief that millions of Christians will disappear from the earth, leaving non-believers behind. Indeed, back then "The Rapture Index," found at www.raptureready.com, which calculated the likelihood that Christ would come back that year, was right off its scale and into "fasten your seatbelts" territory.

For some, that date was a great marketing opportunity. 20th Century Fox chose it to release its remake of *The Omen*, the classic 1970s horror film about a woman who gives birth to the child of Satan. The heavy-metal rock group Slayer used it to launch its Unholy Alliance tour, while the death metal group Deicide, which calls itself "Satan's favourite band," released its newest album on what it called "that most unholy of days." Not to be outdone, best-selling evangelical authors Tim LaHaye and Jerry B. Jenkins also selected June 6, 2006 as a good day to launch their new book, called *The Rapture: In the Twinkling of an Eye / Countdown to the Earth's Last Days*, the latest instalment in their *Left Behind* series. Some Christian retailers reportedly got into the spirit of things by selling paperback editions of earlier *Left Behind* books for $6.66.

What's up with that number, anyway? It comes from the last book of the Bible, where the author writes that the number of the Beast of Revelation is 666. Over the centuries, that has led to widespread speculation about the Beast's identity. For some Protestants, it has been almost any pope (in the sixteenth century, some Catholics thought it was Martin Luther).

More recently, Ronald Wilson Reagan was a candidate (six letters in each word in his name—get it?), as was US president, George Walker Bush Jr. (six letters again). In the 1970s, Henry Kissinger was the beast of choice, and prior to that people thought it was Hitler or Mussolini. Also in the running were the ubiquitous UPC bar codes on everything we buy, while some suggested it was the World Wide Web.

But biblical scholars say John, the (debated) author of Revelation, didn't have any of these people or things in mind when he wrote the book. They argue John was referring to the Roman Emperor Nero, who led a terrible persecution against the early church. This is based on the Hebrew language, where each letter has a numerical value; in Hebrew, Nero's name equals 666—a bit of code that John's first-century readers would have figured out very quickly. But not only that, say scholars: John wasn't writing about the end times at all.

According to Michael Gilmour, who teaches New Testament at Providence College in Otterburne, Manitoba, the book of Revelation isn't about prophecy or the end of the world. It's a pastoral book, he says, written for Christians who, at that time, were experiencing terrible persecution during the reign of the Roman emperor, Domitian. "Many people assume that the book of Revelation is about the future, but John is writing to first century churches," Gilmour says. "He's writing to a marginalized and persecuted church, trying to comfort and encourage them."

Brian Froese, who teaches history at Canadian Mennonite University, agrees. "John was writing to Christians in dark and perilous times, pointing to a future of peace and prosperity," he says. But if that's the case, why do so many people today see Revelation as a blueprint for the end times? Gilmour and Froese say it can be traced back to John Nelson Darby, a nineteenth-century British minister who used verses in the Old and New Testaments to come up with the idea that history is divided into specific periods of time, or dispensations. Over the past 35 years, Darby's ideas have been widely promoted by people like Hal Lindsey, author of *The Late Great Planet Earth* (1970), and the authors of *Left Behind*—people who suggest we are living in the last period of time before Christ returns.

The main problem with this view, Gilmour says, is that it does "violence to the text," and those who subscribe to it have to practice "hermeneutical acrobatics" to make all the different verses from the Old and New Testaments fit into their system. "It pieces disparate things together to make a coherent structure," adds Froese, but he notes that proponents have to take verses "out of context" to make them fit.

Both Gilmour and Froese hasten to add that this doesn't mean that Christians can't apply lessons from the book of Revelation today. We just have to be careful not to view it as "some mysterious *Da Vinci Code*-like puzzle," says Froese. Adds Gilmour: "All we know is that Christ will return, and we should live in this moment, being faithful and ready."

June 2006

The Prayer of Jabez, or, God as cosmic butler

WITH OVER 20 MILLION copies sold, *The Prayer of Jabez: Breaking Through to the Blessed Life* (2000) may be the most popular book ever written about prayer.

In it, author Bruce Wilkinson promises that those who pray a "daring prayer that God always answers" for 30 days in a row will receive personal blessings. The prayer in question is found in 1 Chronicles 4.10, where an obscure Bible character named Jabez is recorded as calling "on the God of Israel, saying, 'Oh, that you would bless me and enlarge my territory and that your hand would be with me and that you would keep me from hurt and harm!'"

In an interview a few years ago, Wilkinson explained how it works: "What happens is, if you keep praying that prayer, you do get answers, and thus far, we've not met anyone who's prayed the prayer for a month who doesn't have a number of stories to tell you." But Wilkinson himself now has quite a story to tell, although you won't find it among the testimonies on his website. His grand plan to build a $190 million US orphanage to house 10,000 children in Swaziland orphaned by AIDS, along with a Bible college, bed and breakfast, game reserve, golf course, and other attractions, fell apart. Apparently, the prayer of Jabez doesn't work all the time—not even for Wilkinson himself.

It all began in 2002, when Wilkinson believed that God was calling him to create a new organization called Dream for Africa and to move to that continent to help with the problem of AIDS. He decided to build a model development project in Swaziland, a country ravaged by the disease, but the plan fell apart when the Swazi refused to give in to his demand for 32,500 acres of land close to two game reserves, or to agree to a complex 40-page plan for the operation after thinking about it for only five days. Faced with failure, Wilkinson quit the continent in December last year, and left the organization he had founded. "I'll put it down as one of the disappointments of my career," Wilkinson told *The Wall Street Journal,* adding that he is still trying to come to grips with the fact that no miracles materialized in Africa—despite his unceasing recitation of the Jabez prayer.

What lessons can be drawn from this story? First, Wilkinson can at least be commended for taking some of the wealth he gained from sales of his book and dedicating it to help the poor. According to a report in *Christianity Today*, the whole experience took a serious toll on him physically, emotionally, spiritually, and financially. Second, no amount of prayer—no matter how sincere—can replace good, experienced international development work. It didn't help that

Wilkinson thought he could do it better than established aid groups. "Because I don't come out of this arena of humanitarian aid, I have a fresh pair of eyes," he said in an interview before it all came crashing down.

But what of the prayer itself? There's nothing wrong with asking God for help in daily life. Petition is an intrinsic part of prayer in every major religion, coupled with adoration, supplication, and thanksgiving. No less an authority than Jesus taught his followers to pray for daily bread and to be delivered from evil. The problem here is how Wilkinson used the prayer of Jabez, portraying God as a cosmic butler who is required to provide an answer if people follow a set formula. As Walter Brueggemann, professor of Old Testament at Columbia Theological Seminary, observes: "This prayer is not an automatic control button, because the God of the gospel is not an automaton. The response and assurance given by God at the end of 1 Chronicles 4.10 is not 'produced' by the prayer; it is the free offer of a generous God who will not be controlled or summoned on call."

Viewing prayer as an easy way to get what we want, no matter how honourable, is also out of step with 2,000 years of Christian experience, which shows that the life of faith involves diligence, hard work, discipline and—sometimes—suffering. Likewise, there is no assurance that following Jesus will result in a wonderful life of physical blessing; just look at the hundreds of millions of Christians in the developing world who live every day with hunger, poverty, disease, and war, not to mention the millions who have been persecuted and killed for their faith.

The idea that God owes believers a happy, healthy, and wealthy life seems to be a uniquely North American idea. It completely overlooks the obvious point that, compared to many people in the poorer parts of the world, we in Canada and the US are already blessed—even if we personally don't make the most money, own the nicest house, or drive the biggest car.

Jabez wasn't the only person to have a prayer recorded in the Old Testament. Agur's prayer, in Proverbs 30.8-9, asks God to "give me neither poverty nor riches; feed me with the food that I need, or I shall be full, and deny you, and say, 'Who is the Lord?' or I shall be poor, and steal, and profane the name of my God." Now that's a prayer worth repeating.

June 2006

The Bible, context, and polygamy

For African Christians, reconciling Christianity with traditional beliefs can be a challenge. This was true for a Kenyan friend of mine studying theology in Winnipeg. He is learning a lot about the Bible, church history, and theology from his Canadian professors. But there's one area where they can't offer much advice: polygamy.

My friend is Maasai and in Kenya, he pastors a Maasai congregation. One characteristic of Maasai culture is the practice of polygamy. In my friend's church, a number of men have more than one wife. For him, it's no big deal. In fact, his father has two wives, his uncle six. And his church is OK with it.

Why? Permitting men with multiple wives to join the church is a practical response for Christians who want to reach out to their community. "Many people want to come to our church, but they won't if they are afraid we will force them to divorce all but one wife if they accept Jesus," he says. Why don't they require the men to divorce all but one wife after they become Christians? Again, it's a practical response. Telling a man to divorce all but one wife would "not only break up a family, it would condemn the woman to poverty," he says. In Maasai culture, he added, a wife belongs to her husband forever, and cannot remarry if he dies or is divorced. "She would end up poor and needy," he says.

I asked him about what it says in the Bible, that marriage is between one man and one woman. My friend pointed out the Old Testament is replete with examples of polygamy, adding "we follow what it says in the book of Timothy,"—a reference to 1 Timothy 3.2, which states that a church leader such as a bishop "must be married only once." To him, that indicates that the early church had polygamous members, and that men with more than one wife can be part of the church—they just can't lead it.

What my friend is doing is interpreting the Bible from his cultural context. Some call this the "Africanization of theology," a process by which Christians on that continent replace the style of church brought over by European and North American missionaries with practices that grow out of the indigenous African experience.

My friend's church isn't the only one in Africa that accepts members who practice polygamy. In a historic vote in 2006, Ethiopia's Meserete Kristos Church, a Mennonite-related group, decided that polygamous converts do not need to divorce multiple wives, and that men with more than one wife can be baptized, although they can't serve as church leaders. In making the decision, leaders of the church say its witness had been handicapped by denying baptism to polygamous converts. "This decision shows concern for the community, and especially for the wives and the children who are affected," says general secretary Mulugeta Zewdie, noting that requiring polygamists to divorce multiple wives often causes extensive suffering for women and children. "The impact of this decision is that the church will be united in evangelizing and in showing concern for the community in polygamous areas," he adds.

For Daryl Climenhaga, an Associate Professor of Global Studies at Providence College in Otterburne, these experiences show that "we can't impose our views on African Christians, even if we believe that God prefers that marriage be only between one man and one woman. We need to respect local cultures and practices." Climenhaga, who also served as a missionary in Zimbabwe, understands how polygamy makes sense in some situations in Africa. "It was well understood in that country," he says. "It was a way of caring for women who might otherwise be uncared for."

When it comes to dealing with the surrounding culture, all Christians need to decide what works in their situation, he says—what makes sense in Kenya, Zimbabwe, or Ethiopia won't necessarily work in Canada, and vice versa. "Christians in every culture have to decide what faith means in their culture," Climenhaga notes. Or, consider Densen Mafinyani, the general secretary of the Zimbabwe Council of Churches, who argued for the inclusion of a local church that practiced polygamy at the World Council of Churches in 1998: "We don't want our Christian faith to be limited by the mindset of Europe, where it came from, a theology too narrow to accommodate what God has done with Africans long before the missionaries came."

March 2007

Treaties as Old Testament covenants

THERE IS A lot of talk about treaties these days in Canada, in particular, calls on the Canadian government to honour treaties. But what is a treaty? According to the Canadian Oxford Dictionary, a treaty is "a formally concluded and ratified document" between states, individuals, or parties. In Canada, there are over 70 treaties with First Nations, including seven in Manitoba.

For many non-Indigenous people, treaties are synonymous with contracts. That's the way I have viewed them—I promise something, and you agree. If it doesn't work out, we void it. But then an article by the leadership of the North American Institute for Indigenous Theological Studies (NAIITS) caught my attention: "When most Christians hear the word 'treaty,' they must recognize that the Old Testament perspective of 'covenant' is invoked in Indigenous people's understanding," they write. "These are not business contracts, promises that can be set aside when a signatory defaults, changes her mind, or in the case of recent and infamous business fiascos, bankrupt the company. Nor can these treaties be unilaterally legislated out of existence."

That description certainly resonates for members of the Abrahamic faiths—Christians, Jews, and Muslims. I'm not a theologian, but the little I remember from classes at Bible college long ago tells me that a covenant, as described in the Bible, is a special thing.

Among other things, a covenant contains agreed-upon terms, agreement by both parties to observe the terms, and a symbol, sign, or ceremony to mark the covenant. It also is forever—at least, as far as God is concerned.

The Old Testament contains a number of covenants, such as the one God made with Noah about never flooding the world again. God makes a covenant with Abraham to multiply his descendants, giving them land, and making them a blessing to the nations. Other covenants are made with the nation Israel at Sinai, with the tribe of Levi, with Joshua and the nation of Israel, with David, and with others. In the New Testament, Christians believe Jesus makes a new covenant to create a different relationship between God and humanity.

For Christians and Jews, these covenants have special meaning. They study them at church and synagogue. They revere and honour them. They see in them a way to understand the nature of God and God's relationship with humanity. If that's the way Indigenous people also view treaties—as covenants—that puts a different spin on things. They are more of a sacred process, not just agreements about land, resources, and money.

When I was a kid, we used to say the old Indigenous proverb: "Never judge a man until you've walked a mile in his moccasins." You don't hear that saying much today, but the principle is still sound; try to see the world through the eyes of another if you really want to create understanding—especially when it comes to seeing treaties the way Indigenous people do.

January 2013

At Christmas time, give that poor innkeeper a break

KENNETH BAILEY, AUTHOR of the groundbreaking book *Jesus Through Middle Eastern Eyes: Cultural Studies in the Gospels* (2008), died in 2014.

Bailey helped me understand that, in order to understand the Gospels, I needed to see them through the eyes of people who lived in that place and at that time. His perspectives were confirmed by my own, very limited, experiences in the Middle East, where I experienced the legendary hospitality of people in that region.

While there, I was invited into many homes, and served coffee, sweets and sumptuous meals. Even the poorest of the poor offered what they could; to fail to show hospitality to a stranger would be unthinkable, a grave offence. What's true today was also true in the biblical world, where the arid desert climate and distance between towns and cities made hospitality even more important—access to food, shelter, and water could mean the difference between life and death. To not extend hospitality was considered an insult, or even an act of hostility. This is why the traditional interpretation of the birth of Jesus in a stable rings so false and makes me wonder: do those of us who live in the Christian West have the nativity story all wrong?

We know the story by heart: Mary and Joseph return to Joseph's hometown of Bethlehem, only to learn there is nowhere to stay. They find shelter in a stable, and Jesus is born. This cold and uncaring reception has become a metaphor for how the Saviour was received by the world—or not received, to put it more bluntly. He was unwelcome and unnoticed, except by the animals and a few poor shepherds.

Is that the way it happened? Bailey says no—there's no way it could be true. In his article "The Manger and the Inn," Bailey notes that what our Bibles translate as "inn" is, in the Greek, the word *kataluma*, which means literally "guest room" and not "hotel." Joseph and Mary did not go hunting for a room at the biblical equivalent of the Holiday Inn—they went to the home of a relative, where they naturally expected to be invited to stay. But when they got there, they found that the house was full with other relatives who, like them, had returned to Bethlehem for the census. It's sort of like what might be happening at any house at Christmas, when many relatives show up. People are sleeping everywhere—rec room, spare rooms, in the office, on the living room couch.

Where would you put up a cousin and his pregnant wife? Not in a hotel, and certainly not in the garage or a tent in the backyard. Joseph and Mary's relatives do neither, says Bailey. Back then, traditional Palestinian homes had two levels: the larger, upper level where the family ate, lived, and slept, and the smaller, lower level for the animals, which were brought into the house for safety at night. The two levels were connected by a short set of stairs, and a manger—a feed trough—was built into the edge of the upper level so the animals could stand up and feed at night if they were hungry.

It was on the edge of that upper level, says Bailey, where Joseph and Mary slept and Jesus was born—not in a smelly stable, but in the comfortable home of loving relatives. If that's the case, then there goes the annual Christmas pageant, with the adoring shepherds and angels gathered around the manger in a barn. But who needs the hassle of messing with centuries of tradition?

Bailey thinks it's important for at least two reasons. Firstly, it takes the terrible weight off that "mean old innkeeper" and all the cruel inhabitants of first-century Bethlehem. "Is the entire village of Bethlehem so hard-hearted that no home is open to a pregnant woman about to give birth?" he asks. Second, it makes the Incarnation "more authentic." Over time, he observes, the birth of Jesus has become so mythologized that it hardly seems real. "The traditional inn-and-stable scene succeeds only in distancing Jesus," he says. "It makes it all so far away and long ago, the make-believe world of Christmas cards and medieval carols. If he had been born in Caesar Augustus' palace, he could hardly be more remote from real life."

The birth of Jesus, he concludes, took place "not in exceptional circumstances, but in a very ordinary setting. We may picture him surrounded by the laughter and bustle and family goodwill of a comfortable if not palatial home. Of course, there are the smells and noises of the animals—but that is part of normal village life, and no one would wish it otherwise . . . Jesus is born in a real, live, warm, loving, crowded home, just as any other Jewish boy might expect to have been . . . In other words, he is one of us."

December 2014

The end of *sola scriptura*?

ON OCTOBER 31, 2017, Protestants around the world marked the 500th anniversary of the Reformation, when, in 1517, Martin Luther is believed to have nailed his 95 theses to the church door in Wittenberg, Germany.

Luther's actions resulted in what have been called the five great *solae* of the Reformation: *sola Scriptura* (Bible alone); *sola fide* (faith alone); *sola gratia* (grace alone); *solus Christus* (Christ alone): and *soli Deo gloria* (glory to God alone). Of the five, *sola scriptura* is the one causing the most problems today, says Dave Schmelzer, director of Blue Ocean Faith, an organization that explores new ways of thinking about and practicing Christianity.

Schmelzer, who lives in California, was a self-described atheist before he became a Christian, received a seminary degree, and planted a church in Cambridge, Massachusetts. For Schmelzer, *sola scriptura* was a powerful way to address the problems in the church of Luther's day. "The problem he was trying to solve was who had the authority to say what God's will was," he says. Luther solved one problem with *sola scriptura*, but he created a new problem. Since his action coincided with the invention of the printing press, many people were able to read the Bible and interpret it for themselves; there was no need to rely on a Pope. But all those new readers ended up interpreting Scripture differently; what was the clear meaning of a passage to some wasn't clear to others. This led to division and discord, and, arguably, to the 9,000 Protestant denominations that exist today.

It also led to heated battles in churches over the centuries about issues such as slavery, divorce, inter-racial marriage, dancing, music, use of alcohol, and women in leadership. In each case, people easily found verses that supported their views, which meant that some people kept slaves, excommunicated divorcees, banned musical instruments in worship, or kept women out leadership. But throughout history new insight and revelations have come along, and certainties changed. Or, as Schmelzer says, "the Bible clearly supported slavery, until it didn't." Change like this is why *sola scriptura* is "showing cracks," he adds.

It's not just that some Christians tend to view the Bible as an instruction manual, a verse-by-verse prescription for how to live, believe, and behave—and who to accept or reject—which concerns Schmelzer. The bigger issue for him is that seeing the Bible this way is "a poor substitute for actually knowing God." The Bible, he says, "can't actually give life . . . for all its amazingness, [it] is just a book, after all, not God."

Dave Schmelzer notes that Jesus viewed religious leaders of the day—those who quoted the scriptures against him—among his opponents. But if that's the case, what will replace the Bible as the final authority for those who hold the *sola scriptura* view? Schmelzer's answer is another of the Reformation's great *solae*: *solus Christus*, or Christ alone. Why does he think that's a better way? He offers a few reasons: it proclaims that Jesus is alive and eager to speak to believers today; it accepts there are multiple ways Jesus can speak to his followers; and it takes the pressure off Christians from having to figure out who to include and who to exclude from the church, based on this verse or that.

Schmelzer doesn't want to throw out the Bible; it's still important. But for him it's just one of the ways God speaks—and it isn't the bottom line. "Combined with hearing from Jesus by way of the Holy Spirit, and with the rich transparent relationships with other people following Jesus, it sounds like we'll be on a good road" with this approach, he says. I asked Schmelzer if he is getting any pushback for his views. "Some call me a heretic, and see this as a very threatening thing," he says, but others find it liberating.

Today the big battle in many churches is whether 2SLGBTQ+ Christians can be welcomed into the community of the faithful. I asked Schmelzer if letting go of *sola scriptura* would help in dealing with this issue. For him, the answer is yes; if *sola scriptura* no longer holds, then Christians don't have to be concerned about verses that exclude people, like those that oppose homosexuality. With *sola Christus*, they can look to Jesus for questions about being open and inclusive. They might find that treating 2SLBGTQ+ persons differently from anyone else is, as Schmelzer says, "not something Jesus would do."

October 2017

Can giving to the needy save you from your sins?

EVER SINCE MARTIN Luther, as legend has it, nailed his 95 theses to the door of Wittenberg church in 1517, Protestant Christians have believed it's grace alone that provides for the forgiveness of sins. One issue that prompted Luther's theses was the sale of indulgences, which promised Christians they could buy favour with God in the afterlife. Luther's reading of the Bible declared that faith in Jesus alone brought salvation; nothing else, however meritorious, could accomplish that.

This is pretty standard stuff for most Protestant Christians today. It's taught in Sunday school and preached from pulpits every weekend. Who would disagree? The earliest Christians, that's who, argues David Downs, associate professor of New Testament Studies at Fuller Theological Seminary in Pasadena, California. In his book *Alms: Charity, Reward, and Atonement in Early Christianity* (2016), Downs notes that Christians until the third century believed in the atoning power of almsgiving—of giving to help the poor.

Using early Christian texts, he shows how early Christians used verses in the Old and New Testaments to promote the idea that giving to help the needy provided spiritual reward—both in this life and in the life to come. One verse they used was Proverbs 19.17: "Whoever is kind to the poor lends to the Lord, and will be repaid in full." Another was 1 Peter 4.8, where believers are told to "maintain constant love for one another, for love covers a multitude of sins." Also 1 Timothy 6.18-19: "They are to do good, to be rich in good works, generous and ready to share, thus storing up for themselves the treasure of a good foundation for the future, so that they may take hold of the life that really is life."

In addition to the Bible, the early Christians' view was shaped by how the Greco-Roman world of that time put a high value on reciprocity—getting back something for being generous. For wealthy givers at that time, this meant being rewarded with highly visible public expressions of gratitude. Since the vast majority of people back then were poor, including Christians, they could not expect such lofty praise. Instead, they believed God would reward them for their generosity, if not in this life then in the life hereafter.

In an interview, Downs says this idea of atoning almsgiving was "very common" in the early church, that "you can attain atonement for sin . . . if you care for the poor." Of course, these early Christians also believed in the saving power of the death and resurrection of Jesus. But, he adds, they "saw no contradiction" between that and the idea that "caring for the poor could alleviate sins." In fact, Cyprian, the bishop of Carthage, developed a chronology of atonement. The death of Jesus forgives all sins before conversion, he wrote, but giving to others helps forgiveness after.

For me, Downs's book is a reminder that Christian belief is not something fixed for all time. Each generation of Christians interprets the Bible in light of their own cultural, political, and economic context. It also makes me wonder if we couldn't use more of that atoning almsgiving today, when the gap between the rich and the poor is growing ever wider and billions of people are poor and hungry. Maybe it wouldn't be such a bad thing to recover a bit of that early Christian belief about being rewarded, here and in the afterlife, for showing mercy to the needy.

March 2019

How the Bible really works

CHRISTIANS HAVE A long history of disagreeing about the Bible. In the nineteenth century, it was about slavery; did the Bible permit it or not? More recently for some churches, it was whether women could be ministers. Now it's 2SLGBTQ+ inclusion; should they be welcomed and affirmed?

Fights like this take place because Christians don't understand how the Bible works. That's the view of Pete Enns, an author and professor of Bible at Eastern University, a Christian school near Philadelphia, PA.

In *How the Bible Actually Works: In Which I Explain How an Ancient, Ambiguous, and Diverse Book Leads us to Wisdom Rather Than Answers—and Why That's Great News* (2020), Enns says problems arise because people see the Bible as an "instructional manual, a rulebook . . . just follow the instructions and you're good to go." But the Bible wasn't designed that way, he says. Treating it as a once-and-forever book of rules "causes the whole Christian enterprise to go off course," since Christians often can't agree on what the instructions say. Instead, says Enns, the role of the Bible is to provide "an invitation to join an ancient, well-travelled, and sacred quest to know God, the world we live in, and our place in it."

Enns provides several reasons for why the Bible can't serve as a one-size-fits-all book of instructions. First, it's an ancient book, the product of a "distant and utterly foreign world" that looks nothing like our world today. The writers of the Bible "lived long ago and far away," says Enns, adding they didn't have us in mind when they were writing. They were "oblivious to our own questions and concerns," he argues, but were intent on asking questions and seeking answers in their own political, cultural, and religious times and places.

Second, if the Bible is an instruction manual, it doesn't do a very good job of telling people "what to think," he says, noting readers can find in its pages competing or contrasting views on various topics. The result: those who claim to follow what they claim is the "clear teaching" of the Bible on one issue or another are on shaky ground—what's clear to one person isn't at all clear to another, and the Bible itself can provide different answers.

Finally, he notes, the Bible doesn't speak with one voice. It was "written by various writers who lived at different times, in different places, and under different circumstances and who wrote for different purposes," he says. These writers "were human beings like us whose perceptions of God and their world were shaped by who they were and when they lived"—just as our perception of God is shaped by the world we live in.

That's why, Enns says, the Bible is best viewed as a "source of Godly wisdom to be explored, pondered, deliberated and put into action," and not as a book of rules. By taking this approach, Christians can be liberated from "a common burden" so many "have unwittingly carried, namely, that watching over us is God, an unstable parent, who is right off the bat harsh, vindictive, at best begrudgingly merciful, and mainly interested in whether we've read and understood the fine print; if not, God has no recourse but to punish us."

How the Bible Actually Works is easy to read. Enns, who also manages a blog called *The Bible for Normal People*, brings a light and humourous touch to a serious subject. This includes his chapter titles, such as "Screwing Up Your Kids Biblically," "Tiptoeing Around the Touchy Almighty," "Dealing with an Inconsistent (and Somewhat Ridiculous) God," and "Standing on a Table Covered in Syrup with My Hair on Fire."

While some will disagree with Enns' approach, *How the Bible Actually Works* can be helpful for Christians who don't feel the Bible is still relevant today, or for those who have given up on it altogether because, as Enns puts it, "they are worn out from dealing with a rulebook Bible." Enns hopes readers find that the Bible is a book that "cheers us on along our own difficult path of faith," inviting people to "look past the words on the page [and] see what God is up to here and now."

August 2019

The not-so-late great planet Earth

Is THE WORLD coming to an end?

What with the news these days, some might wonder if that's the case. But fifty years ago, lots of people didn't question it. They believed the end was nigh, like, within a few years, and all because of *The Late Great Planet Earth* (1970).

Written by evangelical Christian author Hal Lindsey, the book popularized end-times thinking about the apocalypse for tens of millions of people across North America. Lindsey linked the upheavals and challenges of the late 1960s with Bible verses in the Old and New Testaments that proved, he said, the beginning of the end.

Lindsey didn't give a date, but he strongly suggested events like the rapture, where true believers are taken away from the earth to heaven to set in motion a thousand years of tribulation, would take place no later than 1988. He based this claim on the idea that the events foretold in the Bible about the end of the world would occur one generation, or 40 years, from the founding of the state of Israel. That happened in 1948.

Lindsey's book had a profound effect on me as a young teenager. I still vividly remember one evening in the early 1970s, looking up at the stars, believing that I would soon be taken up and away to heaven. Why make long-term plans? After all, the end was coming "soon and very soon," as a popular song at the time put it. But 50 years later, the world is still here and so am I—both a bit worse for wear, but still chugging along.

I'm not the only one thinking about *The Late Great Planet Earth* these days. Over at Religion News Service, Jana Riess is thinking about it, too. The book's fiftieth anniversary "tickles my irony bone," she writes, given that it "expressed a near-total certainty that there would be no earth left by 2020 to mark such milestones." As for why it was so popular, she says, Lindsey's genius was the way he incorporated bleak contemporary realities, casting them as part of God's master plan. "Every crappy and seemingly random thing that was going on in the world was part of a carefully crafted blueprint that God encoded ages ago in the Bible, if people only had eyes to see and ears to hear," she says. "Everything is part of the same long game God is playing," she adds, noting the book helped people make sense of a crazy and out-of-control world.

The popularity of books like *The Late Great Planet Earth* isn't surprising, Reiss argues—then or now. "When the going gets tough, we want to know what's going to happen next," she says, adding books of end-time thinking offer "a weird kind of comfort in that they first acknowledge that, why YES, the world is just as horrible as we've always thought it was, but that those horrors are necessary steps toward something beautiful God's got cooking."

Even though Lindsey got it wrong 50 years ago, that hasn't stopped him from promoting end-times thinking about the pandemic. Today he runs a prophesy website called *The Lindsey Report*. A video on that website says the COVID-19 pandemic—or "pestilence," to use the biblical term—is another sign of the times, along with other factors such as the economic collapse caused by the virus and the "lawlessness" that accompanied some of the Black Lives Matter protests. He isn't alone in his thinking. A poll by The Joshua Fund, an evangelical, charitable organization that educates Christians about Israel, found about 44 per cent of American voters see the coronavirus pandemic and economic meltdown as either a wake-up call to faith, a sign of God's coming judgment, or both.

The word for this kind of end-times thinking is the Greek word *apokalypsis*, or "apocalypse" in English. It means an unveiling, or a revelation. When it comes to revelations, the pandemic has produced some important ones. For example, it revealed the sorry state of elder care in many places in North America. It revealed how little value and importance we, as a society, have placed on those we now consider "essential" workers. It revealed how health crises like the virus disproportionately impact people who are poor and marginalized. In the US, it revealed even more starkly the polarized state of politics in that country, with people dividing along partisan lines over things like staying indoors or wearing masks.

On the other hand, it also revealed some positive things, as *The Guardian* columnist George Monbiot notes in a March column. According to Monbiot, dystopian movies and books about the future get it wrong. "Instead of turning us into flesh-eating zombies, the pandemic has turned millions of people into good neighbours," he writes. There's still a ways to go and things could change, he says, but he has "the sense that something is taking root now, something we have been missing: the unexpectedly thrilling and transformative force of mutual aid."

Maybe this isn't this the end of the world. It could be the beginning of a new and better one.

July 2020

Burning Bibles: A legitimate form of protest?

RIGHT WING AND Christian media lit up this month when Bibles were burned at a Black Lives Matter (BLM) protest in Portland, Oregon.

Blame was quickly laid on anarchists, antifa, "the radical left," and BLM. One conservative commentator compared the protestors to Nazis burning books. Another compared them to the world's despots, writing: "Bible burners want to eradicate the religious truths which have provided believers with pillars of hope and faith, and which have inspired even non-believers to pursue a just and compassionate world. This is why the Bible has always been attacked by the Hitlers, the Stalins, the Maos—and yes, the Xis [Xi Jinping] and the Kims of the world."

While it appears Bibles were burned—it wasn't fake news—it isn't clear who did the burning. The burners wore BLM shirts, but that doesn't mean they were actually affiliated with the protest. As reporter Danny Peterson of the local CBS affiliate noted, "Many of these protests have been a non-homogeneous mixture of people with greatly varying political ideologies, and this night was no exception, from what I could tell."

They might not even have been supporters of BLM. As some have pointed out, they could have been "false flag" protestors—right wing provocateurs sent to disrupt and discredit the protest, which is what many suspect happened during the George Floyd protests in Minneapolis in May. Also worth noting is that the fire was put out by some women identifying as BLM Moms, showing not everyone agreed with the Bible burning.

It's not clear if the Bibles were burned in protest, or just at a protest. But if they were, I can understand why it was done. While it could have been done simply to shock people and get attention—which appeared to work, judging from the media coverage and the widespread reaction—it could also have been done to express anger at how the Bible was used, for a very long time, to support and promote the horrific practice of slavery of Black people in the US and in other parts of the world.

Moreover, you could argue that Donald Trump made the Bible a legitimate target for the protest by using one as a prop—like a weapon, some say—in his now-infamous photo op in front of historic St. John's Church in Washington back in June. By holding the Bible up like a cudgel to support his law-and-order agenda, he made it a player in the BLM issue, and a legitimate object of protest, even burnings.

But it's not only BLM protestors who might feel that way about the Bible.

Women and members of the 2SLGBTQ+ community may also resent it for the way it has been used to support their oppression and marginalization. For people in the developing world, it can represent colonialism and, in a country like South Africa, the cruel system of apartheid. Then there are the Jews: for millennia the Bible was used by Christians to justify terrible pogroms and other acts of murder, violence, and oppression against members of the Jewish community. Some Indigenous people in Canada have conflicted views of the Bible, too. It was used to justify their oppression—taking children away from parents and imprisoning them in residential schools—where many suffered incredible abuses.

Mary Carpenter, an Inuk from Sachs Harbour, Northwest Territories, was forced to go to a church-run residential school as a little girl. The Bible, to her, is a fearsome book that was used to "justify the ill treatment of innocent children." One of the first things the nuns did, who ran the school she went to, was take away the name her parents gave her—Tungoyuq—and replace it with Mary, "a name from their Bible," she says.

It's not surprising many people today—Black, Indigenous, 2SLGBTQ+, female, and others—might have an ambivalent or even hostile view of the Bible. Maybe it's a miracle there aren't more Bible burnings! For those who love the Bible as a source of comfort and inspiration, that hostility might feel hurtful or sacrilegious. But if you step back and remember how the Bible has been so badly used as an instrument of oppression and terror, it's possible to understand why it was burned in Portland last month—and why that may not be the last one we see burning at a protest.

August 2020

The Bible and booze

WHAT ALCOHOLIC DRINK goes best with the first chapter of Genesis? What should you pair with the book of Joshua? What about Revelation? Answers to those questions are found in *Pairings: The Bible and Booze* by Matthew Anderson (2021).

In the book, Anderson, who teaches theology at Concordia University in Montreal, uses drinks as a "fun" way for people to explore the Bible. "I'm always looking for new ways to communicate the old truths of the Bible," says Anderson, an ordained Lutheran minister who was born in Saskatchewan and now resides in Dublin, Ireland, where his wife teaches at a local university.

Anderson hit on the idea of using drinks to help teach about the Bible while drinking a red wine from Chile made from Carménère grapes—grapes that originally came from France. That wine, transplanted in that South American country and now viewed as a local variety, made him think about a story in the Hebrew scriptures, or what Christians call the Old Testament. "I thought of Ruth, a stranger in Israel who was adopted into the family of Israel," he says. "Like Ruth, that wine in Chile crossed borders and was made welcome in that country and culture." From there Anderson began to spin out ideas for a book using wine, beer, and spirits to help people engage the Bible while having fun at the same time.

Anderson is quick to point out he isn't a wine connoisseur. "I grew up in a working-class home where wine was served maybe two times a year," says the long-time Roughriders fan. "Rye and Coke and beer were the drinks of choice. Nothing fancy."

One of the chapters in the book is titled, "When Life is the Bitters: Campari and Soda and the Psalms of Contrition." "To raise a glass of bitters to one's lips is to taste thousands of years of biblical interpretation, worship, monastic meditation, and herbal medicine-making," he writes in the book, adding, "Few drinks have the strong—if somewhat tangled—ties to the Bible as do these." The genealogy of bitters, he notes, includes ancient songs of Jewish worship, Christian monks, Roman politicians, medieval reformers, and nineteenth-century chemists and hucksters. "The feel of bitters is known to anyone who has read or sung Psalm 51," he writes.

In another chapter, titled, "Purists: Laphroaig Single Malt Islay & The Gospel of Matthew," he compares Laphroaig Scotch from the Islay region of Scotland with that gospel. "Matthew is a complex gospel," he writes. "Taking it seriously is not for the faint-hearted. There are notes in Matthew that are quite strong. In fact, they would be surprisingly harsh were they not softened by the warmth suffused elsewhere." This is a lot like Laphroaig Scotch, he says, noting that it, like the Gospel of Matthew, has undertones that "are deep and complex. Not all whiskies are created equal; neither were all gospels."

Anderson's whole book is like this, taking different drinks and Bible passages and finding points of similarity and comparison. Anderson knows not everyone drinks, so also he includes non-alcoholic drinks with each chapter. "I want it to be a fun and educational way to learn more about the Bible, not preachy," he writes, noting that "just as beer is not the same as single malt Scotch, the Bible is not something that can all be lumped together if you want to take it seriously."

Anderson may be on to something. In his book *Drunk: How We Sipped, Danced and Stumbled Our Way to Civilization* (2022), University of British Colombia philosophy professor Edward Slingerland posits that alcohol has played a key role in helping people be creative and understand the world around them. He explains how alcohol has "lubricated innovation and social trust through history."

"Intoxicants provided the spark that allowed us to form truly large-scale groups," Slingerland writes, contributing to the development of civilization by causing humans "to become, at least temporarily, more creative, cultural, and communal." Alcohol does this because it targets the part of the brain devoted to rationality and abstract thinking, anxiety and stress, he says, temporarily dampening those things and allowing humans to play more. "A childlike state of mind in an adult is key to cultural innovation," he states, adding "intoxicants allow us to enter that state."

Maybe the same holds true for having a good drink while studying the Bible. If that's the case, Anderson's new book may be a way to find out. Oh, and what drink goes with Genesis? Apple Cider, naturally. With Joshua? Gin and Tonic—a drink of invaders and colonizers. Revelation? A Bloody Caesar, of course.

November 2021

Rethinking the Great Commission

In 2022 I wrote about a Winnipeg woman who was distressed after receiving a letter from the Jehovah's Witnesses personally addressed to her husband. "I found it intrusive," she said.

The woman said her family has gone to some lengths to make sure their personal information is not publicly available, including signing up for "do not call" lists and not being on the Canada411 website. If the letter, which contained promotional material about the church, had been addressed to "occupant" or "homeowner," she wouldn't have been as concerned. "But this shows that someone has his name and knows where we live," she said. "We are private people. We want our privacy respected."

After the story was published, I received e-mails from others who had received similar letters and also felt the tactic was intrusive. Two writers asked the same thing: why does the group send letters, or knock on doors, at all? If people want to learn more about Jehovah's Witnesses, they can always go online, call, or even visit a Kingdom Hall.

As I thought about their responses, I realized the same question could be posed to any Christian denomination that engages in evangelism. Why do they think they need to do it? Their messages are just a click away, after all.

Upon further reflection, I'm sure they'd respond by pointing me to something called "The Great Commission," found in Matthew 28.19 in the New Testament of the Bible. In that passage, Jesus is quoted as saying to his disciples: "Go therefore go and make disciples of all nations, baptizing them in the name of the Father and of the Son and of the Holy Spirit." Those verses have been the animating force behind hundreds of years of missionary activity, countless evangelistic crusades, and innumerable local outreach efforts. The only problem is Jesus never said what Christians have long believed he said—as a bit of research shows.

As many Christians know, the New Testament was originally written in Greek. But it turns out Greek is a language that can be hard to translate into English. This is true for the passage in Matthew, where the word "go" isn't actually as commanding as we have been told it is. In the original Greek, the word is in what's called an inactive tense—a verb tense that doesn't exist in English. A better translation would be: "As you go" into the world, make disciples.

Jesus is not commanding his disciples to embark on missionary trips or undertake special evangelistic missions. Rather, he is simply telling them to live out their faith as they live their daily lives. But you might not want to take my word for it. That's why I contacted some theologians.

"This is exactly what I've been teaching!" says Scot McKnight, professor of New Testament at Northern Seminary in Lisle, Illinois. "The term behind 'go' is a participle and expresses a situation that is assumed: a kind of 'in your going' or 'as you are going' or 'since you will be going,' that kind of thing," he says.

Paul Doerksen, who teaches theology at Canadian Mennonite University in Winnipeg, agrees. "The word 'go' could be translated as 'having gone,'" he says." "It's not an imperative." When Jesus talks about "making disciples," that's an imperative, he said, adding "God's ultimate concern is that his chosen people are making disciples wherever they find themselves." Referencing Alan Kreider's *The Patient Ferment of the Early Church: The Improbable Rise of Christianity in the Roman Empire* (2016), Doerksen suggests the early Christians never did "outreach" at all, but "attracted people" to the faith by how they lived and cared for each other.

Adds Gordon Matties, former professor of theology at CMU: "There is one main verb, an aorist active imperative, which is 'make disciples.' All the others are participles." The context also helps us understand the verse better, he says, since it's clear from earlier texts in Matthew that the disciples will be harassed and will be forced to move. "It's possible the 'going' isn't something they've chosen to do," Matties says. "It's something that is simply their way of life. So the translation 'as you go' makes sense, but it doesn't convey the passive very well. Perhaps it should be, 'as you're being made to go, make disciples,'" he adds.

In his book *The Rise of Christianity: How the Obscure, Marginal Jesus Movement Became the Dominant Religious Force in the Western World in a Few Centuries* (1997), sociologist Rodney Stark suggested the Christian church grew not because it was evangelistic, but because of how its members cared for each other—especially during epidemics that ravaged the Roman world.

Writes Stark: "To cities filled with the homeless and the impoverished, Christianity offered charity as well as hope. To cities filled with newcomers and strangers, Christianity offered an immediate basis for attachments. To cities filled with orphans and widows, Christianity provided a new and expanded sense of family. To cities torn by violent ethnic strife, Christianity offered a new basis for social solidarity. And to cities faced with epidemics, fires, and earthquakes, Christianity offered effective nursing services."

Perhaps those people who wrote to me about the letters in their mailboxes are right; maybe all Christians need to do today is live in such a way others want to join them. After all, it worked for the early church.

August 2022

6

THE CANADIAN CONTEXT OF FAITH

When "nones" might be "maybes"

Growing up in southern Ontario, my NFL team was the Buffalo Bills. When I moved to Manitoba, I cheered for the Minnesota Vikings. When I lived in Dallas, Texas, I rooted for the Cowboys. It was the same for the CFL: living close to Toronto as a kid, I cheered for the Argos. After moving to Winnipeg, I became a Bombers fan. In hockey, it was the Leafs, followed by the Jets. My sports allegiances weren't fixed—they were fluid. Who I cheered for depended on where I lived.

It turns out that what's true for sports might also be true for religious affiliation, according to Michael Hout, a professor of sociology at New York University. In an article for the *Journal for the Scientific Study of Religion*, titled "Religious Ambivalence, Liminality, and the Increase of No Religious Preference in the United States, 2006-2014," Hout suggests that religious preferences are also not as fixed as some might think. This is especially true for the growing number of people who identify as "nones," people who, when asked in surveys if they identify with a religious group, say they have no affiliation.

With about 20 per cent of Americans saying they have no religious affiliation in 2017, and about 24 per cent of people in Canada saying the same thing, their growing numbers suggest that religion in both countries is in serious trouble. But Hout says we may be drawing the wrong conclusions from the data. Most surveys that ask about religious affiliation, he says, are binary in nature—people are asked if they are in or out at one particular moment in time.

After checking longitudinal results from the US General Social Survey, which checks religious affiliation three times over a period of six years, Hout discovered that religious affiliation is not an immutable thing. While some of the respondents were consistently in the nones camp at each point, others changed their minds and identified with faith groups.

Hout's conclusion? Although it's true that Americans are identifying less and less with organized religion, these results show that nones are "not consistently nonreligious." Based on his research, Hout concludes that 70 per cent of Americans are consistently religious, ten per cent are consistently non-religious, and 20 per cent are in-between. He calls these people "liminals," taken from the Latin word limin, which means "threshold." They are literally on the fence between affiliating or not affiliating with religious groups—they could go either way. The story of the past 25 years is that of a move away from organized religion, Hout acknowledges, "but focusing on the net change misses substantial flux that moves both toward and away from organized religion."

What about Canada? Studies in this country also show that many of the non-affiliated continue to be open to religious belief—they believe in God and pray. They are what University of Lethbridge sociologist Reginald Bibby calls the "ambivalent middle," people who could go either way when it comes to identifying with religious groups. Like in the US, many of these people "haven't slammed the door on possible religious involvement," Bibby says, adding while not everyone who is a none is interested in being part of a faith group, "it does mean significant numbers of Canadians haven't said a final goodbye to religion."

A question that might come to mind, then, is: if liminal people might be willing to identify with religious groups, what might attract them—and what might keep them away? According to an Angus Reid study, 42 per cent of Canadians who are ambivalent about religion say they would be open to greater involvement with a religious group if it met their personal needs. As for what pushes them away, a study in the US finds that about half of nones mention the gulf between science and what their faith groups teach. Other reasons included a dislike for the hierarchical nature of religious groups, and the way groups view 2SLGBTQ+ people. The latter was especially true for younger liminals. If that's the case, religious groups have some thinking to do about ways to attract newcomers—and then keep them, too.

October 2017

When it comes to religiosity, are we measuring the wrong thing?

What if we are measuring the wrong thing when it comes to religiosity? That's the question that came to mind when I read a report about the decline in church attendance in Canada.

I ask the question because that's one of the ways Statistics Canada measures religiosity, along with religious affiliation (what faith you identify with), frequency of participation in religious activities (going to worship services), frequency of participation in private religious or spiritual activities (prayer or devotions) and the importance of religious or spiritual beliefs in how to live one's life.

Of those four markers, attendance at worship services is in steep decline. That's the finding of a 2021 report by the Association for Canadian Studies (ACS) and Leger, a Canadian-owned marketing research and analytics company. Respondents who said they never attend services increased from 30 per cent pre-pandemic to 67 per cent in 2021. And not only that; the poll found 60.5 per cent of Canadians who say they strongly believe in God never or rarely attended a religious service since the beginning of the pandemic.

Those findings echo a survey by the Evangelical Fellowship of Canada. It found that weekly religious service attendance in Canada fell from 11 per cent pre-COVID—a figure that was stable for several years—to nine per cent during COVID. This included online services.

It's easy to blame the pandemic for the decline. After 22 months of interruptions and cancellations to in-person services, it's easy for people to fall out of old habits or develop new ones. But attendance was falling even before COVID-19. According to Statistics Canada, from 1985 to 2019 the number of people who said they attended a group religious activity at least once a month fell by almost half, from 43 per cent to 23 per cent. The pandemic didn't cause the decline, in other words—it just accelerated it. However, not attending services is not affecting the way Canadians view spirituality. Despite the drop in attendance, the poll by ACS and Leger found a third of Canadians still say religion is important in their lives. At the same time, there was only a slight decrease in belief in God.

A survey during the pandemic by Angus Reid found something similar related to attendance. It prompted Angus Reid Institute president Shachi Kurl to say that while some people suffered in terms of spiritual health, "others came out stronger than ever before . . . people saw that God is not in a building, God is also inside us."

The drop in attendance makes me wonder if counting the number of people who attend religious services is at all a good measure. That's the view of Brian Clarke, who teaches at the Toronto School of Theology. "The idea that gathering for weekly congregational worship is the chief form of religious observance is a Christian one," he says, referencing how Christianity has traditionally operated with "saved or unsaved," "heaven or hell" and "member or non-member" categories.

As fewer Canadians identify with organized religion, Clarke is becoming interested in the concept of "lived religion," the study of what people do outside of sanctioned sacred spaces and activities like worship services. For him, it's about looking at what practices people engage in and asking how they appropriate them, refashion them, and cobble ideas and practices from various religious traditions together—with or without attending formal religious services.

Lori Beaman of the University of Ottawa feels similarly. Yet, as someone who studies religion in Canada, she is reluctant to give up counting bodies. By dropping that marker, it would be tough to compare changes in religion in Canada over time. "I think in a perfect world we'd keep the old categories and introduce several more to capture the dynamic nature of religion and nonreligion," she says—things like including alternative spiritual practices like tarot cards, doing yoga or walking a labyrinth.

This will be hard, she acknowledges; how do you measure the spiritual influence of a daily walk in the woods? And yet, it's the same with attendance. Going to services can only provide a limited amount of information about the role it plays in people's spiritual lives. Just being at a service doesn't reveal much about a person's individual spirituality.

Back in the late 1990s, William Closson James addressed this topic in *Locations of the Sacred: Essays on Religion, Literature, and Canadian Culture* (2000). In the book, the professor emeritus of Queen's University said: "To the extent that our culture is secular, or the extent that we exist amidst a plurality of cultural forms infused with religious material, to that extent it is impossible to generalize about a single sacred anchoring point for Canadian culture, as if there were only one." For that reason, he preferred to speak in the plural, of "locations of the sacred" in Canadian life, something he regarded as being "multiple, fluid and impossible to fix in any permanent or lasting way."

Today, as attendance at religious services declines, I look forward to what researchers discover as new ways to understand the many ways Canadians encounter the sacred.

January 2021

A moral and spiritual emergency, or, what Canadians concerned about residential schools can learn from the African-American experience

WHILE THINKING ABOUT the terrible legacy of the residential schools, and the grave injustices against Indigenous Canadians over decades, my mind went back to the 1960s and the US civil rights movement.

Specifically, I thought about June 1963, when US President John F. Kennedy made a televised speech in which he appealed to Americans to accept civil rights as a moral issue. Writing about the speech, Mark K. Updegrove, an ABC News presidential historian, noted Kennedy had been under considerable pressure to stop seeing civil rights only as a legal or legislative issue and see it also, as Martin Luther King, Jr., put it, as a moral cause that needed "moral passion."

Some of the most serious pressure came from his brother, attorney general Bobby Kennedy. Earlier that year the younger Kennedy had met with a group of African American activists in New York City. At that meeting, the group didn't hold back. A young protestor told the attorney general about the beatings he had received for demanding civil rights. He "put it like it was," recalled actress and singer Lena Horne, sharing "the plain, basic suffering of being a negro." He became so worked up that he blurted out he wanted to vomit just being in the same room with Bobby Kennedy. The verbal assault hit Kennedy hard, Updegrove wrote, since he had considered himself an ally of African Americans and supportive of their cause.

After the meeting Kennedy knew he needed to do more. He urged the president to embrace civil rights as a moral issue. John F. agreed, even though many of his advisors cautioned against it. In the speech, the president said civil rights were not a regional, partisan, legal, or legislative issue alone. "We are confronted primarily with a moral issue. It is as old as the scriptures and is as clear as the American Constitution," he stated.

The speech was warmly received by African Americans and other people of colour who faced systemic racism and segregation as a daily reality of life. A few days after, the president invited representatives from various faith groups to a meeting at the White House to talk about civil rights. Among the invited faith leaders was Rabbi Abraham Heschel, one of the leading American Jewish theologians and philosophers of the twentieth century. In accepting the invitation, Heschel referenced the televised speech, asking the president to go further. He suggested Kennedy "demand religious leaders' personal involvement, not just a solemn declaration." "We forfeit the right to worship God as long as we continue to humiliate Negroes," Heschel said. "Church and synagogue have failed, they must repent. Ask religious leaders to call for national repentance and personal sacrifice. Let religious leaders donate one month's salary toward a fund for Negro housing and education. I propose that you, Mr. President, declare a state of moral emergency . . . the hour calls for moral grandeur and spiritual audacity."

Unfortunately, the president did not declare a state of moral emergency or make any other requests of clergy. Despite that, Heschel's comments stick with me. Today our issue is Canada's troubled history with Indigenous people, and the terrible legacy of residential schools. As with the issue of civil rights, the situation today isn't just political or legal, although those are important. Nor is it just about money, although renumeration is a powerful symbol of wanting to make things right.

And it certainly isn't jurisdictional. I think it's time for church leaders to stop debating which dioceses or orders or denominations were most responsible for which schools or who signed which agreement or which group apologized and when. Nobody cares about that, and it dodges the issue. It might be time to declare a moral and spiritual emergency over residential schools and the terrible history of Canada's relationship with Indigenous people. Along with that could come a call to repentance, to seek forgiveness, and to sincerely commit to pursue reconciliation.

Such a call could include plans for a national summit of religious leaders—not just Roman Catholics, who receive the bulk of critical media attention today—but all Christian denominations and other faith groups. For many Canadians, I don't think it matters who was in charge of residential schools; Christianity in general is in disrepute over what was done to children in the name of God.

Of course, this isn't the 1960s. Religion doesn't hold the same place in society today. Prime Ministers no longer naturally turn to religious leaders when addressing issues of national consequence. Something very wrong was done to Indigenous people through residential schools. Surely it's time for someone, or some group, to call this a moral and spiritual issue for the whole nation. Who will make that call?

August 2021

Conversion therapy, residential schools, and the church

In 2022, the federal government unanimously passed Bill C-4, making it illegal to perform or promote conversion therapy. One week after the bill passed, a reported 4,000 churches in this country and the US used their Sunday service to protest the new legislation.

The protest was organized by Liberty Coalition Canada, a conservative Christian organization that aims to defend Canadian freedom that is endorsed by conservative US church leaders, including Franklin Graham. In calling for the action, the Coalition urged "Bible believing churches" to "publicly preach a sermon that specifically proclaims the Biblical truth that homosexuality and transgenderism are serious sins condemned by the law of God." This bill, the Coalition goes on to say, "while purporting to protect individuals from coercion and abuse in the form of 'conversion therapy,' will instead criminalize Christianity in our country."

An attempt to get confirmation of the number of churches that participated in the protest went unanswered by the Coalition, which also promotes "religious freedom from vaccination coercion," has issued a call to end lockdowns, and has posted support for the truckers' convoy in Ottawa.

The Evangelical Fellowship of Canada did not participate or promote the protest. But it has some concerns about the new law. While supporting the government's intent of addressing coercive and abusive practices through conversion therapy, the EFC is concerned the definition of conversion therapy in the bill was too broad and that it risks criminalizing legitimate and sincere religious teaching and practice, says Julia Beazley, director of public policy for the organization. "It's not clear how the bill may be applied to programs offered by religious organizations on matters of human sexuality and human flourishing, or pastoral help for those seeking to align their sexual expression and behaviour with their deeply held religious beliefs," Beazley says. At the same time, she believes it is important for churches to "carefully consider our ministry practices and how we journey alongside those who are questioning their sexual and gender identity."

Whether or not churches agree with it, the question on my mind is: does conversion therapy work? I asked two local psychologists for their opinion. Both said no. "Research says it is harmful to the individual and not successful at creating change over time," says Jason Ediger, who attends River East Church, a Mennonite Brethren congregation in Winnipeg. "If conversion therapy worked, it should also be able to make straight people gay," he says.

Same-sex oriented young people who are part of faith communities where being gay is condemned can also suffer harm, he says. "They may come to believe that their feelings and interests make them bad people. It can create huge distress and confusion for the individual." The premise behind conversion therapy is also wrong, he says. "It's an attempt to fix something that isn't a problem. There are millions of happy, healthy gay people in the world." For him, the practice "goes against the belief in a God who calls us to love all people. So it's failing twice—against science, and against God." If clergy are approached by someone who is struggling with sexual identity, "I would encourage involving a professional with experience and qualifications in mental health," Ediger says, and not to try to deal with it themselves.

Robin Westmacott is a Unitarian Universalist who works with people who want to transition their gender medically. If religious leaders try to change them through a process like conversion therapy, it can cause them to "internalize the criticism and rejection and hate themselves," she says. "It communicates you are not OK as you are and you need to be changed to be accepted by others. There is also fear of God's disapproval and punishment." For Westmacott, conversion therapy is "very damaging and demoralizing, serving only to increase shame. It can take years of therapy to undo that damage, if it is even possible to undo it." She continues, "We have to create safer spaces for sexually diverse people, especially if we mean it when we say we welcome all."

In the nineteenth century, when the Indian Residential Schools were created, their goal was to "kill the Indian to save the child" by forcibly changing them into something they were not—assimilated Christians. Back then, Christians used their understanding of the Bible to support these actions. Today, however, you would be hard pressed to find a church leader in Canada who thinks it was a good policy or practice. Instead, church denominations are united in lamenting the terrible damage it caused for tens of thousands of children.

So why would anyone think something like conversion therapy—an effort to kill the gay in a person—would be acceptable or effective today? Yet some still do. Perhaps in the future more Christians will feel the same way about conversion therapy as they now do about residential schools—as an awful, horrible, and misguided mistake.

February 2022

Christians and "freedom" convoys

In early 2022, when trucks filled downtown Ottawa streets and border crossings across the country, many Canadian Christians were disturbed to see fellow-believers at blockades linking their faith with the flag.

While most participants said their protests were about COVID-19 restrictions, a report by the Edmonton security firm Global Enterprise Security Risk Management, which covertly embedded itself with blockaders at Coutts, Alberta, found some were more interested in "replacing our current democratic system of government with a government that is based upon the principles of the Christian right." The report states: "The rule of law would be replaced with the word of God, as interpreted through right-libertarian ideologies."

The term for that is Christian nationalism, the belief that Christianity and the nation are one, and that the Christian religion should rule Canada. Christian nationalism is most prevalent in the US, where proponents believe that country was singled out by God to be a Christian nation to fulfill God's purposes on earth. Interestingly, the idea has also taken root in Russia, where the head of that country's Orthodox Church sees church and state working together to restore the Russian Christian empire.

Christian nationalism in both countries has been subject to recent critique. In the US, a new report titled "Christian Nationalism and the January 6 Insurrection," says a growing number of American Christians believe in the "unconstitutional idea that the United States should be an exclusively Christian nation." The report, which was produced by the Baptist Joint Committee for Religious Liberty and the Freedom From Religion Foundation, goes on to say that Christian nationalism was most virulently on display during the January 6 insurrection. It existed before that date, the report says, with the groundwork laid by evangelical preachers and conservative media outlets.

The idea is propelled by "a sense of persecution," the report adds—from liberals, the media, and so-called elites, and furthered by language about being in "a battle against tyranny and demonic forces." Critics are labeled "as ungodly and evil at extremist rallies and through videos, websites, and blogs."

Elizabeth Dias and Ruth Graham of the *New York Times* weighed in on April 6, with an article titled "The Growing Religious Fervor in the American Right." They write how political rallies in support of Donald Trump, and his belief in a stolen election, include all the elements of an evangelical church service, including prayers and praise music. They are, Dias and Graham argue, "worship for a new kind of congregation: a right-wing political movement powered by divine purpose, whose adherents find spiritual sustenance in political action." The reporters quote one of the people from the January 6 crowd: "This is a Jesus movement. I believe God removed Donald for a time, so the church would wake up and have confidence in itself again to take our country back."

In Russia, something similar is happening as Patriarch Kirill of the Russian Orthodox Church lends his support to that country's war against Ukraine. Kirill, a close ally of Russian president Vladimir Putin, sees Russia as God's favoured nation, a bulwark against what he sees as a decadent, secular West—particularly over the acceptance of 2SLGBTQ+ rights. He and Putin share a vision of the *Russkiy Mir,* or "Russian world," linking Christianity and Russia together.

Some brave Orthodox priests have spoken out against Kirill and his ideas. Now Orthodox leaders around the world have joined in, releasing a statement on the blog *Religion in Praxis* this month against Christian nationalism in Russia. The signers state that "Christian identity is not singularly, exclusively, or supremely held by a nation, a race, or a civilisation . . . We therefore stand against 'Christian Nationalism,' 'Christian Europe' and the 'Russian World.'" The signers go on to call on other Christians to speak out against "unholy alliances of Christianity and political power, and especially in the context of nationalism, populism, and new forms of totalitarianism. The integrity of the Christian witness is distorted when the appropriation of Christian identity remains uncontested from within Christian traditions."

All Christians, they say, "must support one another in resisting the sacralisation of political communities, and in offering resources to articulate a theology committed to the common good, to truthfulness, and to justice." Reading the statement, I couldn't help but think it doesn't just apply to Russia. Those words could apply in in the US—and in Canada too.

April 2022

Some good news about religion in Canada: Millennials hold on to faith

HERE'S A BIT of good news about religion for a change: not all young people are giving up their faith.

That's the finding of new research by Sarah Wilkins-Laflamme, titled "Religion, Spirituality and Secularity among Millennials: The Generation Shaping American and Canadian Trends." "When we hear about religious decline, we assume that's all young people," says the professor of sociology at the University of Waterloo. "There's still a decent-sized group engaged with faith."

Wilkins-Laflamme's research, published in 2022, found that 24 per cent of Canadian millennials—people born between 1981 and 1996—say they are religious. These are people who are likely to be religiously affiliated, attend religious services, pray, and believe in God according to the teachings of their religion. One possible reason for this is because many are from immigrant families, where religion is still highly valued. "This group of Canadians is the most religiously diverse, ever," she says.

An additional 20 per cent of millennials were categorized as "spiritual seekers." These are people who "have a foot in both worlds," says Wilkins-Laflamme, herself a millennial. They may attend services occasionally and believe in God in their own ways, she says, adding they might also participate in spiritual activities such as yoga, meditation, mindfulness, and being outdoors in nature.

A third group, also at 20 per cent, are what she calls "cultural believers." These are people who identify with a religion—who say they are Catholic, Jewish, Muslim, or Hindu or another group, if asked—but do not actively participate in it. They would be like the person who told her: "I'm Catholic because I was born Catholic. And I wouldn't want to be anything more than Catholic. But nothing more than that."

The largest group are the non-religious millennials, at 36 per cent. These people don't identify with any religion and don't participate in religious activities. There's a good chance they are this way because of their parents. "If parents are non-religious, the kids will tend to be non-religious too," she says, adding "once habits are formed, like not going to worship services, they are hard to break."

Not all had that experience; some millennials grew up in religious homes but decided against it as they grew older, she says. For some, distrust in organized religion is the result of the sex scandals within the church and its history with residential schools. Some can't reconcile science with the faith they were brought up in. Others find it hard to fit religious services and observances into their busy lives if they are going to school and working two jobs. For them, "there's not a lot of time for other things like going to services," Wilkins-Laflamme says.

Altogether, the trends point in one direction: less engagement with organized religion. "More and more Canadians are moving away from religion," she says, adding this includes millennials. "The slope is down, but that's not the whole story." What researchers like Wilkins-Laflamme don't know is what millennials will do when they have children, hit middle age, and confront the realities of aging and mortality. Based on what's happened with their parents' generation, where so many have left religion behind, Wilkins-Laflamme thinks the chance of them becoming religious as they get older isn't great. This portends poorly for religion in general, she observes; if millennials don't bring up their children to be religious, they won't be religious when they grow older, either—each generation will be less religious than the one before. "If parents aren't religious, children won't pick it up on their own," she says.

One group that is doing a better job of seeing families remain faithful and keep attending services are conservative Christian churches. But even they are experiencing challenges. "They are declining slower than mainline churches," Wilkins-Laflamme says. All religious groups, however, face challenges over moral questions due to the changing attitudes of millennials towards issues like abortion and 2SLGBTQ+ inclusion.

Studies in the US show that religious millennials are more progressive than older generations when it comes to legal access to abortion and support for same-sex marriage, while Canadian millennials are even more progressive on these issues than their American counterparts, Wilkins-Laflamme says.

While Wilkins-Laflamme's research was done in 2019 before the pandemic, she doesn't expect things to be different today because of it—except maybe accelerating the changing religious landscape. "We have been seeing these changes for many years now," she says.

September 2022

Canadian evangelicals caught in changing cultural currents

LOTS HAS BEEN written about evangelicals in the US. Less has been published about Canadian evangelicals. Sam Reimer, who teaches sociology at Crandall University in Moncton, New Brunswick, is trying to change that.

In his new book *Caught in the Current: British and Canadian Evangelicals in an Age of Self-Spirituality* (2023), Reimer argues the attention given to U.S evangelicals is due to the fact that the majority of them voted for Trump in the 2016 and 2020 presidential elections. "It's a different story in Canada," he says.

Reimer wanted to know more about what evangelicals in Canada are like, comparing them not to Americans but to their counterparts in the UK. What he found is that evangelicals in Canada are caught in the currents of contemporary culture. "They want to go one way, but they are being pulled in different directions," he says. "There is a difference in what they are saying they believe and what they do, words versus actions."

Through surveys and interviews with Canadian and British evangelicals, Reimer found that their views on the Bible and their leaders as sources of authority and guidance are changing. Now, he says, they are "pulled towards an internal locus for spiritual authority." Instead of following official church doctrines, or its teaching about what the Bible says, they "tend to listen to their own hearts" and are more interested in "finding their own path."

Many still go to church, he says, "but they don't necessarily believe everything the preacher says," on issues like welcome and affirmation of 2SLGBTQ+ people and same-sex marriage, and on medical assistance in dying (MAID). Their denominations and churches may officially be against those two issues, but many Canadian evangelicals don't support those positions, Reimer found. "I am seeing changes in those areas," he says, adding that evangelical denominations and churches can "no longer dictate" what their members are supposed to believe.

This "inward turn," as he calls it, is most prevalent among baby boomers and younger evangelicals, with many evangelicals today seeing spirituality as a "private journey." But this change isn't only happening among the laity—it's happening to evangelical clergy, too. "While the clergy I spoke to embrace evangelical orthodoxy, the presentation of the 'good news' is increasingly experiential, digital, and welcoming of all, while exclusive beliefs and contentious moral positions are toned down," Reimer says. They are doing this because they recognize the world, and their members, have changed. Clergy may still preach official denominational doctrines, but in their pastoral work and in their relations with members they are less judgemental and more accepting of practices and ideas that might be officially forbidden by their denominations.

Why these changes among Canadian evangelicals? Reimer suggests one reason is the current zeitgeist, or the defining mood or spirit of our times, where people feel they should decide their own spiritual path. But Reimer also cites a desire among Canadian evangelicals to "avoid being labelled as intolerant like US evangelicals . . . They are reacting against the portrayal of that group."

As for the future, Reimer thinks Canadian evangelicals would do better to look to the United Kingdom—a country that is further down the secularism road—than to the US for answers. "There is a lot we could learn from them," says Reimer, noting that evangelicals in Canada, as in the UK, are a minority religious group. "We need to accept our minority status in this country," he said, noting that evangelicals in Canada today make up only six to eight per cent of the population, down from 11 per cent a decade or more ago. Canadian evangelical churches should also accept they can't expect to grow through evangelistic efforts, he says. "Evangelicals can expect few people to convert through evangelism . . . conversion today is rare."

The days of traditional church growth strategies—such as starting new churches in suburbs—may be numbered, Reimer suggests. "It's no longer a matter of build it and they will come," he says, adding that many evangelical churches today are "losing more members than they are gaining." If any increases are to be had, it is through immigration, according to Reimer. "Immigration is the doorway to growth," he says. "Immigrants are more religious, more likely to want to go to church." At the same time, churches that want to attract newcomers should "focus on meeting the real needs of people," he says. "Churches should try to provide a strong sense of community and belonging."

August 2023

7

PRACTICES, TRADITIONS, AND NEW WAYS FORWARD

A farewell for those who die by suicide

Glenn (not his real name) was a childhood friend, someone I knew a long time ago but lost touch with. Contact was infrequent, and years went by without connecting at all. Yet we remained friends.

Then I got a call out of the blue telling me Glenn had died by suicide. My immediate thought was: How could that be possible? He seemed like such a well put-together guy—good job, great family, a positive and generous personality. But things change over the course of a life. Slowly the truth comes out: Glenn had struggled with depression for some time. A week ago he decided to end it all.

Glenn is not the first person I knew who has died by suicide. Another friend of mine took her own life after years of feeling inadequate, combined with a deep and pervasive loneliness. No matter how hard she tried, she could not find a lasting and loving relationship. My last memory is of meeting her downtown. We talked for a few minutes on the busy sidewalk, and then my bus came; a short while later she was dead.

Their deaths moved me. What profound sense of desperation drove them to do the unthinkable? Was there anything I could have done to help them? Suicide is troubling for everyone, but it is particularly challenging for people of faith. All the major religions condemn it, considering it a grave affront against the God who gave life to all.

For Christians, it was common for a long time to believe people who committed suicide would go to Hell. The Bible, however, never says that. In fact, when suicide is mentioned in the Bible it never condemns the act. It is silent on the subject of whether it is wrong, and about what happens to that person's eternal soul. Much of what Christians think about suicide comes from people like Augustine, the fourth-century church leader and theologian, who argued the command "Thou shalt not kill" applied equally to the taking of one's own life.

Thomas Aquinas, the thirteenth-century Catholic theologian, added that suicide is a sin against self, neighbour, and God. It is contrary to nature, he stated, since every living thing wants to preserve its own life; it is contrary to our social obligations, since we injure others by killing ourselves; and it is contrary to God's will, since God alone can determine when people die. The poet Dante, following Aquinas's lead, placed those who take their own lives on the seventh level of hell, just two levels above Satan's abode. It was, he suggested, one of the worst acts a person could commit—and one with the gravest consequences.

That idea has pervaded western thinking for a very long time. To the point that, for generations, people who died by suicide could not have a Christian funeral or be buried in a church graveyard. Today, however, most Christians see suicide differently. It's not condoned or condemned; we have come to realize that many people who commit suicide don't do it out of malice, but out of extraordinary pain.

At the same time, more people are willing to speak openly about the subject. One person who did so recently was Russ Toews, a member of the Mennonite Brethren Church of Manitoba. His son, Brad, killed himself. "My first thought was, how can we hide the fact this was a suicide?" he writes in the *Mennonite Brethren Herald*. "But immediately I knew that if we tried, we would never heal. We would have to face this as openly and honestly as possible." For Toews, his son's suicide was sad and tragic, but not eternal condemnation. As he notes: "We do not earn salvation by good works, and we do not lose it simply by leaving a sin unconfessed. God is a gracious God . . . who understands the torment that would lead a person to take such a drastic step."

In 1997, Ron Hynes wrote "Godspeed," a song about the suicide of his songwriter friend Gene MacLellan, writer of the happy song "Snowbird," made popular by Anne Murray. As it turned out, MacLellan struggled with life-long depression, and killed himself in 1995. The song's lyrics say:

Godspeed, Godspeed
Forgive a sweet soul a desperate deed
His was a prison and he was freed
Godspeed, Godspeed

God bless, God bless
What's born out of sorrow or out of distress
Speculation is anyone's guess
God bless, God bless

God only knows what takes a petal from the rose
What makes the dark rivers overflow
What makes a lifetime come and go

But God damn, God damn
You put your hand in the hand of the man
Must have believed he would understand
Forgive a sweet soul a desperate deed
Godspeed, Godspeed

Indeed, "Godspeed" and "God bless" to those who struggle with mental health issues and to those who die by suicide. We could say no less for them.

August 2009

Attaining Moksha, or, whatever happened to yoga's Hindu roots?

Lots of different kinds of yoga are practised by North Americans these days—hot yoga, power yoga, prenatal yoga, Catholic yoga, restorative yoga, Christian yoga, Jewish yoga, and even naked yoga. One thing you don't find much of is yoga that embraces its 6000-year-old Hindu origins.

It's estimated about 1.4 million Canadians, and between 16 million to 20 million Americans, practice yoga. North America-wide, yoga generates billions in sales, once you factor in clothing and other yoga-related accoutrements. For most people, yoga is a way to promote physical and mental health through stretching, postures, and breathing techniques. Attaining Moksha—the Hindu ideal of liberation from worldly suffering and the cycle of birth and rebirth—isn't usually one of the goals. In fact, many yoga practitioners might be unaware of this ancient religious goal.

That is something the Hindu American Foundation would like to change. In 2010, the foundation launched "Take Back Yoga," a campaign designed to help people become more aware of yoga's debt to that ancient faith. The campaign began with an essay posted on the foundation's website, lamenting how North American yoga culture, magazines, and studios had divorced yoga from "the Hinduism that gave forth this immense contribution to humanity." According to Suhag Shukla, managing director of the foundation, the campaign started to call attention to the "commercial appropriation and misappropriation of yoga which purposefully delinks yoga from its roots in Hinduism." While emphasizing that Hindus are glad to share yoga with anyone, she adds, "we simply cannot ignore, contrary to what's done by many Western yoga practitioners, the fact that yoga is rooted in core Hindu concepts of divinity in all of existence, karma, reincarnation, and moksha."

In fact, the kind of yoga practised by most people in the West today has no real basis in traditional Hindu teaching. That's the view of Ian Whicher, who teaches religious and philosophical thought of India, Hinduism, and the Yoga tradition at the University of Manitoba. "There is no real evidence in the Indian tradition for the kind of health- and fitness-oriented practice that dominates the global yoga scene of the 21st century," he says. Whicher would also like to see more people understand and appreciate yoga's deep spiritual roots in Hinduism. "Yoga has a very profound philosophical understanding which links up with our psychological natures, our ethical capacities, and our physiological being," he says. "Yoga is really about liberating our energy and attention to know more and more what life is, who [we are] and what all this universe is."

What do local Hindus think of all this? "Yoga is a gift from Hindus to the world," says Narendra Mathur, president of the Hindu Society of Manitoba. In fact, the Hindu Temple on St. Mary's Road is offering yoga classes to anyone who wants them—free of charge. "It's a service to the community," he says. At the same time, he would be happy if people who do yoga decide to learn more about Hinduism. "Hinduism is linked to yoga," he says. "We invite people to come to the temple to learn more about it."

In the end, can anyone own yoga? Maybe it's become the Hindu equivalent of the Christian celebrations of Christmas and Easter—popular with almost everyone but so thoroughly secularized and commercialized that they are now mostly divorced from traditional religious meaning and significance. As for those who practise yoga, maybe the least they can do while doing their bandha, mudra, and pranayama poses is acknowledge that yoga has Hindu roots. As Boston University religion professor Stephen Prothero says, yoga practitioners should "know where yoga came from and respect those origins. Then, when you chant *Om*, it will resonate not only in the room but down through the ages."

August 2014

"Fuck you, cancer," and other honest expressions of lament

"FUCK YOU, CANCER, you indiscriminate fog of death; you've taken three dear friends too soon over the past four years, two since the fall. Remorseless diseases; I continue to mourn."

So began a Facebook post by a friend of mine, who is a leader in his denomination, a cry of pain at the death of yet another friend. "Fuck you, science," he continued. "You pretend to know so much, think you have answers to big questions, but you know nothing of what is important. We may be dust, we may be spirit, you do not know; and you don't know why our bodies ache to see a friend smile one more time. You know nothing of love."

"Fuck you, religion; you've backed yourself into a corner, defending your existence, quibbling over your own definitions. You have become blind to love and community and laughter and song. You still flog your club membership but you're done."

"Good night, Kirsten. You embraced the stories of so many; always bringing strangers into community. Who you are mattered. The connections you made will continue to bring smiles to this world."

This language might disturb some, but reading his message, I thought of the Psalms in the Bible. My friend's post was a Psalm-like lament, an honest and gut-wrenching fist of anguish aimed at the disease that killed his friend. Those familiar with the Psalms find in them comfort and reassurance during difficult times. But there are also Psalms of lament, where the author writes about disappointment with God.

Take Psalm 13.1-4, for example.

Long enough, God—
you've ignored me long enough.
I've looked at the back of your head
long enough. Long enough
I've carried this ton of trouble,
lived with a stomach full of pain.
Long enough my arrogant enemies
have looked down their noses at me.

Take a good look at me, God, my God:
I want to look life in the eye,
So no enemy can get the best of me
or laugh when I fall on my face. (The Message)

Or these portions of Psalm 42, as translated by Eugene Peterson in *The Message*: "I wonder, 'Will I ever make it—arrive and drink in God's presence?' I'm on a diet of tears—tears for breakfast, tears for supper. All day long people knock at my door, pestering 'Where is this God of yours?'"

Psalms of lament are sometimes called the neglected Psalms. But just like Psalms about lying down in green pastures and sitting beside still waters, they reflect life as we often live it: hard, painful, lonely, dark, depressed. Psalm-like laments, like my friend's Facebook post, are still being written today. Some of the most evocative are being written by Indigenous Canadians, such as residential school survivors, like Dennis Saddleman. His poem "Monster" begins like this:

> I hate you residential school, I hate you.
> You're a monster.
> A huge hungry monster.
> Built with steel bones. Built with cement flesh.
> You're a monster,
> Built to devour innocent Native children.

On July 1, 1967, Chief Dan George silenced a crowd of over 30,000 people in Vancouver with his "Lament for Confederation." "How long have I known you, Oh Canada? A hundred years? Yes, a hundred years. And many, many more. And today, when you celebrate your hundred years, Oh Canada, I am sad for all the Indian people throughout the land." Over the previous one hundred years, he said, "I have seen my freedom disappear like the salmon going mysteriously out to sea. The white man's strange customs, which I could not understand, pressed down upon me until I could no longer breathe." But there was hope. "Oh God! Like the thunderbird of old I shall rise again out of the sea; I shall grab the instruments of the white man's success—his education, his skills—and with these new tools I shall build my race into the proudest segment of your society."

As for me, I have my own psalm of lament for my friend Nancy Patzia who also died of cancer. Only 49, the single mother of two left behind two teenage boys. Near the end, she accepted her fate, dying with a quiet dignity.

Like my friend in mourning, all I want to say is: "Fuck you, cancer."

April 2014

Amble, ramble, or hike: The way is made by walking

My wife was in England a few years ago, teaching a course at a seminary near Manchester. One Sunday afternoon she went with her English friends on an eight-kilometre hike in the countryside. At least, that's what she thought it was. But, she was told, it was not a hike. It was a "ramble." It turns out that the British have more than one word for walking. A ramble, for example, is different than "amble," which is a long walk in a park. A "walk," meanwhile, is something you do to get from your house to the corner store. And a hike only occurs when someone walks 32 kilometres or more.

By that definition, Arthur Boers went on a very long hike—800 kilometres, and just to get to church. Boers, who teaches at Tyndale University College in Toronto, hiked the Camino de Santiago, the Way of St. James, in 2005. The famous and ancient pilgrimage runs from southern France to Santiago de Compostela in northwestern Spain. It ends at a cathedral that is purported to be the final resting place of the Apostle James.

The journey, which crosses four mountain ranges, was "hard and tough," he says. The arduous trip took 31 days, and included a visit to a hospital to treat his badly blistered feet. But although it was hard on his body, it was a refreshing spiritual experience. "Pilgrimage is a way to become totally involved, body and soul," he says. "Very few things we do today engage us so totally."

Boers has written a book about the journey, called *The Way is Made by Walking: A Pilgrimage Along the Camino de Santiago* (2007). The Camino de Santiago is one of the world's oldest and most famous pilgrimages, rivalling Rome and Jerusalem in the Middle Ages. Over the past 1,200 years millions of people have walked the route; today thousands travel it each year. In his book, Boers describes how a simple act like walking can become a spiritual activity, and how Christians today can experience pilgrimage even in the midst of their busy lives.

For Boers, the trip was a time to recall the history of the church, think about major themes of Christian faith, and reflect on the ancient practice of pilgrimage itself. "Pilgrimage is more about the journey than the destination," he says, noting that the days were filled with talking with new friends from around the world he met along the way. At the same time, he had a profound sense of meeting God as he walked, prayed, and reviewed his life. "As I looked back, I had a deep sense of God's presence and comfort in my life," he says.

Some of his fellow pilgrims found it strange that a Protestant would go on a pilgrimage—something that has been traditionally thought of as a Catholic practice. But, Boers says, "the walls of the Reformation are coming down," and more Protestants are thinking seriously about spiritual disciplines like pilgrimage. As well, he notes, many people who do not profess Christian faith at all are being drawn to this ancient form of spiritual practice. "A prominent paradox of my sojourn, and the one that surprised me and taught me the most, is the fact that so few fellow pilgrims I met counted themselves as Christians," he says. Even more surprising is that "these folks ended up teaching me more than I realized I needed to know," he adds.

Not everyone can walk the Camino de Santiago, but Boers believes that everyone can experience pilgrimage in their own lives by walking, or by taking time out of a busy schedule to serve poor people or fix up a house in the inner city. "Whatever expands your sense of spiritual direction can be a form of pilgrimage," he says.

Even something as simple and everyday like going to church can be like a pilgrimage, as long as people go there "with the hope and expectation of meeting God." "Jesus calls us to live out and practice what he taught and modelled, to walk the walk," Boers says. "All pilgrimage unfolds as God leads and we are invited to follow. "The way commended by Christ has to be journeyed. It is made by walking."

December 2014

Giving up on Christmas

EVERY YEAR, IT'S the same thing—people complaining that Christmas is too busy, too commercialized, too hectic, too stressful. For many Christians, the biggest complaint is that Christmas is too secular. Jesus may be the reason for the season, but he gets precious little attention.

Maybe it's time we did something about it. Instead of complaining about how secular Christmas has become, perhaps we should just admit defeat and let it go. Why fight a losing battle? That's the way Digby Anderson felt in 2003, writing for the UK's *Spectator*, when he wrote that "good generals know when it is time to give up an impossible defence and seek a more secure position to hold. It is time to give up Christmas. It is now utterly overrun by the combined forces of sentimentality, irreligion, bad manners, and worse taste . . . we should realise that the cause is lost, at least on this day. The 25th is no longer ours."

I think Anderson was on to something, except that Christmas on December 25 never was "ours" to begin with. It was someone else's holiday, which the church borrowed to celebrate the birth of Christ. A popular holiday in the Roman Empire around December 25 celebrated the winter solstice ("the day of the birth of the unconquered sun") and may have been conveniently Christianized. The first recorded celebration of Christ's birth, consisting of prayer and a mass—a Christ mass—happened in the fourth century. Said one early church leader: "We hold this day holy, not like the pagans because of the birth of the sun, but because of him who made it."

As for when Christ was really born, nobody knows for sure. It may have been in spring, since that was lambing time—a time when, as Luke recorded, shepherds would have been "keeping watch over their flock by night." What about the tree? There's been a lot of controversy over calling it a "holiday" tree, not a "Christmas" tree, but it isn't Christian in origin. It began as a pagan symbol of life, especially in northern climes. The ancient Vikings, for example, honoured evergreen trees as signs of hope that spring would return, and mistletoe was associated with the god Baldur. Druids may have decorated their sacred places with evergreen boughs.

In fact, evergreen trees have only been associated with the Christmas season since the 16th century, initially in Germany. There is an enduring legend that reformer Martin Luther put candles on a tree in his home to remind his children of the starry sky over Bethlehem. According to the British Library, however, "it's pretty certain that Luther had nothing to do with Christmas trees." But he was one of the prime instigators of gift-giving on Christmas

Eve. German settlers in North America introduced Christmas trees here in the 1700s, although the trees only caught on in a major way in the next century.

So that's the date and the tree; what about carols? They pre-date Christianity, too. Wassailing was an Anglo-Saxon practice of singing and drinking meant to honour sacred trees and orchards. The word "carol" originally referred to a dance; in medieval times carols were not necessarily religious in character.

In the early centuries of the Christian church, Latin hymns attributed to writers such as Ambrose, bishop of Milan, became associated with Christmas worship. But such carols were seen with suspicion at the time of the Protestant Reformation, and similarly, when the British monarchy was overthrown in the mid-1600s, singing carols was forbidden by Puritans who saw the practice as ungodly. Most of the carols we sing today are relatively new, dating only from the 19th century.

If Christians give back December 25, then what? Maybe they can choose a different day. December 6 might work. That's the day that some European Christians celebrate the generous St. Nicholas, the prototype for Santa Claus. Or they could join Orthodox Christians in celebrating Christ's birth on January 6. This is also the day when western Christians celebrate Epiphany—the revelation of Christ as God's son and saviour for the world.

It won't happen, of course; Christmas on December 25 is too ingrained in our culture. But that doesn't mean Christians can't choose to celebrate Christ's coming into the world any day they like—or every day, for that matter.

December 2014

The problem with short-term missions: "What's in it for the leper?"

If it's winter, it must be time for short-term mission and service trips. A quick search online shows that groups of Winnipeggers have gone from churches and schools to places like Mexico, Uganda, the Dominican Republic, Ecuador, Bolivia, and Guatemala. (Funny how God seems to call Canadian Christians to southern climes in winter, isn't it?) Each trip can cost participants thousands of dollars, much of it fundraised. In the evangelical church world, many trips are undertaken by youth groups. Service trips by doctors, nurses, dentists, or other trained professionals can make good contributions. But what about other kinds of trips?

In his 2012 book, *Toxic Charity: How Churches and Charities Hurt Those They Help (And How to Reverse It)*, Robert Lupton writes, "Contrary to popular belief, most mission trips and service projects do not empower those being served, engender healthy cross-cultural relationships, improve quality of life, relieve poverty."

Darren Carlson, president of Training Leaders International, agrees: "I have seen with my own eyes or know of houses in Latin America that have been painted 20 times by 20 different short-term teams; fake orphanages in Uganda erected to get Westerners to give money . . . teams who build houses that never get used." Short-term missions, he says, are "fraught with problems, and many wish such trips did not exist, at least in the common form today."

Many of the short-term mission and service trip leaders I talk to agree that the money might be better spent providing jobs for local people. But what about the effect on the participants—aren't their lives changed by the trips? No doubt that can happen, but for most, the effect doesn't appear to be as long-lasting as one hopes. Research by Kurt Ver Beek of Calvin College in the US found there were, in fact, few long-term life changes in the lives of Christian teens following their mission trips—no increases in giving, prayer or spirituality.

Even if some lives are changed, it prompts another question: is it morally right for people in Canada to use poor people as a means of personal and spiritual transformation? American pastor Hugh Hollowell, who operates a ministry for homeless people in Raleigh, North Carolina, raised the issue in a blog post for *Patheos* last November. Hollowell writes about receiving a fundraising letter from a young person, who wanted money for a short-term mission trip to South America. The key "selling point" in the letter was how the trip would "change the lives of the teenagers that go on this trip." When he read it, Hollowell thought back to another encounter between a wealthy missionary and a poor person, many centuries ago: the meeting between St. Francis of Assisi and the leper.

In the story, Francis—a product of wealth and privilege—was riding his horse near Assisi when he came across the leper. Francis got off his horse and gave the leper a kiss of peace and all of his money. Then he got back on his horse and rode away. For Francis, the experience was life-changing, setting him on a course of helping the poor. But what about the leper? He got money and a kiss—neither of which he asked for, Hollowell notes. What he mostly got, says Hollowell, was a chance to play a nameless bit in the inspirational story of St. Francis.

No doubt some trips do very good things, but unless participants and leaders are very careful, they can also cause problems and challenges for the very people they want to help. Plus, the trips can put them on morally shaky ground. Will the people they meet just be nameless others in Facebook selfies and church basement PowerPoint presentations? Or will they be seen as real people who deserve respect and dignity as human beings?

Those are tough questions that require an answer—before boarding the plane. "Let me tell you the truest thing I know," writes Hollowell. "The economically poor do not exist to be agents of your transformation. They are not props in the story of you. And if you don't have a really good answer to the question, 'What's in it for the leper?' I wish you would stay home."

February 2017

Anglican or alien? Priests ponder wearing of vestments

As SOMEONE WHO didn't grow up in the Anglican Church, I can't tell an alb from a surplice from a chasuble from a stole. But after attending an Anglican church for a few years now, I am more familiar with those clerical vestments, though I still couldn't pass a test on what each one was—or what they represent.

For people like me in England, one day it may not matter. The Anglican Church in that country recently decided to let priests wear "lay garments"—normal clothes—rather than traditional vestments while conducting services. One reason given for the change is how British society as a whole is more casual in its dress. Another reason is that non-churchgoers—young people in particular—might be put off by the ornate robes; they may make the wearers look alien and disconnected from modern-day life. Whether or not that's true, there's no doubt that most Canadians today aren't familiar with Anglican clergy vestments.

Vestments have their origin in ordinary street clothes from Roman times. In the Anglican Church, they are worn by bishops, priests, lay readers and others involved in the worship services. While they make the wearers stand out to people unfamiliar with vestments, their role is actually to obscure them—to put the focus on the ministry they are providing, and on Christ.

How do Anglican clergy in Canada feel about vestments? I posed that question to a few of them. "I'm not aware of any national directives of what [clergy] should wear or not wear," says Donald Phillips, the Bishop of Rupert's Land. "There is no written code in the diocese. It is assumed that priests know what to wear [the standard priestly wear]," although "nobody says they have to wear it. But it's understood."

For Phillips, vestments provide an appropriate sense of "mystique or solemnity," although he acknowledged there might be "some wisdom" in what is happening in England. "People have drifted away from church," he says, adding that churches need to be more welcoming of newcomers. "But I'm not sure dispensing with the vestments will change that."

Paul Johnson, Rector and Dean at St. John's Cathedral—the mother church for the diocese—prefers to always wear them: the alb, stole, cassock, surplice, and chasuble. "I like to wear vestments for the symbolism," he says. "It's a visible reminder of what we believe, similar to the stained glass windows." He does dispense with the chasuble, a heavy poncho-like garment, in July and August, however. "It's just too hot, and the cathedral isn't air conditioned," he notes. For him, staying with the traditional "is a good place for me, and it's what the congregation expects."

Jamie Howison is the priest at St. Benedict's Table. St. Ben's, as it is known, offers a looser and less formal style of Anglican worship. What's his take on vestments? "Not only would I go without vestments, I do so on a semi-regular basis," he says of what he wears for presiding over communion at house services, family camps, retreats, or for the church's child-friendly service. For him, it's "all about context." Vestments in a house communion or at camp "simply feel overdone and really rather overly-earnest," he says. For the regular Sunday evening worship service, "they fit."

For Howison, an apt analogy is mealtime. Some days "it's grilled cheese sandwiches and soup at the kitchen table, and some days it is a more formal celebratory meal," he says. For the former, "paper napkins and ragged placemats are fine, but for the latter you set the dining room table with linens and use your best serving dishes, and you quite probably dress differently as well." At a practical (and tongue-in-cheek) level, vestments means he "never has to think about what I will wear to church"—unlike ministers in other traditions, who have to worry about their clothing choice each Sunday.

On a more serious note, "every time I put that stole across my shoulders I am aware that it symbolizes the 'yoke' of my work and vocation," Howison says. "What a privilege, and what a marvelous burden."

August 2017

Panhandling: To give or not to give?

ANYONE WHO WORKS downtown in a major Canadian city encounters panhandlers every day. That was my experience when I worked in downtown Winnipeg; I was asked for money so many times over the years I became inured to the requests. On a typical summer's day, I could be asked for money three or four times during a walk of several blocks.

I rarely, if ever, gave panhandlers spare change. I comforted my conscience by reminding myself I donate regularly to Winnipeg's Siloam Mission, which offers meals, beds, and other services to those experiencing houselessness. I'm sure there are some genuinely needy people out there, but being constantly asked for money can have a deadening effect on the heart and spirit. It's just so much easier to look away or shake your head and say no.

British journalist Tony Parsons felt the same way. Writing in *Arena Magazine* about the many people he daily saw asking for money, he wrote that begging "degrades the spirit. It dehumanizes you as well as them; it brutalizes us all. You learn to walk past these people, you have to, and it makes it easier to turn away from the truly needy . . . [to] harden your heart, put calluses on your soul. They make every cry for help seem like junk mail." I can empathize, even if guiltily so.

For people of faith, those who ask us for money on the streets pose a unique problem. All religions encourage their adherents to be charitable and to give to those in need. But they also teach the value of work and personal responsibility. What to do? Perhaps we should give to everyone in need, and let God worry about how it is used. It's not our money, after all—all of our resources belong to God. But surely God also wants us to give wisely. Giving to someone who may use money to feed a destructive addiction would not be a good investment. Or maybe we can see panhandling as the 21st century equivalent of the Old Testament practice of gleaning. Since not many of us are farmers today, perhaps the change in our pockets can be compared to the grain sheaves that were to be left for the poor.

It's not only individuals that struggle with the question of whether to give to beggars, churches do too. Clergy receive many calls from individuals with the most incredible stories of hardship and need. They sometimes respond, usually after checking the veracity of the story. Other times, they know they are being scammed because other clergy have tipped them off. In some parts of Winnipeg, churches share the names of people who go church to church, exhausting the goodwill of congregations, in order to prevent them from taking advantage of other groups.

One Winnipeg pastor, the late Harry Lehotsky, was well-known for his tireless efforts to help Winnipeg's poor. But even he admitted to being worn out by the constant requests for money. "I've heard countless stories and requests for cash over the years. Some requests are sufficiently creative to be turned into screenplays. After the first few minutes, however, it becomes evident that the engaging pitch is purely the creation of a desperate imagination or a powerful addiction."

For Lehotsky, "the most difficult requests are when you don't know if the person is asking from need or sloth, from addiction or hunger, for their family or their dealer. I can usually offer an educated and experienced guess as to the legitimacy of a request. In the end, I have to balance the limits of my own resources with the trust I have in the request and the relationship I have—or can have—with the person who's asking."

Of course, people who panhandle do so for a variety of reasons. Not all of them are asking for money to feed their addictions. But whether or not people should give to panhandlers is an eternal question that has no easy answers. Lehotsky may have offered the best advice. Over time, he became "more careful giving money to the people who are hurting themselves with my generosity. That way I'll have some left to help those who are helping themselves—with just a little assistance from a stranger."

September 2017

On the benefits of "thoughts and prayers"

AFTER MAJOR TRAGEDIES, the same thing happens over and over: people say they are sending "thoughts and prayers." This happens after natural disasters and, increasingly in the US, after mass shootings. One of the groups most apt to send them are politicians.

In the US, research by Ben Rowen in *The Atlantic* showed from 1995 to 2017 there were 4,139 instances in which a congressperson expressed "thoughts and prayers" in the Senate or House. "Given that the House has averaged 138 days in session a year and the Senate 162 since 2001, this equates to close to one 'thoughts and prayers' entered into the record per workday on the Hill," he writes. In Canada, a search through Hansard going back to 1994 shows that "thoughts and prayers" were shared 540 times in Parliament, mostly by Conservatives.

The practice has also produced a backlash: don't just pray, do something! That's how Connecticut Senator Chris Murphy saw it after the 2017 Las Vegas shooting. To his colleagues who sent thoughts and prayers, but who refused to try to check the proliferation of guns in that country, he tweeted: "Your cowardice to act cannot be whitewashed by thoughts and prayers. None of this ends unless we do something to stop it."

Most would agree that prayer without action is meaningless. But does that mean that sending thoughts and prayers, in themselves, is a bad thing? I don't know what it means to send thoughts. There are some who believe that energy can travel across space to positively impact other people, but this seems to be a minority view. As for prayer, lots of people say they do that. An Angus Reid survey from 2016 found that 86 per cent of Canadians pray at least once a month or more. Fifty-nine per cent of the time they pray to ask God for help; 35 per cent of the time they pray for God to help others. What about the effect of those prayers? The same study found that 44 per cent of Canadians said their prayers are answered "sometimes." Twenty-four per cent said they were answered "often" and 11 per cent said "always."

Not all the benefits of prayer are for others. Praying benefits the one who is doing it. Eighty-six per cent of Canadians said praying added something to their own lives. In his book *The Psychology of Prayer: A Scientific Approach* (2013), Kevin Ladd, a former pastor and associate professor of psychology at Indiana University, confirmed this. For him, a major function of prayer "is the key role it plays in helping people cope with the problems encountered in social living."

Prayer, he says, is significant for helping people deal with things like difficult relationships, illness, and death. Pausing to pray also has a calming effect, generates a sense of peace, and reduces stress. "That prayer helps one better cope and adjust to life's challenges has become increasingly evident over time," he states.

Today we seem to be awash in tragedy and misery—natural disasters, refugee flight, famine, mass shootings. It is easy to be overwhelmed and feel powerless to do anything to make a difference. We want to help, but what can we do? Sometimes prayer might be the only thing, for those who are suffering and also for our own peace of mind. Of course, we shouldn't only send thoughts and prayers; people should also donate money, give blood, volunteer, make a casserole for a neighbour in distress, or do anything else that might make a practical difference in the lives of those who are suffering.

A final word from Kevin Ladd about why people pray. Prayer, he writes, "is a paradoxical spiritual practice that does not guarantee predictably discernible efficacy at every turn. It's not a cosmic vending machine. So why do people pray? Because they have faith that it is the right thing for them to do."

And to that I can only say: "Amen."

October 2017

For some, relics are weird; for others, a way to connect to God

As a Protestant I have to admit: I don't get relics. The idea of lining up to look at the bones or ashes of dead people strikes me as weird, and a little bit morbid. But that doesn't mean it isn't meaningful for many people—especially Roman Catholics.

In Canada this month, people are lining up to see the right forearm of St. Francis Xavier, the sixteenth-century Jesuit missionary, as the relic travels across the country. Although many find the practice strange, the veneration of relics has a long history in the Christian church. One of the first recorded instances goes back to the martyrdom of St. Polycarp, the Bishop of Smyrna (now Turkey), who was killed by the Romans in the second century. After his death, the Romans burned his body to prevent Christians from venerating it. But local believers collected fragments of the body to remember him and others "who have run their race and to prepare those yet to walk in their steps," as stated in the manuscript *The Martyrdom of Polycarp*.

By the Middle Ages, the collection of relics was in full swing. Today, a tourist location is popular because it has a great beach. Back then, when most tourists were pilgrims, relics mattered most. Since having a relic was a great way to boost the economic fortunes of a town or city, competition for them was fierce. The bodies of saints were separated, sold, and even stolen. The body of St. Francis was spirited away and hidden by his friends in Assisi after his death, reportedly to prevent another city from stealing it for its church.

Over time, the Catholic Church came to regulate the trade, display, and veneration of relics, putting them into three groups: first class relics are the body or fragments of the body of a saint; second class are things that a saint owned; third class are items a saint touched or that have touched other relics.

As it turns out, anyone can own a relic, even though the Roman Catholic Church forbids making a profit off their sale. (It's called simony.) A search on eBay shows hundreds for sale such as the "rare and holy relic of Saint Mary Magdalene" ($599), the "holy papal relic of Saint Pius the tenth Pope" ($499), and a medal touched by the American Catholic saint Elizabeth Ann Seton—a bargain at only $9.95. Catholics aren't the only group known for relics, although they probably have the most. Muslims show respect to items like the sandals or hairs from the beard of the prophet Muhammed, while Buddhists can reflect on the Buddha's tooth and ashes.

While relics might still seem strange to me, they are meaningful to many people—like my friend Deborah Gyapong, an Ottawa-based journalist who covers national politics and the Catholic Church. The former evangelical church member once found them to be "weird, macabre, and/or superstitious." Today, as a relatively new Catholic, she finds that relics remind her of the "physicality of our Lord" and of the "concrete, historical reality of saints who followed Jesus, perhaps to martyrdom, and who brought the Light of the Gospel wherever they lived and suffered." Additionally, they help Gyapong understand the "incarnational and historical reality of the mystery of Christ's life, death, and resurrection, and of Christ in us, the hope of glory."

For Father Michel Boutilier, a Jesuit priest and chaplain at St. Paul's High School in Winnipeg, relics help connect him with Jesus. Relics, he says, are not objects of worship. Instead, "they point to Christ—he is the one we worship," he says. He is also quick to note "there is no magic in the relics." Venerating them won't bring you good luck, like winning the lottery. Instead, Boutilier shares, relics are vehicles of "grace that can change our lives. They don't impart grace themselves."

Of course, not every Christian feels this way about relics. Not even all Catholics agree about the place of relics in their faith; it can vary according to age, country, and culture. But at a time when our increasingly secular society seems to be pushing spirituality to the margins, it is understandable to have a tangible need to be reminded there is more to life than things we can only touch and see—there are mysteries beyond our physical comprehension.

January 2018

Faith and chronic illness

WHAT'S IT LIKE to be a person of faith with a chronic illness? That's one of the questions explored by Winnipegger Allison Alexander in her new book *Super Sick: Making Peace with Chronic Illness* (2020), about living with a chronic illness in a society that tells people they need to be healthy, productive, and successful to be valuable.

In the book, Alexander shares about her life-long experience of living with severe Irritable Bowel Syndrome, writing about how chronic illness is not well-represented in TV, movies, books, or video games—or in faith. When it comes to the latter, Alexander has found churches can make being chronically ill both harder and easier. "Some Christians believe that if you're sick it's your fault for not having enough faith, or because of a past sin," she says, pointing to the Christian movement called "prosperity theology" which teaches God wants all Christians to be wealthy and healthy. "That is especially damaging to poor and suffering people, because it suggests if we're not happy, healthy, and wealthy, we must not have enough faith."

On the other hand, being a member of a church that understands and supports her has made being chronically ill easier. These are people "who don't just say 'I'll pray for you,' but offer to bring a meal, or pick up medication, or come sit in the hospital waiting room, or play a video game with me to help distract me, or whatever it is I need," Alexander says. This is "the church as it should be, reminding me that I am loved, valued, and cared for."

Having a chronic illness has also challenged and deepened Alexander's faith. "When you're in intense pain, and you know God has the power to stop it but doesn't, it's difficult to wrap your mind around. Faith is a struggle in this way," she says. On the other hand, her faith is a comfort because "I believe God is suffering with me . . . God cares about what I am going through."

One thing she wishes other Christians knew about chronic illness is "it's not a problem to be solved. Sometimes I just need someone to be there for me and to say 'that sucks' instead of quoting a Bible verse." She also wishes other Christians realized there are limits on what she can do at church, such as being a regular attender. "Telling a sick person you miss them and encouraging them to come to church more often may be the opposite of helpful," she says. "It may just add guilt to their plate."

Since people with chronic illness can't always make it to services, Alexander encourages church leaders to find ways to involve them that don't require their physical presence—something the pandemic has made easier.

"With COVID-19, there has been a huge movement to online services and community that may not have been thought possible before," she says. "I'm hopeful these communities will be kept alive after the pandemic is over, for people like me."

July 2020

Swearing for Christians, or, what to do when life is a "shit-show"

When asked to summarize the Christian gospel in one sentence, Will Campbell, a self-proclaimed, prickly "bootleg preacher" from Mississippi, put it this way: "We are all bastards, but God loves us anyway." American Methodist preacher and theologian Stanley Hauerwas is known for his earthy way of communicating about the faith. "Without cross and resurrection, life is just shit," he says, along with "Jesus is Lord and everything else is bullshit."

In a prayer that went viral last year during the pandemic, when everything seemed to be going off the rails, American Lutheran minister Nadia Bolz-Weber started off by saying: "It's a shit-show down here, Lord." And last month Knox United Church in Calgary put up a sign outside the building inviting people inside for fellowship and coffee that said, "Yes! There is coffee inside the church. No, it's not shitty church coffee."

Some readers may be offended by such inappropriate language used by Christians. But not Allan Rudy-Froese. He not only thinks it's OK, he thinks Christians need to talk more about swearing—and even feel free to swear when and where it's appropriate. Rudy-Froese teaches preaching at Associated Mennonite Biblical Seminary in Elkhart, Indiana. Growing up in a Mennonite home in Saskatchewan where swearing was not permitted, he still remembers the first time he swore in the house. It was a new word he had learned, although he didn't know what it meant. "I got a spanking," he recalls, noting the reaction indicated certain words were powerful and mysterious.

Later, in a Christian high school class, a teacher asked the students to say all the swear words they knew. After the initial shock and titillation of saying the words out loud, the experience "demystified those words, took away their power," Rudy-Froese says. Now, as a professor at seminary and a former pastor, Rudy-Froese wonders if it's time for pastors to offer guidance to their congregations when it comes to colourful language. "There's been an explosion of swearing in movies, books, music, plays, everywhere," he says. "It's all around us."

Rudy-Froese explains that swearing falls into different categories. One is sacred, using the name of God or Jesus or some other religious term. In Canada, this is especially true in Quebec where the strongest swear words are religious in nature, such as "tabarnak" (the tabernacle), "câlice" (chalice), and "ciboire" (the ciborium, a container for the consecrated bread). Another category for swearing involves body parts and is usually sexual in nature. Often these words are connected to sexism and misogyny, or are used to describe bodies in a negative light. "There are so many negative words about bodies," Rudy-Froese says, wondering if this is because people over the centuries have been taught to view the earthly body as inferior to the spiritual body after death.

While not advocating a liberal adoption of swearing, he wonders if Christians today might benefit from having a more positive approach to that kind of language. Swearing can show honesty, frankness, and authenticity, although if used too much it "can become cheap." Plus, Rudy-Froese notes, science says swearing can be good for us. "It can be cathartic," he adds. "Sometimes it just feels good to swear. It can help us let go of tension in the body."

For example, studies have shown that profanity improves pain tolerance and improves stamina. In one study people on bikes who swore while pedaling against resistance had more power and strength than people who used "neutral" words. Another study suggested if you hit your finger with a hammer, you may well feel less pain if you say "shit" instead of "shoot."

So should pastors give congregants a break when it comes to swearing? Maybe. After all, as Rudy-Froese points out, many people already do it, especially younger people, for whom swearing is not as taboo as it was for older generations. Should clergy swear themselves? "If a pastor can say 'shit,' maybe that helps people see him or her as human, not on a pedestal," he says, remembering his own experiences as a pastor when someone swore in his presence. "They would immediately apologize," he says. "I'd tell them not to worry, to set them at ease."

Rudy-Froese cautioned he's not advocating swearing in the pulpit for swearing's sake; that can come across like the preacher is trying to be "too cool." But it could be appropriate in the right context and if the preacher knows the congregation. "You wouldn't want to do it just to offend."

In the end, Rudy-Froese just wants to get a discussion going and stop pretending Christians don't swear. In fact, he's writing a book on that subject now. Working title: *A Guide to Swearing for the Badass Faithful.* "It's not a good title at all, but I have to start somewhere," he says.

February 2022

Parish nursing: A congregational response to the healthcare crisis

MANITOBA NEEDS AS many as 2,000 more nurses to fill vacant positions. Emergency rooms are overloaded. Surgical wait times are up. Patients are waiting in hallways to be seen. The healthcare system is at, or beyond, the breaking point. And it can only get worse as the number of seniors rapidly grows. According to the province's Age-Friendly Manitoba initiative, in 2019 close to 16 per cent of the population were 65 years and older. By 2028, that figure will rise to 31 per cent.

Many of those seniors will prefer to stay in their own homes as long as possible. As the government puts it: "As most older adults aged 65 and over live in the community, communities face opportunities and challenges in responding to their needs and desires." That's an understatement.

There are various ideas being thrown around for ways to fix the problem, such as attracting more nurses from countries like the Philippines or making it easier for foreign nationals to qualify to work in healthcare in the province. One idea I haven't seen come up is parish nursing.

Parish nursing in its contemporary form is a concept pioneered in the US in the 1980s. In a nutshell, it finds congregations employing healthcare professionals, or utilizing retired nurses as volunteers, to attend to the needs of people in congregations or communities. Parish nursing focuses on the whole person, including their spiritual well-being. Today there are thousands of parish nurses involved in faith-based settings around the world, including a few in Canada. Parish nursing doesn't replace traditional healthcare. Instead, it serves to bolster and support it by keeping people, especially seniors, out of the healthcare system as long as possible—keeping them healthy and well in their homes for as long as they can stay there.

In this country, the Canadian Association for Parish Nursing Ministry is a small organization that resources and supports parish nurses. According to the organization, a parish nurse is a registered nurse who is affirmed by a faith community that validates their call to ministry. The people nurses serve may belong to a congregation, but the circle of care can extend beyond to the local community. Through parish nursing, people achieve better health and are better able to cope with life's challenges and transitions.

Core competencies for parish nursing include the ability to assess and intervene with individuals, families, groups, and communities; to make assessments about the physical, emotional, mental, social, and spiritual dimensions of people's health; and the ability to promote positive health practices and behaviours. In plain language, that means things like doing a basic check-up during a home visit, along with checking on medications—making sure people are taking them as prescribed—checking their fridge and cupboards to see how they are eating, and generally ensuring they are doing well enough to continue living independently at home.

If greater care is needed, parish nurses can make referrals for additional medical interventions, or link people with government or other agencies for different kinds of assistance. This could include being an advocate for them in the health care system or something as simple as ensuring seniors' sidewalks are shovelled in winter, or organizing their yard care from spring to fall. Seniors might also need rides to appointments or require small repairs to their homes—things that volunteers from a congregation can assist with.

Since many congregations have retired health care professionals among their members, one model for parish nursing involves congregants volunteering for a few hours or days each week to check in on seniors or other vulnerable people. It's a way for them to continue to use their skills and stay busy in a meaningful way when they still have energy to serve others.

I am not aware of any congregations currently offering parish nursing in Winnipeg, but parish nurses can be found in other parts of Canada. For example, the Upper Ottawa Valley Parish Nurse Initiative Health Council has hired Melissa Jardine-Ridley as a full-time Parish Nurse with the designation of lay minister with the United Church of Canada. The former military senior medical technician and paramedic will serve St. Andrew's United Church in Chalk River, as well as Wesley United and Calvin United Churches in Pembroke, providing services to those churches on a rotating basis. Some Anglican churches in the country also have parish nurses on staff, but a search doesn't turn up any other denominations currently engaged in the practice.

Parish nursing will not solve the healthcare crisis in Manitoba, but at a time when the province is rapidly aging and health needs are growing, every tool in the toolbox is needed to address the growing demand for health services. Parish nursing might just be one of those tools.

March 2023

Author's death prompts reflection on bad things happening to good people

How do we react "when bad things happen to good people"? That is the question Rabbi Harold Kushner set out to answer in 1981 in his book with the same name (2004). Kushner, who died April 28, 2023, at the age of 88, wrote that book after the death of his son, Aaron, from a rare genetic condition called progeria. The illness affects one in four million children and is fatal.

In an interview, Kushner said his son's death at age 14 gave him "a deep, aching sense of unfairness. I had been a good person and always tried to do what was right. I had assumed my side of the bargain, so how could this be happening to my family? If God existed, if He was minimally fair, let alone loving and forgiving, how could He do this to me?" Kushner went on to wonder how to reconcile his belief in an all-loving and all-knowing God with the enormity of suffering in the world. "Can I, in good faith, continue to teach people that the world is good, and that a kind and loving God is responsible for what happens in it?" he said.

When faced with suffering, "I have to face the fact that either God is all-powerful but not kind, or thoroughly kind and loving but not totally powerful," Kushner said in an interview with NPR. He came down on the side of love over power. "I would rather compromise God's power and affirm his love." In Kushner's view, God is not responsible for suffering, nor does God use it to teach humans a lesson or as a test of faith. Instead, it is the natural consequence of living in a world governed by physical laws and human choices. "The theological conclusion I came to is that God could have been all-powerful at the beginning, but he chose to designate two areas of life off limits to his power," Kushner said. "He would not arbitrarily interfere with laws of nature, and secondly, God would not take away our freedom to choose between good and evil." When challenged for how he minimized the traditional view of God's almighty and omniscient power, Kushner replied: "Your God wants the earthquake to happen, the little boy to die? Which one of us is diminishing God?"

The book resonated with many. It also met a need for Kushner, who said he wrote it to give meaning to his son's brief life. And he was clear he never meant for people to give up believing in God because of it. Instead, he believed suffering was a call from God to respond with compassion and action to alleviate it wherever it was found.

One person who appreciates Kushner's work is Alan Green, who used to be the rabbi at Congregation Shaarey Zedek in Winnipeg. "I can certainly relate to his experience, walking through hospital wards," he says. But Green disagrees with Kushner's conclusion. "I never felt comfortable with a theology that imposes limits on the power of God," he says.

For Green, God "is present even in the darkest, lowest, meanest of human circumstances, and to some extent, is responsible for them—which is not to deny the role played by evil people or one's own errors." Kushner's stance is reasonable, he adds, and he understands its appeal. "My stance is much harder to swallow," he says. "But my God is the God of Job, all powerful and sustaining the universe and those who dwell in it with a depth of love and wisdom that eludes human comprehension."

As humans, "we are not meant to understand, rationally, why things happen the way they do, why bad things happen to good people," Green continues. "While I believe we humans are responsible to do everything we can to alleviate suffering—and that emphatically, this is doing God's work—the suffering we cannot prevent is not due to any limitation on the power of God." In other words, Green says, "I see some higher purpose in our suffering, though it often makes God look like a rough character. God, the Divine Physician, in facilitating our healing, sometimes needs to cut in the very places where we hurt the most."

At the same time, Green praised Kushner for "dealing directly and cogently with the greatest theological conundrum of them all." In so doing, he did something "rare," which Green says is to "be a rabbi and a best-selling author." Whether you side with Kushner or with a more traditional view of God's role, both Kushner and Green emphasize that when it comes to suffering, we need to do whatever we can to alleviate it.

May 2023

Do we have too much stuff?

Do WE HAVE too much stuff? That question occurred to me when a new self-storage business opened in my end of town. It's huge—nine buildings with 768 storage units of varying sizes. I wondered, how many people need to rent extra space to store their stuff?

Lots, as it turns out. The self-storage industry in Canada is booming. "Canadian storage markets are bursting at the seams as skyrocketing consumer demand drives the building of new facilities," writes Richard Leach in *Inside Self Storage*, the largest-circulation magazine for storage professionals in North America. "Over the past 10 years, there has been dramatic self-storage growth in nearly every province." Canadians, he goes on to say, were "slower to grasp the self-storage concept" than Americans, but today developers in this country have discovered "the mother lode of gold" as they scramble to provide more storage facilities.

Canada-wide, there are 2,800 self-storage facilities, according to the Canadian Self Storage Association. The US has over 51,000. How does that compare to other countries? "There are between 6,000 and 7,000 everywhere else combined. In the world," says Timothy J. Dietz of the US Self Storage Association. "We're a consumer-driven country, and our economy is very strong. Americans like to hold onto their stuff," he adds.

It's not as though we need the extra space. The average house being built in Canada today is 2,000 square feet. In 1975, it was 1,075 square feet; in 1945 it was just 800 square feet. Since the size of Canadian families is shrinking, we should need less space, but that's not the case. The growth of the self-storage sector suggests we need more.

It's a worrisome trend for Winnipegger Mark Burch, author of *Simplicity: Notes, Stories and Exercises for Developing Unimaginable Wealth* (1995). Through our excessive consumerism "we are smashing the body and shedding the blood of the greatest gift given to us," he says. "Caring for this planet is the way we manifest God's love." Burch, campus sustainability coordinator at the University of Winnipeg, is a proponent of what is called voluntary simplicity—the idea that people should purposefully try to live more simply in order to preserve the planet and their sanity. The term was coined in 1936 by Richard Gregg, who defined it as a "singleness of purpose, sincerity and honesty . . . as well as avoidance of exterior clutter, of many possessions irrelevant to the chief purpose of life. It means an ordering and guiding of our energy and our desires, a partial restraint in some directions in order to secure greater abundance of life in other directions."

For Burch, voluntary simplicity isn't just a way to save money by not buying more stuff. It's also a way to contribute to the good of the earth and its inhabitants. "Discerning how much is enough involves placing our personal consumption of things in the context of environmental sustainability, social justice, and inter-generational equity," he says. "In this realm, we move beyond considerations of what may be expedient or comfortable in terms of our individual lives and consider ourselves to be part of a much larger whole." It's a way, he notes, to "create a world that is more peaceful and equitable."

Simplicity has deep religious roots. The Buddha, St. Francis of Assisi, the Amish, various monastic orders, and Jesus, all advocated it. For Burch, "the ethical and spiritual dimension of this is very important. We need to subordinate our material consumption to spiritual values. We need to take time to remember who we are, why we are here, and what our purpose is." But trying to live more simply today is hard, Burch acknowledges. It's like "swimming upstream all the time" in our materialistic society, he says. Living simply, he adds, "is almost a heroic act today." For that reason, some people join simplicity circles, where they can find support as they attempt to go against the grain.

There's nothing wrong with buying the stuff we need, of course, but our culture never gives us a break. We're always pushed to buy more of this and more of that. Then, after we've gone out and bought too much stuff, we need to rent places to store it. Says Burch: "We need to consume to live, but we shouldn't live to consume." Sounds like good, simple advice to me.

December 2007

8

WHAT'S GOING ON?

"Hug your customers": How churches can welcome visitors

WHEN YOU'RE MARRIED to a pastor, one thing you can't do on Sundays is visit other churches. My wife ended her ministry at our church in June, giving our family a chance to visit other churches to see how they worship. Over the course of the summer we visited five different churches: Alliance, Mennonite, Baptist, and two non-denominational congregations. It was an eye-opening experience.

In all five, the societal changeover from hymns to praise and worship choruses was complete. All of the churches we visited use a contemporary worship style—singing choruses accompanied by a band (guitars, keyboard, drums). At only one church was a traditional hymn sung and none of the churches used hymnbooks or songbooks—in all the churches, the lyrics were only displayed on a screen.

When it comes to singing, you need lots of stamina—people with back trouble or weak knees are in for an uncomfortable time. In all the churches but one the singing lasted 20 minutes or more, with congregants standing the whole time. Not everyone was able to stay on their feet; all around us people—mostly seniors—sat down part way through the package of songs. Neither of those two things surprised me—contemporary worship is becoming a hallmark of many evangelical church worship services today. One thing that did surprise me was how insular these churches were.

During the time we were making our church visits, Canadian soldiers were fighting and dying in Afghanistan, there was war between Israel and Hezbollah in the Middle East, the first election in 46 years took place in Democratic Republic of the Congo, and the international AIDS conference took place in Toronto. But not one of the churches we visited noted these major world issues during the service, including in the pastoral prayer. The only things that were prayed about were the spiritual and personal needs of the members of the congregation.

I was also surprised by how poorly the five churches dealt with visitors. In only one church were we personally greeted by a member of the congregation who did not already know us. The most awkward experience occurred when we arrived about ten minutes early for a service at one church. We took our seats near the front, surrounded by others who completely ignored us as they greeted each other and engaged in animated conversations. We felt like we had wandered into somebody else's family reunion.

Of course, it's wrong to judge a church on the basis of one Sunday morning visit. But first impressions matter; according to church growth specialist Herb Miller, only 12 per cent of first-time visitors will return the following Sunday and eventually become members. One of the key reasons why people come back, he says, is whether or not they are made to feel welcome.

Jane Fisler Hoffman considers herself a "professional" church visitor. As a conference minister with the Illinois Conference of the United Church of Christ, she gets to visit a lot of different congregations. "Nearly every church believes itself to be friendly and welcoming," she says, "but that truth is not always readily apparent to the nervous first-time visitor who has just moved into the area or who is having a new sense of spiritual seeking."

Ways churches can help visitors, she notes, include listing the worship time on the answering machine and website; by putting up lots of signs—regular attenders know where everything is, but visitors don't; and have a "visitor-friendly bulletin," which lists all the responses and instructions. Most important of all, churches should train members to be on the lookout for visitors. "The standard doorway greeters who look at you with that 'are you a first-time visitor or an old-time member I should know?' question in their eyes rarely do more than smile and shake a hand," she says. "Other members should be trained and, if necessary, assigned to watch actively for visitors and help them find childcare, coat racks, and so forth." No church is "too small or remote or too large and busy to take these steps," she adds.

In the business world, "customer service" is quickly becoming the mantra for companies that want to distinguish themselves from competitors. For Jack Mitchell, the owner of successful high-end clothing stores on the east coast of the US, the path to success is simple: hug your customers. Not literally, of course; for him, hugging means doing everything possible to make them feel welcome. In his book *Hug Your Customers: Love the Results* (2003), he offers practical tips on how businesses can make customers feel special and important—and make them want to come back. Hugging, says Mitchell, "involves listening to and caring about the customer, getting so close to the customer that the customer is more important than anything else." But for "hugging culture to work," he adds, "everyone in the organization, from top to bottom, must embrace it."

When someone visits your place of worship, will they feel "hugged"? If they don't come back, I guess you'll know the answer.

September 2006

Thinking about faith and end-of-life issues

A LOVED ONE is rushed to the hospital with a life-threatening illness or condition. The doctors say they could try to save the person you love, but even if they are successful, the results could be devastating—brain damage, or other terrible effects. You are given a few minutes to decide what to do. If that's the first time you've thought about end-of-life issues, you've waited too long.

That's Joel Shuman's view. Shuman, who teaches Christian ethics and bioethics at King's College in Wilkes-Barre, Pennsylvania, says that people should be talking about whether to seek or decline potentially risky life-saving measures before a critical illness strikes. "The first time you think about it shouldn't be when you are in the hospital, and you have five minutes to come up with an answer," he says.

Shuman's perspective on end-of-life issues comes to mind now that the College of Physicians and Surgeons of Manitoba is considering giving physicians the authority to stop or withhold medical treatment—even if the patient or family disagrees. A draft policy written by CPSM says doctors should have the authority to make the final decision about treatments such as withholding or withdrawing respirators, breathing tubes, and feeding tubes, and also about continuing with treatments like dialysis. Families would be given 96 hours' notice of the decision and the right to appeal it through a second opinion or court intervention.

But Shuman, author of *The Body of Compassion: Ethics, Medicine, and the Church* (2003), doesn't think that's the answer—particularly for Christians. The church, he says, should help members think about these important medical and end-of-life issues in advance, helping them adopt a Christian view of medicine that accepts the finitude of life. "This finitude is not to be regretted or lamented," he says. "It is a given, a condition we are born into. It highlights our dependence on God, and on others." Shuman also thinks the church should play a more active role in helping individuals to discern what treatments should be pursued for loved ones. "Those difficult decisions are often put on the shoulders of individual family members," he says. "We should share the burden of making those decisions."

In Calgary, the Care at the End of Life Initiative, a project of the Calgary Health Region, is trying to help people in that city prepare for these tough end-of-life decisions. The Initiative, which is directed by hospital chaplain Bert Enns, aims to help people "think about how their cultural and religious values would affect decisions about the end of life," she says.

According to Enns, how and where people died over the last 30 years has changed dramatically, with frailty due to conditions such as dementia, cardiovascular disease, and Parkinson's shaping the last years of life for many people. "We may be sick enough to die, but live many years," she says. "Yet, at this time, the health care system is not well situated to ensure quality care at the end of life."

The Initiative is preparing a workbook that individuals and groups can use to help them prepare for decisions about the quality of life, and what kind of medical care they want, as their lives draw to a close. "It's a tool that enables people to start a conversation about these issues," she says, noting that it can be especially useful for people who find it hard to talk about death and dying. Another goal of the Initiative is to share the burden of making tough decisions about end-of-life medical care. "Physicians here are asking individuals and society to be more involved in these decisions," she says, adding that families often tell her they have no idea about the burden health care professionals feel over making decisions about what treatments to give and which to withhold.

When it comes to end-of-life and medical care, there are no easy answers. But if faith guides you in life, it should also give guidance when death is a real possibility. Faith groups can play a key role in helping people talk about these difficult issues. As Shuman says: "Medicine is a gift to us. Now we need to have a discussion about how best to use it."

October 2006

Praying for God to take Dad home

It's not easy growing old. Just ask my dad. Now 86, he lives in a nursing home. As a younger man, he worked hard to support his family, running machines at the factory, loading trucks—but now he is frightfully thin, frail, and weak and uses a wheelchair to get around. His hearing isn't very good, he finds it hard to read, and his memory is failing. Sometimes he remembers I am visiting; other times it's a surprise. Sometimes he thinks I'm coming when I'm not, and then he is hurt and angry.

When you're old and frail and in a nursing home, you look forward to little things to make the day more enjoyable—things like eating. Even that small pleasure is denied him. Since he has trouble swallowing, his food is mostly pureed. "It tastes bland," he says. And he's right; in order to achieve the right consistency, the dining hall staff have to add water. Then there's the loneliness. Most of his friends are gone, and so is his wife—she died almost four years ago. They were married for 53 years. Sure, they often argued, sometimes very loudly, but now he has nobody to talk to at all.

Add it all up, and he wonders: why keep on living? In fact, the thing he desires most is to die. Every night he prays that God will take him home. "I just want to go peacefully, in my sleep," he says, adding he can't understand why God won't answer that one simple prayer. I don't blame him for feeling that way. It must be hard to depend on others for the simple necessities in life—getting up, having a bath, getting dressed. It must be hard to be living in a place where you are constantly surrounded by illness, decline and death. It must be tough to feel like you are caught in a real-life version of the movie *Groundhog Day*, each day like the day before. No wonder he has so little interest in living.

Gerhard Friesen is chaplain at a Winnipeg personal care home. My dad isn't alone in his dilemma, he says. "It's normal for people to feel that way. Everything aches, and they've suffered so many losses in life—friends, home, possessions, and sometimes a spouse." He tells them that God will take them home in God's own good time. Friesen also tells them that the church cares for them, even though sometimes it doesn't feel that way. In Winnipeg, churches take turns providing worship services at various nursing homes. Some do a very good job—the music is good, the preachers are relevant. Others don't. They seem to do the minimum that is possible, sending less than their best. "Residents will tell you on Monday morning when the service was bad," says Friesen. "They say, 'They think that's good enough for us.'"

Sitting with my dad a week ago, many thoughts about aging went through my mind. I thought about how, when it comes to people who are elderly, caring is non-negotiable—especially for people of faith. The world's great religions all teach that older people should be respected, honoured, and cared for. I also thought about the huge challenge facing places of worship when it comes to aging. Canada is getting older, and fast. According to Statistics Canada, by 2016 there will be 5.8 million seniors in the country—more older people than ever before. By 2026, one out of five Canadians will be over 65. Are places of worship ready?

Right now, I'd say no. I don't hear a lot about preparing new clergy to deal with issues relate to spirituality and aging. A look at the course listings for three prominent Canadian Christian seminaries shows 23 courses on youth ministry, but only two courses on ministering to older people. That will hardly do in years to come, when many churches have more seniors than young people. But all that faded away as I watched my dad sleep. I knew he was lucky to be in a great personal care home—the staff are friendly, compassionate, considerate, and professional. The level of service is excellent. Still, he wants God to take him home. "I pray that one night I will just lay down and not get up," he says. Some days, I find myself praying that for him, too.

Postscript: My dad got his prayer answered a month later, in February 2009.

January 2009

A personal mystery of Titanic proportions

On weekday mornings in 2011, while working downtown, I have been confronted by the mystery of life. My life, to be precise. It happens when I get off the bus and pass by posters at the MTS Centre Exhibition Hall for the Titanic exhibit. For many, the photos of the great ship are just that: photos. For me, it has prompted a deeper question: Why am I alive?

It's not an academic exercise; if not for a missed reservation for passage on the doomed ship, I might not be here today. The story goes like this. In 1911, my grandfather, also named John Longhurst, emigrated from England to Canada. Like many other emigrants starting a new life in a new country, he left behind his fiancée, Alice Bond—my grandmother. The plan was for him to become established in Canada, then return to England so they could marry.

Early in 1912, he came back and they were married. Apparently, John was a bit of a romantic; he wanted to do something special for his new bride. And what could be more special than booking a honeymoon passage on the maiden voyage of the Titanic? But he was too late; the ship was full. Instead, he made a reservation on the SS Megantic, arriving in Quebec City six weeks later. Had he been in time to book passage on the Titanic, it is likely that one, or both, would have died. And because of a missed reservation, I am alive.

When it comes to averted tragedy, most people don't have a story as dramatic as the Titanic. But everyone can recall near misses of one sort or another, times when the course of our lives could have been completely altered, or ended. When that happens, many people offer thanks to God, Allah, Jehovah, their lucky stars, or whatever universal power they believe in.

Sometimes another thought creeps in: did a higher power really help me avoid that tragedy? Was it all planned to happen that way, right from the beginning? Or was it just luck or blind chance? In my case, did God know the Titanic was going to sink, and so prevented my grandfather from getting a ticket on the doomed ship? Did he have a plan that involved not only John and Alice, but also my father, myself, and my kids—all the way down the line? If that's the case, why did he keep John and Alice off the doomed liner, but allow so many others to sail away to their deaths?

Those are big questions on weekday mornings, especially before a first cup of coffee, and I'm not sure I have good answers. One person who has given this a lot of thought is Bruce Epperly, a process theologian and author of the book *Process Theology: A Guide for the Perplexed* (2011). In a nutshell, process theologians like Epperly believe God does not, and cannot, fully determine the experience of any person on the planet. In this view, God does not determine the most important details of our lives. Instead, the future is as open for God as it is for a person; neither knows exactly what will happen next.

For Epperly, this doesn't diminish God. Instead, it makes God "more alive, creative, and active than a God who has chosen the future in its entirety. A God to whom new things happen can respond to our prayers in ways that make a difference, operating within the causal relationships of the natural world." This is an "open-source, open-system vision of the universe in which God and the world exist in a dynamic, growing and evolving partnership," he adds. If Epperly is right, this means God didn't ordain for the Titanic to hit an iceberg and sink that terrible night in April 1912. He didn't plan for John and Alice not to be able to get passage on the liner, nor for all those people to die. God may not even have known the ship would sink at all.

Bruce Epperly's view is not conventional, but it's catching on as more Christians wrestle with the issue of suffering and pain in the world. Is everything preordained, from beginning to end? Or are we, in Epperly's words, engaged in a dynamic relationship with God where we both react to events, both good and bad? I certainly don't have answers to those questions. All I know is when I get off the bus each morning and see those photos of the doomed ship, I face a mystery of Titanic proportions.

July 2011

Do rocks have rights?

The year 2007 was the 200th anniversary of the beginning of the abolition of slavery. In 1807 the British Parliament signed into law the Abolition of the Slave Trade Act, the first step towards the worldwide eradication of the African slave trade.

Today it's obvious that people should not be bought, sold, and enslaved. Back then the prevailing view was that the slave trade was necessary, even if it was brutal. Stopping it would have negative economic consequences; only a few people believed that slavery was wrong. It took 20 years of tireless work by William Wilberforce, a courageous Christian Member of Parliament in England, before the trade was ended.

The anti-slavery movement is just one example of how humans can be seen to have evolved ethically. Other examples include the civil rights movement in the US, the anti-apartheid movement in South Africa, and the extension of human rights to women, 2SLGBTQ+ people, and people with disabilities. But the human race has often faltered. There are still parts of the world where people are enslaved and there is still much discrimination.

While progress has been made in developing rules to govern human relationships, we have not done as well when it comes to developing an ethic to guide our relationship with the earth. True, there is a growing consensus that we need to change the way we live if humans are to survive, but real change won't occur until we believe that it is morally wrong to pollute the planet. Not wrong because it has negative economic consequences. Not wrong because it will negatively affect our way of life. Not even wrong because we will die if we don't stop dumping on, paving over, and polluting the environment. Rather, wrong because that's no way to treat anyone or anything.

Rocks, in other words, have rights, too. It's a radical shift in thinking. Traditionally, we have mostly thought of rights as belonging to human beings, but more and more ecologists argue that the earth is not to be prized because it sustains life, but because it has value in and of itself. One of the earliest to think this way was Aldo Leopold, considered the father of wildlife management in the US. In his classic essay, "The Land Ethic," Leopold, who died in 1948, suggested that the next human moral evolution would be the expansion of ethics to govern our relationship to the earth. He proposed the following ethic for the way we deal with the environment: a thing is right when it tends to preserve the integrity, stability, and beauty of the earth. It is wrong when it tends otherwise.

More recently, Wendell Berry, a Christian environmentalist, author, and farmer from Kentucky, has added his voice to Leopold's. Berry wants people to see the sacredness of the material world and all of its nonhuman inhabitants. He argues that the earth, and all its aspects, are invested with value not just because they were created by God, but because they are expressions of the divine. "We have lived by the assumption that what was good for us would be good for the world. We have been wrong. We must change our lives, so that it will be possible to live by the contrary assumption that what is good for the world will be good for us . . . we must recover the sense of the majesty of the creation and the ability to be worshipful in its presence. For it is only on the condition of humility and reverence before the world that our species will be able to remain in it."

A number of religious groups are taking the issue of earth care seriously. For example, the Evangelical Environmental Network has created an "Evangelical Declaration on the Care of Creation," which has been signed by hundreds of evangelical leaders. The Coalition on the Environment and Jewish Life proposes actions that Jews can take to show concern for the environment. In 1990 Pope John Paul II called Catholics to take the issue of creation care seriously, stating that "the ecological crisis is a moral issue." Muslims concerned about the state of the earth turn to the Qur'an and the Hadith, which are rich in proverbs and precepts that speak about Muslim responsibility for caring for the earth. Buddhist environmentalists look to the first of the Buddha's five precepts for inspiration: "Do not harm, but cherish all life."

All of this is good. The next step in dealing with environmental crisis may well be a collective decision to extend ethical consideration to the planet itself. Maybe then the day will come when we believe that it is morally wrong to abuse the earth—the same way British Parliamentarians 200 years ago came to believe that it was wrong to enslave human beings.

March 2007

Can a pacifist wear a poppy?

CAN A PACIFIST wear a poppy? The answer is yes—I'm a pacifist, and I wear one. A few others that I know do, too. But others who oppose war have ambivalent feelings about poppies. I think they're afraid that wearing one will suggest that they are, tacitly or otherwise, supporting war and militarism. Some compromise by wearing red buttons that say: "To remember is to work for peace." Every year Mennonite Central Committee distributes thousands of them. It's a good message. But I think a poppy says the same thing—I've never met a veteran who thinks war is a good idea.

I don't wear a poppy to celebrate war. I wear it as a sign of respect for the many men and women who sacrificed years, youth and, for some, their lives during this country's wars. They did not plan those wars. They did not seek them. They did what they thought was right at the time. In the same situation, I might have done the same.

I also wear a poppy for personal reasons. I wear it for my Uncle Harry, who was wounded in Europe in World War Two. Each Remembrance Day he would march with the other veterans to the cenotaph in my hometown, pausing for two minutes to remember the dead. Later, he'd go the Legion and drink and reminisce and cry with his buddies, remembering the friends who never made it home. Uncle Harry, like most vets, never talked about the war, even though I pestered him as a child. He'd just shake his head and change the subject.

I also wear the poppy for my father. Due to a medical condition, he was rejected for military service in 1944. This bothered him his whole life, especially since so many of his high school friends went overseas and some of them were killed. After he died, I went though his belongings. Among his prized possessions I found his certificate for rejection for general service. Why did he keep it all those years? I think it was his way of proving, to himself, at least, that he was no shirker. Maybe it was his special way of keeping faith with friends who served and died.

I wear a poppy for conscientious objectors—for those who bravely decided to go against prevailing opinion by choosing not to participate in the military during this country's wars. During World War Two, 10,782 Canadian men did some form of alternative service on farms, in hospitals, planting trees, building roads and other things, showing there were ways other than fighting to serve their country. Over 3,000 were from Manitoba—more than any other province.

I wear a poppy *because* I am a pacifist. Over my career in international relief and development, much of my work has been in response to hunger and suffering caused by war—people uprooted by conflict, in need of food, shelter, and safety.

Finally, I wear a poppy to show that pacifists can be patriotic, too. Being against war or militarization is not to be anti-Canadian. Service to one's country is not reserved for those who put on a uniform. People can serve in many ways—by volunteering at a food bank, being a Big Brother or Big Sister, cleaning a park, visiting seniors in personal care homes. Things that make the world a bit kinder and—dare I say it?—more peaceful. That's why I wear a poppy. Why do you wear one?

November 2012

Religion and elder orphans

ONE WINTER DAY in the late 1990s, my elderly parents had a problem. There had been a huge snowstorm the day before, and their driveway was filled with snow. They needed to get out for medical appointments but were physically unable to clear the snow. Since they lived in southern Ontario, while I lived in Manitoba, I was no help, I called their church to see if they could find someone to shovel the snow, but the pastor gave me all sorts of reasons why it wouldn't be possible.

I couldn't believe it; my parents had been members of the church since the 1950s, contributing financially and doing volunteer work, and now, in their time of need, nobody was available to help them? I eventually convinced the pastor to send someone, but I felt guilty myself, being so far away. I didn't have the term for it then, but I do now: my parents (now deceased) were elder orphans. That's the name given today to a large and growing number of seniors who have no children close by to care for them as they age. Some of these people never married. Others married but had no children. Or, as in the case of my parents, their children moved far away.

One of the people doing research in this area is Dr. Maria Carney, chief of geriatric and palliative medicine at Northwell Health in New York. Through her research, Carney has found that nearly one-quarter of Americans over 65 are currently at risk of becoming elder orphans, and that close to 33 per cent of Americans age 45 to 63 are single and positioned to join them. Something similar could happen in Canada, where about 27 per cent of Canadians live alone. "It seems that, with increasing longevity and the trend toward having fewer children and families being fragmented, this risk of aging alone is increasing," Carney told CTV's *Canada AM* in May 2015.

This is clearly a growing challenge, but why raise this issue on the faith page? The reason is simple: one group in Canada that should be well-placed to respond to the needs of seniors is the faith community. For some groups, like Muslims, Sikhs, and Hindus, this is not as pressing a problem; adherents of those religions see it as their duty to care for aging parents. But the same is not necessarily true for Christianity.

That is the point made by Linda Mintle in a post on www.beliefnet.com, titled "Are Churches Neglecting the Elderly?" In the post she recounts how her own aging parents had been left on their own by their church, despite years of faithful service to the congregation. "Many churches have become so focused on numbers and youth, that meeting the needs of their senior members are not even on the radar," she writes. Her parents' church has five pastors, but not one of them has pastoral care for seniors in their job description. "The elderly seem to be forgotten," she writes. "And during this time in their lives, when a call or visit would mean so much, the pastors are not taking the time to minister to them."

It's not just churches that have made seniors a low priority; a check of courses offered by six major Christian colleges and seminaries in Canada, including two in Manitoba, shows that while they all offer majors in youth ministry, none offer majors in care for seniors.

This is going to be an issue for congregations in the not-so-distant future. The number of seniors in Canada is growing—people 65 and older are the fastest-growing demographic in the country. At the same time, the number of elder orphans is also increasing. This means two things: those who are without children as they age might consider connecting with a faith community, and faith communities looking for ways to make a difference in their neighbourhoods should start taking this issue more seriously.

June 2016

Welcome to the dark side

In 1610, the famed Italian astronomer Galileo Galilei published a book about the stars and planets he observed in the sky above Padua. Although his homemade telescope was less powerful than most beginners' telescopes sold today, he made some remarkable discoveries about the moon, planets, and the Milky Way. Most people today would have trouble replicating Galileo's ages-old feat, even with modern telescopes—not because the stars and planets are dimmer, but because the earth has become much brighter.

In an article in *The New Yorker* titled "The Dark Side," David Owen notes that a person standing on the observation deck of the Empire State Building in New York City on a cloudless night could not repeat that feat. A person today "would be unable to discern much more than the moon, the brighter planets, and a handful of very bright stars—less than one per cent of what Galileo would have been able to see without a telescope."

Thoughts about Galileo, and about how our view of the heavens has changed over the past 400 years, come to mind this month during Earth Hour. That's when millions of people around the globe turn off unnecessary lights. It got me thinking about the role light plays in religion. Almost all religions use it as metaphor for knowledge, wisdom, justice, and other spiritual ideals and goals. Darkness, on the other hand, has most often been a common metaphor for evil. Since the world's major religions originated before electricity, it's easy to see why light and dark were such important concepts—there was so little light back then. The idea of God as light, piercing and dispersing darkness, would have been immediately understood and appreciated by all.

Today, that image is much less meaningful. If we want light, we simply flick on a switch. We can experience illumination 24 hours a day if we want—something that would have been very difficult, if not impossible, for most people not very long ago. The result? We fail to see light as something special, or even miraculous; it has become just another commonplace thing we take for granted.

If anything, we have too much light these days. The many lights from buildings, streetlights, cars, and other sources in large parts of the developed world has created a condition called "skyglow," the dome of light that appears over major cities and washes out the night sky. This light pollution, as astronomers call it, means that those who study the skies have to go further and further afield to find places dark enough to permit decent stargazing. To see skies like Galileo did, you would have to travel to the Australian outback or the mountains of Peru.

Does this mean that light is no longer a useful metaphor for God or religious understanding? No, but it may have lost some of its power and meaning today. What's so special about light if you can have it whenever you want it? Maybe what we need today is a greater appreciation for something we have so little of—darkness. Instead of looking for God in the light, we need to seek out the dark. Through something like Earth Hour, we can appreciate the dark in a whole new way. Perhaps it is only in great darkness that we can fully see the light.

March 2014

Want to boost girls' self-esteem? Hire more female clergy

In 1990, my church—River East Mennonite Brethren Church in Winnipeg, part of the Canadian Conference of Mennonite Brethren Churches—was the very first church in that denomination in North America to hire a woman to be its lead pastor. At the time, the decision was very controversial, but eventually there was a change of hearts and minds, and it was decided women in the denomination could lead churches. At the time, I was glad for the women who now could follow God's call in their lives to be pastors. Later, when my children were born, it was great to know they were growing up seeing it was normal for women to be clergy—especially my daughter.

Another reason why this is a great idea: seeing women in leadership in religious groups is good for girls' self-esteem. That's the conclusion of a new book entitled *She Preached the Word: Women's Ordination in Modern America* (2018) by Benjamin Knoll of Centre College in Danville, Kentucky, and Cammie Jo Bolin, a PhD candidate at Georgetown University in Washington, DC.

In the book, the authors indicate that research has consistently shown that positive adult role models contribute to the health, education, and overall well-being of young people. This includes learning about gender roles. "When children see a behavior modeled exclusively by men or by women, they internalize that behavior as distinctly masculine or feminine," they say about the world of business, politics, and other places of work, in a press release. "The more children see positions of power occupied only by men, the more they come to think of leadership as an exclusively masculine role." This, they add, can "implicitly generate an association between gender, leadership, and self-confidence."

Knoll and Bolin wondered if what is true in society in general is also true in churches. Does the presence of female church leaders affect the self-worth and empowerment of girls and young women? The answer, they say, is yes. Based on a US-wide survey of churchgoers, "one of our most striking findings is that women who had female congregational leaders in their youth enjoyed higher levels of self-esteem as adults," they say.

What about men? Do they experience less self-esteem if they have a woman as a pastor? Apparently not. "Men who had female congregational leaders frequently growing up have levels of self-esteem that are just as high as those who never had a female pastor or priest," say Knoll and Bolin. Why is this finding about the effect of female church leaders on girls important?

One reason is because "low self-esteem has been linked to higher levels of depression and anxiety as well as lower levels of relationship success, job satisfaction, and motivation for personal improvement." Another is that women whose most influential leaders in church growing up were women are more likely to be employed full-time, and to advance further in university. To the authors, this "strongly suggests" that the lack of women leaders in many churches "is at least partially to blame for the contemporary gender gap" in society. Increasing the proportion of women in pulpits "would not only improve women's psychological well-being, but would also likely help close the gender gap in the workplace and other positions of societal leadership."

If that's the case, then churches have work to do. Research a few years ago in the US by the Barna Group shows that one out of every 11 Protestant pastors is a woman, and that one in five seminary students are female. For religious parents of girls, what might this mean? If you want them to grow up strong and secure, there are many things you can do to encourage them—in and out of religious services. But it might also mean choosing a church or other place of worship where women are given equal access to leadership, including preaching and teaching. It also wouldn't be a bad thing for boys to see that girls can do anything they want, too.

April 2018

"Accidental killers" and cities of refuge

I WAS DRIVING in an unfamiliar part of the city, trying to find an address, when I missed the stop sign. Fortunately, the driver who had the right of way at the three-way stop saw me coming. He put on the brakes. Since it was too late for me to stop, I mouthed the word "sorry!" as I sailed through the intersection. The near accident stayed with me for many days. I imagined hitting the other car broadside, injuring or even killing the other driver. Each time I silently thanked God nothing bad happened.

That experience came back to me when I learned of the tragic death of the eight-year-old boy who was killed while crossing a street in St. Vital on February 13, 2018. My heart went out immediately to the family, and also to the driver. From media reports, it appears to have been an accident. At the time of writing, the driver has not been charged, although police say charges could be laid. Even if there are charges, it's safe to say he or she never set out that morning intending to kill a child.

Why do I feel for the driver? He or she has now become what's known as an "accidental killer," a group none of us wants to belong to. "Accidental killers," like that driver, live with guilt and remorse. Perhaps also with the condemnation and opprobrium from society—possibly without much in the way of help in dealing with the experience.

As author Alice Gregory put it in a riveting article in *The New Yorker* titled "The Sorrow and the Shame of the Accidental Killer," there are self-help books written for almost every human failing, challenge, or inadequacy, but there's nothing for "anyone who has accidentally killed another person. An exhaustive search yielded no research on such people, and nothing in the way of therapeutic protocols, publicly listed support groups, or therapists who specialize in their treatment."

Dr. Jason Ediger, a Winnipeg psychologist who has worked with people who have accidentally killed or injured others, says it isn't a major subject in his profession. "This isn't a specific topic frequently under discussion at present that I'm aware of," he says. "The low numbers of people in one place would make researching a therapy designed specifically for these people quite difficult." I ask him: how do these people cope with what they've done? "They may construct narratives where they were less responsible, they may attempt some effort at penance, they may punish themselves, abuse substances to forget, attempt or complete suicide, withdraw from society and isolate themselves," he says. Some also "try and find meaning in it somehow," but "it is unlikely though that they ever get to a place where they don't regret the outcome or their involvement."

As it turns out, Manitoba Public Insurance does offer financial support so people who cause accidents can get counseling. But the support is not well known. If the person who caused the accident was injured, a case manager would let them know about the service, says MPI spokesperson Brian Smiley. But if they weren't, "they would have to contact" MPI on their own, he says, adding that MPI "relies on brokers" to tell people about various services.

This is not a new issue. In the Hebrew Bible, the people of Israel were instructed by God to designate cities of refuge "so that a slayer who kills a person without intent may flee there" (Numbers 35.11). In these cities, accidental murderers were to be protected from the wrath of family members of the deceased. They could not be harmed. A tribunal would then rule if he or she was eligible for ongoing sanctuary. According to Talmudic commentary, the roads leading to these cities of refuge were to be well marked so those who needed such refuge could find them easily.

In *The New Yorker* article, Maryann Gray, a secular Jew who accidentally killed a child in a car crash, remembers how she felt when she first learned about the cities of refuge. "The Torah was talking about me," she is quoted as saying. "I love that there was a way of recognizing the true devastation that's been wrought, the harm that's been done, without condemning the individual."

I suspect that's what other accidental killers are looking for—a way to live in the world with acceptance, but also with the acknowledgment that something terrible occurred. A place of refuge, in other words.

March 2018

The witches of Winnipeg

I WAS DRIVING home one fine fall day when a sign jumped out at me: Elemental Witchery and Conjure Boutique. Since I travel that stretch of road regularly, I don't know why I hadn't noticed it before. Immediately, I was curious. What is a witchery and conjure boutique? And: there are witches in Winnipeg?

When I contacted owner Dominique Smith, she immediately invited me for a visit. On an unseasonably snowy day in mid-October, I stopped by. After saying I knew nothing about witchcraft, except for the Salem witch trials and Harry Potter, I asked her: What is a witch? "There's no single answer to that question," says Smith, who has been visibly living as one for about a decade. "It's very personal to each person. Some see it as a religion, others as a practice. There's no single body, no head witch or doctrinal group, to give a final answer." All that can be agreed on, she says, is "someone who practices witchcraft is a witch."

For Smith, witchcraft is just like any other religion. "Just because it's not organized, or doesn't have hierarchy or theology, doesn't mean it isn't religious," she says. I wondered why people might want to be witches. For her, the answer is "self-empowerment . . . to be in control of oneself." That's why she was attracted to witchcraft. "I wanted to be in control of my own destiny, not be told what to believe or do."

Witchcraft, Smith went on to say, has traditionally been attractive to people who feel oppressed or subjugated. That's why, she adds, "a majority of witches are women. They know what it is like to have to deal with oppressive structures in society." Smith, who runs the store with her daughter, assured me that witchcraft is not about casting spells on people or trying to do them harm. The kind of magic she promotes is intended to help people become better persons or get ahead in life. For example, the green candles she sells are for getting more money. Blue is for spiritual protection, white is for peace and calm, and red is for love and passion. Smith also sells oils and herbs for use in different ways—things like mandrake, amber, mugwort, and dozens of other plants are lined up in jars behind the counter. Each has "inherent metaphysical qualities."

As for how many witches there are in Winnipeg, "enough to keep me in business," Smith says with a smile, adding nobody actually knows. The majority practice secretly for fear of stigma or even losing their jobs. They are "not out of the broom closet," Smith jokes, adding they come from all walks of life and professions. Many people in the city know a witch, she says. "They just don't know they do," she says.

Smith thinks things are getting better, thanks in part to a more positive portrayal of witches in the media. "Today we are trying to reclaim the term," she says, noting that a few hundred years ago the term "witch" was an accusation that could lead to a death sentence. One way she does that is by teaching classes and hosting a monthly Witch's Coffee Klatch, where people interested in witchcraft gather to talk about magic and conjuring and other things. Due to space, she has to limit the group to 15 people. "I have no problem getting enough," she says, and then concludes, "there's a lot of misunderstanding about witchcraft." Her goal is "to educate people about who we are, break down stigma . . . it's not anything to be afraid of."

October 2019

"I'm ready for flight": Trailblazing Winnipeg pastor chooses MAID

As a pastor, professor, and leader in the Manitoba and Canadian Mennonite Brethren church, former Winnipegger John Regehr was a trailblazer. With encouragement from his wife, Mary, he embraced feminism in the 1950s—long before it became acceptable in the denomination. As a Bible college professor from the '60s to '90s, he promoted an inclusive and accepting kind of Christianity that put him at odds with some of members of the denomination. As pastor, he was open and candid about his personal and theological questions and struggles at a time when people expected church leaders to always be confident and strong.

In light of this, it isn't surprising that Regehr, 93, continued his trailblazing ways when he chose Medical Assistance in Dying (MAID) last November. "He was ready to go," says his son, Rennie, a retired music professor and former first violist with the Winnipeg Symphony Orchestra. "He had lived a full life. He knew it was time."

For John Regehr, a member of the McIvor Mennonite Brethren Church in North Kildonan, the last few years had been difficult. Mary died in 2014. At the age of 90, he needed life-saving heart surgery. The surgery went well, but a few months later he fell and broke his hip. He recovered, continuing to live independently, but over the next few years there were more falls and more trips to emergency.

On October 18, he was admitted to Concordia Hospital with severe pain in his hip. This time it was clear he would never be able to go back home again. "He was exhausted. He had no more projects and didn't want to stay alive for the only purpose of remaining alive," says Rennie. "He didn't want to lie in bed for who knows how long, waiting for death to come." On November 1, he called his children together for a conversation about death. "He asked us if it was OK for him to die," Rennie says. "He wanted our support and blessing."

Regehr's other son, Mark, admits he was taken aback at first. "I was caught off guard when he suggested it," he says. "But I quickly saw his point of view." While finding it hard to hear his request, daughter Jenny was not surprised; her dad had spoken many times about being ready to die. "He had made his mind up," she says.

When Regehr asked medical staff about ways to hasten his dying, they suggested he stop eating—an option that didn't appeal to him. What about MAID; was he eligible? It turned out he was. "His face lit up," Rennie says, remembering his reaction upon hearing he qualified. While the news put Regehr at ease, his family worried his decision might cast a pall over their dad's life of service to the church. As Jenny puts it, she was supportive of her dad's decision but concerned about the reaction of others. "I worried this would define his life's work," she says. But when they saw how convinced he was, they offered their full support.

Since Concordia Hospital doesn't allow MAID, on November 7 Regehr was moved by ambulance to Health Sciences Centre. In his hospital room, Regehr was joined by his family and two pastor friends. Scripture was read and he was asked: "John, can anything separate you from the love of Christ?" He shook his head emphatically and with a strong voice answered: "No!" Then, as Rennie played one of his favourite hymns on the viola, Regehr slipped away.

For Rennie, it was a powerful experience. "To see my Dad surrounded by people who loved him deeply, lovingly participating in a compassionate, painless, and comfortable death was overwhelming. It was wrenching and beautiful all at the same time," he says. Looking back, the children agree MAID was the right thing for their dad. "He was ready to go," says Jenny.

As for the church he served for so long, they say their father wanted his decision to start a discussion in his denomination about death and dying. "When we asked if he wanted us to share this, he said yes," says Jenny. "I saw his decision as the professor giving his last teaching, or the pastor preaching his last sermon," says Mark.

For those who might question Regehr's decision on theological grounds—that only God can decide when someone should die—Rennie says his dad had no doubts. "The inner work had been done long before," he says, noting his dad had spent a lot of time thinking and praying about it. "He had complete trust in a loving and accepting God." Plus, he adds, his dad "felt he had already 'played God' earlier by deciding to have life-saving heart surgery. He felt death had already come calling for him then, but he had not been willing to go."

Before he died, Regehr anticipated some might be critical of his decision based on pro-life grounds. He told his kids that anyone who insisted he should have continued in a "torturous, useless struggle to survive" might not really be pro-life from a caring, compassionate point of view, "but more a slave to that ideology."

Looking back, Rennie says his dad "died in dignity, surrounded by the love of the people he had invited to his passage. He died in a way that was congruent with his theology, with his experience of and with God. And his decision was aligned with who he was as a trailblazer, living slightly ahead of the curve, as a person who thought through issues deeply, and as a person living—and willing to die—by his principles and convictions."

As for Mark, he has decided to honour and remember his father by having something his dad said tattooed on his arm: "My wings are poised. I'm ready for flight." Mark says, "It's what he said when the doctor asked if he was ready to die."

August 2020

Estranged brothers find each other at Pride parade

For 40 years, brothers Peter and Gerhard Thiessen were estranged. Then they found each other, and reconciliation, at a Winnipeg pride parade. The two grew up in a Mennonite church in Manitoba. Their rift began when Gerhard, the younger of the two, came out as gay.

Gerhard had known he was gay since the age of 12, but he kept quiet about it since their church preached anyone who was gay would go to Hell. He desperately wanted to be straight, noting he was "afraid for my soul, and fearing rejection by the church, my family and friends, not to mention the wrath of God and eternal damnation." He remembered the church's pastor condemning anyone who was gay with "venomous" words. "I was shocked and disturbed," Gerhard says. "He was talking about me! I didn't know what to say. I feared what might happen if anyone found out."

Alone and afraid, his thoughts turned to suicide. "If that was the only way to avoid going to Hell, then maybe that was the best course of action for me," he says. In his distress, he approached a church elder for guidance. "I told him I was gay," Gerhard says. "But instead of offering kindness and help, he said I would need to address the congregation and ask forgiveness for having gay thoughts and would need to promise never to act on those thoughts if I wanted to remain a member of this church." This didn't make any sense to Gerhard. He thought: "Wasn't this who I was? Didn't God make me this way? And God didn't make mistakes—right? I wasn't going to confess to the congregation. Instead, I chose to leave the church."

He chose to focus his anger about Christianity at his brother, Peter. "I seemed to be the lightning rod for his anger towards the church," says Peter, who remained a committed churchgoer. But Gerhard's anger didn't bother him; he knew he was right and Gerhard was wrong. "I had God on my side and the Bible made the rules," he says. "It said homosexuality was a choice, and Gerhard would end up in Hell unless he changed his ways."

But in his 50s, Peter began to re-examine his faith and his stance towards the 2SLGBTQ+ community. "I began to rethink a lot of the things I believed in," he says. "One of them was whether people chose to be gay. I realized they didn't. I also realized God loved and accepted people like Gerhard. I knew I needed to reach out and show love and acceptance for him." But Gerhard refused to see him. So Peter wrote a letter of apology for all the hurt he had caused in their lifetime as siblings. Gerhard replied with a letter of his own. "He told me he had never considered me an ally or thought of me as a supportive Christian," Peter says, noting Gerhard found his continued support for the church—the institution that had caused him so much pain—to be very hurtful.

Peter was shocked. "I thought I had been a pretty good Christian all my life, but now I was being evaluated by my brother and had come up very short. I hadn't given any of this a lot of thought, but now I had to," he says. When they eventually did meet, Peter apologized again, but he wanted to do more than just say words; he wanted to put them into action. That's how, in 2019, he came to walk in the Winnipeg Pride parade behind a Mennonite church banner. "At first I didn't think this was a big deal, but as we were marching along people started pointing at the sign and then pointing to us and saying: 'Those are my people!'" Peter says. "It felt freeing and right and I felt proud walking behind a Mennonite sign in the Pride parade."

As Peter walked along, he heard someone call his name from the sidelines. It was Gerhard. He ran into the parade "and gave me the biggest hug I've ever had!" Peter says. "In that moment I felt the weight of those years slip off. The Spirit led me into a whole new world, and it was there I found my brother."

For Gerhard, when he saw Peter in the Pride parade he couldn't believe his eyes. "I never expected to see him there," he says. "When I saw him marching in the parade behind a Mennonite church banner, I was blown away. I was surprised but also very happy. It helped bring to an end a long and painful chapter in my life." He adds, "When we embraced at the parade, it felt wonderful. I had my brother back."

Today Peter attends a Mennonite church that is welcoming of members of the 2SLGBTQ+ community, and Gerhard finds support and acceptance within his own 2SLGBTQ+ community. Now they also have each other.

June 2021

Goalie's decision sparks debate on 2SLGBTQ+ inclusion

Religion can be found everywhere, if you look for it. This includes sports. That's what happened last month when James Reimer, the Manitoba-born goalie for the San Jose Sharks, decided not to wear an 2SLGBTQ+ Pride jersey before a hockey game on March 18. In refusing to wear the jersey—intended as a statement by the NHL to show that everyone, including 2SLGBTQ+ people, is welcome in hockey—Reimer cited his religious beliefs. "In this specific instance, I am choosing not to endorse something that is counter to my personal convictions, which are based on the Bible, the highest authority in life," he said in a statement posted that day.

He went on to say he has a "personal faith in Jesus Christ who died on the cross for my sins and, in response, asks me to love everyone and follow him. I have no hate in my heart for anyone, and I have always strived to treat everyone that I encounter with respect and kindness." He added that he strongly believes "that every person has value and worth, and the LGBTQIA+ community, like all others, should be welcomed in all aspects of the game of hockey."

Reimer developed those convictions in his Evangelical Mennonite Conference (EMC) church in his hometown of Morweena, Manitoba, located 140 kilometres north of Winnipeg. That made me wonder: what does that denomination say about 2SLGBTQ+ inclusion? As it turns out, there is nothing about it in its denominational statement of faith, although the group does regard marriage as being only between a man and a woman. But Reimer wasn't asked to weigh in on same-sex marriage; just on whether members of that community would be welcome in hockey. Which also made me wonder: would 2SLGBTQ+ people be welcome in EMC churches?

The answer is "absolutely yes," says the denomination's executive director, Tim Dyck, adding that everyone is welcome to be part of that group—although they draw the line at performing same-sex weddings. If that's the case, then maybe Reimer could have spared himself all the public relations grief by just wearing the jersey. From what I can tell, it wouldn't have put him offside with the denomination.

One of the hallmarks of the EMC denomination is a commitment to pacifism. It's right there in its statement of faith: "We believe in the life of peace. We are called to walk in the steps of the Lamb of God, the Prince of Peace. Everything about his life, his teachings, and his redemptive death on the cross, summons us to a life of nonviolence. As Christians committed to love and nonviolence, we may not participate in or support anything that will violate this life of peace." While Reimer said he can't wear a Pride jersey because of his religious convictions, he doesn't appear to have any problem wearing jerseys that celebrate the military. In fact, you can buy a "James Reimer San Jose Sharks Adidas Authentic Military Appreciation Practice Jersey (Camo)" at the team's online hockey store. An online search pulls up a 2015 photo of Reimer wearing a military-style jersey at a military appreciation night with members of the Canadian Armed Forces when he was a member of the Toronto Maple Leafs.

Maybe I'm being too hard on Reimer. Few of us are perfectly consistent when it comes to the ways in which we live out our religious beliefs. We all have done and said things that don't line up with the things we were taught in our places of worship. We are all tempted to cherry-pick the verses that line up with our way of thinking and ignore others that don't. People also change; it could be Reimer no longer agrees with the principle of pacifism he was raised with.

When it comes to 2SLGBTQ+ inclusion, religion is being invoked by many people as a reason to exclude members of that community from full welcome and fellowship. Those discussions normally play out on the faith page, or sometimes in other parts of the paper. Rarely do you find them in the sports section, but thanks to Reimer, it's become a sports story, too.

April 2023

Prosperity gospel no guarantee of success or long life

MANY YEARS AGO, when I was in my late teens, a much-loved youth pastor in my hometown was diagnosed with an aggressive form of cancer. Together with others, we prayed for him to be healed. Oh, how we prayed! Fervently, devotedly, as individuals and in groups. We prayed how we had been taught: to claim victory over the dreaded disease in the name of Jesus, believing if we said the right things in the right way our prayers would produce a miracle. And then he died.

Upon hearing the news, I was devastated and confused. Hadn't I been taught the Bible promised health and healing for believers? That Jesus promised abundant life for Christians—not just in heaven, but here on earth, too? That God answered prayers if people had enough faith? It was a tough and challenging time for me. My belief system was rocked. Things didn't turn out the way I had been told. I had to figure out a new way to live as a person of faith in the world. I didn't realize it at the time, but what I had been taught was a prosperity gospel—the belief that it's God's will for Christians to be happy, healthy, and wealthy. All I had to do was "name it and claim it."

I haven't believed that way for a very long time. Over the years I've learned that life is unpredictable, uncertain, and messy, but those who go to Springs Church in Winnipeg still follow a prosperity gospel. Leon Fontaine, Springs' long-time pastor who passed away on November 19, was one of its most popular preachers. In sermons and video messages he said things like: "God has promised us health and healing. That's a fact . . . I've witnessed incredible instantaneous miracles take place, and I've also watched people walk out miraculous recovery from everything from plantar warts to terminal cancer." No matter what you're facing, he said, "the truth remains that you can walk in God's promises of health and healing!"

Fontaine asked in another message: "What if I told you that God doesn't want you to be sick? Many Christians have been taught that whatever happens in their life is God's will. In other words, if one person is healthy and the other is sick—it's God's will. But if you look in the Bible, you'll see that's actually not true." God's will, he preached, was not for people to be "poor, sick, and hurting . . . when the Bible says 'for by grace are ye saved by faith.' The word saved doesn't just mean saved from hell. It means saved from sickness, saved from poverty, saved from early deaths." God's plan was to save Christians from sickness and disease, he said. His grace would keep them healthy and protected "until old age"—as long as people had enough faith and trained their minds to think only positive thoughts. No negative thoughts!

Then Fontaine died suddenly at 59 from cancer. How will people at Springs respond? His passing might prompt some uncomfortable questions for his followers, such as: was what he taught wrong? If Fontaine could die young from cancer, a disease he said God would cure people from, was it all a lie? If it wasn't a lie, here's a troubling thought: did Fontaine not believe what he preached? Or did he not have enough faith to get his own miracle? If a man so close to God couldn't get healed, what hope is there for others? Finally, can this God Fontaine preached about be trusted? For some, his death could prompt a crisis of faith.

Former Winnipegger Kate Bowler is a cancer survivor and author of the book *Blessed: A History of the American Prosperity Gospel* (2013). She acknowledges its appeal, especially when she was in the depth of her cancer treatments. The prosperity gospel, she says, "offers people a guarantee: Follow these rules, and God will reward you, heal you, restore you." But life doesn't always work out that way, she notes. And when it doesn't, followers of the prosperity gospel can suffer doubly.

"Shame compounds the grief," she says, noting they not only feel grief over the loss of a loved one, they also feel guilty because they weren't able to pull them through—a guilt they need to live with for the rest of their lives. "Those who are loved and lost are just that—those who have lost the test of faith," she says.

To be clear, I don't think Fontaine was a fake or a charlatan. I don't think he was preying on the hopes and dreams of others. I believe he sincerely believed what he was preaching. From the tributes pouring in, he sounded like a caring and devoted pastor, husband, father, and friend. But the fact of the matter is there are no guarantees in life. Christians get cancer, too. Sometimes they survive it, sometimes they don't. Sometimes they get a good job, sometimes they are passed over for promotion. Sometimes someone they love dies, sometimes they don't. There is no "gospel," prosperity or otherwise, that offers a formula that works every time for every situation. Or, as Bowler puts it, "there is no cure to being human; finitude is going to be part of this deal . . . at some point, we must say to ourselves, 'I'm going to need to let go.'"

January 2023

God, faith, and tornados

"My little girl asked me, 'Why would God let this happen?'" That's what the Rev. Wes Fowler, senior pastor of First Baptist Church in Mayfield, Kentucky, said after a terrible tornado hit the town in December 2021. He looked at the eight-year-old and said, "I don't know." The tornado, one of the most devastating in the US in recent times, travelled over 250 kilometres through several states, killing 90 people.

Struggling to find meaning and purpose in storms has been a human obsession for probably as long as there have been humans and storms. This includes religious questions, like the one asked by Fowler's daughter. After the Kentucky tornado, I looked to see what people were saying about God and storm and I came across the book *Tornado God: American Religion and Violent Weather* (2020).

I contacted the author, Peter J. Thuesen, a professor of religious studies at Indiana University and Purdue University in Indianapolis. He told me his goal with the book was to explore the relationship between natural disasters and how humans have interpreted their meaning over the ages—with a special focus on the US. In America, which has more tornados than any other nation, storms have prompted a lot of theological reflection about the nature of God, some by the earliest settlers, the Puritans, who often saw them as judgements from God.

As they pushed west, American settlers encountered more fearsome weather. Two major tornados, in Mississippi in 1840 and in Missouri in 1896, prompted a lot of religious soul searching on a national level. The Mississippi storm—called "the Great Natchez tornado"—was seen by some as a sign of the end times, while one minister wrote it was a sign that God was rebuking the sins of the nation.

What they didn't question was the cause. For most it was a matter of divine providence—just as God delivered blessings, God could also cause great storms. Presbyterian theologian Charles Hodge defended this idea in the 1850s by saying it was his "secure conviction that a sparrow cannot fall, nor a sinner move a finger, but as God permits and ordains." Over time, some American church leaders came to espouse a more benign view of God and a more naturalistic view of storms, especially as science began to understand and explain what caused them.

Even if science can explain what causes a tornado to form, people still can't but wonder why it hits where it does—why one home is totally destroyed while another across the street is left standing. Despite the destruction caused by tornados, and their seemingly random and capricious nature, many Christians still see God's hand behind them. "If people believe in a God who controls everything, including the weather, what other explanation could there be but that there's a plan behind it?" Thuesen says.

This is an especially active discussion in the US Bible belt, which overlaps with the geographical area known as Tornado Alley. While some might see this as ironic, many Christians who live there view it as an illustration of faith being tested time and again and emerging victorious. When I told Thuesen he must have received lots of calls from the media about religion and tornadoes, he replied I was the only one. That made him wonder if the growing secularization of America is leading to less theological reflection on events like natural disasters.

What any kind of storm shows, he says, are the "chronic moral failings" in America today—racial and economic inequalities are often exposed by storms which impact poor and marginalized people harder, With every year seeing more storms in the US due to climate change, this will become a more significant issue in the years ahead, he adds.

In the end, tornados remain "an insolvable theological problem" for many faithful, Thuesen says, adding even scientists still regard them as mysterious. As Howard Bluestein, a leading tornado researcher put it, tornados are "one of the last frontiers of atmospheric science."

For Thuesen, tornados raise "age-old puzzles about the origins of the natural world and humans' place in it," adding that questions about the role of the divine in the storms still remain for many people of faith in the US a question found "in the whirlwind."

January 2022

"Who are you to put limits on the love of God?"

The parents reached out to me. They wanted to tell their story about their journey with a trans child. They are long-time members of an evangelical church, one that is theologically conservative when it comes to marriage and 2SLGBTQ+ inclusion and affirmation. They requested anonymity; they still aren't sure who they can tell, or how their church will respond to them. I will call them Barb and Thomas; I'll call their child Sam.

Sam is in their early 20s, a young adult, the eldest of four children in the family. (Sam prefers neutral pronouns.) Since about the age of 14, Sam knew something felt different—they didn't feel like the female gender they had been assigned at birth. They kept quiet for a long time, not telling anyone, not even their parents. Then, a few years ago, they went to their parents to tell their story. "Sam came into the room one night to talk to us," says Barb. "'I need to tell you something," they said. "'I'm trans.'"

While taken by surprise, Barb and Thomas assured Sam they loved them. "We had decided years ago there was nothing our children would do that would end our love for them," Barb says. "Including this." Barb remembers praying that night after Sam broke the news. "I told God I didn't know what to do with this," she says. "I told God I loved my child and I loved God. I said if it's a phase, help us all get through it well. If it isn't, help me make sense of it, since it goes against everything I have been taught at church. I asked God to give me wisdom and clarity. And that I was always willing to learn and be open to new things." For Thomas, it was hard to identify with Sam's experience. "But I could identify with their pain," he says.

Sam wanted surgery to remove their breasts, but Barb and Thomas asked them to slow down a bit. Ultimately, they agreed it was best, as was the process of officially changing their name from a female to a male name. While now happy for Sam, Thomas admits he also "grieved the end of my daughter." Yet he and Barb constantly told Sam "We loved them, that there was nothing they could do that would change that love for them."

Thinking back on the experience, Barb now realizes Sam was in pain for a long time before they told their parents. "I'm sorry they didn't feel they could tell us earlier," she says. But she understands how hard it was for Sam. They didn't know if their parents might reject them due to the family being part of a denomination that didn't allow discussion about supporting 2SLGBTQ+ rights and same-sex marriage.

For Barb, who is a lay leader in her church, this is a challenge. What can she tell her pastor? "I want to be honest, but I don't know what the reaction will be," she says. This could include being asked to step down from her leadership position—which she is OK with, if it comes to that. If Barb and Thomas have to leave their church because of Sam, that will be hard. "But increasingly we just don't feel we fit in our church or denomination anymore," she says.

Sam has already made the move to an affirming church in their city. "I knew I needed a church, a place where I could be accepted for who I am, where people would celebrate joys with me like my new birth certificate, or how happy I was after my top surgery," Sam says. "Those were fantastic days, and I wanted to share those things with my church." Being part of an affirming church brings them a lot of joy. "When I saw my name in the directory, my new name, it made me so happy," Sam says. "That's me!"

When asked what churches can do to support trans people, Sam says: "I just needed someone to talk to, someone to listen to me, to hear what I was going through, to hear where my pain was, where my joy was," they say. When asked what they would say to people who believe what they did was wrong, Sam says: "Who are you to put limits on the love of God? How do you know where God's love ends? Everyone is loved by God. We are all fearfully and wonderfully made. Including me."

Today, Sam's parents are at peace about Sam's decision. "I believe God created us and loves us and wants to be in a relationship with us. That means all of us, including Sam," says Thomas. As for why they are sharing their story, Barb says it's because "we want anyone else having this experience, no matter what their church or denomination, to know they aren't alone."

June 2023

9
FAITHCETERA

The mensch of Malden Mills

When Aaron Feuerstein's textile mill in Lawrence, Massachusetts, burned down in 1995, he could have taken the $300 million in insurance money and walked away into a comfortable retirement. But he didn't. What happened next has been described as incomprehensible in the world of business in the US.

The then-70-year-old told his 3,000 workers that not only would he rebuild the factory—he would pay them for doing nothing until it was finished, and then bring them back to work when it was done. It was a huge decision, costing him more than $25 million in wages and benefits. But it got the mill up and running again, manufacturing Polartec, a highly regarded lightweight thermal material.

The response to Feuerstein's decision was overwhelming. The media lauded him. He was named Person of the Week by ABC News and called "a saint for the 90s" and "the best boss in America" by NBC News. Then-president Bill Clinton invited him to be a guest of honour at a State of the Union address. His actions also earned him the sobriquet the "Mensch of Malden Mills," *mensch* being a Yiddish word for a stand-up kind of guy.

While some considered him a saint, others thought him a fool. They thought he should have taken the money and walked away, or else used the fire as a chance to move the factory to another part of the country or world where labour costs are cheaper. But that wasn't an option for Feuerstein, an observant Jew, who says his core values derive from his faith. In an interview, he said that his religious ideals played the major role in his decision. He quoted the first-century Talmudic scholar Hillel: "In a situation where there is no righteous person, try to be a righteous person." And: "Not all who increase their wealth are wise." Plus, he said, his workers were "depending upon me. The community was depending upon me. My customers were depending upon me. And my family."

In other words, with so many watching to see how he would respond, he had no choice but to do what he believed was the right thing, and his knowledge of what was right was derived from his faith. Make no mistake; Feuerstein didn't pay all those wages just because he felt sorry for his employees. He did it because he was a shrewd businessman. He knew it would take time to rebuild the factory, and that if it was closed for too long they would need to find other work. If he was to get back up and running again, he would need them to come back. He wasn't against layoffs and downsizing, however; a few years after the fire, he closed a money-losing division, moving many employees to jobs elsewhere in the company or providing re-training or employment counselling. Of his fame, Feuerstein was ambivalent. "It speaks poorly for society that standards have decreased to the point that I'm considered superb," he said. "If the average CEO did what he ought to do, I wouldn't be receiving such acclaim."

It was a heartwarming story, but it didn't have a fairy-tale ending—you know, the kind where good people like Aaron Feuerstein do the right thing and everything turns out perfectly in the end. In the early 2000s, Malden Mills filed for Chapter 11 protection; it struggled to service its debt from rebuilding and suffered from losing its market share after the fire. Which raised an interesting question: is there no connection between doing the right thing, according to your religious beliefs, and business success?

In an issue of the *The Marketplace*, a magazine for Christians in business published by Mennonite Economic Development Associates, editor Wally Kroeker reflected on his own family's experience in business. He noted there is "no guaranteed connection between faithfulness and financial success. It was a matter of simple observation that some fine Christians lost their shirts, while some scoundrels seemed to have the Midas Touch . . . I believe God is the author of all good, but how that good is apportioned here on Earth remains the stuff of mystery."

If that's the case, it's still good to be known as a mensch—like the mensch of Malden Mills.

November 2003

Communion on the moon

THE DEATH OF astronaut Neil Armstrong on August 24, 2012, prompted many to recall the first moon mission. But one thing that hasn't come up in recent media coverage is the story of the first communion on the moon, conducted by Armstrong's fellow Apollo 11 astronaut Buzz Aldrin.

It happened on July 20, 1969, the day that Armstrong and Aldrin landed on the moon. Aldrin, an elder in the Presbyterian Church, performed the short communion ceremony, also called The Lord's Supper. "This is the pilot," Aldrin said into his microphone, "I'd like to take this opportunity to ask every person listening in, whoever and wherever they may be, to pause for a moment and contemplate the events of the past few hours and to give thanks in his or her own way." Aldrin then served himself communion, using a kit provided by the pastor of Webster Presbyterian Church in Houston, Texas.

In 1970, Aldrin wrote of the experience. "I opened the little plastic packages which contained the bread and the wine. I poured the wine into the chalice our church had given me. In the one-sixth gravity of the moon, the wine slowly curled and gracefully came up the side of the cup. Then I read the Scripture, 'I am the vine, you are the branches. Whosoever abides in me will bring forth much fruit.' I ate the tiny Host and swallowed the wine. I gave thanks for the intelligence and spirit that had brought two young pilots to the Sea of Tranquility. It was interesting for me to think: the very first liquid ever poured on the moon, and the very first food eaten there, were the communion elements."

According to a 2009 story in the *Washington Post*, Aldrin had hoped that NASA would broadcast the service worldwide. But the space agency decided against it because of a lawsuit filed (and later dismissed) by atheist Madalyn Murray O'Hair after Apollo 8 astronauts read from Genesis while orbiting the moon at Christmas. Later, Aldrin told an interviewer that "if I had it to do over again, I would not choose to celebrate communion. Although it was a deeply meaningful experience for me, it was a Christian sacrament, and we had come to the moon in the name of all mankind—be they Christians, Jews, Muslims, animists, agnostics, or atheists." However, at the time, he said, "I could think of no better way to acknowledge the enormity of the Apollo 11 experience than by giving thanks to God."

The small chalice Aldrin used for the wine went back to Webster Church. Each year on the Sunday closest to July 20 the congregation celebrates what it calls Lunar Communion. Aldrin wasn't the only person to have a religious experience in space. Astronaut Frank Borman, who read from the book of Genesis while orbiting Earth, later said, "I had an enormous feeling that there had to be a power greater than any of us—that there was a God, that there was indeed a beginning." James Irwin, who walked on the moon in 1971, described the lunar mission as a revelation. "I felt the power of God as I'd never felt it before," he said. John Glenn—the first American in space—said about his view from the spaceship: "To look out at this kind of creation and not believe in God is to me impossible."

Glenn's comments might have been made in response to the purported comment from the first man in space—Soviet Yuri Gagarin. It was widely reported that Gagarin, who died in 1968, stated during his flight that he didn't see God in space. However, no record of those comments exist, and his friend, Valentin Petrov, stated that the quote originated from a speech by Soviet leader Nikita Khrushchev. In fact, says Petrov, Gagarin was a baptized member of the Orthodox Church and reportedly told his friend that nobody can go to space and "not have God in his mind and his heart."

As for Armstrong himself, in keeping with the way he maintained a steadfast private life, it is not known if he was religious. But he did say that "mystery creates wonder, and wonder is the basis of man's desire to understand."

October 2012

Christianity and the Great War

The year 2014 was the 100th anniversary of the start of the Great War. It was marked in many ways—historically, politically, militarily, culturally. But little was said about the role Christianity played in the conflict.

That gap is filled by Philip Jenkins, author of *The Great and Holy War: How World War I Became a Religious Crusade* (2015). According to Jenkins, a history professor at Baylor University in Texas, we can't comprehend the Great War until we understand the role religion played in creating and sustaining it. Religion, he writes, is central to "understanding the war, to understanding why people went to war, what they hoped to achieve through war, and why they stayed at war."

The War, he notes, was a "thoroughly religious event in the sense that overwhelmingly Christian nations fought each other in what many viewed as a holy war, a spiritual conflict." In the book, he shows how politicians and the military used religion on both sides to support the conflict, using the language of holy war: crusade, martyrdom, apocalypse, and Armageddon. There were even angels. The War was framed by belligerents on both sides "in thoroughly Christian terms. Each nation saw itself as playing a predestined role that was divinely inspired, and those self-concepts contributed mightily to the outbreak of war," Jenkins says.

On all sides, clergy baptized the struggle, becoming "vocal, even fanatical, advocates." This included the Anglican bishop of London, who said in 1915: "Everyone that loves freedom and honour . . . are banded in a great crusade—we cannot deny it—to kill Germans; to kill them, not for the sake of killing, but to save the world; to kill the good as well as the bad, to kill the young as well as the old . . . to kill them lest the civilisation of the world itself be killed." Or the chaplain to the Speaker of the British House of Commons, who proclaimed that "to kill Germans is a divine service in the fullest acceptance of the word."

In Germany, people felt the same way—but from the other side. As Roger Chickering notes in his book *Imperial Germany and the Great War, 1914–18* (2014), "no sector of the population was more ardent a supporter of the war than the German Protestant Church . . . The fact that France was Catholic and Russia Orthodox supported the belief that Germany was fighting in the name of true—Protestant—Christianity and that the triumph of Germany corresponded to the designs of God." Religion was recruited to the war effort in the US, too. Americans were told that God was summoning them to war against Germany. As evangelist Billy Sunday put it, the War was not just "Germany against America," but "hell against heaven."

Comments like those are uncomfortable for many twenty-first-century ears. They sound more like what we are accustomed to hearing from religious terrorists. But sentiments like these were regularly shared from pulpits in the warring nations in an effort to keep support for the war high. Christian religion also impacted by the end of the war. Churches mirrored the enthusiasm of the general population at the start. But things changed for many when the terrible cost of the catastrophe was known. After such a calamity, who could believe in a loving and generous God anymore?

As Jeremy Paxman notes in his book, *Great Britain's Great War* (2014), soldiers on both sides found their faith tested. "What room was there for religion when those made in God's image were being blown to pieces all around? How could hell be any worse than what they were living through?"

In addition to shaping the war, Christian religion was also shaped by it. The War triggered "a global religious revolution," Jenkins says, and in the process "drew the world's religious map as we know it today." This redrawing of the map included the fall of the Ottoman Empire, which led, says Jenkins, to the "assertive, self-confident, and aggressively sectarian" form of Islam we know today. It also led eventually to the creation of the state of Israel, since Britain was granted control of the region under the League of Nations Mandate for Palestine in 1920, and then publicly committed itself to the creation of a Jewish homeland. This action still reverberates today.

Jenkins' book is a timely reminder of how often religion is recruited to justify and support war. Or, as he terms it, of "how easily ideas of the church militarist emerge in times of crisis." It is also a reminder to Christians that it wasn't so long ago that fanatical religious fervor and language we associate with Islamic extremists today—and condemn—was preached with welcome and praise from many church pulpits.

August 2014

Sermon on the mound: Baseball as a road to God

BASEBALL IS ALMOST back! Opening day for 2014 is March 31, although a few northern ballparks might be a little chilly. The sport's return suggests that winter, at long last, has really been vanquished, even if the evidence outside our windows in Manitoba suggests otherwise. Its return inspires a sense of hope, renewal and new beginnings—which sounds sort of religious, in a way.

In fact, for many people, baseball is a religion. It has all the religious elements: a creation story (replete with dissenting views about how this "faith" really started), falls from grace, redemption, prophets, heretics, deities, icons, rituals, holy books, temples, worship, miracles, sacrifice, miracles, saviours, and sinners. There's even a Vatican-like place called the Baseball Hall of Fame, where "worshippers" can view holy relics, venerate the saints, and re-live the great moments of the faith. As Susan Sarandon's character says in the movie *Bull Durham*: "I believe in the church of baseball. I've tried all the major religions and most of the minor ones . . . and the only church that feeds the soul, day in, day out, is the church of baseball."

William Herzog and Christopher Evans, who teach at Colgate Divinity School in Rochester, New York, seem to agree. The two are editors of the book *The Faith of 50 Million: Baseball, Religion, and American Culture* (2002) a collection of essays that "plumb how baseball illuminates significant patterns of faith and meaning." "People are incurably religious," says Herzog in an interview for *SFGATE.com*. "We have to have some form of religion, and for some people it's baseball. It's only a game, but it has elements that point beyond."

The book's foreword is by theologian Stanley Hauerwas, a baseball fan and professor at Duke Divinity School. He really brings it home for this Mennonite church member when he notes that "being a Cubs' fan and a pacifist are closely linked; namely, both commitments teach you that life is not about winning."

Someone else who sees a link between baseball and religion is John Sexton, President of New York University and author of the book *Baseball as a Road to God: Seeing Beyond the Game* (2013). Sexton, a Yankees fan, decided to combine his interest in religion and baseball into a course at New York University. Also called "Baseball as a Road to God," it's a way to "get students to think about things that they see as mundane in a rich and nuanced way, and to do that through the trigger of something they see as an oxymoron," he says. By using something familiar—baseball—he hopes to help students see the world in a different way, a way that "adds to the richness of your experience of everything in the world." As for baseball itself, Sexton sees that as a metaphor for a rich spiritual life—in baseball, time passes more slowly than in the real world, and since it doesn't use a clock, it could go on forever.

Books on the reading list for Sexton's course include *Shoeless Joe* and *The Iowa Baseball Confederacy* by W.P. Kinsella, *The Natural* by Bernard Malamud, and *The Universal Baseball Association Inc., J. Henry Waugh, Prop.* by Robert Coover. For Sexton, "baseball evokes in the life of its faithful the features we associate with the spiritual life: faith and doubt, conversion, blessings and curses, miracles, and so on. For some, baseball really is a road to God." He admits that, for many—especially for those who aren't religious—baseball is not a spiritual experience. "But if given sensitive attention, it can awaken us to a dimension of life often missing in our contemporary world of hard facts and hard science," he says. "We can learn, through baseball, to experience life more deeply."

March 2014

When Christianity was weird

"ANY RELIGION IS, by definition, crazy to a non-believer." That aphorism was coined by Jeffrey Weiss, formerly a religion reporter at *The Dallas Morning News*. Dubbed Weiss' law, it explains how weird other religions can look to people who are not a part of those faiths—while people inside those belief systems see their world view as completely normal.

I thought about Weiss' law while perusing Larry Hurtado's most recent book, *Destroyer of the Gods: Early Christian Distinctiveness in the Roman World* (2017). Because Christianity has been around so long, and so many people around the world believe it, it seems normal. But there was a time when the religion was considered strange and weird, Hurtado argues. Before Constantine made Christianity the religion of his empire, the new religion was seen as "distinctive, odd, even dangerous in the eyes of some of that time." It was not only weird to the ancient Romans, but also repugnant. "There is a group, hated for their abominations, called Christians," wrote the historian Tacticus. Added another historian, Suetonius: "The Christians are a class of men given to a new and wicked superstition." Said a third, Lucian: "The poor wretches have convinced themselves they are going to be immortal and live for all time."

What were these superstitions and abominations? The idea that a man could die and rise from the dead, of course. The practice of the Eucharist also caused concern—to the Romans, eating Christ's flesh and blood sounded like cannibalism. But there were other reasons, too. Christianity was seen as a threat to the state. By refusing to acknowledge the primacy of the emperor, as adherents of other religions did, Christians appeared disloyal and threatened the stability and legitimacy of the Roman Empire. The new faith also upended behavioral norms. Christians were expected to live by high moral standards—men, for example, were required to be faithful to their wives at a time when it was widely accepted they could have one or more mistresses.

Another radical idea was how Christianity based its identity not on ethnicity or nationality but on a shared religious belief. As well, the new faith elevated the role of women, and rejected practices of giving daughters as child brides. The result was that life for the earliest Christians was very difficult. "Becoming a Christian held no social or economic advantage," writes Hurtado. "Those who wanted to aspire for upward social mobility would have been advised to give Christianity a pass."

How Christianity was once viewed can be instructive for Christians in the West today, Hurtado goes on. "Christianity is no longer the socially dominant force that it once was. Christians are again one kind of religiousness among many others. So, actually, it may well be those Christians and texts of the first three centuries that will be the most instructive about how to live out Christian faith in these circumstances."

Instead of bemoaning the plight of the Christian faith in the secular West, as some are inclined to do, maybe it is better to look back—way back—to a time when Christianity wasn't the dominant force in the world, back to a time when it was just weird. Hurtado's book is a good place to start.

July 2017

Can even Nazis be forgiven? A World War Two story

I STILL FEEL sorry for Mr. Thiessen, all these years later. It couldn't have been easy trying to teach Sunday school to a rambunctious group of junior high boys back in the late 1960s. What made it harder was that we liked to try to stump the teacher with hard questions. One of our favourites was about Hitler. Mr. Thiessen liked to tell us that God loved and offered forgiveness to everyone who asked for it. So, we wanted to know, what if Hitler had asked forgiveness—would he go to heaven, too?

I don't remember what Mr. Thiessen said. But I now know that Christian forgiveness was indeed extended to 21 of the top Nazis prosecuted during the famous Nuremberg trials in 1945—and that four of them took it. This summer I read *Mission At Nuremberg: An American Army Chaplain and the Trial of the Nazis* (2014) by Tim Townsend. The book is about US Army chaplain Henry Gerecke and how he ministered to some of the worst criminals in history.

Before the war, Gerecke was a Lutheran pastor in Missouri. During the war, he served US troops in England and Europe. Since he spoke German, when the war ended he was ordered to Nuremberg, along with Roman Catholic chaplain Sixtus O'Connor, to be a pastor to the 16 Protestant German defendants. O'Connor served the Catholics.

Why did the victorious allies offer spiritual support to Nazis? The Geneva Convention was the main reason. According to the Convention, prisoners of war were entitled to perform religious duties, such as attending worship services, and to be served by ministers of religion. After the war, Gerecke admitted he was terrified of the prospect of being so close to men who had committed such horrific crimes. He had seen American soldiers killed and wounded by the German military. He has also visited the death camps. But he also knew that, as a "representative of an all-loving Father," he needed to go so the prisoners could "be told about the Saviour bleeding, suffering and dying on the cross for them." Along with ministering to the prisoners, Gerecke and O'Connor helped their families, many of whom were destitute.

The book records time Gerecke spent with Fritz Sauckel, chief of slave labour recruitment. Each time the two men met they ended their time kneeling on the floor of the cell in prayer. "Many times, Sauckel asked for God's mercy . . . and called himself a sinner." Before he was executed, Sauckel asked for communion. After the trial, Gerecke wrote that he believed that Sauckel, minister of the interior Wilhelm Frick, foreign minister Joachim von Ribbentrop and Wilhelm Keitel of the German high command, died "as penitent sinners trusting God's mercy for forgiveness." Hermann Goering, head of the German air force, also asked for communion prior to committing suicide. Gerecke refused, not believing he was sincere.

Among the remarkable stories told in the book is the time a rumour circulated that Gerecke would be transferred home because his wife, Alma, whom he had not seen in over two years, wanted him back. One of the defendants wrote her a letter, pleading with Alma to let her husband stay. "Please consider that we cannot miss your husband now," he wrote. "During the past months he has shown us uncompromising friendliness of such a kind that he has become indispensable for us." All the defendants signed it. Gerecke stayed.

According to Townsend, the chaplains believed "that God loves all human beings, including perpetrators, and so their decision [to accept the assignment] was more about how to minister to the Nazis, not whether they should." He adds: "The process of ministering to those who have committed evil involves returning the wrongdoer to goodness . . . for Gerecke and O'Connor that challenge meant using what they had learned about each defendant to spiritually lead him back from the place where he had fallen to a place of restoration." They were attempting to bring "God's light into a dark heart" by giving "Hitler's henchmen new standing as human beings before their impending executions."

Near the end of the book, Townsend wonders if it was really the place of Gerecke and O'Connor to offer forgiveness, especially to men who had committed such cruelty against Jews. "What right does anyone other than those who died in the Holocaust have to forgive anyone" who was part of that Holocaust? The Christian concept of forgiveness "must be strained by the idea of genocide," he adds.

Gerecke, who died in 1961, likely wouldn't have seen it that way, Townsend writes. Those "monsters" at Nuremberg would have been seen by him as men in need of salvation and forgiveness, who needed someone to minister to them: "The Nuremberg chaplains' one single burden was to return these children of God from darkness to the good of their own light."

August 2014

Descendants of Holocaust survivors contemplate "God, faith, and identity from the ashes"

In 2015, Oskar Gröning, the "accountant of Auschwitz," was found guilty of 300,000 charges of accessory to murder. His trial is considered to be one of the last trials of the Nazis who perpetrated the Holocaust.

Already, most who experienced the Holocaust are dead; soon, all will be gone. But the children and grandchildren of Holocaust survivors remain. Their experiences are captured in *God, Faith & Identity from the Ashes: Reflections of Children and Grandchildren of Holocaust Survivors* (2015), a new book edited by Menachem Z. Rosensaft.

In the book, 88 children and grandchildren of survivors share how the Holocaust shaped them theologically, politically, culturally and in terms of their identity, education, and careers. Although none of them experienced the Holocaust first-hand, all were deeply affected by it. "We did not see our families murdered, we were never cold, we were never starved, we were never beaten," says Rosensaft, a child of two survivors. "We grew up in comfort. And yet what we do have, what sets us apart, is that we grew up with our parents and grandparents. We absorbed their stories firsthand."

The book is divided into four sections: God and Faith, Identity, A Legacy of Memory, and Changing the World for the Better. In the first section, the writers reflect on how the Holocaust affected their faith. Some choose to believe in God, while some dismiss completely the idea of a loving or caring God. Others have landed somewhere in between.

Eric Nelson's grandfather lost his parents and two brothers in the concentration camps, yet he kept his faith in God. "It strikes me that, for all my doubts and questions, if my grandfather can go on thanking the God of Israel . . . then surely I ought to consider doing so as well," the Harvard professor writes.

"God was not present in the survivor's home in which I grew up," writes Israeli artist Aliza Olmert. "The missing niche of faith was filled by a socialist worldview and uplifting patriotism."

"Both the God of consolation and the accusation against God live within me," says Rabbi Moshe Waldoks.

Notes former *The New York Times* reporter Joseph Berger: "What God's culpability or at least responsibility was remains a mystery that I'll never resolve."

While reading the book, one thing I found unexpectedly moving was how so many children of survivors grew up without any relatives—in Rosensaft's case, both his parents' entire immediate families were murdered. Similarly, Waldoks writes: "Like many children of survivors, I have been haunted by faceless phantoms of dozens and dozens of aunts, uncles, and cousins."

Growing up, Karen Friedman realized her family was different from her friends. "Their family dynamics and experiences were just different from the rest of ours," writes Friedman, a grandchild of survivors. "I was always aware that my mother never knew what it was like to have grandparents."

In 1984, Elie Wiesel, who survived both Auschwitz and Buchenwald, delivered the keynote address at the first conference for children of Holocaust survivors. "It was you that the enemy sought to destroy," he said. "We were only the instruments. You were the enemy's obsession. In murdering Jews, he wished to prevent you from being born." It would have been natural and logical for their parents to turn their back on the world, "to have opted for nihilism," he went on to say. "And yet we have chosen you."

Now, as the last trials of Nazis are held and the few remaining survivors pass away, these chosen ones have the task of preserving the memory of their parents and grandparents for future generations. "A generation will soon come of age having never heard firsthand testimony from a living Holocaust survivor," says Rosensaft. "The preservation and transfer of memory is the most critical mission that children and grandchildren of survivors must undertake."

The stories in *God, Faith & Identity from the Ashes* show that many of them are taking that mission seriously.

July 2015

Of saints and sacrifice: The story of the English plague village of Eyam

There's a new way to become a saint, according to Pope Francis. In addition to the traditional three paths to sainthood—being martyred for the faith, living a life of heroic Christian virtues, and having a reputation for strong religious devotion—the Pope has added a fourth: sacrificing your life for others.

According to the Vatican, to follow this path to sainthood people need to freely and voluntarily offer their life in the face of certain death, show Christian virtues, and have a reputation for holiness. You need to be Catholic, too, of course—none of the categories apply to non-Catholic Christians.

Around the same time I heard about this new way to sainthood, I learned about a group of Christians who voluntarily gave up their lives to save others. In this case, it happened over 350 years ago, in the English village of Eyam. In September 1665, the local tailor in Eyam received a bolt of cloth from London. At that time, London was dealing with a terrible outbreak of bubonic plague, also known as the Black Death. The cloth was infected with fleas carrying the plague—which nobody knew until people started getting sick. This included the tailor, who was dead in a week.

Understandably, the 350 or so residents of the village wanted to flee to avoid the plague. But the new minister, William Mompesson, convinced them not to go. He preached a sermon pleading with them to stay to prevent the plague from being spread to other towns and villages. He added that if they stayed he would stay, too, doing everything he could do alleviate their suffering. According to the stories told about the event, the residents of Eyam agreed it was their Christian duty to stay quarantined until the disease had passed. They sealed themselves inside their village and awaited their fate.

A stone boundary was created around the town—nobody from inside was allowed out and nobody from the outside could come in. They made arrangements with other communities to leave food and other supplies on the stones; money washed in vinegar (believed to disinfect the coins) was left on a well outside the village for payment.

After a year, the plagued burned itself out, but not before killing over 250 people in Eyam, included Mompesson's wife. The cemetery was so full that the dead had to be buried in nearby gardens and fields. According to historical reports, the brave actions of the villagers prevented the plague from spreading to other places—but at a terrible cost.

In a BBC interview, Dr. Michael Sweet, a disease specialist at the

University of Derby, says the decision by the villagers to quarantine their village "significantly reduced the potential of the spread of the pathogen. Without the restraint of the villagers, many more people, especially from neighbouring villages, would more than likely have succumbed to the disease."

The current rector in Eyam, Mike Gilbert, said in the interview: "There was definitely that hope of heaven that kept them going, but it was phenomenally difficult to simply face it. It wasn't a nice way to die . . . it is almost overwhelming to think what it must have been like. I suspect fear stalked them every day of their lives."

Today Eyam is known as the "plague village." There is a plague museum that tells the story, the well and a boundary stone can still be seen, and the graves of the plague victims inside the churchyard and surrounding area are testaments to the selflessness of the villagers.

History is full of many other examples where people of faith put their lives on the line for others. And not just Christians: Muslims, Jews, and others have put themselves in danger, or lost their lives, to protect people they didn't even know. At a time when so much of the news about religion seems unrelentingly negative or polarizing, it's good to be reminded there are those who show another side of faith—and sometimes those people are called saints.

July 2017

A Hidden Life no more: Austrian conscientious objector Franz Jägerstätter

Claus Von Stauffenberg was the German officer who led an unsuccessful plot to kill Adolf Hitler in 1944. After the attempt failed, he and other plotters, including theologian Dietrich Bonhoeffer, were arrested and executed.

Sophie and Hans Scholl, two German university students, were motivated by their Lutheran beliefs to oppose the Nazi regime. Together with other students, they created the White Rose movement, publishing leaflets expressing their opposition to the regime. They were arrested by the Gestapo and executed in 1943, along with four other members of the group.

We know about these people because of the many movies, books, and documentaries that have been made (including the 2008 movie *Valkyrie*, with its controversial selection of actor Tom Cruise to play Von Stauffenberg.) But scant attention was paid to Franz Jägerstätter until the movie *A Hidden Life* directed by Terrence Malick.

Jägerstätter, who was born in 1907, was an Austrian who found Nazism incompatible with his Catholic faith. When called up to military service in 1943, he declared himself a conscientious objector—despite being warned by friends that he was throwing his life away. As they predicted, he was arrested and thrown in prison. But he was undeterred. From his cell, he wrote: "I can easily see that anyone who refuses to acknowledge the Nazi Folk community, and is also unwilling to comply with all the demands of its leaders, will thereby forfeit the rights and privileges offered by that nation."

But, he went on to say, "it is not much different with God: He who does not obey all the commandments set forth by him and his Church, and who is not ready to undergo sacrifices and to fight for his kingdom either—such a one loses every claim and every right under that kingdom." Anyone who could be both a Nazi and a Christian, he added "would be a great magician . . . I, for one, cannot do so. And I definitely prefer to relinquish my rights under the Third Reich and thus make sure of deserving the rights granted under the kingdom of God."

On August 9, 1943, Jägerstätter was executed—beheaded—leaving behind a wife and three children. He was 36 years old. In June 2007, the Vatican declared him a martyr and in October that year he was beatified in Linz, Austria. His feast day is May 21.

Jägerstätter's comments, written from his prison cell long ago, still speak to people today about the need to take stands against repressive and tyrannical governments—and their wars. "Just as the man who thinks only of this world does everything possible to make life here easier and better, so must we, too, who believe in the eternal Kingdom, risk everything in order to receive a great reward there," he wrote. "Just as those who believe in National Socialism tell themselves that their struggle is for survival, so must we, too, convince ourselves that our struggle is for the eternal Kingdom. But with this difference: we need no rifles or pistols for our battle, but instead, spiritual weapons—and the foremost among these is prayer."

February 2018

Anti-abortion history for religious conservatives not straightforward

The anti-abortion stance of conservative Christians in the US has become part and parcel of the evangelical brand in America. But it wasn't always that way. As Jonathan Dudley noted in a 2012 blog post for CNN, this "uncompromising opposition to abortion" is not "a timeless feature of evangelical Christianity."

According to Dudley, "the reality is that what conservative Christians now say is the Bible's clear teaching on the matter was not a widespread interpretation until the late 20th century." He noted that in 1968, *Christianity Today*—the flagship publication for evangelicalism in the US—published a special issue on contraception and abortion where leading evangelical thinkers explained that the Bible "plainly teaches that life begins at birth."

In the lead article in that issue, Bruce Waltke, then professor of Old Testament at the conservative Dallas Theological Seminary, wrote that "God does not regard the fetus as a soul, no matter how far gestation has progressed . . . the destruction of the fetus is not a capital offense." That same year *Christianity Today* and the Christian Medical Society sponsored a symposium that declined to characterize abortion as sinful, citing "individual health, family welfare, and social responsibility" as justifications for ending a pregnancy. Three years later, in 1971, the Southern Baptist Convention passed a resolution affirming abortion should be legal not only to protect the life of the mother, but to protect her emotional health as well.

Today, Dudley wrote, opinions and resolutions like those would be considered heretical by many evangelicals. "Yet their positions were mainstream at the time, widely believed by born-again Christians to flow from the unambiguous teaching of Scripture," he said.

So, what changed? One of the key figures in the cause is conservative political activist Paul Weyrich, who co-founded the "moral majority" with televangelist Jerry Falwell. In a 2014 article titled, "The Real Origins of the Religious Right," in *Politico Magazine*, Randall Balmer, a historian of American religion, wrote that Weyrich was looking for a way to secure evangelical support for right wing political issues. Back then, Balmer says, American evangelicals had largely stayed out of the political arena in any organized way. "If he could change that, Weyrich reasoned, their large numbers would constitute a formidable voting bloc—one that he could easily marshal behind conservative causes," Balmer wrote.

But this moral majority needed a standard around which to rally. For nearly two decades, Weyrich had been trying to find one—things like pornography, prayer in schools, the proposed Equal Rights Amendment to the Constitution, and abortion. "I was trying to get these people interested in those issues and I utterly failed," Balmer quoted Weyrich as saying. But he was able to capitalize on growing uneasiness about abortion.

Beginning with the 1980 presidential election that saw Republican Ronald Reagan defeat Democrat Jimmy Carter, "leaders of the religious right hammered away at the issue, persuading many evangelicals to make support for a constitutional amendment outlawing abortion a litmus test for their votes," Balmer said. (Actually, Balmer maintains that racism—opposition to desegregation of whites-only schools, including the evangelical school Bob Jones University—was the real reason for evangelicals getting involved in right-wing politics. Since that wouldn't be an acceptable strategy, abortion was selected as a safer route.)

Which brings us back to evangelical activism around abortion today. There may be good reasons to oppose abortion. But for evangelicals in the US, and maybe in Canada, too, one of the reasons isn't that they have always been against abortion, or that they have always interpreted the Bible as supporting that cause. To put it another way, just as the issue of abortion itself isn't simple or straightforward, neither is the history of evangelical opposition to it.

October 2018

Sunday morning monarchists: Musings after the death of Queen Elizabeth

WHAT DOES THE Queen's death mean for Christianity in Britain and beyond? That's the question posed by English writer Paul Kingsnorth in his article on *Substack*, titled "Intermission: Last Post for Christian England."

Like millions of others, Kingsnorth, who lives in Ireland, watched the Queen's funeral. It was filled, he writes, with "a dense mat of symbolism, replete with historical meaning, anchored in a very particular nation and time period." And what did it symbolize? "Above all, I think, it symbolised something that our culture has long stopped believing in, and as such can't really process effectively, or even perhaps quite comprehend." That thing people no longer believe in is the "ancient notion of sacral kingship," he states.

In that sacral kingship model, authority flows downward from God to the monarch; their earthly power is derived from the spiritual plane. It was the foundation on which the political structure of most ancient societies was built—and the kind of society in which the Bible was written. While the Queen appeared to believe this, and maybe her son, King Charles III, does too, few other people today do, Kingsnorth writes. "The understanding now is that authority flows upward from below, from 'the people' and into the government. In this model there is no sacred centre, and there is no higher authority to whom we answer," he goes on.

In other words, leaders answer to the people who elect and de-elect them. This isn't to say people don't believe in God. Many in England and beyond still do. It's just that the majority don't believe in a sacred, God-ordained monarchy. It's a vestige of time, long ago in the past. "Whether we know it or not, it (the funeral of the Queen) marks the final passing of this worldview," Kingsnorth says. "There is no sacral kingship now."

There may be no "sacral kingship" in general society anymore, but the idea of monarchy still hangs on in many churches today. That's where one may still hear God described as a king and Jesus as Lord, along with talk about the reign of God. This was something that bothered theologian William Johnson Everett, long before the Queen died. Back in 1989 he wrote an article in *Christian Century* noting that most people in the world lived in democratic societies six days of the week—but for an hour on Sunday mornings spent time in the world of absolute monarchy.

Titled "Sunday Monarchists and Monday Citizens?" Everett observed how Christians talk and sing at church about a king and lord who reigns, but the rest of the week inhabit a world where they elect their leaders and have a voice in decisions affecting their lives. "They are monarchists in worship and democratic republicans in daily life," he wrote. It's no surprise the Bible uses monarchical language, he said; that was the political system its writers knew.

At a time when western Christians, and Christians in many other countries, live in democracies, Everett wondered: "How has this fervent Christian anomaly survived two centuries of republican and democratic development? Isn't it past time that we reconstructed our Christian thought in order to engage the world in which we actually live?" If Christians are to be relevant in the contemporary world, Everett said, they need to re-examine their language about God when it comes to the political terms they use to describe God. He compared that process to how feminists in many churches dismantled the use of exclusively male language in Christianity. He suggested something similar should happen when it comes to terms like king, lord, crown, and reign. What might this new language look like? Everett suggested looking to Jesus, who acted more like a modern political leader while on Earth. His leadership was "powered by listening," was "founded in covenant bonding," and his "election was rooted in self-sacrifice," he said.

In 1999, Everett, an American, expanded on these ideas in his book *The Politics of Worship: Reforming the Language and Symbols of Liturgy*. In that book, he doesn't go so far as to say we should call God or Jesus the "president." But he does suggest a shift in thinking to no longer seeing God as reigning over the faithful. Rather, God should be seen as "presiding" over them like a president or perhaps a prime minister—mobilizing, encouraging, visioning, and moderating in an effort to reach a goal. For him, this kind of God, one who "presides in the spirit of service," does not require praise "like a narcissistic king." Gratitude, yes, and respect too. But not the kind of respect that would "become the basis for the kind of kowtowing associated with ancient and modern despots alike," he wrote.

Many may find those words challenging. God as prime minister? Jesus as president? The terminology may be too limiting. But just as the Queen's death may be a watershed moment for how the United Kingdom and the Commonwealth view the monarchy, perhaps it can also spark some new thinking by Christians about images and metaphors for God.

September 2022

"No Randy Kehler, no Pentagon Papers"

In 1971, Daniel Ellsberg was working as a military analyst for the RAND corporation when he leaked the Pentagon Papers—top-secret documents revealing the US government's history of lies to the American public about the Vietnam War. Their publication helped turn the tide of public opinion against that war. The leak also resulted in a landmark Supreme Court ruling in favour of press freedom in that country and led, indirectly, to the downfall of then-President Richard Nixon.

Ellsberg, who died June 14, 2023, at the age of 92, changed the course of history. But none of it might have happened without the influence of a young man named Randy Kehler—and therein lies a tale about standing up against injustice and having the courage of one's convictions. His story is also an example of how small acts can lead to big consequences.

Kehler was a Harvard University graduate when, in 1969, he was drafted into the US military. He refused to go and because of that decision, he was sentenced to two years in prison. Before beginning his prison term, Kehler spoke at a War Resisters League meeting at Haverford College near Philadelphia about his willingness to go to prison because of his opposition to the war. That speech would have passed into obscurity except for who was in the audience that day: Daniel Ellsberg.

Ellsberg, who had been growing disillusioned with the government's escalation of the war, had begun attending anti-war events like the one at the college. Kehler's speech had a profound impact on him. "It wasn't what he said exactly that changed my worldview," Ellsberg recalled later. "It was the example he was setting with his life. How his words showed that he was a stellar American, and that he was going to jail as a very deliberate choice."

After hearing Kehler speak, Ellsberg wrote that he "left the auditorium and found a deserted men's room. I sat on the floor and cried for over an hour, just sobbing. The only time in my life I've reacted to something like that." The thought that went through his mind was: "We are eating our young." Hearing that speech prompted Ellsberg to leak the Pentagon Papers. "If I hadn't met Randy Kehler, it wouldn't have occurred to me to copy [the Pentagon Papers]," Ellsberg said. "His actions spoke to me as no mere words would have done. He put the right question in my mind at the right time."

Kehler ended up spending 22 months in jail. After his release, he went on to work for various anti-war groups. He also became a war-tax resister, refusing to pay taxes to protest US spending on the military. For that decision, he and his wife, Betsy Corner, had their house seized and sold by the IRS in 1991. Looking back on his life, Kehler, now 79, said in a 2021 interview, "I don't regret anything. I've had an amazing and blessed life." That included a 15-month stint teaching refugees who had escaped war in Africa. The experience of seeing how little most people in the world had to live on, and the impact of war on civilians, helped turn him against the Vietnam War. "I had learned, in a very poor third-world country, what the effect of our weapons would be in such villages," he said. From there, "it was just a series of steps to disconnect myself from the war, especially as a draft-age young man."

For Kehler, it was all about standing up for his convictions. "If we are silent, if we don't speak out against what we don't believe in, we are complicit," he said. "Until we understand what our own complicity is, we can't stop being complicit. Just raising your voice is one way. A letter to the editor is one way. It doesn't mean you have to go to jail. Just stand up and be counted."

While Kehler is not a religious person, his actions echo precepts from the world's religions about standing up against injustice and for those suffering because of it. It reminds me, as a Christian, of the words of Jesus, who spoke about how a small mustard seed—or a speech at a long-forgotten War Resisters League meeting—can grow into a plant that changes the world. It also speaks to the religious wisdom that God sometimes chooses small things and unknown or obscure people to make big things happen. Their words or actions are like ripples that radiate after a pebble is thrown into a pond; we never know where or how far they will go. As for Kehler, he has a copy of Ellsberg's book, titled *Secrets: A Memoir of the Vietnam War and the Pentagon Papers* (2003). In it is a handwritten note from Ellsberg that says, "No Randy Kehler, no Pentagon Papers."

June 2023

Mennonite Historical Society apologizes to Indigenous people

In July 2023, I was part of a tour commemorating history. I didn't expect to see history made at the same time.

It happened in Abbotsford, British Columbia, the last stop on the "Memories of Migration: Russlaender 100 Tour," commemorating how 21,000 Mennonites came to Canada from the Soviet Union between 1923 and 1930. During the tour, Richard Thiessen, president of the Mennonite Historical Society of British Columbia, apologized, on behalf of the Society and Mennonites in that province, to representatives of the Semá:th First Nation (also known as the Sumas First Nation) near Abbotsford, for how they had suffered due to the draining of Sumas Lake.

In the apology, made in a traditional longhouse at the First Nation, Thiessen acknowledged how some of the Mennonite immigrants who arrived in BC's Fraser Valley a century ago took advantage of the draining of that lake—a lake that had been a resource and source of life for the First Nation for generations. The lake was emptied by the BC government in the early 1920s to create fertile farmland for the new settler arrivals. It was seen as "positive opportunity" by those Mennonite immigrants, Thiessen said, but it was "nothing like that for your people."

In fact, it had "a devastating impact on your people," he said. "You were displaced from your dwellings, and your traditional fishing and hunting grounds were taken from you. In so many ways, your lives were changed forever." On behalf of those who "care about our Mennonite story," Thiessen said he was sorry "that our mothers and fathers didn't see you when they settled here 100 years ago" and "for the role our settler ancestors played in this devastating chapter of your lives." In response, Dalton Silver, chief of the Semá:th First Nation, accepted the apology and said it was "a step in the right direction." Silver added he hoped the apology would be the "start of a new journey of friendship and reconciliation together."

The apology by the Historical Society is the latest in a line of expressions of regret and requests for forgiveness made by Canadian churches and church-related groups to Indigenous people. The first apology appears to have been made by the United Church in 1986. Presented by the church's General Council in Sudbury to Indigenous Elders from across Canada, it expressed regret for how that church, in its "zeal to tell you of the good news of Jesus Christ," ignored the value of Indigenous spirituality. It went on to ask forgiveness for confusing "western ways and culture with the depth and breadth and length and height of the gospel of Christ" and for imposing "our civilization as a condition for accepting the gospel."

Another apology was made by Roman Catholic oblates in 1991, when they apologized for their role in residential schools. This included apologizing for "the part we played in the cultural, ethnic, linguistic, and religious imperialism" against Indigenous people.

In 1993, Primate Archbishop Michael Peers apologized on behalf of the Anglican Church of Canada, saying he was "sorry, more than I can say," for taking children from their families to residential schools, for "trying to remake you in our image," and for the abuse many suffered in the schools. In 2019, Canadian Anglicans followed up with an apology for causing spiritual harm to Indigenous people. They also passed a motion that year to designate August 6, the date of the 1993 apology, a special day in the Church's liturgical calendar. And in 2022 Justin Welby, the Archbishop of Canterbury and the head of the worldwide Anglican Church, came to Canada to apologize for the Church of England's legacy of colonialism and the harm done to Indigenous peoples.

In 2021, the Canadian Conference of Catholic Bishops apologized on behalf of the whole church in Canada. Last year Pope Francis came to Canada to apologize on behalf of the worldwide Catholic Church.

Mennonites apologized in 2014 when leaders from various Canadian Mennonite denominations acknowledged Indigenous people had experienced "much hurt and much suffering" due to residential schools and other abuses. "We regret our part in the assimilation practice that took away language use and cultural practice, separating child from parent, parent from child, and Indigenous peoples from their culture," the Mennonite leaders said, adding they regretted how "the Christian faith was used, wrongly, as an instrument of power, not as an invitation to see how God was already at work before we came." They closed by saying "we commit ourselves to walk with you, listening and learning together as we journey to a healthier and more just tomorrow."

Apologies like these, along with others, are important. But as Dalton Silver, Chief of the Semá:th First Nation noted, they are just steps in the right direction, not an arrival at the destination. There's much more work to do. Or, as the Anglican Church put it recently: "Today, the journey of reconciliation continues—through listening, truth-telling, repentance, and healing with Indigenous peoples, both within and beyond the Church."

August 2023

Why your brain wants to help one person but not millions

Right now, over 800 million people in the world don't have enough to eat. Did you want to turn the page after reading that sentence? If yes, you can claim that it's your brain's fault. That's the view of psychologist Paul Slovic of the University of Oregon, who has done research into why people do (and don't) donate. Slovic discovered people are often overwhelmed when faced by huge needs like 800 million hungry people. It's much easier, he found, for people to give to help one person, not many.

Through his research, Slovic showed one group of people a picture of a little girl suffering from starvation. He then asked how much they were willing to donate to help her. He told another group about the starving girl, adding there were millions more like her. The result? "People who were shown the statistics along with the information about the little girl gave about half as much money as those who just saw the little girl," he says.

On a rational level, this doesn't make sense. You'd think hearing about millions who are hungry would cause people to give more because of the huge need, but it doesn't work that way. Big numbers de-motivate people. We feel overwhelmed by the enormity of the need, believing "nothing I can do will make a big difference," Slovic says. In fundraising circles, this is known as the "singularity effect," the idea that people are more willing to help a single, identifiable victim than multiple, non-identified ones. It's not a conscious thing; people don't actively decide not to help. The response occurs at an unconscious level. It's what our brains automatically do when confronted by enormous needs. As Slovic puts it: "As the numbers grow, we sort of lose the emotional connection to the people who are in need."

Jamil Zaki, a professor of psychology at Stanford University and the director of the Stanford Social Neuroscience Laboratory, has also researched in this area. He specializes in what he calls "compassion collapse." When we hear about big disasters, with large numbers of homes destroyed and people killed, injured, or made houseless, we can be left "strangely unmoved," he says, once again blaming our brains. "Human empathy has been built, over thousands of generations, to respond to certain triggers—for instance, a child's cry or an anguished face," Zaki says. "People do empathize more naturally with one person's visible, heart-wrenching sorrow than with descriptions of massive tragedies, and human emotion does have a limited range." He adds, "A single victim produces these signs of distress, which tug at us and inspire our help. Groups give us statistics, which land flat, triggering little, and thus benefiting less from others' compassion."

If you need an example of how this works, just recall the reaction to the 2015 photo of the dead body of two-year-old Alan Kurdi, the Syrian child washed up on a beach by the Mediterranean Sea. The Syrian civil war had been going on for a long time, producing millions of refugees and untold suffering, before that terrible picture went viral. But when the photo was published, hearts were moved. It generated a global outpouring of assistance.

Of course, compassion fatigue also plays a role. How much suffering can we absorb? Wildfires, floods, school shootings, the war in Ukraine. Sometimes we just want to turn off the news. Which brings us back to the millions of people who are hungry, and the role of people of faith.

Our brains may be hard-wired not to respond to the needs of millions, but every major religion requires its adherents to feed the hungry. It's a divine imperative, a hallmark of sincere belief, and it seems to be working. Religiosity is a key factor in determining whether or not people donate, and how much—people of faith donate more and more often than non-religious people. One reason that is the case is people of faith are more likely to hear about needs around the world at religious services—in sermons, sharing, or the prayers of the people. (Which means the downturn in attendance at religious services is a cause of concern for faith-based aid groups.) Our brains may be hardwired not to help millions, but our faith and various scriptures compel us to respond to people who are hungry. Maybe that makes all the difference.

July 2022

Acknowledgements

Most of the columns included in this book were originally published in the *Winnipeg Free Press*, but some were published or republished in other periodicals such as the *MB Herald*. They have been edited and, in some instances, updated for this collection. In a few cases original terminology has been retained to offer a feeling of the time, but in other places it has seemed appropriate to make changes for overall consistency. This is the case with the acronym 2SLGBTQ+, the term adopted throughout this book, although there are many variations we could have used. The publisher recognizes the changing landscape regarding terminology and extends this perhaps interim solution to the 2SLGBTQ+ community with respect.

The author and publisher have made all reasonable efforts to cite appropriately the sources within this book. Readers are encouraged to consult the bibliography for publication information about quoted print materials. The publisher and author welcome any corrections or additional information.

Bibliography (Selected): Books Cited

Alexander, Allison. *Super Sick: Making Peace with Chronic Illness*. Mythos & Ink, 2020.

Anderson, Matthew. *Pairings: The Bible and Booze*. Novalis, 2021.

Armstrong, Karen. *The Battle for God: A History of Fundamentalism*. Ballantine, 2001.

Armstrong, Karen. *A History of God: The 4,000 Year Quest of Judaism, Christianity and Islam*. Ballantine, 1994.

Atwood, Margaret. *The Handmaid's Tal*e. McClelland & Stewart, 1985.

Bailey, Kenneth. *Jesus Through Middle Eastern Eyes: Cultural Studies in the Gospels*. SPCK, 2008.

Bessey, Sarah. *Jesus Feminist: An Invitation to Revisit the Bible's View of Women*. Howard Books, 2013.

Blum, Edward J., and Paul Harvey. *The Color of Christ: The Son of God and the Saga of Race in America*. University of North Carolina Press, 2014.

Boers, Arthur. *The Way is Made by Walking: A Pilgrimage Along the Camino de Santiago*. Intervarsity Press, 2007.

Bowler, Kate. *Blessed: A History of the American Prosperity Gospel*. Oxford University Press, 2013.

Bowman, Sharon. *Preventing Death by Lecture!* Bowperson, 2001.

Burch, Mark. *Simplicity: Notes, Stories and Exercises for Developing Unimaginable Wealth*. New Society Publishers, 1995.

Carrette, Jeremy, and Richard King. *Selling Spirituality: The Silent Takeover of Religion*. Routledge, 2004.

Chickering, Roger. *Imperial Germany and the Great War, 1914-18*. Cambridge University Press 2014.

Downs, David. *Alms: Charity, Reward, and Atonement in Early Christianity*. Baylor University Press, 2016.

Ellens, J. Harold. *The Destructive Power of Religion: Violence in Judaism, Christianity, and Islam*. Bloomsbury, 2007.

Ellsberg, Daniel. *Secrets: A Memoir of the Vietnam War and the Pentagon Papers*. Penguin, 2003.

Enns, Pete. *How the Bible Actually Works: In Which I Explain How an Ancient, Ambiguous, and Diverse Book Leads us to Wisdom Rather Than Answers—and Why That's Great News*. HarperCollins, 2020.

Epperly, Bruce. *Process Theology: A Guide for the Perplexed*. Bloomsbury, 2011.

Everett, William Johnson. *The Politics of Worship: Reforming the Language and Symbols of Liturgy*. Wipf and Stock, 1999.

Halberstam, Joshua. *Everyday Ethics*. Penguin, 1994.

Herzog, William, and Christopher Evans, eds. *The Faith of 50 Million: Baseball, Religion, and American Culture*. Westminster John Knox Press, 2002.

Hurtado, Larry. *Destroyer of the Gods: Early Christian Distinctiveness in the Roman World*. Baylor University Press, 2017.

James, William Closson. *Locations of the Sacred: Essays on Religion, Literature, and Canadian Culture*. Wilfrid Laurier University Press, 2000.

Jenkins, Philip. *The Great and Holy War: How World War I Became a Religious Crusade*. HarperOne, 2015.

Jenkins, Philip. *The Lost History of Christianity: The Thousand-Year Golden Age of the Church in the Middle East, Africa, and Asia—and How It Died*. HarperOne, 2009.

Keller, Phillip. *A Shepherd Looks at Psalm 23*. Zondervan, 1974.

Kelly, Kevin. *The Inevitable: Understanding the 12 Technological Forces that Will Shape Our Future*. Penguin, 2017.

Knoll, Benjamin, and Cammie Jo Bolin. *She Preached the Word: Women's Ordination in Modern America*. Oxford University Press, 2018.

Kreider, Alan. *The Patient Ferment of the Early Church: The Improbable Rise of Christianity in the Roman Empire*. Baker, 2016.

Kushner, Harold. *When Bad Things Happen to Good People*. 1981. Knopf Doubleday, 2004.

Ladd, Kevin. *The Psychology of Prayer: A Scientific Approach*. Guilford, 2013.

LaHaye, Tim, and Jerry B. Jenkins. *The Rapture: In the Twinkling of an Eye / Countdown to the Earth's Last Days*. Tyndale House, 2006.

Lindsey, Hal. *The Late Great Planet Earth*. Zondervan, 1970.

Long, Thomas. *Accompany Them with Singing: The Christian Funeral*. Westminster John Knox Press, 2013.

Lupton, Robert. *Toxic Charity: How Churches and Charities Hurt Those They Help (And How to Reverse It)*. HarperOne, 2012.

McHugh, Adam. *Introverts in the Church: Finding Our Place in an Extroverted Culture*. InterVarsity Press, 2009.

Miller, Donald. *Blue Like Jazz: Nonreligious Thoughts on Christian Spirituality*. Thomas Nelson, 2003.

Mitchell, Jack. *Hug Your Customers: Love the Results*. Hachette, 2003.

Packard, Josh, and Ashleigh Hope. *Church Refugees: Sociologists Reveal Why People are DONE with Church but Not Their Faith*. Whitaker House, 2015.

Paxman, Jeremy. *Great Britain's Great War*. Viking, 2014.

Peck, M. Scott. *The Road Less Traveled*. Simon & Schuster, 1978.

Penningroth, Phil, and Barbara Penningroth. *A Healing Divorce: Transforming the End of Your Relationship with Ritual and Ceremony*. AuthorHouse, 2001.

Piela, Anna. *Wearing the Niqab: Muslim Women in the UK and the US*. Bloomsbury, 2021.

Polkinghorne, John. *Science and the Trinity: The Christian Encounter with Reality*. Yale University Press, 2004.

Putnam, Robert. *Bowling Alone: The Collapse and Revival of American Community*. Simon & Schuster, 2001.

Reimer, Sam. *Caught in the Current: British and Canadian Evangelicals in an Age of Self-Spirituality*. McGill-Queens University Press, 2023.

Rosensaft, Menachem Z., ed. *God, Faith & Identity from the Ashes: Reflections of Children and Grandchildren of Holocaust Survivors*. Jewish Lights, 2015.

Sagan, Carl. *Pale Blue Dot: A Vision of the Human Future in Space*. Ballantine, 1997.

Savulescu, Julian, and Ingmar Persson. *Unfit for the Future: The Need for Moral Enhancement*. Oxford University Press, 2012.

Sexton, John. *Baseball as a Road to God: Seeing Beyond the Game*. Gotham, 2013.

Shuman, Joel. *The Body of Compassion: Ethics, Medicine, and the Church*. Wipf and Stock, 2003.

Slingerland, Edward. *Drunk: How We Sipped, Danced and Stumbled Our Way to Civilization*. Little Brown Spark, 2022.

Stark, Rodney. *The Rise of Christianity: How the Obscure, Marginal Jesus Movement Became the Dominant Religious Force in the Western World in a Few Centuries*. HarperOne, 1997.

Thiessen, Joel. *The Meaning of Sunday: The Practice of Belief in a Secular Age.* McGill-Queen's University Press, 2015.

Thuesen, Peter J. *Tornado God: American Religion and Violent Weather.* Oxford University Press, 2020.

Tickle, Phyllis. *The Great Emergence: How Christianity is Changing and Why.* Baker, 2012.

Townsend, Tim. *Mission At Nuremberg: An American Army Chaplain and the Trial of the Nazis.* HarperCollins, 2014.

Tutu, Desmond. *God Is Not a Christian: And Other Provocations.* HarperOne, 2011.

Weintraub, David. *Religions and Extraterrestrial Life.* Springer, 2014.

Wilkinson, Bruce. *The Prayer of Jabez: Breaking Through to the Blessed Life.* Multnomah Books, 2000.

OPPOSING VIEWPOINTS® SERIES

The Future of Warfare

Garrett Winter, Book Editor

GREENHAVEN PUBLISHING

Published in 2026 by Greenhaven Publishing, LLC
2544 Clinton Street,
Buffalo NY 14224

First Edition

Articles in Greenhaven Publishing anthologies are often edited for length to meet page requirements. In addition, original titles of these works are changed to clearly present the main thesis and to explicitly indicate the author's opinion. Every effort is made to ensure that Greenhaven Publishing accurately reflects the original intent of the authors. Every effort has been made to trace the owners of the copyrighted material.

Cover image: Dmytro Sheremeta/Shutterstock.com

Cataloging-in-Publication Data

Names: Winter, Garrett, editor.
Title: The future of warfare / edited by Garrett Winter.
Description: First edition. | New York : Greenhaven Publishing, 2026. | Series: Opposing viewpoints | Includes index.
Identifiers: ISBN 9781534510159 (pbk.) | ISBN 9781534510166 (library bound)
Subjects: LCSH: War--Forecasting. | Military art and science--Forecasting. | Military art and science--Technological innovations.
Classification: LCC U21.2 F888 2026 | DDC 355.02--dc23

Manufactured in the United States of America

Website: http://greenhavenpublishing.com

Contents

Chapter 3: How Dire Is the Threat of Nuclear Weapons?

Chapter 4: Can Global Peace Ever Be Achieved?

The Importance of Opposing Viewpoints

Perhaps every generation experiences a period in time in which the populace seems especially polarized, starkly divided on the important issues of the day and gravitating toward the far ends of the political spectrum and away from a consensus-facilitating middle ground. The world that today's students are growing up in and that they will soon enter into as active and engaged citizens is deeply fragmented in just this way. Issues relating to terrorism, immigration, women's rights, minority rights, race relations, health care, taxation, wealth and poverty, the environment, policing, military intervention, the proper role of government—in some ways, perennial issues that are freshly and uniquely urgent and vital with each new generation—are currently roiling the world.

If we are to foster a knowledgeable, responsible, active, and engaged citizenry among today's youth, we must provide them with the intellectual, interpretive, and critical-thinking tools and experience necessary to make sense of the world around them and of the all-important debates and arguments that inform it. After all, the outcome of these debates will in large measure determine the future course, prospects, and outcomes of the world and its peoples, particularly its youth. If they are to become successful members of society and productive and informed citizens, students need to learn how to evaluate the strengths and weaknesses of someone else's arguments, how to sift fact from opinion and fallacy, and how to test the relative merits and validity of their own opinions against the known facts and the best possible available information. The landmark series Opposing Viewpoints has been providing students with just such critical-thinking skills and exposure to the debates surrounding society's most urgent contemporary issues for many years, and it continues to serve this essential role with undiminished commitment, care, and rigor.

The key to the series's success in achieving its goal of sharpening students' critical-thinking and analytic skills resides in its title—

Opposing Viewpoints. In every intriguing, compelling, and engaging volume of this series, readers are presented with the widest possible spectrum of distinct viewpoints, expert opinions, and informed argumentation and commentary, supplied by some of today's leading academics, thinkers, analysts, politicians, policy makers, economists, activists, change agents, and advocates. Every opinion and argument anthologized here is presented objectively and accorded respect. There is no editorializing in any introductory text or in the arrangement and order of the pieces. No piece is included as a "straw man," an easy ideological target for cheap point-scoring. As wide and inclusive a range of viewpoints as possible is offered, with no privileging of one particular political ideology or cultural perspective over another. It is left to each individual reader to evaluate the relative merits of each argument—as he or she sees it, and with the use of ever-growing critical-thinking skills—and grapple with his or her own assumptions, beliefs, and perspectives to determine how convincing or successful any given argument is and how the reader's own stance on the issue may be modified or altered in response to it.

This process is facilitated and supported by volume, chapter, and selection introductions that provide readers with the essential context they need to begin engaging with the spotlighted issues, with the debates surrounding them, and with their own perhaps shifting or nascent opinions on them. In addition, guided reading and discussion questions encourage readers to determine the authors' point of view and purpose, interrogate and analyze the various arguments and their rhetoric and structure, evaluate the arguments' strengths and weaknesses, test their claims against available facts and evidence, judge the validity of the reasoning, and bring into clearer, sharper focus the reader's own beliefs and conclusions and how they may differ from or align with those in the collection or those of their classmates.

Research has shown that reading comprehension skills improve dramatically when students are provided with compelling, intriguing, and relevant "discussable" texts. The subject matter of these collections could not be more compelling, intriguing, or urgently relevant to today's students and the world they are poised to inherit. The anthologized articles and the reading and discussion questions that are included with them also provide the basis for stimulating, lively, and passionate classroom debates. Students who are compelled to anticipate objections to their own argument and identify the flaws in those of an opponent read more carefully, think more critically, and steep themselves in relevant context, facts, and information more thoroughly. In short, using discussable text of the kind provided by every single volume in the Opposing Viewpoints series encourages close reading, facilitates reading comprehension, fosters research, strengthens critical thinking, and greatly enlivens and energizes classroom discussion and participation. The entire learning process is deepened, extended, and strengthened.

For all of these reasons, Opposing Viewpoints continues to be exactly the right resource at exactly the right time—when we most need to provide readers with the critical-thinking tools and skills that will not only serve them well in school but also in their careers and their daily lives as decision-making family members, community members, and citizens. This series encourages respectful engagement with and analysis of opposing viewpoints and fosters a resulting increase in the strength and rigor of one's own opinions and stances. As such, it helps make readers "future ready," and that readiness will pay rich dividends for the readers themselves, for the citizenry, for our society, and for the world at large.

Introduction

> *"I know not with what weapons World War III will be fought, but World War IV will be fought with sticks and stones."*
>
> *- Albert Einstein*

Like everything else in this world, warfare has evolved. We have all seen films depicting hand-to-hand combat in ancient times, with primitive weapons such as clubs, spears, bows and arrows, and slings. These weapons could be quite effective.

However, warfare changed forever with the historically recent inventions of gunpowder, dynamite, land vehicles, and airplanes. It is common knowledge that the invention of the atomic bomb helped to end World War II. In recent times, as British inventor Frank Whittle has noted, "A nation's ability to fight a modern war is as good as its technological ability." Now, in the 21st century, autonomous weapons such as drones and robots do battle in conflicts around the world.

The future of warfare is before us, and it's not pretty. Strategy, which is crucial in all wars, will assume an even more important role when robots engage in battle with other autonomous actors: "Victorious warriors win first and then go to war, while defeated warriors go to war first and then seek to win," said Sun Tzu in *The Art of War*, penned in the 5th century BC.

Of course, war is ugly, and only getting uglier. Combat is in reality (as opposed to romanticized cinematic accounts) so hideous that it led poet Walt Whitman, who ministered to the wounded and dying during the American Civil War, to write that "The real war will never get in the books." In his account of this war, Whitman depicted "a heap" of amputated arms and legs outside a makeshift Union hospital. Today, governments do not want their citizens to witness how awful war can be. The use of the body bag, which completely hides a combatant's corpse, has been a boon to the reputations of countries obsessed with invading other nations.

The United States has become somewhat war-weary, simply because it has lost two of its recent land wars, in Vietnam and Afghanistan. After Richard Nixon pulled out of Vietnam, the North Vietnamese overran their southern counterparts, and in 1975, Saigon fell. Anyone who has seen the musical *Miss Saigon* knows of the chaos and despair that followed. More recently, Joe Biden's ending of the 20-year war in Afghanistan was also chaotic and defeatist. The Taliban now runs the country as a theocracy; women have been reduced to second-class citizens.

Such failures suggest why it is to the benefit of countries to hide the true nature of war from its citizens. War is big business, and hiding its brutality is big business as well. It is not good for the public to witness a war going badly. It is not good for the money machine that benefits from such wars, either. What is this money machine? It consists of bankers, weapons makers, uniform suppliers, military boot makers, rations suppliers, and many more military supply corporations that thrive off taxpayer dollars. L3Harris Corporation, for example, supplies military radios, which are indispensable during combat. The corporation issues stock and has a market cap of $41 billion.

Almost 100 years ago, an American general named Smedley D. Butler diagnosed the true nature of war from the inside, in a book he wrote called *War Is a Racket*. Such truth-telling among the higher-ups is rare. After all, they do not personally engage in combat, and they usually benefit from warfare. Here is how he opened the book: "War is a racket. It always has been. It is possibly the oldest, easily the most profitable, surely the most vicious. It is the only one international in scope. It is the only one where the profits are reckoned in dollars and the losses in lives."

Later the general assessed the true cost of war: "The general public shoulders the bill. And what is this bill? ... Newly placed gravestones. Mangled bodies. Shattered minds. Broken hearts and homes. Economic instability. Depression and all its attendant miseries. Back breaking taxation for generations and generations."

Though those on the outside seldom consider it, war is always about money. The U.S. involvement in the Middle East is about preserving Big Oil. Countries have gone bankrupt prolonging war. During the Ukraine War, the Russian government allegedly did not inform families that their loved ones had died on the battlefield. Instead, they would list these soldiers as "missing." The reason? Putin had promised to pay the families of dead soldiers 5 million rubles (about $54,000 dollars) as compensation.

General Butler asks of those who profit from war: "How many of these war millionaires shouldered a rifle? How many of them dug a trench? How many of them knew what it was to go hungry in a rat infested dugout? How many of them spent sleepless, frightened nights, ducking shells and shrapnel and machine gun bullets?"

The book was written in 1935, in the aftermath of World War I and with World War II looming. Those millionaires are now billionaires. We must not underestimate the capacity of certain humans to profit from others' misery. Whether the powder keg is oil in the Middle East or an estimated $15 trillion dollars in mineral and rare earth deposits in Ukraine, the motivation is there.

Is it hyperbole to say that World War III is already underway? Unlike the last world war, some experts say, there is no mushroom cloud. Instead "hybrid war" is the new paradigm, fought with "a mix of cyberattacks, disinformation, and economic manipulation." Many experts believe that this global conflict has begun; Russia's invasion of Ukraine is seen as the starting point.

However, the world has grown smaller, and its interconnectedness along with the rise of social media has made it harder for countries to hide the human cost of war. Like Russia, the United States has been concealing the blood and guts and human misery associated with war for generations. It is not in a country's best interest to be candid about murdering other humans. Most citizens are not worried about attacks in far off nations. Unless the horror is shoved in their faces, they go on about their daily activities, working their jobs and providing for their families. The poorer they are, the more they squeak by from day to day, the less they can afford to pay attention to what their government is doing 9,000 miles away. However, the American war machine hurts the impoverished more than others. In his book, *War Made Invisible: How America Hides the Human Toll,* Norman Solomon writes about a major drone operation outside of Syracuse, New York, only miles away from one of the poorest inner-cities in America. A small slice of the Pentagon's $800 billion budget could change many lives. Instead, the military industrial complex thrives and the poor wither, Solomon suggests.

Solomon points out that despite the public's weariness with war, the United States has essentially been continuously at war since 9/11. However, our government has learned from past mistakes. The U.S. now attempts to avoid or cover up casualties so that its military interventions can proceed without objection.

New strategies and cutting-edge technology have aided this duplicitous effort. The key is to limit or even end American casualties while inflicting pain on those whose voices are not heard across the ocean. Consider the American military's strategy of "by, with, and through." This policy places the onus for combat on local actors rather than American soldiers. Americans support, say, an operation against terrorism in a Middle East country, but they don't engage in active fighting. Thus locals prosecute the war, while Americans stay safely out of the fray.

New technologies also minimize American deaths and keep Americans out of body bags and sensationalist news stories. A typical attack drone may require over 100 humans to support its mission, but none of these people are in danger. If a drone crashes or is shot down, no American is injured, killed, or taken prisoner—and drones cost far less to build than manned aircraft. It's a win-win situation for the military.

In *War Made Invisible,* Solomon places much of the onus for hiding the reality of war on the American media. If, as Whitman wrote, the real war would never get into the books, it certainly hasn't been broadcast on television. Solomon writes, "To the shame of U.S. media outlets … coverage of [recent] conflicts has been sparse to the point of standard journalistic malpractice in relation to American warfare. The impeding factors include self-censorship, desires for career advancement, and concerns about job security, amid pressure from nationalism, commercialism, and professional conformity." In short, Solomon argues that the American media is not just embedded in the military, but in bed with them. It does not pay to buck a billion dollar industry, and whistleblowers face prison terms and career suicide.

Among the American media's many sins, Solomon argues, is that the industry, along with the military, has no interest in the collateral damage of war, the many civilians whose lives are disrupted, destroyed, and ended by American operations abroad. "On the TV networks," Solomon writes, "with rare exceptions, war victims were not to be seen and war opponents were not heard."

For these and many more reasons, it would seem that the future of war is all but assured. As philosopher George Santayana wrote many years ago, "Only the dead have seen the end of war."

Opposing Viewpoints: The Future of Warfare presents a wide range of viewpoints that expand upon, clarify, and debate many of the above-mentioned issues. It provides a valuable resource for those readers who want to investigate the complex issues involved in the ever-changing nature of warfare.

OPPOSING VIEWPOINTS® SERIES

Chapter 1

Will There Be a World War Three?

Chapter Preface

By now, we realize that it was quaint of those who fought in "The Great War" of 1914 to 1918 to think of it as "the war to end all wars." And yet, this was what those who fought in World War I believed. Of course, World War II followed only 20 years later. That war upped the ante on technology and brutality and ended with the atomic attacks on Hiroshima and Nagasaki. That humankind has since come to its collective senses and avoided a World War III is somewhat miraculous.

However, we can't give too much credit to humans for things such as empathy, caring, decency, or civilized behavior. The truth is that "mutually assured destruction" is what has kept our world from obliterating itself. Every country knows that should it launch a nuclear attack, the response will be immediate and devastating. In short, it is likely that there will be little left afterwards. As bloodthirsty, aggressive, and heartless as the world's current dictators are, the one positive they all cling to is life itself.

No one, authoritarians included, wants to be vaporized. After all, as the saying goes, "You can't take it with you."

Mutually assured destruction did not stop the so-called "proxy wars" of the Cold War era. These hostilities, such as those fought in Korea and Vietnam, were ideological conflicts between communist and democratic powers, the Soviet Union and the United States, with some Chinese influence. The superpowers were actually at war with one another, but they had to attack conventionally, even though both possessed enough nuclear warheads to destroy the planet.

The end of the Soviet Union in 1989 ushered in a moment of relative peace before the rise of Vladimir Putin, who wanted nothing more than to reacquire lost satellites such as Belarus and Ukraine. His full-scale invasion of the latter country in 2022, which he had hoped to last only weeks, dragged on and on, as Ukraine put up a courageous fight. Most observers believe that Ukraine is not Putin's endgame, and that victory in Ukraine will lead to additional attacks on the other breakaway Soviet states.

As Putin shows more and more frustration with the slow pace of his invasion, there have been whispers about the use of nuclear weapons, but even he has not yet shown poor enough judgment to employ this solution. Meanwhile the European Union and the United States have entered the fray by proxy, supplying Ukraine with weapons, provisions, and hope.

Donald Trump's ascension to the U.S. presidency has had a chilling effect on Ukraine's prospects. A long-time Putin supporter, Trump has sought to distance himself from NATO and the European Union. In April of 2025 he pulled millions of dollars from pro-democracy programs in the former Soviet republics as part of Elon Musk's DOGE (Department of Government Efficiency) efforts. Trump's stinginess is part of his master plan to put more of the onus for defense on Europe, but it is also clearly supportive of Russia, given that Putin has waged a disinformation and propaganda campaign as part of his own martial strategy. Propaganda has always been an important tactic in war time, and Putin has used it effectively. Trump's cancellation of funds for programs such as "promoting democratic culture" in Armenia and "advancing critical civic engagement" in Uzbekistan are clearly designed to aid his Russian friend.

Whether Russia's invasion of Ukraine will lead to a third world war is uncertain, but there are other powder kegs continuing into the second quarter of the 21st century that could also trigger global conflict. Despite numerous efforts at peace negotiations, Israel's invasion of Gaza in response to the massacre of its citizens by Hamas in 2025 wages on. Thousands upon thousands of Palestinian innocents, including women and children, are dying. Again the United States has been involved by proxy, mostly in supporting Israel with military aid. Iran entered the fray by sending hundreds of drones and missiles toward Israel in 2024, but most were deflected or destroyed.

There is a famous quotation from the old Pogo comic strip that runs, "We have met the enemy and he is us." Is it possible that the United States, longtime defender of freedom around the globe, is now its own worst enemy? Americans have always believed that it is other countries that threaten the peace. However, as author Oliver Markus Malloy has observed, "Global surveys show that the world sees Trump's America as the #1 threat to world peace. Not Isis. Not China or Russia or North Korea."

With Donald Trump's posturing about taking Greenland and Panama "one way or the other," one wonders if the concept of the United States as the "good guy" and "the world's policeman" is now as quaint and outdated as those naïve beliefs about World War I.

Viewpoint 1

> *"I have told the government of Israel that aiming for security while neglecting peace is an illusion."*

A Third World War Is Possible

The United Nations General Assembly

The United Nations General Assembly reports on a speech by Charles Michel, head of the European Council, at the United Nations General Assembly (UNGA), in September 2024. Noting that there are significant conflicts in three different parts of the world—Ukraine, Sudan, and Gaza—Michel worries that these powder kegs could erupt into a global war. Michel insists on the dignity of all humans, including victims who have had their lives shattered in Gaza, Sudan, and Ukraine. He deplores the use of food deprivation in war zones and calls for greater, more diverse representation on the U.N. Security Council, which he declares has been rendered ineffective. Michel concludes by addressing the subject of climate change and the need to act upon it. The UNGA is a platform for discussing global problems. It is the main deliberative, policy-making, and representative organ of the United Nations, where its 193 member states convene to debate and vote on international issues.

As you read, consider the following questions:

1. Why does Michel believe that a third world war is possible?

"'A Third World War is possible', says Charles Michel at the UN General Assembly," United Nations Regional Information Centre for Western Europe, September 30, 2024. Reprinted by Permission.

2. What does Michel believe is paralyzing the United Nations Security Council?
3. How would Michel change the Security Council?

A Third World War is possible. We must urgently come to our senses," stated Charles Michel, President of the European Council, on 26 September at the United Nations General Assembly.

In his speech, the head of the European Council defended peace, democracy and international humanitarian law. These are core values and priorities for the EU in a world where "we feel helpless as we watch three major conflicts mix into an explosive cocktail," he stressed.

"In Ukraine, a permanent member of the Security Council has launched an illegal and unprovoked war. This an attempt to impose the law of force rather than the force of law. (…) The European Union will support Ukraine for as long as necessary."

"The Palestinian People Have a Right to Their Own State."

Addressing the situation in Gaza, Charles Michel weighed his words: "Freedom and solidarity. By virtue of these same principles, we condemn the despicable terrorist attacks by Hamas. We demand the unconditional release of all hostages. Israel has the right to defend itself while respecting international law and the principle of proportionality. We call for an immediate ceasefire in accordance with the order of the International Court of Justice."

"The endless escalation must stop. It is irresponsible to drag Lebanon into this spiral. Our appeals, also addressed to the Israeli government, have so far been in vain. This cannot continue. We support the existence of a strong and democratic State of Israel, living in peace and security alongside the Palestinian people, who must also have their own viable and stable State.

The Palestinian people deserve respect and dignity. I have told the government of Israel that aiming for security while neglecting peace is an illusion. That cannot work. Peace is the best guarantee of security. A world fueled by vengeance and collective punishment is a less secure world. The Palestinian people have the right to their own State. Denying it this right will fuel threats to the security of Israelis indefinitely. This, in turn, will fuel polarisation in the world. It will make the world more dangerous and undermine a multilateral system that cannot tolerate double standards."

A Plea for Respect for International Law and Cooperation

Continuing on the subject of the civil war in Sudan, Charles Michel described a conflict in which "as always, women are paying the highest price." He spoke of "a massive humanitarian disaster: 20,000 deaths, millions of people in crisis and displaced. The entire Horn of Africa is at risk of tipping into chaos. (...) The arms deliveries must stop. We can put an end to this conflict if we want to."

To conclude on the subject of conflicts, the President of the European Council said: "The life of a child killed in a school bombing is precious—in Ukraine, in Gaza or elsewhere. The dignity of a woman who has been raped is sacred in times of both war and peace. In Sudan, Ukraine or elsewhere. Depriving an entire population of food is a war crime—in Ukraine, Gaza, Sudan or elsewhere. A crime is a crime. No matter who commits it, no matter where it is committed. Our indignation is only sincere if it is universal."

Security Council Reform

Charles Michel has condemned current acts of destabilisation: "One thing is clear: Iran and Russia follow the same playbook of nuclear threats, imperialist ambitions and support for ruthless and lawless terrorist groups to destabilise their neighbours and countries further afield."

It is in this context that "the United Nations Security Council must free itself from the right of veto that is paralysing it in its

Is World War Three Imminent?

With Israel's invasion of Gaza passing its one-year anniversary, the Middle East appears more unstable than at any time in the past 12 months.

Israel's response to Iran's unprecedented missile attack on its territory—itself a retaliation for the targeting of senior figures from its Lebanese proxy Hezbollah—means the two nations are now in direct confrontation.

Due to the "complex web of alliances and rivalries" across the Middle East, conflicts between Iran and Israel could see the US brought directly into the fighting, said *The Independent*. Trump has been a vocal hawk against Iran, so his assumed second presidency will do little to temper concerns.

The US and UK are "increasingly concerned" that Russia is sharing secret information and technology with Iran, which could "bring it closer to being able to build nuclear weapons, in exchange for Tehran providing Moscow with ballistic missiles for its war in Ukraine", Bloomberg reported.

Iran's "loose allies" Russia, North Korea and China are "watching events and there is an outside possibility of World War Three, given the conflict in Ukraine", said *The Mirror*.

"Others believe that has already started—it just looks different in what modern analysts call 'hybrid warfare', which is not only fought in the trenches but behind the scenes, with covert military operations, destabilising missions, disinformation campaigns, election interference and hacking".

"Are We Heading Towards World War Three?," *The Week*, **accessed on April 23, 2025.**

current form. The Security Council is not representative. It is hardly legitimate. Above all, it is no longer effective. The Security Council increasingly resembles one of the living dead. (…) The Security Council needs to be reformed. It must be reformed by making it more inclusive. Africa and Latin America in particular must be given permanent seats. Regional organisations must be more closely involved in UN decision-making processes, including by giving them a systematic consultative voice on the Security Council."

Sustainable Development, Technology, International Financial Architecture

In the second part of his speech, Charles Michel stressed the need to help developing countries cope with climate change.

He warned about the evolution of artificial intelligence: "Data and artificial intelligence are instruments of power, and even of economic and political subjugation and dominance. And now, also, weapons of war. We need to manage this progress on a global scale. We support the efforts of the Secretary General of the United Nations in this direction."

As for the reform of the Bretton-Woods institutions envisaged at the Future Summit, Charles Michel stated that "the international financial architecture must reduce inequalities, not magnify them. When Kenyan farmers do not have access to micro-credit at affordable rates, this is not merely a detail. It is a global development issue."

The President of the European Council also participated in a series of parallel events and held bilateral meetings in New York with several heads of state, including Ukrainian President Volodymyr Zelenskyy.

Viewpoint 2

> *"Resurgent autocrats run their country without concern for human and economic harm, deceiving both their own population and the international community."*

Autocratization Paves the Way for More and Bloodier Conflicts

Vanessa Boese and Sebastian Hellmeier

In this viewpoint, Vanessa Boese and Sebastian Hellmeier discuss the rise of autocracies in the 21st century world and the dangerous consequences of this pattern. The world has gone through periods of increased democratization, as well as increased autocratization. However, the current trend, they show, is toward less freedom and fewer rights worldwide. The rise of authoritarians is dangerous. Democracies typically don't wage war on each other, but autocracies and dictatorships do. Global trends have endangered peace and caused untold human and economic harm. Drastic measures are needed in order to protect democracy and limit global damage. Vanessa Boese is a postdoctoral research fellow in the research unit Transformations of Democracy at the WZB Berlin Social Science Center, Germany. From 2021 to 2023, Sebastian Hellmeier was a research associate in the research group Transformations of Democracy at the WZB and Research Associate at the Varieties of Democracy Institute at the University of Gothenburg.

"Autocratization and Its Consequences," by Vanessa Boese and Sebastian Hellmeier, The WZB, accessed on May 23, 2025. Creative commons.

As you read, consider the following questions:

1. According to the authors, what two pathways has recent autocratization followed?
2. What five countries have recently experienced coups?
3. According to the authors, how do countries typically regress into autocracy?

In many parts of the world, democracies are under siege. Globally, we are in an ongoing wave of autocratization. In our research, we monitor current transformations of democracy around the world and analyze statistics to track these developments and place them in a historical context. Some of our findings are summarized in the annual Democracy Reports published by the Varieties of Democracy Institute based at the University of Gothenburg, Sweden. According to the most recent report, the number of democracies worldwide barely equaled the number of autocracies: 89 states with democratic governments face 90 autocratic governments. The 90 autocracies are home to 70 percent of the world's population, whereas only 30 percent of people worldwide are governed democratically. The number of autocracies—that is, systems of government without free and fair elections and without a minimum of civil liberties—has been increasing steadily since around the turn of the century, a trend that continues today.

Using comparative data on the quality of democracy worldwide, we observe autocratization in the last 20 years along two pathways. First, autocratization processes unfold in (formerly) democratic countries such as Hungary, where the elected government undermines democratic norms and institutions by curtailing freedom of the press, for example, or by redrawing electoral districts in a way to help the current government win a disproportionate share of seats in parliament, making it extremely difficult for voters to oust incumbents from power. In the worst case, such erosion leads to the collapse of the democratic system. Second, we see countries already ruled by authoritarian regimes becoming even more repressive. For example, freedom of the press and civil liberties in Russia were further restricted before and during the attack on Ukraine. As a result, existing autocratic institutions are being expanded and consolidated.

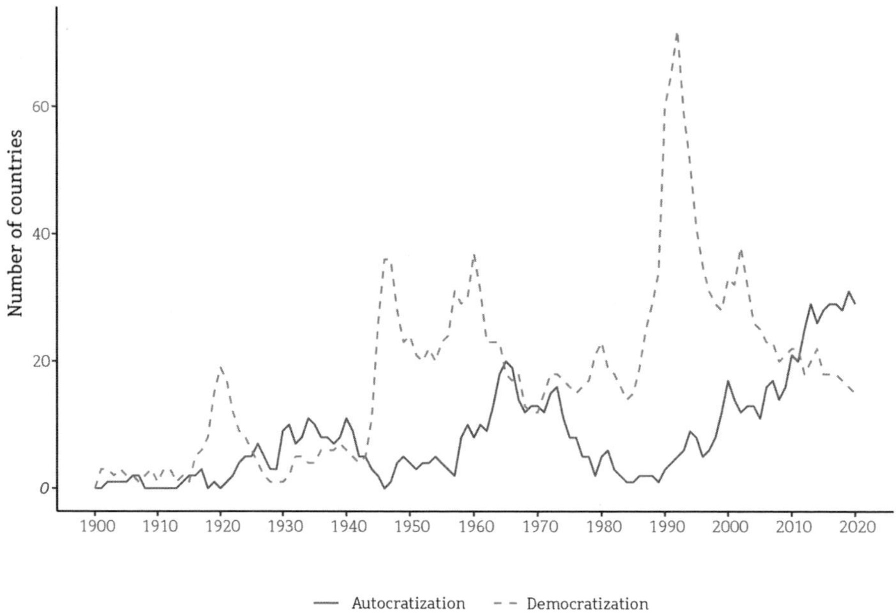

Source: https://www.wzb.eu/en/article/autocratization-and-its-consequences

The magenta colored line in Figure 1 shows the number of countries (both democracies and autocracies) in which the quality of democratic institutions has declined significantly since 1900. We refer to this as episodes of autocratization. Three waves of autocratization are notable: the first around World War II, the second during the 1960s and 1970s, and finally the third wave starting around the end of the Cold War. The figure highlights the vast extent of the current wave of autocratization: Never in the entire 20th century was there a time in which as many countries were simultaneously subject to autocratization as in 2021. For comparison, the dashed line in the figure shows the number of countries undergoing episodes of democratization.

Again, three global waves of democratization emerge, running in opposite directions to the waves of autocratization. The first two waves occurred after World War I and World War II, the third after the end of the Cold War. Currently, the number of countries undergoing democratization is decreasing, and these countries tend to be small with little economic power, such as the island nation of Fiji. By contrast, the countries threatened by autocratization are much larger (India, for example). As a result, we find democracy to be in a critical situation and the current wave of autocratization to be of historic proportions, notwithstanding the high level of democratization found in many countries when viewed over the long term.

Autocratization in Action

The loss of democratic quality is also called regression or erosion. What characterizes the current wave of autocratization is that erosion is gradual, proceeding at a slow pace. In previous waves, it was often the military that came to power through a coup d'état. Another characteristic is that illiberal actors often fuel pre-existing trends toward polarization to further divide society and weaken democratic institutions. High degrees of polarization (also referred to as toxic polarization) and autocratization form a vicious circle: society increasingly splits into two opposing camps, and public discourse is characterized by a rhetoric of "us" versus "them." One example of such toxic polarization is the growing division of U.S. society along party lines. When elections occur at such a toxic level of polarization, political content fades into the background, and candidates tend to be elected based on their affiliation with one of the two camps. Their democratic (or anti-democratic) stance loses significance for voters. If anti-democratic actors come to power in this way, they vilify the members of the other group, driving polarization and autocratization even further.

But even in already authoritarian countries, a dismantling of partially existing democratic rights and freedoms is underway. The year 2021 saw at least five successful coups d'état worldwide—a striking increase compared with the average of 1.2 coups per year since 2000. Five of these coups occurred in autocracies and helped to expand and consolidate autocratic structures: in Myanmar, Chad, Mali, Guinea, and Sudan.

One hallmark of contemporary autocratization is the strategic use of disinformation by anti-democratic actors. This can be observed in all regimes (democratic and autocratic). On the one hand, it includes strategies aimed at influencing public opinion to one's own advantage, for example by spreading fake news via social media and the press. On the other hand, it even includes the manipulation of official statistics, such as death tolls in the coronavirus pandemic or economic performance measures.

Renaissance of Violent Autocrats?

What are the consequences of the current wave of autocratization? Research has clear answers to this question. First and foremost, autocratization paves the way for more (and bloodier) conflicts. According to Kant's idea of perpetual peace, democracies do not attack other democracies. For a resurgent autocrat like Putin, however, the idea of attacking other states is no longer out of bounds, with the invasion of Ukraine being a case in point. Even in domestic conflicts such as the war in Syria, it is evident

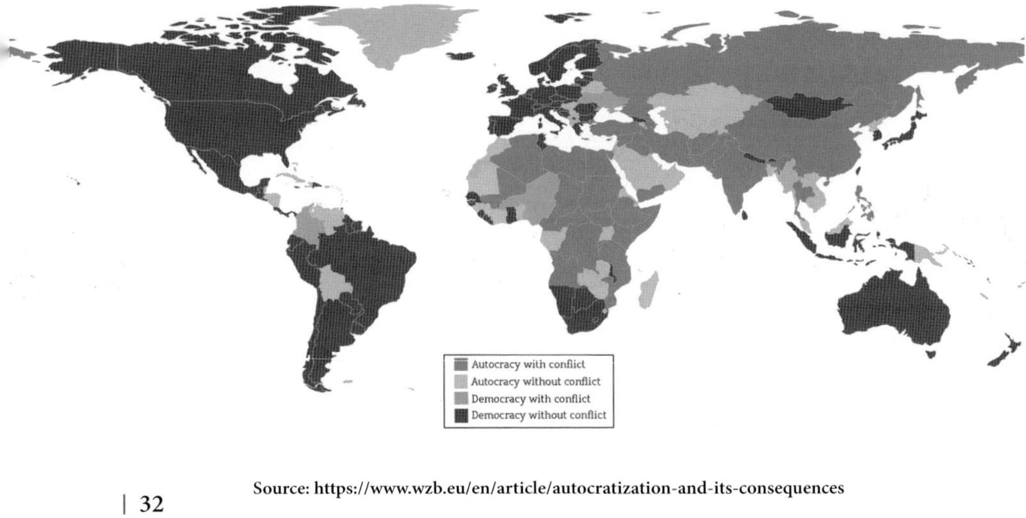

Source: https://www.wzb.eu/en/article/autocratization-and-its-consequences

that there are more casualties when autocracies are involved in the conflict. The world map below shows democracies as well as autocracies, indicating whether they were involved in armed conflict (domestic and international) in 2021. Most democratic countries were peaceful in 2021 (dark purple). For autocracies, however, we find the opposite: the majority of autocratic states were involved in armed conflict in 2021.

Second, democratic political institutions function as a kind of economic safety net offering protection against economic meltdowns (such as crises or excessive exploitation of natural resources by dictators). If this net is not in place, autocrats whose power is unchecked by parliaments or the judiciary can cause lasting economic damage to their country.

Third, as mentioned earlier, data manipulation and disinformation in the digital age, aside from obviously misleading the population, means an enormous challenge for liberal democracies trying to pursue evidence-based policies. The example of Covid mortality rates illustrates that a scientific evaluation and international comparison of anti-Covid measures is impossible if the statistics from autocratic countries contain manipulated figures. As a consequence, joint international efforts to address crises are hampered.

The current wave of autocratization involves more and economically stronger countries than in the past 120 years. Targeted disinformation, toxic polarization, and autocratization reinforce each other, creating a vicious cycle that affects both democratic and authoritarian regimes. The possible effects of the autocratization wave can be observed in Russia, for example: Resurgent autocrats run their country without concern for human and economic harm, deceiving both their own population and the international community. This development needs to be further monitored and evaluated in order to explore the extent to which the expected consequences actually materialize. In addition, targeted measures are needed to protect democracy in affected countries.

A Failed Embrace

There has been hardly any focus on foreign policy during this election season. Yet, Donald Trump has convinced his supporters that he alone can keep America safe.

"I will prevent World War III," he has repeated over and over, contrasting his track record as president with that of President Joe Biden and Vice President Kamala Harris.

But the exact opposite is true. A Trump foreign policy presidency will make global conflict far more likely during the next four years. It will make America less safe at home and abroad.

The GOP candidate is basing his whole foreign policy on his supposed ability to bend his dictator pals to his will by personality, tariffs, or threats. Never mind that he failed utterly to do so during his time in office, setting the stage for today's wars.

...

Trump bragged of his "love letters" and summits with North Korea's Kim Jong Un—but the dictator refused to halt his nuclear program, and has continued to expand his nuclear arsenal and test intercontinental missiles.

Trump failed to get Iran's supreme leader to agree to a dialogue, so instead canceled U.S. participation in the Iran nuclear deal negotiated by President Barack Obama. That deal, known as the JCPOA (Joint Comprehensive Plan of Action), had flaws. But had Trump remained in the deal, Iran would be a year away from having several bombs' worth of enriched uranium rather than two to three weeks away.

And even the much-touted Abraham Accords, which led to the recognition of Israel by two Gulf states, laid the ground for today's explosive violence in Gaza and the West Bank.

The deal was negotiated by Trump's son-in-law, Jared Kushner, who relied heavily on Benjamin Netanyahu, despite the fact that the Israeli leader was facilitating the transfer of millions of Arab dollars to the Hamas terrorist group in Gaza, because he thought he could buy them off. Had Kushner done minimum homework, he would have realized he couldn't afford to ignore the issue of political rights for the Palestinians.

"Trump Says Only He Can 'Prevent World War III,' but His Embrace of Autocrats Endangers the USA," by Trudy Rubin, *The Philadelphia Enquirer*, **Oct. 27, 2024.**

References

Boese, Vanessa A./Edgell, Amanda B./Hellmeier, Sebastian/Maerz, Seraphine F./ Lindberg Staffan I.: "How Democracies Prevail: Democratic Resilience as a Two-stage Process." In: *Democratization*, 2021, Jg. 28, H. 5, S. 885-907. DOI: 10.1080/13510347.2021.1891413.

Boese, Vanessa A./Alizada, Nazifa/Lundstedt, Martin/Morrison, Kelly/Natsika, Natalia/ Sato, Yuko/Tai, Hugo/Lindberg, Staffan I.: Autocratization Changing Nature? Democracy Report 2022. Varieties of Democracy Institute (V-Dem) 2022.

Knutsen, Carl Henrik: "A Business Case for Democracy: Regime Type, Growth, and Growth Volatility." In: *Democratization*, 2021, Jg. 28, H. 8, S. 1505-1524.

Lührmann, Anna/Lindberg Staffan I.: "A Third Wave of Autocratization Is Here: What Is New about It?" In: *Democratization*, 2019, Jg. 26, H. 7, S. 1095-1113.

Maerz, Seraphine F./Edgell, Amanda/Wilson, Matthew C./Hellmeier, Sebastian/Lindberg, Staffan I.: A Framework for Understanding Regime Transformation: Introducing the ERT Dataset. V-Dem Working Paper 2021, 113. Online: https://ssrn.com/abstract=3781485 (last accessed 6/31/2022).

Viewpoint 3

> *"Turning the pages while flying over our increasingly disorderly planet, I find the similarities to our times inescapable, both in the overwhelming arguments against conflict and growing chance it might occur."*

We Must Act Now to Prevent World War III

Frederick Kempe

Frederick Kempe argues that undue optimism in global affairs is a cause for concern, just as it was before the outbreak of World War I. Governments ignore significant issues at their own peril. Kempe finds four major "delusions" about the current state of the world that might presage a future global conflict. They are: U.S.-Chinese military conflict cannot occur; Europe is just fine on its own without U.S. aid; Middle Eastern problems can be contained; and the U.S. will continue to be a global leader. Denial of these problems is not the answer. The U.S. is still strongly positioned, but China will soon be the world's largest economy, and the U.S. must be flexible and adaptable to prevent a worldwide catastrophe from occurring. Frederick Kempe is president and chief executive officer of the Atlantic Council. Before joining the Council, Kempe was a prize-winning editor and reporter at the Wall Street Journal for more than twenty-five years.

"Preventing World War III," by Frederick Kempe, Atlantic Council, November 17, 2018. Reprinted by permission.

As you read, consider the following questions:

1. How was the thesis of the book *The Great Illusion* proven wrong?
2. According to Kempe, what is the problem with organizations such as the United Nations, the World Bank, the IMF, and NATO?
3. In what ways, according to Kempe, have Middle Eastern issues begun to threaten the entire world?

My reading choice aboard a fourteen-hour flight from DC to the United Arab Emirates, in a nod to this week's centennial of World War I armistice, was Norman Angell's 1909 book, *The Great Illusion*.

Its thesis, proven catastrophically wrong a few years later with the deadliest war in human history, was that great power conflict had grown obsolete. The rising forces of globalization, economic integration and technological advance, the Nobel Peace Prize laureate argued, made such conflict unthinkable among nations with so much to lose and little to gain.

Turning the pages while flying over our increasingly disorderly planet, I find the similarities to our times inescapable, both in the overwhelming arguments against conflict and growing chance it might occur. On the Great War's anniversary, it's a good time to ask: How can we prevent a World War III among countries with even more devastating, technologically advanced might and economic interdependence?

Angell's *Great Illusion* turned out to be tragic delusion. By failing to anticipate the prospect of war between a rising Germany and a declining United Kingdom, the U.S. and others took too few steps to prevent it. Similarly, events are unfolding today on four continents where delusional thinking could cloud the necessity for strategic response and preventive action.

Those delusions, detailed below, are 1) U.S.-Chinese military conflict is inconceivable; 2) Europe is fine and U.S. transatlantic engagement of reduced significance; 3) Middle Eastern problems can be contained, and 4) that U.S. global leadership is assured.

And don't forget it was only after a second World War that the U.S. and its allies responded by creating a set of alliances, institutions, practices and relationships that have since brought the world one of its longest periods of peace and progress.

The United Nations, the World Bank, the IMF, NATO, the European Coal and Steel Community, our Asian alliances and more were this period's legacy. Though they were designed to adapt, they have been slow to do so to accommodate rising powers and address emerging risks, thus increasing the chance of conflict.

"Our predecessors recognized that global cooperation must evolve to survive," writes IMF managing director Christine Lagarde.

So, what does survival look like across "the four delusions?"

Delusion #1: U.S.-Chinese military conflict is inconceivable

"Today," writes strategist Graham Allison, "the intensifying rivalry between a rising China and a ruling United States could lead to a war that neither side wants and that both know would be even more catastrophic than World War I."

Those tensions have increased in no small part due to Chinese leader Xi Jinping's increased flexing of economic and military muscle, and President Trump's determination to push back, born more by a sense of grievance than of history.

In Asia this week for three major summits, Vice President Mike Pence rallied allies and warned of a new Cold War if Beijing didn't give ground to Trump on major economic, military and political issues when they meet at end-November on the margins of the G20 in Argentina.

What's most required seems least likely: a strategic dialogue aimed at creating structures and habits that would prevent, defuse and manage crises.

Delusion #2: Europe is fine, and U.S. presence there of reduced significance

Europe is not fine, and U.S. presence has rarely been more urgently required.

The current picture has contradictions. The U.S. has increased its commitments and NATO has lifted its performance in the face of the Russian threat, which is good. Not good are divisions between key European allies and President Trump alongside strains within Europe.

From October 25-November 7, NATO was engaged in Trident Juncture, its biggest military exercise since the Cold War, with some 50,000 personnel, 65 ships, 250 aircraft, and 10,000 vehicles engaged in the mock defense of Norway after an invasion by a "near peer" adversary.

Four days later President Trump's visit to Paris for the World War I centennial sullied this demonstration of allied camaraderie as he skipped much of the observance, including a symbolic walk down the Champs Elysee with allies. In Trump's presence, French President Macron warned against the dangers of nationalism and called earlier for "a true European army" to reduce dependence on the U.S. In France and Germany, talk of European "strategic autonomy" is growing.

That approach will only divide Europe further, as both Nordic and Central European states want nothing of it. Their greatest worry: that the U.S. won't be there when Russia tests them.

Delusion #3: The Middle East's problems can be contained

The lesson of global terrorism and the refugee waves that have inflamed European politics is that what happens in the Middle East doesn't stay in the Middle East. A growing U.S. confrontation with Iran, the ripples from the brutal Khashoggi murder in Saudi Arabia, and ongoing civil wars in Yemen, Libya and Syria have significantly increased the immediate risks.

Message to the U.S. and its European and regional allies: don't let these crises go to waste.

It's time for a deeper global effort to forge a more sustainable, strategic response to contain and then end the region's wars and unlock the human potential of its young population.

This is a hard fix, given regional animosities and American weariness of Middle East engagement. It will take the sort of institution-building and peace-making—between Iran and Saudi Arabia, between Israel and the rest—that remade Europe after World War II.

Growing efforts to end the Yemen war, including an end to U.S. aerial refueling efforts on Friday, are a good starting point, supporting UN Special Envoy for Yemen Martin Griffiths. What's expected early next year is the Trump administration's long-anticipated peace plan for Israel.

It's also the right time for the Trump administration's Middle East Strategic Alliance, a U.S.-led security and economic pact with Sunni-Arab states to counter Iran, informally dubbed 'Arab NATO.'

Delusion #4: U.S. global leadership is assured

The window is closing on our ability to shape a future to our liking.

The United States has dynamism, resources, human capital and sources of attraction that could extend its global leadership. However, with China on track to surpass the U.S. as the world's biggest economy, it has far less leverage and relative resources than it had in 1945.

That means U.S. leaders will have to summon even more strategic and collaborative vision, renewing alliances, adapting current institutions and preventing major conflict.

To think U.S. leadership can be assured otherwise would be the mother of all delusions.

> *"The reality is that Putin is no more interested in being drawn into World War III than his NATO counterparts."*

Giving Ukraine NATO Membership Is the Best Way to Prevent World War III in Europe

Ian Bond

In this viewpoint, Ian Bond observes that while inclusion in NATO was considered for Ukraine back in 2008, nothing has happened between then and now. This lack of action has emboldened Vladimir Putin, who considers Ukraine to be part of Russia. Some fear that accepting Ukraine into NATO might trigger World War III, but Bond refutes this idea, arguing that Putin has no interest in such a global conflict. Europe's procrastination in accepting Ukraine and like nations into NATO is a dangerous abdication of duty, Bond believes. Ian Bond is Deputy Director at The Centre for European Reform (CER). He joined the CER as foreign policy director in April 2013. Prior to that, he was a member of the British diplomatic service for 28 years.

As you read, consider the following questions:

1. What is the "hedgehog" strategy attributed to Israel?

"Giving Ukraine NATO Membership Is the Best Way to Prevent World War III in Europe," by Ian Bond, Centre for European Reform, June 10, 2023. Reprinted by permission.

2. According to Bond, why can't Ukraine adopt the Israeli strategy?
3. What is Bond's measured suggestion for accepting Ukraine into NATO?

When they met in Bucharest in April 2008, NATO leaders discussed the membership aspirations of Georgia and Ukraine and declared "these countries will become members of NATO". Fifteen years later, as NATO leaders prepare to meet in Vilnius on July 11th and 12th, neither country seems any closer to membership. Vladimir Putin's war against Ukraine may have cost Russia dearly, but he can feel satisfied about one thing: few in NATO seem to want to give membership to countries that are under attack or do not control all their territory. Even those like the UK and US that backed Ukraine's membership bid in 2008 have got cold feet.

Western leaders should think again, however. Four months after the Bucharest Summit, Russia invaded Georgia—not because NATO's offer of membership provoked Russia, but because its perceived indecision did. Bringing Ukraine and other countries caught between the alliance and Russia into NATO would be a better way of stabilising the region than the various alternatives mooted, such as neutrality, a 'hedgehog' strategy, or guarantees provided by a 'coalition of the willing'.

Even after the war started, Ukraine explored neutrality as a possibility, and some Western analysts promoted the idea. There have been various models of neutrality in Europe, some of which have worked better than others. The problem is that neutrality would not address Putin's belief that Ukrainians are really Russians and that Ukraine has no right to exist as a sovereign entity independent of Russia.

Some Western analysts have suggested that Ukraine's best option is to emulate Israel's 'hedgehog strategy'—deterring future attacks through military power. Western governments might even promise it a 'qualitative military edge'—something which the US is obliged by law to give Israel, ensuring that it always has access to better weapons and more advanced military technology than its Arab neighbours.

There are two problems with the Israel model. One is financial: Ukraine, with its economy in ruins, could hardly maintain the kind of defence budget needed. Israel's military spending exceeded 10 per cent of GDP in every year from 1967-1994. The other is that Israel has its own nuclear deterrent, while Ukraine does not. None of Ukraine's partners would encourage Kyiv to follow Israel down the nuclear path.

If Ukraine cannot benefit from a NATO guarantee, perhaps a coalition of the states most interested in its success could provide an alternative? The UK and Sweden, for example, agreed in May 2022 that in the event of an attack on one of them, they would "upon request from the affected country assist each other in a variety of ways, which may include military means". That does not constitute a legally binding guarantee of help, but such an agreement would give Ukraine more certainty than it now has. The question is whether Putin would take a guarantee seriously, unless the US stood behind it—which it has so far shown no interest in doing.

NATO membership would have clear advantages over any of these options. Unlike the neutrality option, it does not leave Ukraine reliant on Russia's good will for its future security. By sharing the burden of defending Ukraine and deterring further Russian attack among all the NATO allies, it makes the costs bearable for all, rather than forcing Kyiv to devote an excessive proportion of its GDP to defence. And by bringing Ukraine under NATO's nuclear umbrella, it removes any incentive for Ukrainian president Volodymyr Zelenskyy or a successor to develop a national nuclear weapons programme. A NATO defence guarantee can be put in place as quickly as allies can be persuaded to ratify Ukraine's accession to the alliance (with bilateral guarantees from interested allies as a stop-gap until the ratification process is complete).

The main objection to taking the plunge seems to be the fear that it will automatically trigger World War III. In a good example of the Russian technique of 'reflexive control', Putin has used Russian propaganda to increase this fear, with a view to getting the West to act in line with his interests rather than its own. The reality is that Putin is no more interested in being drawn into World War III than his NATO counterparts.

Still, accidents happen. So one option for reducing the risk of an 'unintentional' Russian attack on NATO forces in Ukraine would be to apply the Article 5 guarantee for the time being only to the territory currently under Ukrainian administration. NATO would be able to move air defence forces, logistic support and the like into Ukraine, and tell the Kremlin that an attack by Russian forces on Ukrainian-administered Ukraine would trigger Article 5. NATO could put in place a 'ratchet' arrangement to extend the guarantee automatically to newly liberated areas once Ukrainian administrative control was firmly re-established there.

NATO membership would not in itself end Russia's assault on Ukraine. But—despite repeated bouts of nuclear sabre-rattling—Putin has been reluctant to confront the West directly. He has not forgotten that NATO has powerful conventional and nuclear forces of its own. The US worried in the early stages of the war that Russia might attack facilities in Poland from which Ukraine was being supplied, but Putin has not done so, even though the flow of weaponry has significantly increased over the last 15 months.

Making a bold offer of membership for Ukraine (and ideally for Georgia and Moldova too) is what NATO should do at Vilnius, but all the indications are that it will not. Its hesitation gives Putin hope that one day, with a friendlier US president in the White House, the West will stop supporting Ukraine militarily and Russia will be victorious NATO should disabuse him of that idea. If it does not, it will show that when it comes to understanding how to stabilise parts of Eastern Europe threatened by Russian imperialism, it has not learned the lesson of its disastrous mistake in Bucharest.

Periodical and Internet Sources Bibliography

The following articles have been selected to supplement the diverse views presented in this chapter.

Peter Aitkin, "What Would World War III Look Like?," *Newsweek*, December 9, 2024. www.newsweek.com/world-war-3-nuclear-war-military-defenses-prediction-1997440.

Mike Gallagher, "Pentagon Has Two Years to Prevent World War III," *The Wall Street Journal*, November 13, 2024. www.wsj.com/opinion/two-years-to-prevent-world-war-iii-trump-sec-def-needs-to-overhaul-bureaucracy-cut-waste-.

Leo Glasgow, "World War III Has Already Begun," *The Cornell Sun*, March 15, 2024. cornellsun.com/2024/03/15/glasgow-world-war-iii-has-already-begun/.

Doug Most, "How Close Are We to World War III?" *BU Today*, March 28, 2022. www.bu.edu/articles/2022/how-close-are-we-to-world-war-iii/.

Peter Oleson, "Preventing World War III by Preparing for It," Pacific Forum, January 7, 2025, pacforum.org/publications/pacnet-2-preventing-world-war-iii-by-preparing-for-it/.

Richard Overy, "Why It's Too Late to Stop World War 3—According to One of Britain's Greatest Military Historians," *The Telegraph*, February 4, 2025. www.yahoo.com/news/why-too-stop-world-war-120000865.html.

Rick Perlstein, "Everything You Wanted to Know About World War III but Were Afraid to Ask," *The American Prospect*, September 18, 2024. prospect.org/world/2024-09-18-everything-you-wanted-to-know-about-world-war-iii/.

Xin Ping, "Is World War III Inevitable?," Embassy of the People's Republic of China in the United States of America, December 12, 2024. us.china-embassy.gov.cn/eng/zggs/202412/t20241219_11505462.htm.

Tanner Stening, "With Tensions Now Flaring in the Middle East and in Europe, Can the Two Crises Snowball into One Global War—World War III, as Some Might Call It—or Are They Contained Within Their Respective Spheres of Influence?,"

Northeastern Global News, January 25, 2024. news.northeastern.edu/2024/01/25/world-war-russia-ukraine-israel-hamas/.

Isabel van Brugen, "World War III Has Already Begun, Claims Russian State TV," *Newsweek*, June 5, 2024. www.newsweek.com/world-war-3-vladimir-solovyov-ukraine-nato-russia-1908442.

John West, "Can NATO Prevent a Third World War?," *News Decoder*, July 29, 2024. news-decoder.com/decoder-can-nato-prevent-a-third-world-war/.

George Will, "World War III Is Already Underway. Not That Harris or Trump Has Noticed," *The Washington Post*, October 16, 2024. www.washingtonpost.com/opinions/2024/10/16/world-war-presidential-election-harris-trump/.

OPPOSING VIEWPOINTS® SERIES

Chapter 2

What is the Future of Technology in Warfare?

Chapter Preface

Even when unarmed, there is something sinister in the appearance of a drone. These flying robots, with their bulbous noses and sleek, tapered bodies, can hover in the sky for extended periods of time, patiently searching for a target. When a payload of Hellfire missiles is added to the equation, a drone becomes a lean mean killing machine.

Though drones have been operational for decades, it wasn't until the last quarter century or so until the United States began using them as weapons. Until that point, the prevailing notion was that using drones as murder weapons was unethical. According to Hugh Gusterson, in his book *Drones: Remote Control Warfare*, both the CIA and the FBI were unenthusiastic about killer drones. "Their reluctance to commit to what has become standard military practice … speaks eloquently to the speed with which norms about remote killing have changed in only a few years," he writes. But 9/11/2001 was the catalyst that launched a thousand (and more) drones. The world was a different place after Osama Bin Laden's deadly attack on America's iconic buildings.

According to Gusterson, the CIA's chief lawyer ignored warnings to evacuate his building on 9/11 and spent the day writing an executive order, eventually signed by President George W. Bush, which authorized targeted killings of Al Qaeda operatives and their allies. "Thus the United States began to use drones" in warfare. These activities have slowed at times, but have not ceased in the quarter century since.

The problem with using unmanned aircraft to assassinate enemy combatants is essentially the same as with all warfare. Collateral damage is bound to occur, and instead of winning hearts and minds, as the U.S. Army liked to say, attacks that went awry and resulted in civilian casualties created lifelong enemies. In addition to the numerous successful drone missions in the Middle East, there were many that were abject failures. According to Gusterson, "Particularly incendiary was a 2006 strike on a school that Pakistani media reported as having killed seventy children."

But President Bush, and later Obama, were both sold on drone warfare. Drones were politically advantageous, in that they could attack enemies without putting American lives at risk. There would be no headlines in American media about casualties resulting from such attacks. Drones had the effect of sanitizing war, at least from the perspective of the attackers.

Unmanned drones were also much less expensive than their manned counterparts. Despite a high percentage of these drones crashing, especially early on in their use, such failure was still preferable to the loss of an expensive aircraft—to say nothing of the lives that could be lost in such catastrophes. Manned crashes could lead the American news cycle for days. Drone crashes would not.

Drones are also effective as an intimidation tool. David Rhode, who was kidnapped and imprisoned in Pakistan by the Haqqani Network, an Islamic militant organization, reports that above all, his guards feared drone attacks, to the point where they were paranoid about any locals who might be spies enabling drones to target them. Rhode writes that while such drones were effective in eliminating some senior militants, he "was left with the impression that drone strikes were not a long term solution." Nevertheless, drones continue to be used in ever-increasing numbers by an ever-increasing number of countries and hostile entities. In October of 2022, Hamas began its invasion of southern Israel by using commercial drones to take out Israeli guard towers.

During the Russian invasion of Ukraine, both sides used drones to target the other. Also in October of 2022, a video posted online by Ukraine purported to show the first recorded instance of drone-on-drone combat, in the Donetsk region of Ukraine, with the Ukrainians claiming victory.

Such battles are likely only the early instances of what may eventually become commonplace, as more and more autonomous robotic vehicles encounter and attack each other. The Russia-Ukraine conflict has already been called the "first drone war." There will undoubtedly be many more, and the victors will be determined not by warriors, but by engineers and software designers. May the best robots win.

Viewpoint 1

> *"There is an argument that AI has the potential to go beyond shaping the character of war and change the nature of war itself because wars will be fought by robotic systems, not people."*

Is Artificial Intelligence Changing the Nature of War?

Maj. Gen. P. K. Mallick

In this viewpoint, retired Major General P.K. Mallik discusses the evolving nature and character of warfare, drawing on the theories of Carl von Clausewitz. Clausewitz distinguished between the fundamental nature of war, which remains violent and political, and its character, which changes with technology and societal factors. Mallik highlights the impact of artificial intelligence and autonomous systems on military operations, suggesting that these advancements could significantly alter how wars are fought, potentially leading to a future where machines play a central role in combat. He presents differing viewpoints on whether the essence of war is changing, with some experts arguing that while the character of warfare is evolving due to technological innovations, the fundamental nature of war remains constant. Mallik emphasizes the need for military organizations to adapt to these changes while acknowledging that despite technological advancements, human decision-making will

"Is Artificial Intelligence (AI) Changing the Nature of War?," by Maj. Gen. P. K. Mallick (Retd), Vivekananda International Foundation, January 18, 2019. www.vifindia.org/article/2019/january/18/is-artificial-intelligence-changing-the-nature-of-war. Reprinted by permission.

continue to be crucial in warfare. P.K. Mallick is a retired Major General in the Indian army. A winner of COAS Gold Medal Essay Competition and second prize winner four times at USI Essay Competition, Mallick is a prolific writer. He regularly contributes to defense-related journals and has published a large number of papers.

As you read, consider the following questions:

1. What are the two main aspects that differentiate the nature and character of war, according to Clausewitz?
2. How might AI influence the organization and planning of military operations?
3. What are the two schools of thought regarding whether the nature of war is changing?

The professional military body differentiates between an objective nature and a subjective character of war by drawing upon Clausewitz. Nature of war describes what war is and character of war describes how it is actually fought. Nature of war is violent, interactive between opposing wills and fundamentally political. War's character is influenced by technology, law, ethics, culture, methods of social, political, and military organization and other factors that change across time and place. Character of warfare changes in concert with the tools that become available and how they influence the ways militaries organize themselves to fight wars.

In his book *On War*, Carl von Clausewitz highlighted how failing to understand the character of war leads to disaster. He chastised Prussian generals for using the old tactics of Frederick the Great against a Napoleonic army waging a new type of warfare. They had not appreciated the changes in how war was being fought or in the character of war. Future development and deployment of human-machine teams and autonomous weapons systems represents such a shift in the character of war.[1]

In [the] near future we will see significant advances in autonomy and machine learning, to include the emergence of robots working together in groups and as swarms. New and powerful robotic systems will be used to perform complex actions, make autonomous decisions, deliver lethal force, provide intelligence, surveillance, and reconnaissance, coverage and speed response times over wider areas of the globe. Military organizations must plan now for this new era of warfare. Governments must be prepared for the political, strategic and ethical dimensions of this shift in the character of war.[2]

Major technological breakthroughs that could occur in robotics as well as information, cognitive, and material sciences are, by themselves, truly revolutionary. Military applications of Artificial Intelligence (AI) have the potential to change the very nature of war. At the strategic level, this could affect how the armed forces organize ground forces, how it fights and what types of major weapon systems it will need. At the operational and tactical levels, [an] enemy's AI capabilities could dictate specific weapon systems design, the development of new types of units to address his AI capabilities and how brigade to squad level units conduct tactical operations.[3]

Today, we are at a major inflection point, one in which technology is reshaping the way wars are fought. The future of warfare will be shaped by the role of smaller drones; robots on the battlefield, offensive cyberwar capabilities, extraordinary surveillance capabilities both on the battlefield and of particular individuals, greater reliance on special operations forces operating in non-conventional conflicts and militarization of the space.

There is an argument that AI has the potential to go beyond shaping the character of war and change the nature of war itself because wars will be fought by robotic systems, not people. AI has the potential to engage in planning and decision making that were previously human endeavours. U.S. Defense Secretary James Mattis speculated in February 2018 that AI is "fundamentally different" in ways that raise questions about the nature of war. The character of warfare will clearly change, and these changes could significantly influence the Clausewitzan elements that frame our understanding of war's nature.

No one is arguing that warfare is not changing. Where people disagree is whether the nature of warfare, the character of warfare, or both are changing. An analysis is done in this paper whether AI will change the nature and character of warfare.

AI and the Character of War

The character of warfare changes in concert with the tools that become available and how they influence the ways militaries organize themselves to fight wars. AI systems have the potential to increase the speed with which countries can fight. Even if humans are still making final decisions about the use of lethal force, fighting at machine speed can dramatically increase the pace of operations.

There are several military applications of AI currently in development ... The neural networks can utilize imagery databases and classify particular scenes (such as a mountain), allowing for a more accurate assessment of specific locations. The processing power that is possible with narrow AI systems has the potential to increase the speed of data analysis. Image recognition can achieve faster, more accurate results than humans can achieve today.

Gen. Mark Milley, Chief of Staff for the US Army, says the character of war is changing in real time and the US Army is trying to keep up with it. Milley said, "The character of war, though, gets to how you fight, with what weapons you fight, what terrain you fight on, the doctrine you fight with, how you do leader development, how you organize yourselves to fight. The character of war is changing very significantly." AI and machine learning can also help in that information gathering and decision-making process. The private sector is just now beginning to explore what its capabilities are and the military is watching closely. "How fast artificial intelligence comes upon us as a society across the world, and how that gets adapted to use in military operations, I think, will have a fundamental impact. It's too early to tell right this minute, but it's fast approaching," Milley said. He said experts are torn on just how fast. Some say it's 5-10 years out, some say 50, and still others say it's more than a century away. It doesn't matter how far out it is; what matters is that it's coming, and it benefits us to get there first.

Successful implementation of AI might lead to new concepts of operation that could influence force structure and force employment, or how militaries organize themselves and plan operations. One possibility is the use of large numbers of smaller platforms, known as swarms, for military operations. Algorithms and control systems designed to enable 'swarming' already exist in the private sector and in academia. Expensive, high quality platforms could become vulnerable to swarms of sensors and lower-cost weapons platforms that are effectively networked together. AI could thus help bring quantity back into the equation in the form of large numbers of robotic systems.

Another potential application for AI that could shape the character of war is coordination through layers of algorithms that work together to help manage complex operations like expert systems. AI could accelerate trends that challenge these long running force structure imperatives, such as the need to defeat adversaries with advanced anti access, area denial (A2/AD) networks with tolerable costs.

Two Schools of Thought

There are two schools of thought. One feels that nature of war is not changing. The other finds that with the rapid development of AI the nature and character of warfare are definitely changing.

Opinion—Nature of War Is Not Changing:

"The nature of war is immutable." –Lt. Gen. Van Riper

"The essential nature of war has not changed, is not changing, and will never change." –Lt. Gen. Dubik

"The nature of warfare and conflict between nations and states is fundamentally unchanging ... However, the character of warfare is changing just as societies, political entities and technologies change." –Vice Admiral Cebrowski

Military professionals swear by one of today's most sacred mantras by the Prussian Clausewitz: The character of war is changing, but the nature of war is not. Pro-Clausewitzans believe war, by its nature, is violent, chaotic and prone to escalation. This has always been and will always be the case. Colin Gray has written, "Many people confuse the nature of war with its character. The former is universal and eternal and does not alter, whereas the latter is always in flux." But does it mean that nature of war is eternal and unchanging? Clausewitz himself seemed less sure about this than many of his followers. [Gray] further writes, "Clausewitz, for once, is less than crystal clear. The great Prussian wrote, confusingly, that 'the nature of war is complex and changeable.'"[4]

People from this school of thought remain extremely skeptical that war's objective nature can be modified. Traditionalists say, war has always been violent, chaotic, destructive, and murderous—and will thus always be so. They contend war is inherently human, a clash of wills, politically driven. Technology cannot mitigate its essence or shed reliable insights to remove its uncertainty. Historian Williamson Murray is skeptical the Information Age can dissipate war's nature, especially battlefield uncertainty. He contends that war's nature includes the fog and the friction of war, and that the arguments contending its nature can be altered are false.[5] Murray argues, "No amount of computing power can anticipate the varied moves and the implications of an enemy's capacity to adapt in unexpected ways."[6]

The claim that has been made many times in the past is that AI and other technologies will enable military commanders to have "a qualitatively unsurpassed level of situational awareness and understanding heretofore unavailable to strategic commanders." This has not happened. The chaos of war, its fog, friction, and chance will likely never be deciphered, regardless of what technology is thrown at it. As long as humans are responsible for directing war, for writing code, and for fielding and maintaining machines, warfare will remain an instrument of policy to be made by warriors. How can AI, deep learning, autonomous systems work with or without humans to achieve the military objectives that create the conditions ultimately required for a political resolution of conflict? Those warriors may have machine augmentation, delegate decisions to cyber assistants and operate more remotely; but they will be directing the fight. While AI-enabled technologies will be able to gather, assess and deliver heretofore unimaginable amounts of data, these technologies will remain vulnerable to age-old practices of denial, deception and camouflage.

Brad D. Williams, in an introduction to an interview he conducted with Amir Husain, asserts, "Generals and military theorists have sought to characterize the nature of war for millennia, and for long periods of time, warfare doesn't dramatically change. But, occasionally, new methods for conducting war cause a fundamental reconsideration of its very nature and implications." Williams then cites "cavalry, the rifled musket and Blitzkrieg as three historical examples."[7]

Franz-Stefan Gady argues that in today's tech-crazed world, where many of us see technological solutions as a panacea to just about anything, defense analysts have a tendency to overestimate the impact of technological changes and new innovations on warfare.[8] Regardless of the tools of warfare, they remain tools. While they will be the primary tools of the warfighter, the decision to enable the warfighter to employ those tools will come from political leaders bent on achieving a certain goal with military force. The violence of warfare will never change.[9]

All the modern armed forces face the same challenge. In spite of spending billions in upgrading existing capabilities, very few of these platforms were designed to seamlessly integrate AI or partner with autonomous robotic systems. This means retro-fitting is required, making emergent technology an integration problem. Culturally, it is also likely to take significant time and effort for the armed forces to adapt entrenched command and control approaches to absorb the shock generated by the introduction of artificial intelligence and autonomous systems.[10] Advanced militaries have to be careful to avoid a situation where military technical determinism guides strategic thinking. Technological superiority does not guarantee military success. Sun Tzu warned, "tactics without strategy is the noise before defeat." Technology without integration, or a conceptual underpinning, is the hype before the letdown. Technology enables tactical actions to advance a strategy—but technology cannot replace tactics. Artificially intelligent, autonomous machines are almost certain to create new integration challenges. AI is likely to be among the greatest military integration challenges due to the additional complexities it creates for network architectures.

Despite some rapid advances in AI development it is estimated that it could take until 2060–2070 for it to reach the level of maturity required to satisfy many imagined military purposes. While this should not prevent militaries from taking heed of artificial intelligence's potential applications, it also should not distract from resolving urgent force modernization challenges like network capacity and combat system integration.[11]

Opinion—Nature of War Is Changing:

The most significant elements of war—violence, human factors, fog and friction and chance—will always remain. War's essence as politically directed violence will remain its most enduring aspect, even if more machines are involved at every level. As technology advances at rapid pace the nature and character of war will be changed. In the upcoming military revolution of autonomy, we will have to consider new sources of combat power and assess how they impact each level of war.[12] Autonomy will change the nature of war in several ways. These are:

- It could weaken the role of political direction by forcing response delegation to lower echelons for faster forms of attack.
- Autonomy can lessen the ability of governments to gain the support and legitimacy of their populations, while

making it easier for foreign governments to manipulate their adversary's populations.
- Deep learning forms of AI will augment the intuition and judgment of experienced commanders.
- Automated technologies could reduce popular support for professional military institutions, which paradoxically could free governments to employ force more readily since the political consequences are reduced.
- As with the earlier ages, friction and uncertainty will endure.
- The age of autonomy can introduce new forms of friction while reducing human factors in tactical contexts.[13]

The nature of war has definitely changed since the Cold War; globalization, violent non-state actors, identity wars, non-trinitarian (irregular) wars, and Information Technology (IT) have fundamentally altered [the] nature of war. Anti-Clausewitzans believe that Clausewitz's theories are passé, not having kept up with revolutionary technological and social changes. The new thinkers argue that capabilities in robotics, AI, and human-machine teaming will change more than just the way warfare is waged. As US Deputy Secretary of Defense, Bob Work identified AI and human performance enhancements as potential breakthroughs in defense technology: "We believe we are at an inflection point at artificial intelligence and autonomy." He later told an AI conference, "I am starting to believe very, very deeply that it is also going to change the nature of war."[14]

Technology has started changing lots of fundamentals of warfare. The lethality of modern weapons has emptied out the battlefield. What can be 'seen' by sensors of diverse types can be targeted by increasingly precise direct and indirect fires. AI has the potential to sharply enhance defense, continuing to empty out the battlefield and turning it into a no-man's zone where automated systems and semi-autonomous devices wage attrition warfare. The Russo-Ukraine war in the Donbas hints that in future wars between state-based military forces, tactical units will need to remain unseen to survive and that they will now 'occupy' territory principally through long-range firepower. If both sides have intelligent machines, war may become simply a case of machines being violent to other machines.

Drone crews firing missiles at insurgents from 3,000 miles away or navies blockading countries and starving their people into submission do not experience war the same as those infantry soldiers did years ago. The experience of violence in some wars has become one sided, while wars are now increasingly waged against civilians well behind any defensive front lines. If a nation's borders cannot be penetrated and its critical centers of gravity attacked using kinetic means, perhaps non-kinetic means are the offensive style of the future. In that case war's changing nature comes into play.

Application of information warfare by strategic competitors against the US political system hints at new cyber techniques that AI may greatly enhance. Instead of destroying another's capabilities and national infrastructures, they might be exploited and used as bearers to spread confusion and dissent amongst the populace. In this century, starvation may not be necessary to collapse a nation; AI may offer more effective methods. War may no longer be violent and murderous but it may still be, as Clausewitz wrote, a "true political instrument."[15]

Over the years, ex-US Secretary of Defense Jim Mattis, an avid reader of military history and theory, has cultivated a reputation for deep thinking about the nature of warfare. He came to a few conclusions about what he calls the "fundamental" nature of combat. He said, "It's equipment, technology, courage, competence, integration of capabilities, fear, cowardice—all these things mixed together into a very fundamentally unpredictable fundamental nature of war. The fundamental nature of war is almost like H_2O, ok? You know what it is." However his opinion about change in nature of war has changed. He said, "I'm certainly questioning my original premise that the fundamental nature of war will not change. You've got to question that now. I just don't have the answers yet." Mattis further said, "The character of war changes all the time. An old dead German [Carl von Clausewitz] called it a 'chameleon.' It changes to adapt to its time, to the technology, to the terrain, all these things." As Mattis put it, "If we ever get to the point where it's completely on automatic pilot and we're all spectators, then it's no longer serving a political purpose. And conflict is a social problem that needs social solutions."[16]

But should the technology develop the way it is expected to, removing a man from the loop could allow machine warfare to be fully unleashed. Mattis and his successors will have to grapple with the question of whether AI so radically changes everything that war itself may not resemble what it has been for the entirety of human history.

Present Status

At the present state of development, AI technologies are immature. Modern unmanned aircraft in service can operate autonomously, but cannot yet execute the sorts of complex missions that manned equivalents can achieve. Land robots are clumsy on uneven terrain. Concepts fail to deliver significant breakthroughs in autonomous decision making. There is considerable wariness that the hype and publicity surrounding deep learning will not pan out as dramatic breakthroughs.

The present developments of AI technologies in [the] military domain has not reached the level when it can be said that it would change the nature of war. In fact, it is in a nascent state of development. However the scenario is changing fast. Despite best efforts, no nation-state can ever be fully prepared for the character of the next war. As such, potential military applications of emergent technology should not be viewed as a panacea for the chaos, friction, and chance that will continue to define war in the future. Regardless of the possibilities offered by technological advances, success in the next conflict is likely to be just as reliant on human genius.[17]

References

"From a Clausewitzan Perspective, that War Is Human Fundamentally Defines Its Nature." Carl von Clausewitz, *On War*, trans. Michael Howard and Peter Paret (Princeton, NJ: Princeton University Press, 1989).

Joint Force Development, Joint Operating Environment JOE 2035: The Joint Force in a Contested and Disordered World (Suffolk, VA: Joint Chiefs of Staff, 2016).

See CRS Report R45178, "Artificial Intelligence and National Security," by Daniel S. Hoadley and Nathan J. Lucas and Peter Singer; "Getting to Grips with Military Robots," *The Economist*, January 25, 2018; and Aaron Mehta, "AI Makes Mattis Question Fundamental Beliefs About War," C4ISRnet.com, February 17, 2018.

Colin Gray, *Modern Strategy* (New York: Oxford University Press, 1999).

Admiral William A. Owens, *Lifting the Fog of War*, with Edward Offley (New York: Farrar,Straus, and Giroux, 2000).

Williamson Murray, *America and the Future of War: The Past as Prologue* (Stanford, CA: Hoover Institution Press, 2017).

Brad D. Willimas, "Emerging 'Hyperwar' Signals 'AI-Fueled, Machine-Waged' Future of Conflict," C4ISRnet.com, August 7, 2017, available at www.c4isrnet.com/dod/2017/08/07/emerging-hyperwar-signals-ai-fueled-machine-waged-future-of-conflict/.

Franz-Stefan Gady, "'The Fog of Peace': Why We Are Not Able to Predict Military Power." February 04, 2015, available at thediplomat.com/2015/02/the-fog-of-peace-why-we-are-not-able-to-predict-military-power/.

General John R. Allen, US Marine Corps (Retired) and Amir Husain, "On Hyperwar," available at www.usni.org/magazines/proceedings/2017-07/hyperwar.

F. G. Hoffman, "Will War's Nature Change in the Seventh Military Revolution?," *Parameters* 47(4) Winter 2017–18, available at ssi.armywarcollege.edu/pubs/parameters/issues/Winter_2017-18/5_Hoffman.pdf

Mark Gilchrist, "Emergent Technology, Military Advantage, and the Character of Future War," July 26, 2018, available at www.realcleardefense.com/articles/2018/07/26/emergent_ technology _military _advantage_and_the_character_of_future_war_113655.html.

F. G. Hoffman, "Will War's Nature Change in the Seventh Military Revolution?," *Parameters* 47(4) Winter 2017–18, available at ssi.armywarcollege.edu/pubs/parameters/issues/Winter_2017-18/5_Hoffman.pdf

Kareem Ayoub and Kenneth Payne, "Strategy in the Age of Artificial Intelligence," *Journal of Strategic Studies* 39, no. 5-6(2016): 793-819, doi.org/10.1080/01402390.2015.1088838.

Sydney J. Freedberg Jr., "War without Fear: DepSecDef Work on How AI Changes Conflict," *Breaking Defense*, May 31, 2017.

"The Tenth Man—War's Changing Nature in an AI World," October 15, 2018, available at madsciblog.tradoc.army.mil/90-the-tenth-man-wars-changing-nature-in-an-ai-world/.

Aaron Mehta, "AI Makes Mattis Question 'Fundamental' Beliefs about War," February 17, 2018, available at www.c4isrnet.com/intel-geoint/2018/02/17/ai-makes-mattis-question-fundamental-beliefs-about-war/.

Maj Gen P K Mallick, VSM, "Artificial Intelligence In Armed Forces—An Analysis," *CLAWS Journal*, Winter 2018.

Viewpoint 2

> *"The use of drones for military purposes has been a significant game changer in recent conflicts. Swarm drones with AI have led to disruptive effects in warfare, as seen during recent Nagorno-Karabakh and Syrian conflicts."*

Technology Will Have a Profound Impact on Future Warfare

Geospatial World

This viewpoint discusses—through an interview with Lieutenant General Chandi Prasad Mohanty, Vice Chief of the Indian Army Staff—the significant impact of advancements in digital technologies, such as artificial intelligence and big data, on military operations and global security, particularly in the context of China's growing economic and military influence in the Indo-Pacific region. The viewpoint highlights India's efforts to enhance regional stability through cooperation and capacity building while addressing non-traditional security challenges. The Indian Army is adapting to modern warfare by integrating these technologies into various military applications, including surveillance and logistics, and is also focusing on self-reliance in defense production. This viewpoint also notes the importance of space capabilities and the recent relaxation of guidelines for acquiring geospatial data. This acquisition could

"Disruptive Technology Will Have Profound Impact on Future Warfare," *Geospatial World*, July 19, 2021. geospatialworld.net/article/disruptive-technology-will-have-profound-impact-on-future-warfare/.

improve military operations, but it also raises security concerns regarding sensitive information. For almost a quarter of a century, Geospatial World has been instrumental in strengthening geospatial ecosystems at business, national, regional and global levels. Pursuing its vision of "making a difference through geospatial knowledge in the world economy and society," it continues to advance global sustainability through its consulting, events, and media divisions.

As you read, consider the following questions:

1. What role does the Tri-Services Defense Space Agency (DSA) play in enhancing India's military capabilities in space?
2. How is the Indian Army planning to use drones in warfare and counter their use by adversaries?
3. What are the implications of the recent relaxation in guidelines for acquiring geospatial data for the Indian Army?

Q: How do you assess the impact of China's economic and military expansion, and its belligerence on the global security scenario; and how can we ensure peace and stability in the Indo-Pacific region?

A: China has taken umpteen steps in recent years to modernize its military and has improved its capabilities to exert influence far beyond its maritime or continental borders. Unprecedented economic growth over the last few decades has enabled China to secure overseas investment, resources and power. Debt diplomacy coupled with overt military belligerence in South and East China Seas, as well as Eastern Ladakh, have led to an environment of uncertainty and volatility in the region.

The Indo-Pacific signifies the confluence of the Indian and Pacific oceans, and is home to over 64% of world population,

62% of global GDP and 50% of global trade. India is a pivotal force in this region and is steadfastly working to achieve peace and stability through cooperation in maritime security, open trade, connectivity and risk mitigation amongst the littoral states. Capacity building of all stakeholders in the region has been a priority for India in countering non-traditional security challenges, such as crime, piracy, drugs, arms and human trafficking, and Climate Change. 'Quad' as a grouping of like-minded countries which share the global commons is an attempt towards a 'free and open' Indo-Pacific region.

Q: Modern technologies like Artificial Intelligence, Machine Learning, Big Data, Internet of Things and GIS are playing an important role in warfare. How can our defense forces adapt faster to the changing technologies?

A: Disruptive technologies would bring about a quantum change in the way future wars are fought. Enhancement in digital technologies like AI, ML, Big Data, IoMT (Internet of Military Things) and GIS is bound to change the way information is acquired, collated, analyzed and disseminated. These are dual use technologies that would have a profound impact on future warfare.

The Indian Army is abreast with these advancements and is adopting measures to identify the domains where these technologies can be assimilated. Some of these domains include lethal autonomous weapon systems, unmanned patrolling and ISR, threat modeling, war game simulation and training, supply chain and logistics, and predictive maintenance. After having identified the military fields of application, modes of induction through IDEX, Make II, TDF (Technology Development Fund) and R&D have also been identified. There are measures/steps under progress for Tri-Services application of these technologies in an integrated and joint manner. There is an endeavor to improve our teeth to tail ratio by incorporating these technologies to reduce our logistics footprint.

Q: Recent border clashes have highlighted the value of satellite data and analytics more than ever. How is the Indian Army enhancing this capability, and does it plan to utilize the commercial satellite industry to support it in this endeavor?

A: Space offers immense force-multiplication capability for the Armed Forces, hence dependence on Space for military application is rapidly increasing. ISRO, under the Department of Space (DoS), drives India's civil and commercial Space requirements. The Tri-Services Defense Space Agency (DSA) under HQ IDS has been created to enhance peaceful exploitation of the Space domain for military purposes. DSA is mandated to fulfil its charter in conjunction with ISRO, DoS and DRDO. The Government of India's recent decision to open the Space domain to commercial enterprises and directions to ISRO to handhold them is a positive step and should provide the much-needed additional avenues for strategic users to build capability.

Q: Conventional wars are increasingly being replaced by hybrid approaches to conflict, often stopping short of war. In this hybrid construct, both Space and cyber are opening up new frontiers in warfare. How is the Indian Army adapting to these changes?

A: While methods of prosecuting military operations have forayed into non-kinetic domains like cyber, space and human psychology, conventional wars still remain a possibility, even though it may not be a 'total war'. The Indian Army is adapting well to this transformation and there does exist seamless coordination between various stakeholders. A robust cyber framework is in place to cater to cybersecurity requirements of various organizations.

As far as utilization of space capabilities is concerned, necessary measures are in place to harness it in the fields of surveillance, ISR, communication, etc. The capability exists to exploit it as a primary source of information as well as to act as redundancy in communication. The technology demonstrations in Space have exhibited our capabilities and would also act as a deterrent to our potential adversaries.

Q: Drones are causing disruption in warfare. Can you elaborate on the Army's plans on utilizing drones and countering their use by adversaries?

A: The use of drones for military purposes has been a significant game changer in recent conflicts. Swarm drones with AI have led to disruptive effects in warfare, as seen during recent Nagorno-Karabakh and Syrian conflicts. Their versatility emanates from the variety of payloads and flexibility afforded due to endurance and range of operations. Drones have not only resulted in enhanced battlefield situational awareness but also facilitated the operational tempo. We have been employing UAVs of foreign origin for quite some time for communication, ISR, electronic warfare, etc. The indigenous drone ecosystem is still evolving in terms of production of micro/mini/tac drones and in areas of manned/unmanned teaming.

Counter-drone solutions are also keeping pace with continuously evolving drone technologies. The varieties of drones available in different shapes, size, speeds and capabilities makes it a challenge to counter them with a single method. The aspects of detection, identification and location technologies are also difficult due to low radar cross-section, slow speed and size. The various stakeholders in the Army have been assigned with clearly defined goals in short and medium terms to defeat the adversary drone/unmanned systems. Towards this end we have had demonstrations of some promising prototypes which are under development.

Q: While self-reliance in defense production is a must, the requirement of state-of-the-art weapon systems in a timely manner cannot be over emphasized. How can there be a balance between these seemingly conflicting requirements?

A: India has been amongst the top three military spenders in the world, importing most of its requirements from foreign countries. However, with 'Atmanirbhar Bharat' (self-reliant India), a concerted effort has been made to promote self-reliance in the field of defense technology and indigenous production. Some of the aspects include issuing a positive list of indigenization, raising FDI (foreign direct investment) limit in the defense sector and spending a proportion of capital budget for domestic capital procurement.

Notwithstanding the self-reliance mantra, a proportion of state-of-the-art systems can also be inducted in order to retain technological edge, without waiting for the domestic industry to mature.

A long-term integrated perspective plan of the defense requirements would give the industry a clear picture of future requirements and provide a level playing field. Steps like establishment of a nodal agency like Indigenous Defense Equipment Export Association, switching from low value items to high value indigenous combat platforms like tanks, armored fighting vehicles, guns, aircraft, helicopters, destroyers and frigates would also encourage potential foreign buyers. Ultimately, [the] defense industry matures over a period of time and an entire ecosystem has to be set up to support the process.

Q: The Government of India recently promulgated new guidelines for acquiring and producing geospatial data services including maps. How do you see the Army benefitting from the recent relaxation in the rules, and are there any security concerns?

A: The new guidelines promulgated by the Department of Science and Technology have subsumed all the existing Ministry of Defense/other ministerial guidelines and have liberalized mapping and acquiring geospatial data to a much greater extent. This would definitely result in enhanced participation by private players and make acquisition of geospatial data by the industry a lot easier.

However, there are concerns due to relaxation in guidelines for acquisition of geospatial data which is a prime resource for national security requirements. These concerns have been highlighted to the ministry from time to time for incorporation of regulatory mechanisms to ensure availability of data to legitimate entities. Although the aspects of liberalization of data acquisition and ease of doing business are well acknowledged, the same should be done with the requisite regulatory mechanism in place to prevent pilferage of sensitive geospatial data.

Viewpoint 3

“"The story of warfare through the ages is one in which innovation regularly makes combat faster and more intense. So think twice before accepting the proposition that AI will make escalation uncontrollable."

AI May Not Drastically Change Warfare

Hal Brands

It is undeniable that AI will change the landscape of war in some way—and, indeed, has already begun to do so. However, in this viewpoint, Hal Brands argues that the fears many people have of AI escalating war to unfathomable heights may be out of proportion with reality. Brands is a senior fellow at the American Enterprise Institute, where he studies US foreign policy and defense strategy.

As you read, consider the following questions:

1. How has AI already begun to change warfare?
2. What factors does the author believe will mitigate the effects of AI on warfare?
3. What are some problems AI could potentially cause?

"6 Ways AI Will Change War and the World" by Hal Brands, American Enterprise Institute, June 09, 2024.. Reprinted by permission.

Artificial intelligence will change our everyday lives in innumerable ways: how governments serve their citizens; how we drive (and get driven); how we handle and, we hope, protect our finances; how doctors diagnose and treat diseases; even how my students research and write their essays.

But just how revolutionary will AI be? Will it upend the global balance of power? Will it allow autocracies to rule the world? Will it make warfare so fast and ferocious that it becomes uncontrollable? In short, will AI fundamentally alter the rhythms of world affairs?

It is, of course, too soon to say definitively: The effects of AI will ultimately hinge on the decisions leaders and nations make, and technology sometimes takes surprising turns. But even as we are wowed and worried by the next version of ChatGPT, we need to wrestle with six deeper questions about international affairs in the age of AI. And we need to consider a surprising possibility: Perhaps AI won't change the world as much as we seem to expect.

1) Will AI make war uncontrollable?

Consider one assertion—that artificial intelligence will make conflict more lethal and harder to constrain. Analysts envision a future in which machines can pilot fighter jets more skillfully than humans, AI-enabled cyberattacks devastate enemy networks, and advanced algorithms turbocharge the speed of decisions. Some warn that automated decision-making could trigger rapid-fire escalation—even nuclear escalation—that leaves policymakers wondering what happened. If war plans and railway timetables caused World War I, perhaps AI will cause World War III.

That AI will change warfare is undeniable. From enabling predictive maintenance of hardware to facilitating astounding improvements in precision targeting, the possibilities are profound. A single F-35, quarterbacking a swarm of semiautonomous drones, could wield the firepower of an entire bomber wing. As the National Security Commission on Artificial Intelligence concluded in 2021, a "new era of conflict" will be dominated by the side that masters "new ways of war."

But there's nothing fundamentally novel here. The story of warfare through the ages is one in which innovation regularly makes combat faster and more intense. So think twice before accepting the proposition that AI will make escalation uncontrollable.

The US and China have discussed an agreement not to automate their nuclear command-and-control processes—a pledge Washington has made independently—for the simple reason that states have strong incentives not to relinquish control over weapons whose use could endanger their own survival. Russia's behavior, including the development of nuclear-armed torpedoes that could eventually operate autonomously, is a greater concern. But even during the Cold War, when Moscow built a system meant to ensure nuclear retaliation even if its leadership was wiped out, it never turned off the human controls. Expect today's great powers to exploit the military possibilities AI presents aggressively—while trying to keep the most critical decisions in human hands.

In fact, AI could reduce the risk of breakneck escalation, by helping decision makers peer through the fog of crisis and war. The Pentagon believes that AI-enabled intelligence and analytical tools can help humans sift through confusing or fragmentary information regarding an enemy's preparations for war, or even whether a feared missile attack is indeed underway. This isn't science fiction: Assistance from AI reportedly helped US intelligence analysts sniff out Russian President Vladimir Putin's invasion of Ukraine in 2022.

In this sense, AI can mitigate the uncertainty and fear that pushes people toward extreme reactions. By giving policymakers greater understanding of events, AI might also improve their ability to manage them.

2) Will AI help autocracies like China control the world?

What about a related nightmare—that AI will help the forces of tyranny control the future? Analysts such as Yuval Noah Harari have warned that artificial intelligence will reduce the costs and increase the returns from repression. AI-equipped intelligence services will need less manpower to decipher the vast amounts of intelligence they gather on their populations — allowing them, for example, to precisely map and remorselessly dismantle protest networks. They will use AI-enabled facial recognition technology to monitor and control their citizens, while employing AI-created disinformation to discredit critics at home and abroad. By making autocracy increasingly efficient, AI could allow the dictators to dominate the dawning age.

This is certainly what China hopes for. President Xi Jinping's government has devised a "social credit" system that uses AI, facial recognition and big data to ensure the reliability of its citizens—by regulating their access to everything from low-interest loans to airplane tickets. Ubiquitous, AI-assisted surveillance has turned Xinjiang into a dystopian model of modern repression.

Beijing intends to seize the "strategic commanding heights" of innovation because it believes AI can bolster its domestic system and its military muscle. It is using the power of the illiberal state to steer money and talent toward advanced technologies.

It's not a given, though, that the autocracies will come out ahead.

To believe that AI fundamentally favors autocracy is to believe that some of the most vital, longstanding enablers of innovation—such as open flows of information and tolerance for dissent—are no longer so important. Yet autocracy is already limiting China's potential.

Building powerful large language models requires huge pools of information. But if those inputs are tainted or biased because China's internet is so heavily censored, the quality of the outputs will suffer. An increasingly repressive system will also struggle, over time, to attract top talent: It is telling that 38% of top AI researchers in the US are originally from China. And smart technology must still be used by China's governing institutions, which are getting progressively less smart—that is, less technocratically competent—as the political system becomes ever more subservient to an emperor-for-life.

China will be a formidable technological competitor. But even in the age of AI, Xi and his illiberal brethren may struggle to escape the competitive drag autocracy creates.

3) Will AI favor the best or the rest?

Some technologies narrow the gap between the most and least technologically advanced societies. Nuclear weapons, for instance, allow relative pipsqueaks like North Korea to offset the military and economic advantages a superpower and its allies possess. Others widen the divide: In the 19th century, repeating rifles, machine guns and steamships allowed European societies to subjugate vast areas of the world.

In some respects, AI will empower the weak. US officials worry that large language models might help terrorists with crude science kits to build biological weapons. Rogue states, like Iran, might use AI to coordinate drone swarms against US warships in the Persian Gulf. More benignly, AI could expand access to basic healthcare services in the Global South, creating big payoffs in increased life expectancy and economic productivity.

In other respects, however, AI will be a rich man's game. Developing state-of-the-art AI is fantastically expensive. Training large language models can require vast investments and access to a finite quantity of top scientists and engineers—to say nothing of staggering amounts of electricity. Some estimates place the cost of the infrastructure supporting Microsoft's Bing AI chatbot at $4 billion. Almost anyone can be a taker of AI—but being a maker requires copious resources.

This is why the middle powers making big moves in AI, such as Saudi Arabia and the United Arab Emirates, have very deep pockets. Many of the early leaders in the AI race are either tech titans (Alphabet, Microsoft, Meta, IBM, Nvidia and others) or firms with access to their money (OpenAI). And the US, with its vibrant, well-funded tech sector, still leads the field.

What's true in the private sector may also be true in the realm of warfare. At the outset, the military benefits of new technology may flow disproportionately to countries with the generous defense budgets required to develop and field new capabilities at scale.

All this could change: Early leads don't always translate into enduring advantages. Upstarts, whether firms or countries, have disrupted other fields before. For the time being, however, AI may do more to reinforce than revolutionize the balance of power.

4) Will AI fracture or fortify coalitions?

How artificial intelligence affects the balance of power depends on how it affects global coalitions. As analysts at Georgetown University's Center for Security and Emerging Technologies have documented, the US and its allies can vastly outpace China in spending on advanced technologies—but only if they combine their resources. Beijing's best hope is that the free world fractures over AI.

It could happen. Washington worries that Europe's emerging approach to generative AI regulation could choke off innovation: In this sense, AI is underscoring divergent US and European approaches to markets and risk. Another key democracy, India, prefers strategic autonomy to strategic alignment—in technology as in geopolitics, it prefers to go its own way. Meanwhile, some of Washington's nondemocratic partners, namely Saudi Arabia and the UAE, have explored tighter tech ties to Beijing.

But it's premature to conclude that AI will fundamentally disrupt US alliances. In some cases, the US is successfully using those alliances as tools of technological competition: Witness how Washington has cajoled Japan and the Netherlands to limit China's access to high-end semiconductors. The US is also leveraging security partnerships with Saudi Arabia and the UAE to place limits on their technological relations with Beijing, and to promote AI partnerships between American and Emirati firms. In this sense, geopolitical alignments are shaping the development of AI, rather than vice versa.

More fundamentally, the preferences countries have regarding AI are related to their preferences for domestic and international order. So whatever differences the US and Europe have may pale in comparison to their shared fears of what will happen if China surges to supremacy. Europe and America may eventually find their way into greater alignment on AI issues—just as shared hostility to US power is pushing China and Russia to cooperate more closely in military applications of the technology today.

5) Will AI tame or inflame great-power rivalry?

Many of these questions relate to how AI will affect the intensity of the competition between the US-led West and the autocratic powers headed by China. No one really knows whether runaway AI could truly endanger humanity. But shared existential risks do sometimes make strange bedfellows.

During the original Cold War, the US and the Soviet Union cooperated to manage the perils associated with nuclear weapons. During the new Cold War, perhaps Washington and Beijing will find common purpose in keeping AI from being used for malevolent purposes such as bioterrorism or otherwise threatening countries on both sides of today's geopolitical divides.

Yet the analogy cuts both ways, because nuclear weapons also made the Cold War sharper and scarier. Washington and Moscow had to navigate high-stakes showdowns such as the Cuban Missile Crisis and several Berlin crises before a precarious stability settled in. Today, AI arms control seems even more daunting than nuclear arms control, because AI development is so hard to monitor and the benefits of unilateral advantage are so tantalizing. So even as the US and China start a nascent AI dialogue, technology is turbocharging their competition.

AI is at the heart of a Sino-American tech war, as China uses methods fair and foul to hasten its own development and the US deploys export controls, investment curbs and other measures to block Beijing's path. If China can't accelerate its technological progress, says Xi, it risks being "strangled" by Washington.

AI is also fueling a fight for military superiority in the Western Pacific: The Pentagon's Replicator Initiative envisions using thousands of AI-enabled drones to eviscerate a Chinese invasion fleet headed for Taiwan. Dueling powers may eventually find ways of cooperating, perhaps tacitly, on the mutual dangers AI poses. But a transformative technology will intensify many aspects of their rivalry between now and then.

6) Will AI make the private sector superior to the public?

AI will undoubtedly shift the balance of influence between the public and private sectors. Analogies between AI and nuclear weapons can be enlightening, but only to a point: The notion of a Manhattan Project for AI is misleading because it is a field where money, innovation and talent are overwhelmingly found in the private sector.

Firms on the AI frontier are thus becoming potent geopolitical actors—and governments know it. When Elon Musk and other experts advocated a moratorium on development of advanced AI models in 2023, official Washington urged the tech firms not to stop—because doing so would simply help China catch up. Government policy can speed or slow innovation. But to a remarkable degree, America's strategic prospects depend on the achievements of private firms.

It's important not to take this argument too far. China's civil-military fusion is meant to ensure that the state can direct and exploit innovation by the private sector. Although the US, as a democracy, can't really mimic that approach, the concentration of great power in private firms will bring a government response.

Washington is engaging, albeit hesitantly, in a debate about how best to regulate AI so as to foster innovation while limiting malign uses and catastrophic accidents. The long arm of state power is

AI Is Already at War

In the world of microelectronics, experts often talk about Moore's law: the principle that the number of transistors on chips doubles every two years, resulting in exponentially more capable devices. The law helps explain the rapid rise of so many technological innovations, including smartphones and search engines.

Within national security, AI progress has created another kind of Moore's law. Whichever military first masters organizing, incorporating, and institutionalizing the use of data and AI into its operations in the coming years will reap exponential advances, giving it remarkable advantages over its foes. The first adopter of AI at scale is likely to have a faster decision cycle and better information on which to base decisions. Its networks are likely to be more resilient when under attack, preserving its ability to maintain situational awareness, defend its forces, engage targets effectively, and protect the integrity of its command, control, and communications. It will also be able to control swarms of unmanned systems in the air, on the water, and under the sea to confuse and overwhelm an adversary. The United States cannot afford to fall behind.

But the national security apparatus cannot afford to be reckless, either. Without proper safeguards, AI models could cause all kinds of unintended harm. Rogue systems could even kill U.S. troops or unarmed civilians in or near areas of combat. The United States therefore finds itself facing a conundrum. The stakes of slowing AI down are unacceptably high, but so are the stakes of racing ahead without needed precautions.

U.S. policymakers appear to understand this paradox. Congressional leaders know that if they were to regulate AI with too heavy a hand, they could prompt the best AI innovators to leave the United States to work where there are fewer restrictions, and the United States would then fall behind its competitors. But both Democratic and Republican policymakers also know that some regulation and oversight is essential to ensuring that AI adoption is safe and responsible. The House of Representatives and the Senate are holding sessions to educate their members and scheduling hearings to get advice from experts. These efforts to build bipartisan consensus before legislating should be applauded.

"AI Is Already at War," by Michèle Flournoy, CNAS, October 24, 2023. www.cnas.org/publications/commentary/ai-is-already-at-war.

active in other ways, as well: The US would never allow Chinese investors to buy the nation's leading AI firms, and it is restricting American investment in the AI sectors of adversary states. And when Silicon Valley Bank, which held the deposits of many firms and investors in the tech sector, spiraled toward insolvency, geopolitical concerns helped initiate a government bailout.

One should also expect, in the coming years, a greater emphasis on helping the Pentagon stimulate development of militarily relevant technologies—and making it easier to turn private-sector innovation into war-winning weapons. The more strategically salient AI is, the less willing governments will be to just let the market do its work.

We can't predict the future: AI could hit a dead end, or it might accelerate beyond anyone's expectations. Technology, moreover, is not some autonomous force. Its development and effects will be shaped by decisions in Washington and around the world.

For now, the key is to ask the right questions, because doing so helps us understand the stakes of those decisions. It helps us imagine the various futures AI could shape. Not least, it illustrates that maybe AI won't cause a geopolitical earthquake after all.

Sure, there are reasons to fear that AI will make warfare uncontrollable, upend the balance of power, fracture US alliances or fundamentally favor autocracies over democracies. But there are also good reasons to suspect that it won't.

This isn't to counsel complacency. Averting more dangerous outcomes will require energetic efforts and smart choices. Indeed, the primary value of this exercise is to show that a very wide range of scenarios is possible—and the worst ones won't simply foreclose themselves.

Whether AI favors autocracy or democracy depends, in part, on whether the US pursues enlightened immigration policies that help it hoard top talent. Whether AI reinforces or fractures US alliances hinges on whether Washington treats those alliances as assets to be protected or as burdens to be discarded. Whether AI upholds or undermines the existing international hierarchy, and

Robots Were Invented as a Warning

"Listen Josef," said the Czech playwright Karel Čapek to his brother. "I have an idea for a play."

Josef, an artist of some renown, was painting furiously and unimpressed by his brother's intrusion. "What kind of play?" he asked, sharply. Karel set out the plot. In the future, humans have created synthetic, humanoid creatures to increase productivity in the factories and fight wars on the battlefield. Built as slave workers, they will eventually rise up and wipe out the human race.

Josef was indifferent to the idea. "Then write it!" he said. But Karel was stuck. He could not think of the appropriate word to describe his artificial workers. "Call them roboti," said Josef. This was the Czech word for serf or forced labourer.

Karel decided the word robot was a perfect fit. The play, *Rossum's Universal Robots (RUR)*, premiered in Prague in January 1921. The exchange with his brother was relayed by Karel Čapek in a newspaper some years later, reflecting on how he introduced the word robot to the world when the play premiered in January 2021 – now exactly 100 years ago.

The play was a hit. An original work of science fiction, it fed into early 20th-century fears about technology's role in the drive for mass production after the first world war. *RUR*'s bold and nightmarish vision of a future where humanity is under threat by robots caused a sensation ....

Čapek's robots acted as a warning rather than a prediction. *RUR* asked that we consider where a relentless pursuit of technological progress might lead humanity. Today, 100 years later, humanity, for the most part, remains firmly in control of its machines. But, who knows, perhaps *RUR*'s 200-year anniversary will see both humans and robots joining in the celebrations.

"One Hundred Years Since a Hellish Vision of Technology Spawned that Fateful Word: Robot," by Simon Lowe, January 10, 2021. www.theguardian.com/technology/2021/jan/10/art-meets-tech-to-mark-first-100-years-of-the-robot.

how much it changes the relationship between the private sector and the state, depends on how wisely the US and other countries regulate its development and use.

What's beyond doubt is that AI opens inspiring vistas and terrible possibilities. America's goal should be to innovate ruthlessly, and responsibly, enough so that a basically favorable world order doesn't change fundamentally—even as technology does.

Periodical and Internet Sources Bibliography

The following articles have been selected to supplement the diverse views presented in this chapter.

Ross Andersen, "Never Give Artificial Intelligence the Nuclear Codes," *The Atlantic Monthly*, May 2, 2023. www.theatlantic.com/magazine/archive/2023/06/ai-warfare-nuclear-weapons-strike/673780/.

Catherine Caruso, "The Risks of Artificial Intelligence in Weapons Design," Harvard Medical School, August 7, 2024. hms.harvard.edu/news/risks-artificial-intelligence-weapons-design.

Raluca Csernatoni, "Governing Military AI Amid a Geopolitical Minefield," *Carnegie Endowment for International Peace*, July 17, 2024. carnegieendowment.org/research/2024/07/governing-military-ai-amid-a-geopolitical-minefield?lang=en.

Avi Goldfarb and Jon Lindsay, "Artificial Intelligence in War: Human Judgment as an Organizational Strength and a Strategic Liability," Brookings, November 2020. www.brookings.edu/articles/artificial-intelligence-in-war-human-judgment-as-an-organizational-strength-and-a-strategic-liability/.

Kai-Fu Lee, "The Third Revolution in Warfare," *The Atlantic Monthly*, September 11, 2021. www.theatlantic.com/technology/archive/2021/09/i-weapons-are-third-revolution-warfare/620013/.

Eric Lipton, "As A.I.-Controlled Killer Drones Become Reality, Nations Debate Limits," *The New York Times*, November 21, 2023. www.nytimes.com/2023/11/21/us/politics/ai-drones-war-law.html.

Tshilidzi Marwala, "Militarization of AI Has Severe Implications for Global Security and Warfare," UNU, July 24, 2023. unu.edu/article/militarization-ai-has-severe-implications-global-security-and-warfare.

Paul Mozur and Adam Satariano, "AI Begins Ushering in an Age of Killer Robots," *The New York Times*, July 12, 2024. www.nytimes.com/2024/07/02/technology/ukraine-war-ai-weapons.html.

Peter R. Orszag, "Silicon Valley and the Military Need to Bury the Hatchet," *The Washington Post*, February 11, 2025. www.washingtonpost.com/opinions/2025/02/11/defense-silicon-valley-military-technology/.

Raj M. Shah and Christopher M. Kirchhoff, "The United States Is Not Ready for the New Era of Warfare," *The New York Times*, September 13, 2024. www.nytimes.com/2024/09/13/opinion/ai-drones-robot-war-pentagon.html.

Reuben Stewart and Georgia Hines, "Algorithms of War: The Use of Artificial Intelligence in Decision Making in Armed Conflict," Humanitarian Law & Policy, October 24, 2023. blogs.icrc.org/law-and-policy/2023/10/24/algorithms-of-war-use-of-artificial-intelligence-decision-making-armed-conflict/.

Koichiro Takagi, "Artificial Intelligence and Future Warfare," Hudson Institute, November 23, 2022. www.hudson.org/defense-strategy/artificial-intelligence-future-warfare.

OPPOSING VIEWPOINTS® SERIES

Chapter 3

How Dire Is the Threat of Nuclear Weapons?

Chapter Preface

There was a brief period, following the break-up of the Soviet Union and the purported end of the Cold War, when the threat of nuclear weapons did not hang over the planet like the sword of Damocles. Various authors such as Steven Pinker wrote books about how the late 20th century was the least violent time in human history.

While many have taken issue with Pinker's optimism, there can be no doubt that for a few years, despite numerous minor conflicts around the globe, the world seemed a more peaceful place. American political theorist Francis Fukuyama wrote a much-celebrated book, *The End of History and the Last Man,* in which he claimed that the worldwide ascension of liberal democracies and free-market capitalism signaled a triumph over autocracy and dictatorship and marked a new era in human civilization.

Conversely, from this point in time forward, many of these liberal democracies entered a period of regression back to less liberated status. Russia, Hungary, Belarus, the United States and many more have experienced a slide toward "autocratization."

With this movement away from democracy and the power of the people has come a more dangerous world, one in which dictators and autocrats such as Vladimir Putin of Russia, Xi Jinping of China, and Kim Jong Un of North Korea have made bellicose gestures toward their neighbors. Russia has invaded Ukraine, China has its sights set on Taiwan, North Korea is continuously working on its missile program, and Donald Trump of the U.S. has taken an aggressive stance toward Greenland and Panama.

The world is becoming more dangerous by the day.

During the relative peace of the '90s, the infamous "Doomsday Clock," which metaphorically tracks how close we are to annihilation, moved from a low of two minutes to midnight in 1953—when the Cold War was at its iciest—all the way back to seventeen to midnight in 1991.

The clock was a creation of Albert Einstein, J. Robert Oppenheimer, and the Manhattan Project scientists who developed the first atomic weapons. Each year since 1947, a group of scientists has set its hands. Such threats as nuclear weapons, climate change, biological threats, and new technologies—including artificial intelligence—have influenced their decisions.

In the fearful year of 2025, that notorious clock was set down to a mere 89 seconds before the darkest of hours. It was reduced from 90 seconds in the previous year. Setting the clock a single second closer to doomsday, the scientists wanted to send "a stark signal." Because they believe that the world is ever closer to a catastrophic, existential event, "a move of even a single second should be taken as an indication of extreme danger and an unmistakable warning that every second of delay in reversing course increases the probability of global disaster."

These scientists cited the war in Ukraine as one of the driving forces of their decision: "The conflict could become nuclear at any moment because of a rash decision or through accident or miscalculation." They also felt that the conflict in the Middle East threatened "to spiral out of control into a wider war without warning." In addition, countries that have nuclear weapons "are increasing the size and role of their arsenals, investing hundreds of billions of dollars in weapons that can destroy civilization." Finally, they observed that nuclear non-proliferation efforts were collapsing and that countries such as Iran have been developing new nuclear programs.

So, to paraphrase a famous line from *The Godfather*, "Just when we thought we were out of danger, they pulled us back in."

According to Sarah Scoles, in her book *Countdown: The Blinding Future of Nuclear Weapons*, "the United States is currently in the middle of a giant nuclear modernization program, reinvesting in its atomic infrastructure like it hasn't in decades." The program had been allowed to deteriorate during the period of negotiated non-proliferation with post-Soviet Russia. It is estimated that to upgrade its nuclear program, the United States will spend almost

$2 trillion over the next 30 years. The world has moved a long, dangerous way from Ronald Reagan's and Mikhail Gorbachev's joint statement that "A nuclear war cannot be won and must never be fought."

In her book, Scoles quotes atomic scientist Aaron Arnold, who observes, "If you think about how many … nuclear weapons are out there, it's insane that we haven't had an accident or haven't gotten into a hot war."

Is it just a matter of time, as Arnold seems to say, or can a nuclear holocaust be avoided?

VIEWPOINT 1

> *"Security guarantees and nuclear umbrellas both illustrate an important point: even countries that have committed to nonproliferation understand that they live in a nuclear world."*

The Threat of Nuclear War is Rising Again

CFR Education

This viewpoint provides an overview of the nuclear world in the 21st century. There are nine countries that have or are suspected of having nuclear weapons. While it is doubtful that the major powers will use these weapons, countries such as North Korea are wild cards. Numerous pacts and treaties have been created to deal with the threat of nuclear weapons. Given that these weapons are the most powerful ever created, countries that do not possess them must align with those that do for protection. CFR Education aims to close the global literacy gap by providing free, nonpartisan resources to help middle, high school, and higher education students gain the knowledge, skills, and perspective to navigate today's interconnected world.

As you read, consider the following questions:

1. What nine countries possess, or are suspected of possessing, nuclear weapons?

"The Nuclear World," Council on Foreign Relations, last updated July 27, 2023. education.cfr.org/learn/reading/nuclear-world. Reprinted by permission.

2. How has Israel tried to keep its hostile neighbors from acquiring nuclear weapons?
3. What are nuclear umbrellas?

Think of the nuclear world as a map of where all the nuclear weapons in existence are located. The map looks the way it does because of two powerful yet competing goals. On the one hand, most countries support a nuclear weapons-free world; that support has resulted in a universal ban on nuclear weapons. On the other hand, because of the security, prestige, and power associated with the possession of nuclear weapons, a small number of countries still possess nuclear arsenals, and that number has increased over the past seventy years.

Which Countries Have Nuclear Weapons?

Although the number of nuclear weapons in the world has shrunk since its peak in the 1980s, more countries now have nuclear weapons. Nine countries are known or believed to possess nuclear weapons: the United States, China, France, India, Israel, North Korea, Pakistan, Russia, and the United Kingdom. Those countries are called nuclear weapons states. Several other countries started nuclear weapons programs but gave them up, either voluntarily or because of external pressure. A few have had nuclear weapons and later destroyed them or turned them over to another nuclear state.

Because countries do not reveal their military secrets, knowing exactly how many nuclear weapons each country possesses is difficult. However, all countries experience some level of security leaks, and a few decades of careful research has produced a generally accurate picture of nuclear arsenals globally.

Russia and the United States Have the Biggest Nuclear Arsenals

Approximately 91 percent of all nuclear warheads, or individual weapons, belong to the United States and Russia combined, each having roughly four thousand in its stockpiles.

During the Cold War, the United States and the Soviet Union together amassed some sixty thousand weapons. Nuclear annihilation was a persistent threat, because each country possessed enough nuclear weapons to destroy the other several times over. Though the threat of a nuclear war is less immediate now than it was during the Cold War, it has not disappeared and is rising once again. As the number of countries that possess nuclear weapons grows along with the tension between nuclear weapons states, so does the potential for catastrophic conflict.

Which Countries Are a Nuclear Threat Today?

Nuclear conflict involving any of the five original nuclear powers—the United States, China, France, Russia, and the United Kingdom—is unlikely but remains a possibility. Although the number of weapons held by these countries has declined, most are reluctant to pursue complete disarmament because they see nuclear weapons as important components of their security posture. After all, nuclear weapons are the most powerful weapons ever created and few countries want to give them up.

In addition to those five countries, four other countries have acquired nuclear weapons since the Nuclear Nonproliferation Treaty (NPT) went into effect.

Israel: Believed to Have Nuclear Weapons

Though Israel has never confirmed its status as a nuclear weapons state, it is believed to possess a considerable number of nuclear weapons. It never joined the NPT, the major treaty trying to halt the spread of nuclear weapons, but it has taken action to stop nearby countries from building a nuclear arsenal. Israel bombed suspected nuclear reactor sites in Iraq (1981) and Syria (2007).

Israel has also signaled that it would attack Iran if it feels threatened by the country's nuclear program. Iran's 2015 deal with China, France, Germany, Russia, the United Kingdom, the United States, and the European Union, limited Iran's nuclear development and eased some international tension. However, in 2018, the United

States withdrew from the agreement and reinstated sanctions against Iran, though the other parties involved have stuck to the agreement so far.

India and Pakistan: Rival Neighbors and Nuclear Powers

Sharing an 1,800-mile border, India and Pakistan have fought several conventional wars over 100,000 square miles of disputed territory. Both countries possess nuclear weapons. Neither joined the NPT, and both appear to be modernizing and adding to their stockpiles. Many policymakers and experts fear that nuclear war could break out between the two countries—or, even more concerning, that Pakistan could lose control of a nuclear weapon to terrorists.

North Korea: The World's Biggest Nuclear Threat

Although North Korea is believed to have a small arsenal, its continued nuclear tests have raised widespread concerns over possible nuclear conflict. It withdrew from the NPT in 2003 and conducted its first nuclear test in 2006. Since then, it has threatened to use its nuclear weapons against the United States, Japan, and South Korea.

Which Countries Ban Nuclear Weapons?

Some countries and regions have developed nuclear weapon-free zones.

Since the 1960s, some countries have come together to create nuclear weapon-free zones (NWFZs), specified areas where countries pledge not to build, receive, test, or store nuclear weapons. NWFZs do not prevent peaceful nuclear technology use.

The idea of setting up an area where nuclear weapons are banned was introduced in 1958, when Poland suggested a plan to create an NWFZ in Central Europe. But NWFZs officially got their start through the NPT, which recognized the right of countries to make those zones (as twenty-one Latin American countries did in the Treaty of Tlatelolco in 1967).

Five treaties have created NWFZs in Africa, Central Asia, Latin America, Southeast Asia, and the South Pacific. Together, those zones span the entire Southern Hemisphere and parts of the Northern Hemisphere.

Additionally, three treaties create a nuclear weapons–free global common space for research, exploration, and the general advancement of humankind:

- The Seabed Treaty bans weapons of mass destruction on the ocean floor.
- The Antarctic Treaty bans any military activity in Antarctica, including the testing of nuclear weapons.
- The Outer Space Treaty bans weapons of mass destruction from the earth's orbit, the moon, or any other object in outer space.

Which Countries Have Security Guarantees to Help Protect Them Against Nuclear Weapons?

The global divide isn't as simple as nuclear and nuclear free.

Many countries without nuclear weapons want to protect themselves against nuclear threats without developing nuclear weapons themselves. One way to do that is through a security guarantee, a pledge from a country to protect an ally using military means. A security guarantee extends the perceived security a nuclear arsenal provides to allied countries that do not possess nuclear weapons. Because of that provision, a security guarantee provided by a nuclear-armed country is also called a nuclear umbrella. The U.S. nuclear umbrella covers several countries.

- Australia: Since 1951, the United States and Australia have been part of a collective security alliance, but the related treaty is nonbinding and its language not as strong as that in the North Atlantic Treaty: whether the alliance requires the U.S. military to actually come to Australia's defense is unclear. Still, most experts consider Australia to be protected by the U.S. nuclear umbrella.

- Japan: In 1951, at the end of the Allied occupation, the United States and Japan signed a security treaty that provisionally allowed the United States to maintain armed forces in and around Japan. In 1960, the two countries revised that agreement, which then allowed the United States to set up military bases in Japanese territories in exchange for U.S. protection and security, including nuclear weapons.
- South Korea: Two months after fighting stopped in the Korean War in 1953, the United States and South Korea signed a mutual defense treaty creating a military alliance that continues to this day.
- North Atlantic Treaty Organization (NATO) members: NATO member countries that do not have nuclear weapons (i.e., all except France and the United Kingdom) are protected by the umbrella.

A nuclear umbrella is also meant to be a tool of nonproliferation: if countries without nuclear weapons are protected under a security guarantee from a nuclear-armed country, then those countries will be less inclined to start nuclear weapons programs of their own.

Security guarantees and nuclear umbrellas both illustrate an important point: even countries that have committed to nonproliferation understand that they live in a nuclear world. The different ways countries deal with that reality—acquiring nuclear weapons, declaring NWFZs, or seeking security guarantees—reflect the paradoxical goal of most countries: a peaceful future secured by weapons as necessary.

Viewpoint 2

> *"The very existence of nuclear weapons is a threat to future generations, and indeed to the survival of humanity."*

Nuclear Weapons Are an Intolerable Threat to Humanity

International Committee of the Red Cross

This viewpoint argues that nuclear weapons cannot be tolerated in our world. The International Committee of the Red Cross has seen firsthand the devastating effects of nuclear attacks on Japan. There is no humanitarian response, the organization's members believe, that can adequately deal with the effects of nuclear war. The devastation from nuclear weapons is so overwhelming that all such attacks must be prevented. Therefore, it is the responsibility of every person to advocate for an end to nuclear proliferation. The International Committee of the Red Cross (ICRC) is a neutral, independent organization ensuring humanitarian protection and assistance for people affected by armed conflict and other violence.

As you read, consider the following questions:

1. What would be the effects of a nuclear detonation?

"Nuclear Weapons—an Intolerable Threat to humanity," the International Committee of the Red Cross, July 8, 2018. Reprinted by permission.

2. According to the authors, why is a future nuclear attack possible?
3. According to the viewpoint, how should people advocate for an end to nuclear proliferation?

Nuclear weapons are the most terrifying weapon ever invented: no weapon is more destructive; no weapon causes such unspeakable human suffering; and there is no way to control how far the radioactive fallout will spread or how long the effects will last.

A nuclear bomb detonated in a city would immediately kill tens of thousands of people, and tens of thousands more would suffer horrific injuries and later die from radiation exposure.

In addition to the immense short-term loss of life, a nuclear war could cause long-term damage to our planet. It could severely disrupt the earth's ecosystem and reduce global temperatures, resulting in food shortages around the world.

Think Nuclear Weapons Will Never Be Used Again? Think Again

The very existence of nuclear weapons is a threat to future generations, and indeed to the survival of humanity.

What's more, given the current regional and international tensions, the risk of nuclear weapons being used is the highest it's been since the Cold War. Nuclear-armed States are modernizing their arsenals, and their command and control systems are becoming more vulnerable to cyber attacks. There is plenty of cause for alarm about the danger we all face.

No Adequate Humanitarian Response

What would humanitarian organizations do in the event of a nuclear attack? The hard truth is that no State or organization could deal with the catastrophic consequences of a nuclear bomb.

The Red Cross' First-Hand Experience

In August 1945, in the aftermath of the atomic bombings of Hiroshima and Nagasaki, the Japanese Red Cross, supported by the ICRC, attempted to bring relief to the many thousands of dying and injured. The magnitude of the needs made us feel helpless and the International Red Cross and Red Crescent Movement has been a strong advocate for a world free of nuclear weapons ever since.

Legal Response to the Nuclear Threat

Since these atomic bombs were dropped on Hiroshima and Nagasaki in 1945, the ICRC has been calling for a ban on nuclear weapons to ensure that these dark events are never repeated. For decades, States have committed to preventing the spread of nuclear weapons and achieving nuclear disarmament through a number of international agreements, including the nuclear Non-Proliferation Treaty. Yet it was only in July 2017 that a treaty banning nuclear weapons was adopted. It was a historic and long-awaited step towards their elimination.

What Can We Do?

We are all responsible for making sure that decision makers understand that nuclear weapons have no place in the world we want for ourselves or for future generations. People like you are the only ones who can make a difference.

You can raise awareness of what is at stake by:

- Putting the issue of nuclear weapons on the agendas of civic, religious, social and other organizations you're part of,
- Spreading the word by sharing this page and other reliable postings on your social media platforms, and
- Writing letters to local media to share these concerns.

Depending on where you live, you can urge political leaders and those who can influence them to:

- Fulfill long-standing commitments to nuclear weapon reductions and elimination,

- Join the Treaty on the Prohibition of Nuclear Weapons, and
- Work urgently to reduce the growing risks that nuclear weapons will be used.

Nuclear Stockpiles in 2024

The Stockholm International Peace Research Institute (SIPRI), which signed the MOU with Hiroshima Prefecture, launched the SIPRI YEARBOOK 2024 and announced the latest status of the nuclear forces.

As of January 2024, the total number of nuclear stockpiles is 12,121. It decreases by 391, compared with the number for January 2023. The US and Russian nuclear stockpiles together continue to constitute around 90% of the total.

The SIPRI YEARBOOK analyzes that the decline "is only due to the USA and Russia dismantling retired warheads. Global reductions of operational warheads appear to have stalled, and their numbers are rising again."

Country	Deployed Warheads	Stored Warheads	Retired Warheads	Total Inventory (As of January 2024)	Total Inventory (As of January 2023)
USA	1,770	1,938	1,336	5,044	5,244
Russia	1,710	2,670	1,200	5,580	5,889
UK	120	105	-	225	225
France	280	10	..	290	290
China	24	476	-	500	410
India	-	172	..	172	164
Pakistan	-	170	..	170	170
Israel	-	90	..	90	90
North Korea	-	50	..	50	30
Total	3,904	5,681	2,536	12,121	12,512

While the total number of the US and Russian nuclear weapons decreased, Russia increased the number of deployed warheads. China increases 90 warheads and "might have started to deploy a small number of its warheads (c. 24) on their launchers." India and North Korea are expanding their nuclear weapon inventories. North

Korea has assembled perhaps 50 warheads, although it "might have produced enough fissile material to build up to 90 nuclear warheads."

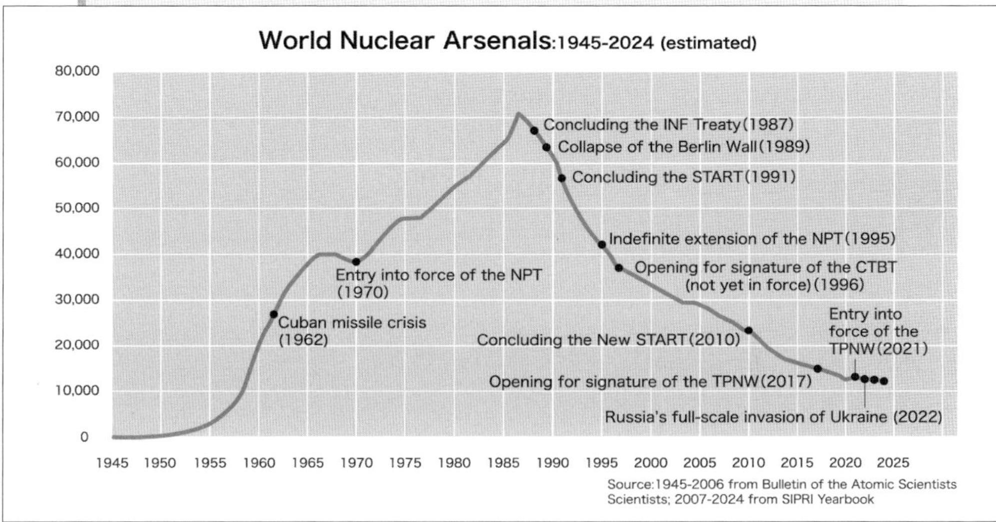

"Status of World Nuclear Forces," Hiroshima for Global Peace, accessed on May 28, 2025. www.pref.hiroshima.lg.jp/site/peace80-en/status-nuclear-forces.html.

Viewpoint 3

> *"The war has shown that Russia does not have a sufficient arsenal of high-precision conventional weapons to mitigate many of the threats to it, or to break the resistance of a country as large as Ukraine."*

Russia Lacks the Firepower to Carry Out Its Threats

Alexander Gabuev

In this viewpoint, Alexander Gabuev writes about the changes that Russia, led by Vladimir Putin, has made to its guidelines for the use of nuclear weapons. Facing attacks from Ukraine that are bolstered by Western allies, Russia is now seeing Ukraine attack within Russian soil. This was not a problem for Putin before the war, and so, in a sense, he has created a new concern. In response, he has lowered the bar for using nuclear weapons. Most experts do not believe Russia will use weapons of mass destruction unless pushed to the brink, but the U.S. and Europe both must be careful about how much they arm Ukraine, so as not to provoke Putin into using extreme measures. Alexander Gabuev is director of the Carnegie Russia Eurasia Center, where he leads a renowned team of analysts who were formerly part of the Carnegie Moscow Center, which was forced to close by the Kremlin in early 2022 after nearly three decades of operation.

"How Serious a Threat Is Russia's New Nuclear Doctrine?," by Alexander Gabuev, Carnegie Politika, October 3, 2024. carnegieendowment.org/russia-eurasia/politika/2024/09/russia-nuclear-doctrine-blackmail?lang=en. Reprinted by permission.

As you read, consider the following questions:

1. What is the difference between Russia's new nuclear doctrine and the old?
2. How has Ukraine successfully fought back against Russia?
3. How has the U.S. been testing Russia's "red line"?

Russian President Vladimir Putin has announced imminent changes to the country's nuclear doctrine. Those changes, announced in public comments at the start of a Security Council meeting on September 25, amount to a lowering of the threshold for the use of nuclear weapons.

The specific wording of the new version of the doctrine will only be known once the corresponding decree is published, but Putin listed the main innovations in his short speech. The first proposal is that aggression against Russia by any non-nuclear state, but "with the participation or support" of a nuclear one, should be considered a joint attack. The second defines the conditions for the possible use of nuclear weapons: Moscow will be prepared to use them "upon receipt of reliable information of a massive launch of air and space attack weapons and their crossing of the state border," including strategic and tactical aircraft, cruise missiles, drones, and hypersonic aircraft.

Finally, nuclear weapons may be used in response to an attack on Russia and Belarus using conventional weapons if that attack poses a "critical threat to sovereignty." Under the current version of Russia's nuclear deterrence policy, approved by Putin in June 2020—just four years ago, but in a very different pre-war era—Moscow is only prepared to use nuclear weapons in response to an attack using conventional weapons specifically against the Russian Federation, and only in cases "when the very existence of the state is threatened."

It was no coincidence that Putin made his comments on the eve of a meeting between U.S. President Joe Biden and his Ukrainian counterpart Volodymyr Zelensky, where a decision was due to be made on allowing Kyiv to use Western missiles to strike deep into Russian territory. That conversation is just the latest episode in an extremely worrying trend for the Kremlin in which the West is expanding its aid for Ukraine while showing increasing disregard for Russia's red lines. In response, the Russian leadership wants to show that its statements should be taken more seriously, and a tougher nuclear doctrine is one of the few tools available to do that. There's no guarantee that this step will help, however.

Only a couple of years ago, it was hard to imagine Western military personnel ever bombing the headquarters of the Russian Black Sea Fleet, or that such an event could possibly take place without sparking a war between Russia and NATO. Yet that is precisely what happened one year ago, when the Ukrainian armed forces launched a strike on Sevastopol using British Storm Shadow missiles. Flight missions for these missiles, as Putin himself stated, could only have been assigned by NATO military personnel. A leaked conversation, apparently between German air force officers discussing the reasons for Berlin's refusal to supply Kyiv with long-range Taurus missiles, revealed similar concerns.

But those strikes against Sevastopol did happen, and now the Russian leadership is ramping up its rhetoric in an attempt to stop the West from allowing Ukraine to fire NATO missiles into internationally recognized Russian territory. According to Putin, such permission would mean that "NATO countries, the United States, and European countries are fighting Russia." In other words, even the president indirectly recognizes the difference between legally established Russian territory and territory captured from Ukraine, including Crimea. That recognition—a position that if publicly voiced in Russia by anyone else would carry the risk of a prison sentence for discrediting the army—is compelling evidence that while NATO is successfully deterring Russia, Russia is not so successful at deterring NATO.

The problem is that right from the very beginning of the full-scale invasion of Ukraine, Putin—who had envisaged that it would all be over in a matter of days—has deployed extremely harsh threats against the West. "Russia will respond immediately, and the consequences will be such as you have never seen in your entire history," he said in his address on February 24, 2022, as the invasion began. At first, Western leaders took him at his word, but it soon became clear that Putin would not achieve his maximal goals in Ukraine and that the Ukrainians, with Western help, could rout Russia on the battlefield and force it to retreat.

Washington then began to test the red lines that Moscow had initially proclaimed. Russia continued to threaten the West with a high price for intervention in the war, but in practice there was little it could do about Western aid to Kyiv, which over the two-and-a-half years of war has grown from modest supplies of small arms and Javelin anti-tank missiles to multibillion-dollar packages that include artillery, air defense, tanks, and F-16 fighters.

The West is trying to nudge Russia's red lines as carefully as possible, via long discussions, media appearances, and communication with Moscow through intelligence channels. This approach irritates Kyiv, but it reduces the risk of an emotional response from Putin. After all, the pyramid of U.S. interests is topped by the security of the United States itself, followed by the security of its formal allies, and only then the interests of friends and partners, which right now include Ukraine.

Washington also believes that unless the Kremlin finds itself on the brink of military defeat in Ukraine, the risk of the use of nuclear weapons remains low. But it is still doing what it can to avoid getting into dangerous situations. Despite Ukrainian drone attacks on the Kremlin and Russian radar stations, which are elements of its nuclear shield, the White House has no intention of changing its cautious approach.

In other words, the nuclear shield has insured Russia against NATO's large-scale involvement in the war, but below that threshold the West is doing more and more to support its Ukrainian allies. The war has shown that Russia does not have a sufficient arsenal of high-precision conventional weapons to mitigate many of the threats to it, or to break the resistance of a country as large as

What Drives North Korea's Militarization?

North Korea's guiding philosophical principles have been *juche* (self-reliance) and *songun* (military-first politics). The military plays a central role in political affairs and its position has been steadily elevated through the Kim dynasty. North Korean leadership believes that hostile external forces, including South Korea and the United States, could mount an attack. As a result, in Pyongyang's eyes, the only way to guarantee national survival is to develop asymmetric military capabilities to thwart its perceived threats. In the decades since the Korean War armistice, the regime in Pyongyang has grown increasingly isolated, in large part due to its ongoing nuclear pursuits and other military provocations. The North's economy and impoverished population of twenty-five million are more and more cut off from the global economy, with limited means to acquire much-needed hard currency. Despite Pyongyang's reputation as a pariah state, Kim Jong-un remains committed to a national strategy of building up the economy and nuclear capabilities jointly. Because Kim has struggled to deliver on his economic promises, he seeks to consolidate his rule by demonstrating unquestioned military might. The nuclear program thus has a dual purpose: to deter external threats and to bolster the image of Kim. Since Kim Jong-un assumed power, the country has shed the ambiguous language surrounding its nuclear and missile development, instead vowing to conduct tests whenever it sees fit. Punitive measures taken against Pyongyang seem to have only emboldened Kim's commitment to strengthening the military. And although diplomatic engagement has in the past temporarily slowed North Korea's rate of testing, it has not resulted in denuclearization.

"North Korea's Military Capabilities," by CFR.org editors, Council on Foreign Relations, last updated June 28, 2022. www.cfr.org/backgrounder/north-korea-nuclear-weapons-missile-tests-military-capabilities.

Ukraine. The Kremlin therefore faces the difficult question of how to restore the effectiveness of Russia's deterrent.

The upcoming changes to the nuclear doctrine are intended to be part of Russia's response. But the changes announced by the president, although verbally lowering the threshold for nuclear use, leave the Kremlin with plenty of room for maneuver and interpretation.

As a result, the most likely scenario for the ongoing war is not a nuclear attack, but increasingly large-scale attacks by Russia and Ukraine against each other with drones and missiles. The latter will be a growing problem for Russia, since Kyiv is actively developing its missile program with the help of Western countries. Ukrainian ballistics could become a much more serious threat as early as next year. As for deterrence and retaliation against the West, the Kremlin is likely to double down on using its toolkit of sabotage, arson, and targeted killings on NATO territory. The transfer of sophisticated Russian weapons to Western adversaries, such as the Houthis in Yemen, is another option on the escalation ladder—but such a bold move will come with its own cost, including pushback from partners vital for the Kremlin's war economy, such as Saudi Arabia.

The irony is that the supposed threats from Ukraine that Putin used to justify the upcoming invasion at the end of 2021 were at the time purely hypothetical and scarcely believable. Yet during the course of the war, many of them have become reality, like self-fulfilling prophecies. By attacking Ukraine, Putin himself created a problem that did not exist before. It's a problem that will haunt the Kremlin in a multitude of ways for many years to come.

Viewpoint 4

> *"North Korea's nuclear progress and the failure of international responses could encourage other countries to acquire nuclear weapons."*

North Korea is a Nuclear Threat

CFR Education

This viewpoint, which is designed as a classroom simulation to help students think through real-world scenarios and the options they present, provides a fictionalized overview of North Korea's nuclear capabilities and its increasing ability to cause harm to other nations. Since its first nuclear test in 2006, the rogue nation has steadily grown as a threat to the rest of the world, and experts believe it now has missiles capable of reaching the United States. North Korea's goals are to prevent another country from striking it, as well as to unify the Korean peninsula. After the Korean War of the 1950s, no peace treaty between the North and South was ever signed. The viewpoint discusses three possible responses to North Korea's military posturing: to engage in negotiations, to assess more punitive sanctions, and to launch a preemptive strike. Not only are these potential solutions all flawed, but North Korea has the support of China and Russia to varying degrees, which complicates matters greatly. CFR Education aims to close the global literacy gap by providing free, nonpartisan resources to help middle, high school, and higher education students gain the knowledge, skills, and perspective to navigate today's interconnected world.

"North Korean Nuclear Threat Educator Overview," by CFR.org editors, Council on Foreign Relations, last updated June 28, 2022. www.cfr.org/backgrounder/north-korea-nuclear-weapons-missile-tests-military-capabilities. Reprinted with permission.

As you read, consider the following questions:

1. How have officials concluded that North Korea now has missiles capable of reaching the west coast of the United States?
2. What actions by the United States does North Korea view as a threat to their country?
3. What are the pros and cons of the three potential solutions to the Korean quandary?

Case Overview

Fictional, set in the present day. The Democratic People's Republic of Korea (North Korea) has for decades pursued its nuclear ambitions to the dismay of both Western countries and its neighbors in East Asia. It recently announced the successful launch of a satellite from a three-stage rocket, and U.S. and allied intelligence services conclude that North Korea now possesses the reentry technology for an intercontinental ballistic missile that could reach the North American west coast. The director of national intelligence has concluded that the missile launch, combined with North Korea's ongoing nuclear tests and its mastery of warhead miniaturization technology, means the country is capable of following through on past threats to fire a nuclear-armed missile against the United States. The president has called an emergency meeting of the United Nations Security Council to present this new intelligence and discuss an international response to North Korea's enhanced capabilities.

Decision Point

U.S. intelligence officials now believe, based on debris recovered from a recent North Korean satellite launch, that North Korea has the technology needed to reach the west coast of North America. The launch came days after Kim walked away from nuclear negotiations with the United States. Kim cited concerns over proposed inspections of its nuclear sites. The U.S. director of national intelligence has concluded that the launch means that the country is now capable of following through on past threats to fire nuclear-armed missiles at the United States. The United States has requested a meeting of the UN Security Council to present this new intelligence and discuss an international response to North Korea's enhanced capabilities.

...

Policy Options

North Korea's pursuit of a nuclear weapons program is motivated principally by the desire to develop a deterrent against an attack by external forces, particularly the United States or South Korea. North Korea's threats have been directed primarily toward the United States and its allies. The Kim regime regards the U.S. military presence in South Korea (which hosts nearly 28,000 U.S. troops as of September 2023) as an obstacle to a North Korea–led unification of the peninsula. It also sees the United States as the most dangerous military threat it faces.

The most important priority for the UN Security Council on this matter is eliminating North Korea's nuclear weapons program. The Security Council is a core part of global efforts to stop the spread, or proliferation, of nuclear weapons. Among other things, it is charged with responding to violations of the NPT. Most frequently, the Security Council acts by imposing sanctions on any country or group that violates the treaty. Since North Korea's withdrawal from the NPT in 2003, the Security Council has been at the center of international efforts to halt the country's nuclear development. After Pyongyang's first nuclear test in 2006, the Security Council unanimously approved a series of sanctions that have grown increasingly severe in response to tests.

North Korea already has the capability to hit South Korea and Japan with nuclear missiles. Advancements in its nuclear technology and missile capabilities could pose a serious security threat not just to the United States but also to its allies. Furthermore, the capabilities could pose a threat to the Asia-Pacific region more broadly. A nuclear attack by North Korea on one of its rivals could destroy cities and kill millions of people, potentially triggering a devastating conflict in the region.

North Korea's nuclear progress and the failure of international responses could encourage other countries to acquire nuclear weapons. Countries such as Japan and South Korea could face domestic political pressure to respond to acquire nuclear weapons of their own to deter North Korea. Such pressure would be a defeat for global nonproliferation efforts. Likewise, it would make any conflict in Northeast Asia far more destructive.

Any response to North Korea's nuclear development will need the approval of all five of the Security Council's veto-wielding permanent members (P5). Although the Security Council has been unanimous in its past condemnations of North Korea's nuclear endeavors, the diverging interests of the P5, especially of China, Russia, and the United States, could get in the way of any new action. China has offered only a mixed record of supporting and upholding sanctions against North Korea. It values North Korea as a buffer between itself and the thriving capitalist democracy of South Korea. Russia has increasingly seen North Korea as a strategic partner, especially since the war in Ukraine began. Both countries have reasons to oppose harsh penalties against North Korea.

With those concerns in mind, the Security Council has a few options it could pursue in response to the North Korean nuclear threat.

Condemn testing and call for negotiations to resume

The UN Security Council could adopt a resolution condemning North Korea's latest missile test. This resolution could also call on it not to test or use missiles or nuclear weapons in the future. This resolution could also outline consequences if North Korea does not comply. Potential consequences include additional sanctions. The Security Council could further call for North Korea to return to negotiations over its nuclear program. In exchange, such negotiations could offer sanctions relief, economic aid, or a formal peace treaty ending the Korean War. Such negotiations could take place between the United States and North Korea alone, under the previous framework of the Six Party Talks, or in a new format. If an agreement is achieved, the Security Council could also call on North Korea to admit outside inspectors to monitor the agreement's progress.

This is the least ambitious option, but it is the most likely to pass. If successful, this option could reduce the threat of North Korean nuclear missiles and avoid rising tensions or even war. However, this option cannot guarantee any results. North Korea has ignored similar resolutions. Past negotiations have failed or led to broken promises from North Korea. The Security Council risks giving North Korea aid or sanctions relief and receiving nothing in return. At best, failed negotiations would result in no change to the situation. At worst, they could lead to the Kim regime increasing its nuclear development, damage the United Nations' reputation, and bring the world closer to nuclear conflict.

The Security Council could choose to pursue negotiations first; should they prove unsuccessful, it could then resort to one of two other options.

Adopt new sanctions

The UN Security Council could adopt a new round of sanctions against North Korea. This could further limit the country's access to fuel, raw materials, and luxury goods. The Security Council could also call for states to crack down on North Korea's illegal activities abroad to restrict its access to funds and nuclear materials.

Expanding sanctions would be driven by the assumption that the best path forward is to isolate North Korea until its government collapses or changes. The Security Council has approved sanctions in response to past nuclear tests, but so far these have not stopped North Korea's nuclear development. Stronger sanctions could finally produce change. However, there is no guarantee that sanctions will have the desired effect. Sanctions have already put North Korea's economy in a dire situation. Additional pressure on the economy could lead to further worsening conditions for North Koreans rather than any policy change on nuclear weapons.

Moreover, sanctions take time to have an effect. During this time, North Korea's nuclear program would continue to pose a threat.

Authorize preventive military strikes

The UN Security Council could adopt a resolution calling on North Korea to denuclearize and authorize member states to enforce that resolution by force. This would lead the United States and possibly its other allies to launch a preventive military strike. This strike would be aimed at destroying as many missile and nuclear-related sites and as much equipment as possible. Even if these strikes could not completely eliminate North Korea's nuclear program, they could set it back for the foreseeable future. Given the current phase of North Korea's nuclear weapons development, this option would likely require a large-scale military operation to succeed.

This option offers a crucial benefit. It could reduce the threat of North Korea's missiles and nuclear weapons for years to come. Preventive strikes would also demonstrate a strong international commitment to nonproliferation. They could further send an effective warning to North Korea and others against developing nuclear weapons in the future.

However, China borders North Korea and has signed a security treaty with North Korea. It is unlikely to allow any military action by the United States or its allies. Moreover, a military intervention comes with significant risks. A preventive strike cannot guarantee the destruction of all North Korean nuclear capabilities. A military strike also risks a North Korean retaliation that could escalate and have devastating results. South Korea's densely populated capital, Seoul, is particularly vulnerable to North Korea's military because of how close it is to the border with the North. Even limited retaliation by North Korea could lead to many deaths and a high level of destruction in Seoul. Moreover, if North Korea fears losing its nuclear weapons, it could also decide to use them first.

Viewpoint 3

> *"...the more we don't use nuclear weapons, the better they work."*

The US Doesn't Need More Nuclear Weapons

Sveta Yefimenko

In this viewpoint, Sveta Yefimenko writes about the United States's plan to upgrade its nuclear arsenal over the next few decades. The upgrade was delayed for many years as the country focused on the war on terror, but China and Russia have both upgraded their arsenal, and the U.S. feels the need to respond. Some politicians have called for the U.S. to not only upgrade, but also expand its nuclear arsenal. Yefimenko believes that expansion is misguided. While Yefimenko acknowledges that an upgrade is overdue, she argues that expansion is a recipe for disaster. Sveta Yefimenko is a political copywriter and researcher. She holds a BA in Political Science from the University of Colorado Denver and a PhD in Russian Studies from the University of Exeter. Her current research focuses on how war narratives inform nation building and collective memory in Russia.

As you read, consider the following questions:

1. What are the three legs of the U.S. nuclear triad?

"Opinion—The US Doesn't Need More Nuclear Weapons," by Sveta Yefimenko, E-International Relations, October 10, 2023. Reprinted by permission.

2. What three reasons does Yefimenko cite to support her argument that the U.S. does not need more nuclear weapons?
3. When Yefimenko refers to Henry Kissinger as "that great paragon of world peace," how does she mean it?

For the first time since the conclusion of the Cold War, the US has embarked on a concerted and long-overdue effort to modernize its strategic and tactical nuclear arsenal. The 2022 Nuclear Posture Review identified modernization or replacement of nuclear weapons and all three legs of the nuclear triad—strategic bombers, ballistic missile submarines, and underground silos housing intercontinental ballistic missiles—as a top priority. The US Department of Defense released a fact sheet which noted that most nuclear systems in the US are currently "operating beyond their original design life, risking system effectiveness, reliability, and availability." Updating nuclear warheads and delivery systems is a time-consuming and expensive process that's projected to take the next two decades and hundreds of billions of dollars to complete.

The modernization program was delayed for decades as Washington dedicated military resources to the Global War on Terror. America's nuclear program was conceived and designed in a geopolitical landscape that differed dramatically from today's; terrorism, cyberattacks, and nuclear-capable adversaries like Russia and China contour the current threat environment. This is in striking contrast to the optimism immediately following the Cold War, when there was hope of normalizing relations with Moscow and China's "peaceful rise" was seen as a positive development. The push toward modernization comes in the context of Russia's invasion of Ukraine and increased competition with China as both nuclear peers aggressively modernize their own arsenals. For example, Russia recently claimed to have tested the Burevestnik, a low-flying cruise missile that can carry a nuclear warhead and is also nuclear powered (which means that it can remain airborne for days) while China's rapid nuclear build-up includes fast breeder reactors, new nuclear silos, and more sophisticated nuclear submarines.

As the relationship between Beijing and Moscow grows closer, so does the threat of nuclear conflict. The rising tension has led some analysts to call for the US to go beyond mere modernization by significantly expanding its stockpile of nuclear missiles. Robert Peters at The Heritage Foundation, a conservative think tank, writes that we have entered a new nuclear age in which the US is tasked with deterring both Russia and China, as well as an aggressive North Korea. Given the higher stakes, Peters argues, the US needs not only more but more varied nuclear weapons to match the adversaries' nuclear forces. Peters concludes: "After more than three decades of shrinking nuclear arsenals due to arms control measures, it might finally be time for the United States to consider expanding the size of its strategic arsenal given Russian and Chinese actions." Matthew Costlow advanced a similar position in the Wall Street Journal. Costlow posits that, since post Cold War enemy nuclear arsenals have undergone rapid modernization and the Pentagon estimates that China's arsenal will quadruple by 2030, the US needs "nuclear expansion" to maintain effective deterrent capability.

Expanding the US nuclear arsenal is misguided for three reasons. First, the US already has assured destruction capability. Second, a nuclear buildup courts geopolitical conflict that can lead to nuclear crisis. Finally, the world has nuclear weapons to spare. Let's examine each of these reasons in detail.

Firstly, the US already possesses assured destruction capability. Historically, Washington's nuclear policy has prioritized deterrence based on assured destruction, with most defence experts agreeing that the approach has been a resounding success since no country has attacked the US with nuclear weapons. Even in the event of a massive nuclear strike on American nuclear targets by a nuclear peer like Russia or China, the US would have sufficient weapons left for a retaliatory strike that can effectively wipe out both the adversary's military infrastructure and economic base. Indeed, a nuclear retaliatory strike is guaranteed to hit cities and kill millions of civilians even if it were intended to strike solely military targets. Since the American nuclear arsenal was designed to withstand a worst-case scenario (such as absorbing a massive nuclear attack and then retaliating with devastating destruction), the nation would have sufficient nuclear power to conduct effective counterforce strikes even if a competitor's arsenal is numerically larger. America doesn't need parity for effective deterrence; it just needs enough weapons for assured destruction. Put simply, the more we don't use nuclear weapons, the better they work.

Secondly, a nuclear build-up courts geopolitical conflict that can lead to nuclear crisis. Is expanding the nuclear stockpile a provocation or a rational reaction to enemy threats? Well, it's complicated. If the US expands its nuclear arsenal, Russia and China are likely to respond in kind in order to keep pace, skyrocketing global tensions, further straining relations, and risking a crisis that can swiftly turn nuclear. The looming nuclear danger already dwarfs the height of the Cold War. China, which has never been party to a nuclear-arms agreement, is on track to become a nuclear peer with the US by 2035 and the New Strategic Arms Reduction Treaty (START) with Russia—which limits each nation to 1,550 warheads—is set to expire in 2026. Given Washington's modernization aims, Beijing and Moscow are both determined to ensure that their nuclear forces can penetrate US missile defences. If New START expires without a follow-up treaty, both Russia and the US may upload hundreds of additional warheads onto their launchers. Negotiations for a successor treaty broke down following Russia's invasion of Ukraine, and it's likely that political tension will continue to impede further dialogue. Yet as Charles L. Glaser, James M.

Acton, and Steve Fetter have recently argued in Foreign Affairs, increasing nuclear threat capabilities is likely to add more fuel to the three-way arms race with Russia and China, which means that the US may have to fight both superpowers simultaneously. For more than 50 years, China presented Washington with a distinct but separate foreign policy challenge from, first, the Soviet Union and now, Russia. As the two nations grow closer, united in part by what they regard as American global "hegemony", a deepening of hostilities can lead to aggression that risks nuclear war.

Lastly, the world has nuclear arms to spare. Following years of Trump-era secrecy, the Biden administration's declassification of stockpile numbers reveals that America's current nuclear arsenal clocks in at 1,670 deployed strategic warheads, with thousands more languishing in reserve or retirement. For comparison, Russia has 1,674 actively deployed warheads and China has 410 reserve warheads. However, the actual number of nuclear weapons necessary to inflict civilization-ending destruction is a modest 100. Any more than that, and we're in for nuclear winter on an uninhabitable planet, to say nothing of diminishing returns. Consider this: a global nuclear exchange could kill 500 to 600 million people in minutes. Even Henry Kissinger, that great paragon of world peace, had mused, "What is the sense in developing a weapon that can destroy a city twice over?" While some defence experts have countered this logic by pointing out that many of America's land-based missiles are scattered across sparsely populated regions to draw fire from opponents, thereby exhausting the adversary's supply of atomic ammunition, it's worth pointing out that this strategy would kill millions of people and make America's hinterland uninhabitable for many generations.

To summarize, while modernizing the US nuclear arsenal is a long-overdue necessity, expanding it would be a mistake. Adding more nuclear weapons to America's stockpile is a costly and unnecessary endeavour that would make the world less safe by increasing the chances of nuclear catastrophe. Even with a complete overhaul of America's nuclear program, enough of the Russian and Chinese arsenals would survive a first strike to utterly topple America's economy and society in retaliation, leaving radioactive ruins where New York, Chicago, and San Francisco once stood.

Periodical and Internet Sources Bibliography

The following articles have been selected to supplement the diverse views presented in this chapter.

William Alberque, "An Unreal Pain: Russia's New Nuclear Doctrine Delivers Headlines, But Not Change," Stimson, February 3, 2025. www.stimson.org/2025/an-unreal-pain-russias-new-nuclear-doctrine-delivers-headlines-but-not-change/.

Brad T. Gericke and Donna Wilt, "Nuclear weapons on the battlefield are a growing risk. US and allied militaries should prepare now," Atlantic Council, November 5, 2024. www.atlanticcouncil.org/blogs/new-atlanticist/nuclear-weapons-on-the-battlefield-are-a-growing-risk-us-and-allied-militaries-should-prepare-now/.

Francesca Giovannini, "The Role of Nuclear Weapons in the 21st Century," Harvard Kennedy School Belfer Center for Science and International Affairs, Spring 2022. www.belfercenter.org/publication/role-nuclear-weapons-21st-century.

Jakub Graca and Justyna Gotkowska, "NATO's Nuclear Deterrence: Is It Time for Change?" OSW, June 6, 2024. www.osw.waw.pl/en/publikacje/osw-commentary/2024-06-19/natos-nuclear-deterrence-it-time-change.

Ulrich Kühn, "The Fall Crisis of 2022: Why Did Russia Not Use Nuclear Arms?," *Defense and Security Analysis*, January 2, 2025. www.tandfonline.com/doi/full/10.1080/14751798.2024.2442794#abstract.

Adam Lowther and Stephen Cimbala, "Future Technology and Nuclear Deterrence," *Wild Blue Yonder*, February 3, 2022. https://www.airuniversity.af.edu/Wild-Blue-Yonder/Article-Display/Article/2071083/future-technology-and-nuclear-deterrence/.

Michael Mandelbaum, "The Future of Nuclear Weapons," *Naval War College Review* Vol. 35, No. 5 (September–October 1982), pp. 58-79. www.jstor.org/stable/44636217?seq=1.

Rishi Paul, "Bluff and Bluster: Why Putin Revised Russia's Nuclear Doctrine," European Leadership Network, November 25, 2024. europeanleadershipnetwork.org/commentary/bluff-and-bluster-why-putin-revised-russias-nuclear-doctrine/.

Miles Pomper, David Santoro, and Nikolai Sokov, "The Future of NATO's Nuclear Posture and Arms Control in Today's More Dangerous World," Middlebury Institute of International Studies at Monterey, September 2024. nonproliferation.org/wp content/uploads/2024/09/ op62_the_future_of_natos_nuclear_posture.pdf.

Steffan Puwal, "Should Artificial Intelligence Be Banned from Nuclear Weapons Systems?," Nato Review, April 12, 2024. www.nato.int/docu/review/articles/2024/04/12/should-artificial-intelligence-be-banned-from-nuclear-weapons-systems/index.html.

Madeline Zutt and Michal Onderco, "How emerging technologies impact the future of nuclear risk and arms control," European Leadership Network, September 1, 2020. europeanleadershipnetwork.org/commentary/how-emerging-technologies-impact-the-future-of-nuclear-risk-and-arms-control/.

OPPOSING VIEWPOINTS® SERIES

CHAPTER 4

Can Global Peace Ever Be Achieved?

Chapter Preface

> *"And they'll say we're disturbing the peace, but there is no peace. What really bothers them is that we are disturbing the war."*
>
> *--Howard Zinn*

The irony in today's world is that one must be brave to protest for peace. The forces that rise up against those who would demand an end to conflict are powerful, wealthy, and driven. They are seemingly as motivated as the "peaceniks" they oppose.

For one thing, war is big business. It makes people rich even as it destroys the lives of others. Among the largest American defense contractors are corporations such as Lockheed Martin, RTX Corporation (formerly Raytheon Technologies Corporation), Boeing, and General Dynamics. The British corporation BAE Systems is another major player. In China, corporations such as the Aviation Industry Corporation of China and the China Aerospace Science and Industry Corporation are major players. Russia's largest war contractor at the time of the invasion of Ukraine is Rostec. It employs hundreds of thousands of Russian citizens. The future of war and the big money companies that feed the beast is on the rise, not the decline.

In 2025, Lockheed Martin was valued at over 100 billion dollars. Much of its income derives from the taxes of the ordinary U.S. citizen. The company's headquarters is located less than fifteen miles from the nation's capital, a prime location from which to lobby American lawmakers.

No less of an expert on war, general and former President Dwight D. Eisenhower famously warned the country to "guard against the acquisition of unwarranted influence, whether sought or unsought, by the military–industrial complex." His sage advice has largely gone unheeded in the 21st century. The military budget of the United States was $850 billion in the year 2025.

Protesting against this swollen budget and the damage it does worldwide has long been a dangerous gesture. In 1846, writer Henry David Thoreau refused to pay his taxes in part due to his non-support of the Mexican War. He was thrown in jail. He spent only a night in incarceration, but the message from the powers that be was clear: citizens must pay their taxes, and the government can use the revenue in any manner it sees fit. In his now famous essay, "Civil Disobedience," Thoreau wrote, "Men generally, under such a government as this, think that they ought to wait until they have persuaded the majority to alter [unjust laws]. They think that, if they should resist, the remedy would be worse than the evil. But it is the fault of the government itself that the remedy *is* worse than the evil. *It* makes it worse."

It is true that those who demand peace from their government, when they work together, can have a powerful effect. The Vietnam War protests of the 1970s may well have compelled Washington to bring the war to an end. The four students who were shot dead by National Guard troops during an anti-war demonstration at Kent State University in 1970, are proof of the dangers. And no one ever speaks of the additional nine students who were wounded during the assault, including one who was paralyzed for life.

For some, protesting war is nearly as dangerous as combat.

Take the 2024 protests against the Israeli-Hamas conflict that began with the murder of over 1,000 Israeli citizens. There can be no doubt that Hamas ushered in this terrible time with its initial attack. However, the zeal with which Israel, under Benjamin Netanyahu, has fought back is unlike anything seen in the region.

Israel has a right to defend itself, certainly—but its troops have killed over 50,000 Gazans as of this writing, many of them women and children.

Naturally, the war's brutality has sparked protests worldwide, especially on college campuses, which have taken the lead in anti-war protests. Major protests at universities such as Cornell, Columbia, and Stanford have been covered on network news. The war in Gaza may well have had an impact on the 2024 election, where anti-Biden sentiment and Donald Trump's promise that he would end the war helped put him over the top. Voters with Middle-Eastern roots in Michigan, for example, punished Democrats for their inability to bring about an end to the war.

In 2025, however, the Trump administration began detaining immigrant students who were prominently involved in the pro-Palestinian protests. Claiming that these students were aiding the terrorist activities of Hamas, Trump instructed U.S. Immigration and Customs Enforcement (ICE) to gather up students from colleges such as Columbia, Tufts, and the University of Alabama and hold them in detention centers in Louisiana. In most cases, no charges have been filed against them. Their sin was living legally in the U.S. while attending college and protesting American foreign policy. Supporters say that these students' first amendment rights are being violated, while authorities insist that their efforts are undermining U.S. aims.

Protesting in America is once again becoming dangerous. Apparently autocrats are not inclined to "give peace a chance."

Viewpoint 1

> *"...societal resilience refers to a country's ability to adapt, withstand, and recover from various challenges, shocks, and disruptions while maintaining its essential functions and safeguarding social wellbeing."*

These Five Countries Are Leading the Way in Positive Peace

Georgina Ullman

In this viewpoint, Georgina Ullman describes five countries that have shown marked success in achieving positive peace on a scale measured by an independent think tank. These five countries are Uzbekistan, Armenia, The Gambia, Taiwan, and Ireland. The notion of "Positive Peace," as opposed to simply "peace," suggests that these countries have not only curtailed violence, but that they have also created a stable and resilient environment that can resist future urges toward warfare. While issues such as corruption and human rights have not been completely solved, these countries are moving away from autocracy and toward economic, environmental, and social wellbeing. Georgina Ullman is a Communications Associate at the IEP and is completing her Bachelor of Arts in Politics, International Relations and Socio-Legal studies at the University of Sydney. Her areas of interest include international security studies and media politics and communication.

"The Five Countries Leading the Way in Positive Peace," by Georgina Ullman, Vision of Humanity, November 13, 2024. www.visionofhumanity.org/the-5-countries-leading-the-way-in-positive-peace/. Reprinted by permission.

As you read, consider the following questions:

1. What is the Positive Peace Index?
2. How has Uzbekistan, a former Soviet republic, moved toward positive peace?
3. What factors played a role in Taiwan's improved Positive Peace Index score?

As levels of conflict have reached an all-time high since World War II, societal resilience is more relevant than ever to navigate this new international norm.

According to the Positive Peace Report 2024, released by the independent think tank the Institute for Economics & Peace (IEP), societal resilience refers to a country's ability to adapt, withstand, and recover from various challenges, shocks, and disruptions while maintaining its essential functions and safeguarding social wellbeing. This resilience is closely tied to the notion of Positive Peace, which has been shown to correlate strongly with a broad spectrum of economic, environmental, and social wellbeing indicators.

The Positive Peace Index (PPI) serves as a comprehensive measure of societal resilience across 163 countries, covering 99.7% of the world's population. It provides valuable insights into the factors that contribute to peaceful societies and allows for quantitative comparisons between nations. The PPI is based upon eight Pillars of Positive Peace, which all contribute to the notion of Positive Peace. By examining the PPI, we can identify areas of improvement and take advantage of shared strengths to promote non-violent conflict resolution and enhance overall development and wellbeing.

Five Countries that Have Made Significant Strides in Improving Their Societal Resilience

Recent data from the report highlights five countries that have made significant strides in improving their societal resilience between 2013-2022. Uzbekistan, Armenia, The Gambia, Taiwan, and Ireland each improved their PPI scores by 7% or more, demonstrating remarkable improvements in various aspects of Positive Peace.

Uzbekistan

Uzbekistan recorded the largest percentage improvement in Positive Peace of all countries in the past decade, with a 9.9% improvement in the country's PPI score. Uzbekistan has undergone significant transformations since 2015, implementing deep administrative reforms and moving away from post-Soviet isolationism. Other key changes include liberalising the exchange rate regime, easing visa requirements, and introducing tax reforms to attract international investments. The country has also made efforts to reduce state intervention in the economy and private affairs.

While corruption remains a challenge, Uzbekistan has made progress in this area, particularly through the implementation of the "On Anti-Corruption" legal framework. These reforms have led to significant improvements in telecom infrastructure, youth employment, education and training (NEET), and international tourism indicators. There have also been improvements in the areas of government openness and transparency, regulatory quality and group grievance.

Armenia

Armenia recorded the second highest improvement in the Russia and Eurasia region, with a 9.2% increase in its PPI score. The country saw improvements across all domains of Positive Peace, with the most significant in their telecom infrastructure index, which coupled with an improvement in the quality of information indicator, resulted in the overall improvement in the Free Flow of Information Pillar.

The country has also been implementing strategies to combat corruption, establishing a Corruption Prevention Commission and adopting new laws to reform its anti-corruption framework, improving the control of corruption indicator.

The Gambia

The Gambia improved its Positive Peace score by 7.1% in the period of 2013-2022, showing progress in all domains and six of the eight Pillars of Positive Peace. The nation has undergone a significant political transition, moving from an autocratic regime to a multiparty republic following the election of President Barrow in 2016.

Under the new administration, The Gambia has focused on improving academic freedom, the judiciary, and the online environment. A notable achievement was the passage of the Access to Information Bill in 2021, which recognises access to information as a legal right.

Taiwan

Taiwan has earnt the title of top performer in the Asia-Pacific region, improving its PPI score to rank 32nd globally. The country saw improvements in all demands of Positive Peace and all but one of the Pillars of Peace. The only area that declined was in Good Relations with Neighbours, largely due to escalating tensions with China.

The Pillar that saw the most improvement was the Well-functioning Government Pillar, which was largely driven by a 50% improvement in the government openness and transparency indicator. This was mostly due to the successful COVID-19 response by the government, and the will to bring civil society closer to the law-making process. Further, the Taiwanese government is taking strides in addressing important indicators such as improving the country's Free Flow of information Pillar and telecom infrastructure index indicator.

Ireland

Ireland, which already ranks high on the PPI in 7th place, further improved its Positive Peace score by 6.7% since 2013. The country recorded substantial improvements in the Structures domain, with a 19.1% increase, and a 3.1% improvement in Attitudes. However, there was a slight decline in the Institutions domain.

In particular, Ireland displayed significant improvements in the Sound Business Environment Pillar, recording a 23.6% improvement since 2013, largely bolstered by improvements in the GDP per capita indicator. The country also saw significant improvements in the Acceptance of the Rights of Others Pillar, particularly on the group grievance and gender inequality indicators, which improved by 26.9% and 15.2% respectively.

Viewpoint 2

"Although each of these countries still face domestic and international challenges, their successes can help guide other countries."

Sustainable Peace Can Be Achieved

Vision of Humanity

This viewpoint centers around three countries, Bhutan, Peru, and Timor-Leste, that are leading the way in implementing sustainable peace. These three countries differ greatly geographically, culturally, and economically, suggesting that the future of peace is possible anywhere on the globe with the right set of circumstances and forward-thinking leaders. A key factor in the development of each country is increasing socio-economic practices to enhance the lives of citizens. All three countries mentioned in the viewpoint have made strides toward doing so. Founded in 2008, Vision of Humanity is a destination for peace studies, providing analysis, data, and editorial through a lens of peace, security and development. They are non-partisan, reaching more than 1.5 million unique visitors each year with intelligent insight, resources, and media.

As you read, consider the following questions:

1. How has Bhutan improved the country's political culture?

"3 Countries Highlight Ways to Implement Sustainable Peace," Vision of Humanity, November 21, 2018. www.visionofhumanity.org/three-countries-structures-institutions-attitudes-can-implemented-sustain-peace/. Reprinted by permission.

2. What factors have allowed Peru to achieve major gains in culture as compared with its neighbors?
3. As one of the newest countries in the world, how has Timor-Leste worked to improve the lives of its citizens?

Unique solutions for sustainable peace are demonstrated in these three countries that vary geographically, culturally and economically.

Bhutan, Peru, and Timor-Leste are three countries highlighting how unique structures, institutions and attitudes can be implemented for sustainable peace. Although each of these countries still face domestic and international challenges, their successes can help guide other countries.

Bhutan

Renowned for conceiving Gross National Happiness, a metric that has been codified as a national priority in the country's constitution, Bhutan leads South Asia in Positive Peace.

A 2007 royal decree legalised political parties in order to improve the country's political culture.

In 2008, Bhutan elected its first National Assembly, marking the successful transition from an absolute monarchy to a constitutional monarchy.

A well functioning government is one of the eight pillars of Positive Peace, and provides the opportunity for peaceful attitudes and institutions to be implemented from the top-down.

The government also runs an online web portal, the National Portal of Bhutan, that contains a range of practical information on legislation, requirements and licenses for businesses that could be essential for entrepreneurs.

Bhutan's per capita income has grown steadily from US$340 in 1980 to US$5570 in 2011.

Socioeconomic development programs, funded by hydroelectricity exports and foreign aid, have enabled Bhutan to dramatically improve its poverty and education rates.

Targeted government programs such as the Rural Economy Advancement Program (REAP) and National Rehabilitation Program (NRP) have provided monetary and infrastructural aid to marginalised communities.

Levels of human capital continue to improve in Bhutan, with 6,000 educators in the country today, compared to 40 in the 1960s.

In collaboration with India and Bangladesh, Bhutan, the only carbon neutral country, is working on hydropower projects that continue to expand the country's capacity to generate and export energy.

Peru

After decades of military coups, violent insurgencies, social unrest and macroeconomic challenges, Peru has emerged as one of Latin America's most prosperous countries.

Although Peru still faces challenges, the country has made strides towards the attitudes, institutions and structures that sustain peace. Prudent monetary, exchange and investment policies have allowed Peru to weather international economic crises and commodity price declines.

The country's economy grew at an average annual rate of 6.1% between 2002 and 2012, which has increased per capita income levels and reduced poverty.

Peru's High-Level Anti-Corruption Commission seeks to prevent and combat corruption by coordinating government anti-corruption efforts and proposing policy solutions.

This promotes a sound business environment, which has been on track and improving since macroeconomic reforms in the 1990s halted hyperinflation.

Compared to its neighbours, Peru's homicide rate is low. In 2004, after decades of border disputes, Peru and Chile signed a statement expressing their intent to forge closer ties and develop bilateral relations.

The improvement of relations with regional neighbours is one welcome step towards regional peace improvements, but internal relationships are improving too.

The Commission of Truth and Reconciliation was set up to establish justice surrounding the country's internal conflict during the 1990s.

More recently, in 2011, the Peruvian Congress passed a law requiring the consultation of indigenous and rural communities before developments or projects involving their ancestral territories, which in the past has been a source of much conflict.

Timor-Leste

Having only gained independence in 2002, Timor-Leste is one of the world's youngest countries. In 2002, Timor-Leste elected their first president and in 2017 the country peacefully transferred power for the second time.

Timor-Leste's National Election Commission (CNE) and Technical Secretariat for Electoral Administration collectively ensure lawful elections, register voters and administer civic education.

This initiative boosted the country's success in the 'well-functioning government' pillar of Positive Peace.

Between 2005 and 2017, the young country experienced the Asia-Pacific region's largest improvement in Equitable Distribution of Resources, illustrating the country's development gains.

Although almost half of the Timorese population live below the national poverty line, the government is committed to improving the socioeconomic prospects of subsistence farmers.

In 2016, the Ministry of Agriculture and Fisheries' introduced a US$21 million project aimed at increasing smallholder agricultural productivity.

Further, the Government investment in education and workforce development through programs such as the Education Sector Support Project (ESSP) have led to an 8.8%

improvement in High Levels of Human Capital on the Positive Peace Index.

The ESSP partnership has constructed and rehabilitated 2,100 classrooms, giving capacity for 65,000+ students to attend school.

Viewpoint 3

> *"Afghanistan ranked as the world's least peaceful country for six years in a row but has been surpassed in this year's edition of the Peace Index by South Sudan, Sudan and Yemen which now holds that unenviable distinction."*

Peaceful Nations Generate Economic Value

Luca Ventura

In this viewpoint, Luca Ventura looks at the countries that are achieving a more positive peace and those that are declining. Peaceful countries, he writes, have a tendency to generate positive economic value, as they can focus on serving their populace and not on external warfare. However, peacefulness is on the decline in more countries than it is on the rise. Western Europe has led the way in achieving higher levels of peace, but the military expenditures in these countries are substantially increasing, likely from the Russian threat. Even so, there is a great benefit to peace beyond the economic. Peaceful countries, Ventura writes, tend to be more productive, informed, and educated. Luca Ventura is a writer at Global Finance Magazine and Vanity Fair Italia.

"World's Most Peaceful Country 2024 Global Peace Index," by Luca Ventura, *Global Finance*, June 12, 2024. gfmag.com/data/most-peaceful-countries/. Reprinted by permission.

As you read, consider the following questions:

1. How does Ventura quantify the economic cost of violence?
2. How is the global peace index determined?
3. According to the viewpoint, what factors undermine global peacefulness?

Peace, some people say, starts with a smile. Peaceful societies enjoy greater income growth, stronger currencies and higher foreign investment—not to mention political stability and a greater sense of happiness among their citizens.

The economic impact of violence on the global economy is quantifiable: in 2023, it accounted for $19.1 trillion in purchasing-power parity (PPP) terms, or 13.5% of total global GDP—that's $2,380 less economic output for each person on the planet. This represents an overall increase of $158 billion from the year before, and was largely driven by a 20% increase in GDP losses from conflict. Meanwhile, expenditure on peacebuilding and peacekeeping efforts totaled just $49.6 billion, less than 0.6% of total military spending.

These are the most significant takeaways from the 2024 Global Peace Index, the world's leading measure of global peace. Compiled by the international think-tank Institute for Economics and Peace (IEP), it covers 163 independent states and territories home to 99.7% of the world's population. The ranking, which is based on 23 indicators grouped into three criteria (societal safety and security; extent of ongoing domestic and international conflict; and degree of militarization), shows 65 countries recording improvement and 97 showing deterioration, more than any year since the inception of the Global Peace Index in 2008.

Global Peace by Region

In total, the level of global peacefulness decreased this year by 0.56% according to the IEP researchers. That might not seem like much, yet it is worth noting that it is the twelfth time that the average has declined, for an overall reduction of 4.5% since the index was launched. Meanwhile, the number of refugees and internally displaced persons has rocketed to 95 million, with 16 nations with at least 5% of the population are either refugees or internally displaced.

It should be no surprise that political instability and unresolved internal conflicts are major factors undermining global peacefulness. Afghanistan ranked as the world's least peaceful country for six years in a row but has been surpassed in this year's edition of the Peace Index by South Sudan, Sudan and Yemen which now holds that unenviable distinction. Ukraine—which last year recorded the largest deterioration in the index, falling 14 places to the 157th spot—dropped 2 positions further, to 159. Needless to say, the conflict in Gaza also has had a negative impact on global peacefulness, with Israel and Palestine recording the first and fourth largest deteriorations in the ranking, respectively. Ecuador, Gabon and Haiti were the other nations that experienced a sharp decline.

On the whole, last year saw 162,000 deaths due to conflict, marking the second-highest toll in three decades. The wars in Ukraine and Gaza were responsible for nearly 75% of these fatalities with Ukraine alone accounting for over half (83,000 deaths) while Gaza saw at least 33,000 deaths by April 2024. Another worrying trend is that conflicts are becoming more internationalized: 92 countries are now involved in external conflicts in some form—the respective figure from the 2008 index was just 33.

Even more concerning, the Institute for Economics and Peace researchers point out, many of the factors that typically precede major conflicts are more pronounced today than they have been since the end of the Second World War. There are currently 56 active conflicts, the most since the late 1940s, with fewer conflicts being settled, militarily or through peace agreements.

Regional Distribution of Peaceful Countries

Regionally, North America recorded the largest average deterioration of all the regions, with a drop of almost 5% primarily driven by increases in violent crime and fear of violence in both Canada and the US. Home to four of the ten least peaceful countries in the world, the Middle East and North Africa (MENA) is the least peaceful region globally. Sub-Saharan Africa, the second least peaceful region, also recorded a fall in peacefulness this year.

Elsewhere, Central America and the Caribbean's average fell slightly by 0.17%, with seven out of 12 countries declining in their scores and five countries improving. Notably, El Salvador and Nicaragua recorded respectively the first and third-highest improvements globally. South America declined too (by 3.6%) as a result of deteriorations in the Safety and Security and Ongoing Conflict domains.

Western Europe remains the world's most peaceful region overall, with seven nations placing in the top 10, including the top three slots. Europe's strength arises from its relatively low internal conflict and political instability and high socio-economic development, buoyed by longstanding efforts to develop peaceful societies at home. Still, last year, the continent recorded its largest year-on-year increase in military expenditure since the index's inception. Behind Western Europe, Asia-Pacific is the second most peaceful region, with the overall score deteriorating by 0.1%.

The only regional improvement in peacefulness, by 0.6%, occurred in the Russia and Eurasia region, largely due to the bounce-back effect from the steep decline experienced after Russia's full-scale invasion of Ukraine in February 2022. Still, the overall levels of peacefulness in the region remain very low compared to its historical averages.

Positive Peace From The World's Most Peaceful Countries

Amid widespread global turmoil, perhaps the more peaceful nations show a way forward. While countries like Iceland and

New Zealand may benefit from their geographic isolation—making them more culturally cohesive and less exposed to territorial disputes—several nations in the top positions of the index fought vicious wars at one point in history, but today are integral members of the world's most peaceful region, Europe. Elsewhere, Singapore and Malaysia illustrate the impact of democratic institutions and economic growth, as well as the ability to draw important lessons from a past marked by struggle and poverty, on bolstering peace.

While the institutions that manage societies—at least in terms of global averages—have generally improved and become more efficient and transparent, conflicts and violent protests stemming from opposing political views have increased across the world over the past decade, they have accelerated during the Covid-19 pandemic, and have continued after. Peaceful societies are not weighed down by the costs and burdens of violence, political instability and corruption, and they are more productive, informed and educated.

Top 10 Most Peaceful Countries According to the Global Peace Index

#10 | MALAYSIA

Ranking as the third most peaceful country in the Asia-Pacific region, Malaysia holds the top global position in the Ongoing Domestic and International Conflict domain and ranks third in the Militarization domain. Remarkably, this nation of about 33 million people has climbed 9 spots from last year, entering the top 10 for the first time. When the Peace Index was launched in 2008, Malaysia stood at the 32nd position.

A multicultural society with a diverse mix of Malay, Chinese, Indian and indigenous communities, Malaysia benefits from government policies promoting tolerance and encouraging inclusivity. Crime rates are low compared to other countries in the region, and a prosperous economy helps reduce poverty and inequality. Additionally, since gaining independence in 1957, Malaysia has enjoyed relatively stable governance, fostering a more harmonious social and political environment.

#9 | SLOVENIA

A legend says that when God distributed the land to all the nations, Slovenians were overlooked because there were so few of them (they are still just 2.1 million). To apologize, he gave them a little piece of paradise he saved for himself. Slovenia's territory—half of which is covered by forests—boasts one of the greatest levels of biodiversity on the continent: with only one-hour drive from the capital Ljubljana, you can either swim in the Adriatic Sea or climb the Julian Alps. It is the only country from Central Europe to place in the top 10, making it the most peaceful nation in the CEE region.

Along with Slovenia, the Czech Republic, Hungary and Croatia too make it into the top 20, and Bulgaria, Slovakia and Latvia into the top 30. Of the 36 ranked countries in Europe, 13 had improvements in peacefulness and 23 saw deteriorations. The only European countries in the bottom half of the index are Cyprus (at number 88), Türkiye (139) and, perhaps surprisingly to some, France (86).

#8 | DENMARK

Sometimes gaining one or two spots and sometimes losing them, since 2008 Denmark never dropped below the fifth place in the Global Peace Index—that is until this year. Now ranked 8th, Denmark's drop is more a result of other countries' improvements than a significant decline in its own score, which has decreased by only 0.037% from last year.

Such relatively minor changes in the ranking only tell us that the kingdom is doing well. A safe country to travel and live in, Denmark is characterized by a high degree of political stability, freedom of the press and respect for human rights. It also boasts a high level of income equality and is frequently ranked as one of the happiest nations in the world.

To safeguard all that happiness and those excellent standards of living, this nation of less than 6 million spends a lot. In 2018, to counter the threat of Russia's increasing military activity in eastern and northern Europe, Denmark reached a landmark cross-party political deal to increase its defense budget by 20%, on course to match its Nordic neighbors Sweden's and Norway's expenditure levels and reach the NATO membership target of 2% of national GDP in military spending. As a result, Denmark's overall standing in the Peace Index is weighed down by its performance in the militarization domain, where it ranks 24th in the world. Things are likely to stay that way: in 2023, Denmark announced plans to invest the equivalent of $21 billion in defense over the next 10 years, a figure that was increased by an additional $5.1 billion in 2024.

#7 | PORTUGAL

Portugal marches to the beat of its own drum when it comes to peace and safety. Over the past few years, this nation of about 10 million people has emerged as one of the biggest climbers of the Global Peace Index, moving from the 18th spot it held in 2014 into the top 10.

Ranking above the industrialized nations' average in terms of housing, work-life balance, personal security and environmental quality, Portugal is also considered one of the top expat destinations due to its overall quality of life. Even better, there is no need to break the bank to enjoy the Portuguese way of living: the republic remains one of the most affordable destinations on the continent.

#6 | SWITZERLAND

Switzerland is exactly as one would expect: a place with an exceptionally high degree of safety in society, superior political stability, and close to inexistent international conflict. However, its surprising degree of militarization (total active and reserve army personnel number approximately 147,000 out of a population of about 8.9 million) keeps this nation from rising into the top 5. Switzerland—along with other well-ranking peaceful nations such as Canada, Singapore, Norway and the Netherlands—is also among the world's top weapons exporters per capita.

Still, by most measures, Switzerland remains a prosperous country where linguistic and religious diversity is embraced. In ninth place in the United Nation's Happiness Report, it also ranks above the average among OECD nations when it comes to subjective well-being, income, health and education and environmental quality.

#5 | SINGAPORE

While the Global Peace Index report shows an increasingly violent world, Singapore has become more peaceful. Way more peaceful: when the ranking was first launched in 2008 Singapore occupied the 22nd spot. What prompted this remarkable jump? The IEP points out that the largest improvements in the ranking are usually broadly based while large deteriorations in peace are usually driven by just a few indicators.

So, while Singapore scored highly in societal safety and security and low levels of ongoing domestic and international conflict, holding it back from the highest tier of the ranking—like Switzerland—is its militarization level. Why does Singapore need so many people in its police and military forces and why is its arms expenditure so high? The city-state depends on seaborne trade for its prosperity, so having the naval resources to ensure the smooth passage of vessels through the Strait of Malacca, the narrow stretch of water that serves as a gateway between the Indian and Pacific Oceans, is crucial.

#4 | NEW ZEALAND

After holding on to the number two spot in the index since 2017, New Zealand slipped two spots to number four in last year's edition of the Global Peace Index, and that's where we find it this year too. Scoring almost perfect marks in the domains of societal safety and domestic and international conflict, this peaceful country is widely considered a wonderful place to live. Still, due to an increase in weapons imports and exports and upgrades on armed personnel

Can There Ever Be World Peace?

Historians might quibble over the exact details, but by most accounts, there are no periods in history that have been free from war. Much of recorded history has also been filled with imperial or colonial occupations, where a powerful nation uses force to rule over other nations.

In some of the relatively peaceful periods in history, including certain periods under the Roman Empire, and the so-called "long peace" after World War II, the relatively war-free state of politics was due to there being one super-powerful nation that had a particularly strong imperial influence over the rest of the world. If the only reliable way to avoid war is to have global empires ruling by force, then the prospects for any meaningful world peace seem a bit grim.

One thing that needs to be figured out, if we (humankind) are ever going to manage a more peaceful world, is how we can peacefully move on from historical injustices. There's a moral dilemma involved in this. On one hand, if people keep holding grudges, for the wrongs that they or their people have suffered in the past, or for present-day

carriers, New Zealand's score in the militarization domain fell by 6% in last year's edition of the index.

At around the same size as the United Kingdom but with a population of roughly 5.2 million people, New Zealand ranks above the average among OECD members in education, healthcare, jobs and earnings. All this, however, comes also at a cost: the shortage of affordable housing is increasingly making it difficult for people with low incomes to buy homes, with the gap between rich and poor considered the top economic issue facing New Zealand by 20% of its citizens.

#3 | AUSTRIA

Since the end of the Cold War, this small landlocked country of about 9 million moved from its peripheral position at the borderline between East and West closer to the center of a united Europe. As

> disadvantages that stem from those wrongs, then peace is always going to be tenuous. Real, lasting, stable peace requires trust and solidarity among people. Those things quickly unravel if old grudges are constantly resurfacing.
>
> On the other hand, the moral value of peace seems undermined if, in order to attain peace, we require people to simply ignore or become content with the unjust suffering that has been inflicted on them. This intuition is captured in the slogan "no peace without justice". So, the question is whether we can right historical wrongs and establish the conditions for a future-looking peace, without reigniting the conflicts that surround those wrongs. Different practical approaches to addressing this challenge have been tried, like "truth and reconciliation commissions", and "reparation movements" for historical injustices.
>
> It may be that the hope of world peace hinges in part on people's creativity (and courage) in trying to figure out how to get more communities to buy into these kinds of peace-building endeavours.
>
> **"Can There Ever Be World Peace?," by Dr. Robert Simpson, University College London, March 29, 2022. www.ucl.ac.uk/culture-online/case-studies/2022/mar/can-there-ever-be-world-peace.**

a young member of the EU and outside of NATO, Austria prided itself on trying to get along with rival political blocs and embracing new forms of cooperation with its neighbors.

However, while Austria performs well in many measures of wellbeing such as income, jobs and housing, social tensions have been growing in recent years fueled especially by anti-migrant campaigns of the popular right-wing Freedom Party (FPÖ). When in November 2020 an ISIS sympathizer shot and killed 4 people and injured 23 others in the city center of Vienna, the government responded by unveiling broad anti-terror measures that included the ability to keep convicted individuals behind bars for life and facilitate electronic surveillance for those who are released. As a consequence, Austria experienced one of the largest deteriorations in peacefulness in Europe owing to a worsening of the terrorism impact indicator. Additionally, amidst the COVID-19 pandemic, its capital has been the epicenter of significant protests against both lockdown measures and the government's mandate to enforce compulsory vaccination for all citizens. Since then, the support for the FPÖ has only grown: today it is the country's leading political party.

#2 | IRELAND

Ireland is one of the wealthiest, most developed and happiest nations in the world. It is also quite peaceful: in 2020, it managed to gain seven positions and land in the fourth spot of the Global Peace Report, the highest position it had ever attained in the ranking. In the following years, it occupied either the third or the second position, which is where we find it today.

Make no mistake: Ireland did not become a peace-loving nation overnight—centuries of tense relations with the United Kingdom can attest to that. Today though, due also to its longstanding independent status and neutral army (meaning that it is not a member of NATO), the Irish Republic is routinely ranked as one of the safest countries in the world. That does not mean it has become immune from political and social turmoil—during the pandemic, for example, Ireland saw its share of violent anti-lockdown demonstrations.

On page 84 of its study, the IEP reveals a striking piece of data: when it comes to the economic cost of violence, Ireland performs better than almost all countries in the world. Ranking 159th out of 163 nations, the toll is just 2.86% of the GDP compared to the global average, 13.5%. Only Malawi, Bangladesh, Indonesia and Madagascar perform slightly better in this domain.

#1 | ICELAND: The Most Peaceful Country in The World

Icelanders can sleep well at night: they live in the most peaceful nation in the world. No news is good news when it comes to tranquil Iceland: it is the 17th year in a row that it retains the number one spot—since the index began in 2008. With no standing army, navy or air force and the smallest population of any NATO member state (about 390,000 people), Iceland also enjoys record-low crime rates (to the extent that policemen generally don't carry firearms), an enviable education and welfare system, and ranks among the best nations in terms of jobs and earnings and subjective sense of wellbeing.

But did we say that Icelanders' idyllic peace faces no threats? In 2022, the Reykjavík police arrested four people in connection with preparations for a suspected terrorist attack. That was the first year that the country recorded any of such activity. Luckily, no further incidents have been reported since then.

Viewpoint 4

"The UN can be and should be criticized for its inability to act where needed or for its inability to stop action deemed damaging to peace and security, but it has an ability to adapt and reinvent itself in line with emerging global challenges that shouldn't be undermined."

The United Nations Has Shown the World How to Behave Peacefully

Anette Sonnback

In this viewpoint, Anette Sonnback discusses the United Nations' (UN) 75-year history and its role in maintaining international peace and security, highlighting the challenges and successes of its peace operations, nuclear disarmament efforts, and humanitarian interventions. Sonneback examines the structure and function of the UN Security Council, noting the influence of its five permanent members and the criticisms regarding its decision-making processes and effectiveness, particularly in conflict situations like Syria and Iraq. Sonnback emphasizes the UN's normative power in shaping global standards of acceptable behavior. It has done so through initiatives such as the Nuclear Non-Proliferation Treaty and the "responsibility to protect" principle, which aims to prioritize human security over state sovereignty. Sonnback

"How Successful Has the UN Been in Maintaining International Peace and Security?," by Annette Sonnback, E-International Relations, November 8, 2020. Reprinted by permission.

argues that while the UN faces significant challenges, it has also achieved notable successes in fostering cooperation among nations and adapting to emerging global issues. Anette Sonnback is co-founder and director of A Path for Europe, a nonprofit think tank based in Berlin. Her areas of interest include European Union (EU) affairs and security, EU neighborhood policy and enlargement, governance and democracy.

As you read, consider the following questions:

1. Who are the five permanent members of the UN Security Council with veto power?
2. What is the primary responsibility of the UN Security Council?
3. What does the "responsibility to protect" principle entail?

This year, the United Nations (UN) is celebrating its 75th year. Born out of war, the UN has sought to curtail plagues of a past characterized by two world wars. Based on the idea of liberal institutionalism where multilateral institutions are to facilitate inter-state cooperation, the UN intended to bring the major military powers together with the main task of maintaining international peace and security (Weiss 2018: 174, Hanhimaki 2015: 18). This has, however, been fraught with difficulties that this essay will address along with the challenges and opportunities with different peace and security initiatives, in an attempt to evaluate the UN's success in its main task. It will specifically focus on peace operations, nuclear disarmament and humanitarian intervention, some of the main areas through which the UN is maintaining international peace and security (UN 2020a). As one main actor in global governance, I conclude that the real success of the UN has been in its role as a normative power, guiding the global understanding of acceptable behavior.

UN's Role in Maintaining Peace and Security—A Tense Security Council and Ambiguous Peace Operations

The UN Security Council (UNSC) is the organ with the primary responsibility for maintaining international peace and security. Outlining its structure and function is an essential first step for determining its success. It consists of 15 members, 5 of which are permanent and have veto power (the P5), namely the United States, the United Kingdom, Russia, China and France. These were considered the main military powers when the UN was founded and their veto right would prevent them from going to war against each other, while creating a necessary balance when taking decisions on security issues that would be collectively enforced (Goodrich 1965: 430). This illustrates how the constellation itself was based on peace and security considerations, and there has in fact never been a direct physical war between the P5 since the UN's beginning. Despite a period of inaction during the Cold War, many UNSC resolutions have also been passed to support peace processes, solve disputes, respond to illegitimate uses of force and enforce sanctions in situations where peace and security has been threatened. This involvement ranges from Bosnia in 1993 to Afghanistan in 2001 to its Anti-Piracy resolution in 2008 (Mingst and Karns 2011: 108). UNSC resolutions have been central for tackling conflict situations and have also demonstrated that extensive joint action can be taken to respond to crisis, such as in the case of Iraq's occupation of Kuwait in 1990 where it condemned its action and authorized states to "use all necessary means" to stop the occupation (Mingst and Karns 2011: 105). Such examples would challenge the realist assumption that there is an inherent collective action problem in international relations and the system of anarchy. Nevertheless, the UNSC has attracted vast criticism for upholding procedures that impede robust action in important situations where international law has been violated but the P5 disagree, such as in Syria (Nadin 2017), as well as for keeping an outdated permanent membership and for being undemocratic (Weiss & Kuele 2014). In the mentioned example of Iraq 1990, the agreed resolution authorized a US-led military operation, but UN oversight was weak and the autonomy of US action as well as the lack of inclusion of supportive states outside of the Council in the decision-making process is one example that points to the undemocratic structure of the Council as well as the continued importance of powerful states during interventions, rather than the UN itself (Ebegbulem 2011: 25). Furthermore, Security Council vetoes have not always managed to stop nations from proceeding with their endeavors, which was the case with the US' invasion of Iraq, 2003 (Morris & Wheeler 2007: 221). This shows that the individual interests of some states make them deviate from institutional constraints, pointing to flaws in the theory of liberal institutionalism that laid the basis for the UN. Such examples spark doubt about the credibility of the UN and UNSC and disrupt the balance that the composition of UNSC is to uphold, which is one important obstacle to its success in maintaining peace and security.

Beyond internal tensions, the UN has an active presence in the world through peace operations, which has become central for the UNSC and its approach to maintaining peace. The mandates range from protecting civilians to supporting state-building efforts, a list that has become more extensive in its attempt to improve the strategy towards sustainable peace. There is no mention of peace operations in the UN Charter, and the concept of peacekeeping has adapted in line with shifting nature of war and understanding of security, leading up to today's multidimensional peace operations (Williams & Bellamy 2013: 415). Traditionally, the presence of UN forces was to be approved by all parties in the host country, they were to be impartial, lightly armed, with the main goal to maintain a truce. The peace has indeed been kept between states such as Israel-Syria or Iraq-Kuwait, indicating the success of UN deployment for preventing interstate conflict (Mingst and Karns 2011: 130). With the increase of intrastate wars in the 1990s however, conflicts had become more complex, requiring a more complex response. Peacekeepers were deployed in situations where there was no peace to keep, and they encountered atrocities that put both them and civilians in danger, demanding greater military response (Bellamy & Hunt 2015: 1277, Doyle & Sambanis 2008: 2). Their mandate therefore expanded and started bordering on enforcement, as was the case of Bosnia in the 1990s. One problem was the discrepancy between the expectations of the operations and the actual capabilities in form of manpower or resources, showing a political unwillingness to transform the operations to more robust ones (Thakur 2006: 62, Autesserre 2019). Bosnia was a clear example of the failure that can ensue when undertaking ad hoc responses to a situation that does not match the original mandate, as it might lead to the inability to perform the envisioned tasks entrusted upon peacekeepers as they are prevented by nation state reluctance (Crossette 1999). This shows the importance of broad member state support of missions in today's complex conflict situations and the need for nations to be willing to adapt to challenges that might arise.

Underlying UN peace operations is the ideal of a liberal democratic peace, which has been a further hindrance to success in some contexts. Afghanistan is a telling example, where democratization, rule of law and economic restructuring was promoted (Saikal 2012: 219), showing a disregard for every state's right to "choose its political, economic, social and cultural system" (UN Declaration 1965). The state-building efforts saw the quick establishment of governance structures based on Western ideals. It was a rushed affair that eventually failed as the government was neither representative nor accountable (Saikal 2012: 226). Postcolonialism offers a valid critique of the ideational dominance of Western values and understandings, and its failure to recognize imperialist tendencies in the vision that liberal peace is universally applicable and desirable (Nair 2017). Imposing structures in a top-down fashion can have important consequences in fragile situations where society is multidimensional. The conception of peace should not be equated with liberalism but rather promoted in a balanced effort through combined considerations for basic democratic principles with local understandings of governance. This is called hybrid peacebuilding by authors such as Richmond (2009: 578). Only then will the UN enable long-term success as it would empower the local community through an inclusive bottom-up approach.

Beyond Peacekeeping—Recognizing the Normative Power of the UN

The active presence of the UN in the world through its different missions has resolved disputes, inhibited escalation of conflict and spurred peace in some situations, but the inherent problems that were highlighted continue to attract criticism. The failure of the UN to foster long-term peace in settings with complex conflict-dynamics shows an important limitation to the claim to success (Sambanis 2008: 29). An alternative area in which its role as a peace and security defender has been more successful, and in my view most successful, is through the spread [of] important norms that have ranged from expanding the security agenda to upholding a nuclear taboo. A telling example is the role of the Nuclear Non-Proliferation Treaty (NPT). As authors such as Scott Sagan argue, norms embedded in the NPT shape "states' identities and expectations and even powerful actors [become] constrained by the norms they [have] created" (Sagan 1997: 76). The NPT regime helped establish shared understandings of what was considered prestigious, legitimate or delegitimate and states thereby chose to disarm rather than be classified as rogue nations by the international community (Sagan 1997: 80). It has also constrained both Russia and the US in their attempts to modernize their arsenals. Even in cases where the norm has been contested, such as when [the] US recognized India as a nuclear weapons state, it never seriously challenged the core assumptions of the nuclear non-proliferation norm (Carranza 2019: 14). Critics would disagree and argue that the accomplishments in the area of nuclear disarmament has been weak, as with collective security (MacKenzie 2015: 489), but the UN's efforts have evidently hindered armament and possible escalation, pointing to a major success for maintaining peace and security in the world.

Beyond nuclear disarmament, there is also the shared understanding of illegitimate and legitimate uses of force. The UNSC holds strong authority in this realm, which again points to the normative power of the UN in its role for maintaining international peace and security (Mingst and Karns 2011: 100). Even though tensions can run high between states in the Security Council, this shared understanding has enhanced the risks that an aggressor might face when "breaking" these norms, as the response from the international community can take the form of international condemnation, coordinated sanctions or even humanitarian intervention. This last point particularly derives from the enhanced focus on human rights and human security within the UN, as well as the shifting nature of war after the Cold War (Bellamy 2013: 488). The principles of sovereignty and non-interference came into question with the atrocities committed during intrastate conflicts such as in Rwanda and Bosnia. The "responsibility to protect" principle (R2P) was thereby born during the 2005 World Summit, which came to mean that all states have a responsibility to protect civilians from genocide, ethnic cleansing, war crimes or crimes against humanity (UN 2020b). In cases where a state couldn't or wouldn't fulfil this function, humanitarian intervention by the international community would be legitimate. This is in line with the human security agenda that was promoted by the UN in the 1990s, as the security of individuals was to be prioritized over the protection of the state (Hampson 2013: 279). While it contradicts the thesis of realism with its focus on self-interested states, there have been debates on this new role for the UN and how successful it has actually been to use force to support human security objectives (Hampson 2013: 286). One main criticism is about the questions of interpretation. Who dictates when this responsibility is to be invoked? There have also been instances where unlawful intervention has been done in the name of R2P, such as in the case of Russia's intervention in Georgia where they claimed to protect Russian citizens (Allison 2009: 178). However, the jointly accepted humanitarian intervention in Libya 2011 based on the R2P norm is an important example that illustrates how normative shifts driven by the UN can bring nations together to protect peace and security in the world. Both China and Russia agreed to humanitarian intervention, despite their traditional opposition to it, which stopped Qaddafi from proceeding with possible crimes against humanity (Bellamy 2013: 500). Beyond operational successes, the fact that the international community has agreed to legitimize action to protect human beings as such rather than states, and that there is a general understanding that states should not stand idly by while atrocities are committed, remain two key achievements for the UN in the realm of peace and security.

Conclusion—A Tale of Success?

The naiveté that liberal institutionalism has been charged with is confirmed by the difficulty to cooperate in areas that are so clearly still part of the realm of national interests (Weiss 2018: 178). Despite this, history has shown that UN nations, and the P5, are agreeing on important resolutions and overcoming their differences. States have also acted in line with the normative frameworks that the UN has promoted. The UN can be and should be criticized for its inability to act where needed or for its inability to stop action deemed damaging to peace and security, but it has an ability to adapt and reinvent itself in line with emerging global challenges that shouldn't be undermined (MacKenzie 2015: 490). Such adaptability gives constructivism right in its understanding that process affects interests, which thereby transforms structure (Wendt 1992: 393). This understanding explains how the UNCS has been able to legitimize certain norms and practices, even when they intrude into the realm of national sovereignty (Williams & Bellamy 2013: 416). The UN is indeed the sum of its parts, composed of member states with their individual interests, but state interaction in this institutional context continues to shape states' evolving interest, enabling policy change that corresponds with its task of maintaining peace and security.

References:

Allison, R., 2009. The Russian case for military intervention in Georgia: international law, norms and political calculation, *European Security*, 18(2), 173-200.

Autesserre, S., 2019. *The Crisis of Peacekeeping: Why the UN Can't End Wars* [online]. Foreign Affairs. Available at: https://www.foreignaffairs.com/articles/2018-12-11/crisis-peacekeeping [Accessed 19 August 2020].

Bellamy, A., 2013. The Responsibility to Protect. In: ed. Williams, P. *Security Studies, An Introduction*. Routledge: New York, 2013, 486-503.

Bellamy, A., and Hunt, C., 2015. Twenty-first century UN peace operations: protection, force and the changing security environment. *International Affairs* 91(6), 1277–1298.

Carranza, M., 2019. The stability of the nuclear nonproliferation norm: a critique of norm-contestation theory. *The Nonproliferation Review*, 26(1-2), 7-22.

Crossette, B., 1999. U.N. Details Its Failure to Stop '95 Bosnia Massacre [online]. *The New York Times*. Available at https://www.nytimes.com/1999/11/16/world/un-details-its-failure-to-stop-95-bosnia-massacre.html [Accessed 19 August 2020].

Doyle, M., and Sambanis, N., 2008. Peacekeeping Operations. In: Daws, S., and Weiss, T. *The Oxford Handbook on the United Nations*. Oxford University Press: Oxford.

Ebegbulem, J., 2011. The Failure of Collective Security in the Post World Wars I and II International System. *Transcience*, 2(2), 23-29.

Goodrich, L., 1965. The Maintenance of International Peace and Security. *International Organization*, 19(3), 429-443.

Hampson, F., 2013. Human Security. In: ed. Williams, P. *Security Studies, An Introduction*. Routledge: New York, 2013, 279-294.

Hanhimaki, J., 2015. *The United Nations: a very short introduction*. Oxford University Press: New York.

MacKenzie, D., 2015. Forever adaptable: The United Nations system at 70. *International Journal*, 70(3), 489-498.

Mingst, K., and Karns, M., 2013. *The United Nations in the 21st Century*. Westview Press: Boulder.

Morris, J., and Sheeler, N., 2007. The Security Council's Crisis of Legitimacy and the Use of Force. *International Politics*, 44, 214–231.

Nadin, P., 2017. How the UN Security Council failed Syria [online]. *The Interpreter*. Available at https://www.lowyinstitute.org/the-interpreter/how-un-security-council-failed-syria [Accessed 19 August 2020].

Nair, S., 2017. *Introduction Postcolonialism in International Relations Theory* [online]. E-International Relations. Available at: https://www.e-ir.info/2017/12/08/postcolonialism-in-international-relations-theory/ [Accessed 19 August 2020].

Pugh, M., 2013. Peace Operations. In: ed. Williams, P. *Security Studies, An Introduction*. Routledge: New York, 2013, 393-408.

Richmond, O. P., 2009. A post–liberal peace: eirenism and the everyday. *Review of International Studies*, 35 (3), 557–580.

Sagan, S., 1997. Why Do States Build Nuclear Weapons?: Three Models in Search of a Bomb. *International Security*, 21(3), 54-86.

Saikal, A., 2012. The UN and Afghanistan: Contentions in Democratization and Statebuilding. *International Peacekeeping*, 19(2), 217-234.

Sambanis, N., 2008. Short- and Long-Term Effects of United Nations Peace Operations. The World Bank Economic Review, 22(1), 9-32.

Thakur, R., 2006. *The United Nations, Peace and Security*. Cambridge: Cambridge University Press.

Weiss, T., 2018. *International Organizations and Global Governance*. Routledge: London.

Weiss, T., and Kuele, G., 2014. The Veto: Problems and Prospects [online]. E-International Relations. Available at: https://www.e-ir.info/2014/03/27/the-veto-problems-and-prospects/ [Accessed 19 August 2020].

Weiss, T., and Thakur, R., 2010. *Global Governance and the UN: An Unfinished Journey*. Indiana University Press: Bloomington.

Wendt, A. (1992). Anarchy is what States Make of it: The Social Construction of Power Politics. *International Organization*, 46(2), 391-425.

Williams, P., and Bellamy, A., 2013. UN Security Council and Peace Operations. In: eds. Weiss, T., and Wilkinson, R., 2013, 1st ed. *International Organizations and Global Governance*. Routledge: London.

UN, 2020a. Maintain International Peace and Security [online]. UN. Available at: https://www.un.org/en/sections/what-we-do/maintain-international-peace-and-security/index.html [Accessed 19 August 2020].

UN, 2020b. R2P and the UN [online]. UN. Available at: https://www.un.org/en/chronicle/article/r2p-and-un [Accessed 19 August 2020].

UN Declaration, 1965. Declaration on the Inadmissibility of Intervention in the Domestic Affairs of States and the Protection of Their Independence and Sovereignty. Res. 2131 [online]. Available at: https://undocs.org/pdf?symbol=en/A/RES/2131(XX) [Accessed 19 August 2020].

UN Peacekeeping, 2020. Historical timeline of UN Peacekeeping [online]. UN. Available at: https://peacekeeping.un.org/en/historical-timeline-of-un-peacekeeping [Accessed 19 August 2020].

Viewpoint 5

> *"So the world would by no means be more peaceful without religion—on the contrary! In addition to the potential for conflict and violence, religions also harbour an enormous, often overlooked potential for peace."*

Religion Can Both Extend and Resolve Wars

Markus Weingardt

In this viewpoint, Markus Weingardt begins by admitting that religion has often prolonged wars. He distinguishes between conflicts of interest, which usually involve land, wealth, etc., and conflicts of values, which incorporate religion and philosophy. Because conflicts of values are about higher ideals, there is often no "red line" that antagonists won't cross, Weingardt says. However, secular wars are all too common, he writes: no religious motive is needed to spur conflict. Religion has tremendous potential for ending conflict as well as motivating it. Weingardt concludes by calling on religious leaders to "become more aware of their peace competences," and to get more involved in promoting peace. Markus Weingardt, Ph.D., is a peace and conflict researcher and a freelance writer.

"Would the World Be More Peaceful Without Religion?," by Markus Weingardt, Stiftung Weltethos, April 4 2024. www.weltethos.org/en/would-the-world-be-more-peaceful-without-religion.

As you read, consider the following questions:

1. Why do those in power often attempt to transform conflicts of interest into conflicts of values?
2. What are some conflicts, according to Weingardt, which religion has helped to resolve?
3. According to Weingardt, why are religious "actors" often more able to bring about peaceful resolutions than secular mediators?

Islamist Hamas indiscriminately massacres people, Patriarch Cyril I declares the Russian invasion of Ukraine a holy war, Hindu nationalists burn down Christian and Muslim villages and Buddhist nationalists carry out pogroms against the Rohingya. War and terror, murder and manslaughter around the globe, and all too often in the name of a god, a religion. No wonder many people believe that the world would be more peaceful without religions of any kind. But would it really be? Would we then really have, as the British bestselling author Ian McEwan says, "a world of humility before the sanctity of life"?

In the Battle for the Higher: Religion in Conflict (of Values)

There is no doubt that religious actors contribute to the intensification and prolongation of violent conflicts. However, religious beliefs or differences are rarely the cause of conflicts. Peace research largely agrees on this. But in order to understand the role of religions in conflicts, it is important to first understand the mechanisms of conflicts.

Rather, religion is used to ideologically charge conflicts of interest and transform them into conflicts of values. Conflicts of interest revolve around land, natural resources or power, for example. Conflicts of values, on the other hand, are about a "higher idea" that goes beyond personal interests and one's own physical survival. Value conflicts revolve around what is "valuable" for me—as an individual or group—such as beliefs, world views and cultural identities. In such conflicts of values, people are much more likely to be mobilised to fight violently; their willingness to commit themselves, their readiness to use violence and, not least, their willingness to make sacrifices increases almost without limit.

There is usually a "red line" in conflicts of interest. If this is achieved, the parties to the conflict, leaders and followers alike, begin to weigh things up: What can I gain and what can I lose? What are the opportunities and risks? If these risks appear too great or incalculable, people tend to refrain from violent conflict. In conflicts of values, however, this "red line" has disappeared or at least shifted very far upwards. Because this is about something "higher", something bigger, about all or nothing, without compromise. And in the fight for this greater goal, every effort and every sacrifice is considered appropriate, even required—and all violence is permitted.

Potential for Conflict: The Power of Ideologies

Maximum commitment, a willingness to use violence and a readiness to make sacrifices—rulers and powerful people recognised these effects in conflicts of values thousands of years ago. And that is why they have always endeavoured to transform conflicts of interest into conflicts of values. This transformation usually takes place by charging various secular ideologies: First and foremost nationalism, but also separatism, ethnicism, communism and others. Violence can also be justified and legitimised in the name of democracy, freedom and human rights.

Yet the "ideologies" of religions also lend themselves to being charged and transformed, and religiously charged conflicts are particularly dangerous. Because then it's no longer just about my values or beliefs, but about good and evil, about a battle of the good (us!) against the bad (the others), for "the good" and against "the bad". In such a struggle, violence is then not only considered legitimate, but even becomes a duty, and non-violence is now seen as cowardice, as treason, as sin.

In the Battle Between Good and Evil: Non-Violence as Sin

Conflicts can be religiously charged, as the central scriptures of all major religions contain traditions in which violence is positively connoted, presented as divine will or even demanded by God himself. Political and religious authorities can still draw on these texts today to legitimise their violence. Of course, only a few (those with the necessary religious education and scepticism) care that their theological, cultural or political context has to be ignored. Because what an eternal God said or did back then can it be wrong today?

Although religions can be used to justify and escalate conflicts, they are by no means necessary. If there were no religions, there would still be enough secular ideologies and justifications to fuel conflicts and legitimise violence or war. This is shown, for example, by Putin's motif of a "Russki Mir" (Russian world). And let us not forget that the overwhelming majority of victims of war and violence in the 20th and 21st centuries were victims of secular conflicts: from the First and Second World Wars to the violent regimes of Stalin, Mao and Pol Pot to conflicts in Vietnam, Rwanda, Congo and, last but not least, Ukraine.

Concrete Potentials: Religions as Peacemakers

So the world would by no means be more peaceful without religion—on the contrary! In addition to the potential for conflict and violence, religions also harbour an enormous, often overlooked potential for peace. They have skills, experience, specific opportunities and successes in de-escalating conflicts and overcoming war and violence! The examples are many and varied:

- In 1992, the Catholic lay movement Sant'Egidio brokered a comprehensive peace agreement during the Mozambican civil war, which claimed millions of victims.

- The outbreak of a war of incalculable proportions between Argentina and Chile was averted in 1978 by a last-minute intervention by the Vatican and a "peace and friendship treaty" was negotiated.
- During the terrible genocide in Rwanda in 1994, it was the local Muslim community that almost collectively refused to accept the violence and offered protection to thousands of refugees, hiding them, providing them with food and saving their lives.
- The Philippine dictator Marcos was brought down in 1986 by a peaceful mass movement initiated and organised primarily by church representatives.
- The Liberian Women's Peace Movement, a coalition of Christian and Muslim women's initiatives, exerted pressure until the civil war was contained and the despotic ruler Charles Taylor was forced out of office.
- In Cambodia, the Buddhist monk Maha Ghosananda initiated a peace and reconciliation movement in 1979 after the reign of terror of Pol Pot and the Khmer Rouge, which developed into an important force in politics and society.
- In the Colombian peace process from 2012 to 2016, church representatives played a key role as mediators behind the scenes.
- Franco-German reconciliation after the Second World War was first and foremost initiated by the churches on both sides of the Rhine, long before politics took up the issue. And the "peaceful revolution" in the DDR would hardly have come about so (peacefully) without the diverse work of the churches.

An Advance of Trust that Opens Doors: The Key to Peace

Analysing these and dozens of other examples[1] reveals an astonishing fact: religious peace actors often enjoy the trust of the conflict parties—across religious, cultural and ethnic boundaries, even when conflict parties and mediators belong to different religions. An advance that opens doors, sometimes just a crack, which then needs to be widened with wisdom and perseverance. This opens up spaces and room for manoeuvre and negotiation in which decisive progress can ultimately be made in peace processes.

Of course, the trust placed in religious peace actors is not blind trust. It has to be earned. A high level of expertise and professional competence is essential. This means both precise knowledge of conflicts in their breadth and depth as well as expertise in constructive conflict management. And peace actors must be credible in their words and actions in order to be accepted as mediators at all. But the leap of faith is based on other factors that are not so easy to acquire:

- A religious motivation for peace is understandable, as the ideas of rejecting violence and reconciliation have been handed down in all religious traditions. Even if you don't share these convictions, the motives are familiar or at least not completely alien.
- Religious actors are often seen as independent, altruistic and fair. Corruption, self-enrichment or nepotism are rarely attributed to them.
- They are often connected to the conflict parties in a way that enables them to gain a deeper, emotional understanding of the conflict. This bond is usually based on a common geographical origin, but can also be of a spiritual nature.
- Religious actors are often more competent and more capable of speaking, especially in deeper conflict dimensions such as guilt, injury, trauma, honour, grief, understanding or reconciliation.
- Religious peacemakers are considered harmless because they do not work with political, economic or even military pressure and coercion, but rely solely on their power of persuasion. And finally, they are seen as persistent and

Neutrality Is Essential in Peace Negotiations

Russia's ambassador to the UN in Geneva on Tuesday accused Switzerland of losing its "neutrality," saying Moscow is not against peace negotiations with Ukraine but would not take part in something led by the traditionally neutral Swiss.

Russia does "not see any possibility" that Switzerland would take the lead and organize a peace summit, Gennady Gatilov told a meeting in Geneva with reporters.

Gatilov claimed "Switzerland is quite far away from neutrality" as it not only adopted the EU sanctions on Russia but also froze 7.7 billion Swiss francs (over $8.52 billion) in financial assets belonging to Russians, calling it "stolen money."

"We are not against (peace) negotiations," he said, explaining that the Swiss lack of neutrality is the reason why Russia would not take part in talks in Switzerland.

Switzerland earlier this year said it could host a peace summit for the Russia-Ukraine war possibly in Geneva and announced plans

reliable actors who do not give up their commitment even in great danger and sometimes fight for peace for many years.

The leap of faith in favour of religious actors may seem surprising at first glance, but it corresponds to a rational conflict logic. Secular forces—whether politicians, supranational actors or non-governmental organisations—usually have a much harder time here. They are usually subject to great suspicion about their true motives, perhaps hidden interests, especially if they come from abroad or are financed from there.

However, religious actors must also prove themselves worthy of the trust placed in them and confirm the positive attributions in the course of peace processes. Even if this is not always successful, the successes are numerous and remarkable. They show the enormous

> to invite members of the BRICS group—Brazil, Russia, India, China, South Africa, Egypt, Ethiopia, Iran, and the United Arab Emirates—and countries from the Global South.
>
> According to Gatilov, inviting the Global South has one purpose, namely to get these countries' support behind Ukrainian President Volodymyr Zelenskyy's peace formula, which is "unacceptable" for the Kremlin.
>
> This week, Swiss Foreign Minister Ignazio Cassis said that details of the proposed Ukraine peace conference, which was planned to take place in the summer, are still unclear.
>
> "Between now and mid-April, we will decide what we are going to do," Cassis told Swiss public radio RTS.
>
> "Do we go ahead with the summit? Do we postpone it? Do we hold two of them, so that both lines of reasoning can move forward at the same time? We are currently in this intermediate or exploratory phase."
>
> **"Russia Says Switzerland 'Far' from Neutrality, Can't Lead Peace Process with Ukraine," by Beyza Binnur Dönmez, Anadolu Agency, last updated March 26, 2024. www.aa.com.tr/en/russia-ukraine-war/russia-says-switzerland-far-from-neutrality-cant-lead-peace-process-with-ukraine/3175705.**

potential for peace that is inherent in religions and which is far from being exhausted.

Peace Through Religion: Opportunity and Responsibility

You don't have to be religious, nor do you have to like religions to recognise their contributions and potential in terms of peace policy. Since religions have such important peace competences, however, we must be keen to use them in the interests of peace and for the good of mankind and to integrate them into politics. Because this potential is both an opportunity and a responsibility:

All religious communities are called upon to become more aware of their peace competences, to develop them professionally and to offer them proactively in peace processes. And politicians would be well advised to increasingly involve such religious peace actors in peace processes, as the different competences and possibilities of secular and religious actors can complement each other perfectly. What's more, as the former German Federal Minister for Development and Economic Cooperation, Gerd Müller, rightly recognised: "Without the contribution of religions, we will not be able to overcome the global challenges."[2]

References:

1. For more detail see Markus Weingardt: Religion Macht Frieden. Bonn 2010.
2. Bundesministerium für wirtschaftliche Zusammenarbeit und Entwicklung BMZ: "Gemeinsam mehr erreichen." Press release from 17 February 2016.

Periodical and Internet Sources Bibliography

The following articles have been selected to supplement the diverse views presented in this chapter.

Anonymous, "In Today's Troubled World, Building Peace 'Humanity's Greatest Responsibility', Secretary-General Stresses, Outlining Organization's Priorities for 2024," United Nations, February 7, 2024. press.un.org/en/2024/sgsm22127.doc.htm.

Benedikt Gieger and Mario Truss, "Young People's Voices Are Key to Securing Global Peace and Security," World Economic Forum, February 18, 2025. www.weforum.org/stories/2025/02/young-people-voices-securing-global-peace-and-security/.

Børge Brende and Bob Sternfels, "Global Cooperation Has Flatlined. Here's How to Reinvent It for a New Era," World Economic Forum, January 19, 2025. www.weforum.org/stories/2025/01/global-cooperation-flatlined-how-reinvent-it/.

Celestine Bohlen, "Seeking the Road to Peace in the Middle East," *The New York Times*, October 7, 2024. www.nytimes.com/2024/10/07/world/middleeast/israel-hamas-gaza-peace.html.

Jiayi Zhou, Jaïr van der Lijn and Jingdong Yuan, "China, Russia and the Future of Peacebuilding," Stockholm International Peace Institute, April 18, 2024. https://www.sipri.org/commentary/topical-backgrounder/2024/china-russia-and-future-peacebuilding

Joseph R. DeTrani, "U.N. Must Do More to Foster World Peace," *The Washington Times*, September 4, 2024. www.washingtontimes.com/news/2024/sep/4/un-must-do-more-to-foster-world-peace/.

Mary Kate Aylward, Peter Engelke, Uri Friedman, and Paul Kielstra, "Welcome to 2034: What the World Could Look Like in Ten Years, According to Nearly 300 Experts," Atlantic Council, January 12, 2024. www.atlanticcouncil.org/content-series/atlantic-council-strategy-paper-series/welcome-to-2034-what-the-world-could-look-like-in-ten-years-according-to-nearly-300-experts/.

Muhammad Babar, "I Grew Up in a Nation Without Free Speech. Here's What I Hope College Protesters Learn," *USA Today*, May

20, 2024. www.usatoday.com/story/opinion/voices/2024/05/20/college-protests-on-gaza-remind-me-how-precious-free-speech-is/73674144007/.

Michele L. Norris, "Can We Give 'Peace' a Chance Again?," *The Washington Post*, October 28, 2022. www.washingtonpost.com/opinions/2022/10/28/peace-movement-language/.

Soraya Chemaly, "The Grit and Resilience of Student Protesters," *The Nation*, April 30, 2024. www.thenation.com/article/activism/student-protesters-gen-z-resilience/.

Stephen M. Walt, "The Realist Guide to World Peace," Foreign Policy, December 23, 2022. foreignpolicy.com/2022/12/23/a-realist-guide-to-world-peace/.

For Further Discussion

Chapter 1

1. After reading the viewpoints in this chapter, do you believe that World War III is already underway?
2. After reading the viewpoints in this chapter, what do you believe is the possibility of a future war on a larger, global scale?
3. After reading the viewpoint by Ian Bond, do you agree that Ukraine should join NATO, or is this a move that will further antagonize Russia?

Chapter 2

1. After reading the viewpoints in this chapter, are you optimistic or pessimistic about the use of technology in warfare?
2. After reading the viewpoints in the chapter, how prepared do you believe India is to engage in modern warfare?
3. After reading the viewpoints in the chapter…

Chapter 3

1. After reading the viewpoints in this chapter, do you think that nuclear warfare is likely in the future?
2. After reading the viewpoints in this chapter, do you believe that North Korea and Iran are imminent nuclear threats? If so, what do you believe should be done about it?
3. After reading the viewpoint by Sveta Yefimenko, do you agree or disagree that the U.S. does not need more nuclear weapons?

Chapter 4

1. After reading the viewpoints in this chapter, do you believe that world peace is a possibility?

2. After reading the viewpoint by Anette Sonnback, do you feel that the United Nations has done all it can to maintain global peace?
3. After reading the viewpoint by Markus Weingardt, what is your opinion on religion's effect on war?

Organizations to Contact

The editors have compiled the following list of organizations concerned with the issues debated in this book. The descriptions are derived from materials provided by the organizations. All have publications or information available for interested readers. The list was compiled on the date of publication of the present volume; the information provided here may change. Be aware that many organizations take several weeks or longer to respond to inquiries, so allow as much time as possible.

American Enterprise Institute for Public Policy Research (AEI)

American Enterprise Institute
1789 Massachusetts Avenue, NW
Washington, DC 20036
phone: (202)862-5800
email: tyler.castle@aei.org
website: www.aei.org

The American Enterprise Institute is a conservative public policy think tank that sponsors original research on the world economy, US foreign policy and international security, and domestic political and social issues. AEI is dedicated to defending human dignity, expanding human potential, and building a freer and safer world. Its scholars and staff advance ideas rooted in their belief in democracy and free enterprise.

The Association for the Advancement of Artificial Intelligence (AAAI)

2275 East Bayshore Road
Suite 160
Palo Alto, California 94303
phone: (650) 328-3123
website: www.aaai.org

Founded in 1979, the Association for the Advancement of Artificial Intelligence (AAAI) (formerly the American Association for Artificial Intelligence) is a nonprofit scientific society devoted to advancing the scientific understanding of the mechanisms underlying thought and intelligent behavior and their embodiment in machines. AAAI aims to promote research in, and responsible use of, artificial intelligence. AAAI also aims to increase public understanding of artificial intelligence, improve the teaching and training of AI practitioners, and provide guidance for research planners and funders concerning the importance and potential of current AI developments and future directions.

Center for Arms Control and Non-Proliferaton

820 1st Street NE, Suite LL-180
Washington, D.C. 20002
phone: (202) 546-0795
email: info@icanw.org
website: armscontrolcenter.org

The Center for Arms Control and Non-Proliferation is a national nonpartisan nonprofit dedicated to enhancing peace and security through expert policy analysis and thought-provoking research. Its mission is to reduce nuclear weapons arsenals, halt the spread of nuclear weapons, and minimize the risk of war by educating the public and policy makers. The Center was founded in 1980. Since then, the Center's expertise on reducing the threats of war and nuclear weapons has been sought by the media and policymakers—supported by the tax-deductible contributions of foundations and individuals.

Cato Institute

1000 Massachusetts Avenue NW
Washington, D.C. 20001
phone: (202) 842-0200
web site: www.cato.org

The Cato Institute is a libertarian public policy research organization—a think tank dedicated to the principles of individual liberty, limited government, free markets, and peace. Its scholars and analysts conduct independent research on a wide range of policy issues.

Center for American Progress (*CAP*)

Address: 1333 H Street NW, 10th Floor
Washington, DC 20005
phone: 202-682-1611
website: www.americanprogress.org

The Center for American Progress is a public policy research and advocacy organization which presents a liberal viewpoint on economic and social issues. Its website includes a range of articles on various contemporary issues.

International Campaign to Abolish Nuclear Weapons (ICAN)

Place de Cornavin 2
1201 Genève, Switzerland
phone: +41 22 788 20 63
email: info@icanw.org
website: www.icanw.org

ICAN is a broad, inclusive campaign, focused on mobilizing civil society around the world to support the specific objective of prohibiting and eliminating nuclear weapons. The ICAN international structure consists of partner organizations, an international steering group and an international staff team. ICAN was awarded the Nobel Peace Prize in 2017.

The National Defense Industrial Association (NDIA)

2101 Wilson Boulevard
Suite 700
Arlington, VA 22201
phone: (703) 522-1820
email: info@NDIA.org
website: www.ndia.org

The National Defense Industrial Association drives strategic dialogue in national security by identifying key issues and leveraging the knowledge and experience of its military, government, industry, and academic members to address them. NDIA formed from a merger between the American Defense Preparedness Association, previously known as the Army Ordnance Association, founded in 1919, and the National Security Industrial Association, founded in 1944. For more than 100 years, NDIA has provided a platform through which leaders in government, industry, and academia can collaborate and provide solutions to advance the national security and defense needs of the nation.

The United Nations (UN)
760 United Nations Plaza
New York City, N.Y. 10017
phone: (212) 963-4475
website: www.un.org

The United Nations is an international organization founded in 1945. Currently made up of 193 Member States, the UN and its work are guided by the purposes and principles contained in its founding Charter. The UN has evolved over the years to keep pace with a rapidly changing world, but it remains the one organization on Earth that allows nearly all the world's nations to gather together, discuss common problems, and find shared solutions that benefit all of humanity.

The United States Department of Defense (DOD)
1400 Defense Pentagon
Washington, DC 20301
phone: (703) 697-9312
website: www.defense.gov

The Department of Defense is America's largest government agency. While the U.S. military traces its roots back to pre-Revolutionary times, the department has grown and evolved with our nation. Its mission is to provide the military forces needed to deter war and ensure our nation's security. The Department of Defense oversees the U.S. Army, Navy, Air Force, Marines, and more.

Win Without War

Washington, D.C.
phone: (202) 656-4999
email: info@winwithoutwar.org.
website: winwithoutwar.org

Win Without War is a diverse network of activists and organizations working for a more peaceful, progressive U.S. foreign policy. They believe that by democratizing U.S. foreign policy and providing progressive alternatives, we can achieve more peaceful, just, and common sense policies that ensure that all people—regardless of race, nationality, gender, religion, or economic status—can find and take advantage of opportunity equally and feel secure.

Bibliography of Books

Alessandro Arduino. *Money for Mayhem: Mercenaries, Private Military Companies, Drones, and the Future of War*. Lanham, MD: Rowman & Littlefield, 2023.

Tanner Billings. *Biosecurity in Warfare*. Buffalo, NY: Cavendish Square Publishing, 2023.

Joseph O. Chapa. *Is Remote Warfare Moral?: Weighing Issues of Life + Death from 7,000 Miles*. New York, NY: Hachette Book Group, 2022.

Chi-Hao Cheng and James Tsui. *An Introduction to Electronic Warfare: From the First Jamming to Machine Learning Techniques*. London, UK: River Publishers, 2021.

Louis A. Del Monte. *War at the Speed of Light : Directed-Energy Weapons and the Future of Twenty-First Century Warfare*. Lincoln, NE: Potomac Books, 2021.

Roberto Di Pietro, et al. "New Dimensions of Information Warfare." Cham, Switzerland: Springer, 2021.

Brent M. Eastwood. *Humans, Machines, and Data: Future Trends in Warfare*. 2021.

Matthew C. Ford and Andrew Hoskins. *Radical War: Data, Attention and Control in the Twenty-First Century*. New York, NY: Oxford University Press, 2022.

Andrew Futter. *Global Third Nuclear Age Clashing Visions for a New Era in International Politics*. Routledge, 2025.

Edward Geist. *Deterrence under Uncertainty: Artificial Intelligence and Nuclear Warfare*. Oxford, UK: Oxford University Press, 2023

James Johnson. *AI and the Bomb: Nuclear Strategy and Risk in the Digital Age*. Oxford, UK: Oxford University Press,Oxford University Press, 2023.

Manousos E. Kambouris. *Hybrid Warfare 2.2: Where Biothreats Meet Irregular Operations and Cyber Warriors in the 21st Century*. Cham, Switzerland: Springer, 2024.

M. Susan Lindee. *Rational Fog: Science and Technology in Modern War*. Cambridge, MA: Harvard University Press, 2020.

Philip M. Seib. *Information at War: Journalism, Disinformation, and Modern Warfare*. Cambridge, UK: Polity Press, 2021.

Raj M. Shah and Christopher Kirchhoff. *Unit X: How the Pentagon and Silicon Valley Are Transforming the Future of War*. New York, NY: Scribner, 2024.

Frank L.Smith III, et al. *Cyber Wargaming: Research and Education for Security in a Dangerous Digital World*. Washington, DC: Georgetown University Press, 2024.

Chris Stephen. *The Future of War Crimes Justice*. London, UK: Melville House, 2024.

Tim Sweijs and Jeffrey H. Michaels, editors. *Beyond Ukraine: Debating the Future of War*. London, UK: Hurst & Company, 2024.

Geoffrey F. Weiss. *The New Art of War: The Origins, Theory, and Future of Conflict*. Cambridge, UK: Cambridge University Press, 2021.

Mikael Weissmann and Niklas Nilsson, editors. *Advanced Land Warfare: Tactics and Operations*. Oxford, UK: Oxford University Press, 2023.

Index

M

N

P

R

S

T

U

W

X

Z